SPIRITUALITY AND SOCIAL WORK

SPIRITUALITY AND SOCIAL WORK

Selected Canadian Readings

Edited by

John Coates,

John R. Graham,

and Barbara Swartzentruber,

with Brian Ouellette

Canadian Scholars' Press Inc.

Toronto

Spirituality and Social Work: Selected Canadian Readings
edited by John Coates, John R. Graham, and Barbara Swartzentruber, with Brian Ouellette

First published in 2007 by
Canadian Scholars' Press Inc.
180 Bloor Street West, Suite 801
Toronto, Ontario
M5S 2V6

www.cspi.org

Canadian Scholars' Press Inc. gratefully acknowledges financial support for our publishing activities from the Government of Canada through the Book Publishing Industry Development Program (BPIDP).

Library and Archives Canada Cataloguing in Publication

Spirituality and social work : select Canadian readings / edited by John Coates, John R. Graham, and Barbara Swartzentruber ; with Brian Ouellette.

Includes bibliographical references.
ISBN 978-1-55130-329-1

1. Social service--Canada--Religious aspects. 2. Social service--Religious aspects. 3. Spirituality.
I. Coates, John, 1948- II. Graham, John R. (John Russell), 1964- III. Swartzentruber, Barbara, 1960- IV. Ouellette, Brian, 1951-

HV530.S668 2007   361.30971   C2007-901926-9

Cover design: Aldo Fierro
Cover art: "Red Leaves on Yellow." © Elena Ray.
Interior design and layout: Brad Horning

07 08 09 10 11   5 4 3 2 1

Printed and bound in Canada by Marquis Book Printing Inc.

Canada

TABLE OF CONTENTS

Section 4: Diversity and Faith Traditions

DEDICATION

BRIAN OUELLETTE

MAY 23, 1951–DECEMBER 9, 2005

Brian Ouellette died suddenly and unexpectedly, due to a brain aneurysm, on 9 December 2005. Brian provided exemplary leadership in Canada in the area of spirituality and social work, and was working with us on this book when he died. This book is dedicated to him.

Brian was one of the co-founders of the Canadian Society for Spirituality and Social Work, and played a significant role in developing and organizing the first four Canadian Conferences on Spirituality and Social Work (2002–2005). In July 2000 at the IASSW/IFSW conference in Montreal, Brian met with Barbara Swartzentruber (Renison College), John R. Graham (University of Calgary), and John Coates (St. Thomas University) to discuss an area of shared interest and commitment—spirituality and social work. Together they agreed to plan a conference and, aided by a grant from SSHRC (of which Brian was the co-applicant) and the cooperation of the Faculty of Social Work at the University of Toronto and the CASSW, the First Canadian Conference on Spirituality and Social Work took place at the University of Toronto in May 2002. In planning for conferences, Brian always remembered the needs of students and practitioners, and strove to "get academics out of their heads" and to strengthen the theoretical and research focus of students and practitioners. In addition to all the "behind the scenes" activity, Brian's contributions included advising practitioners and students who were interested in preparing and presenting at the conference, focusing on the interests and participation of students and practitioners, and giving presentations on his teaching and research.

Many members of the Society for Spirituality and Social Work (USA) knew Brian, as he attended several conferences, including the 2005 conference in Tucson, where he introduced the idea of a joint Canadian/

American conference. Brian pursued this when he returned to Canada, where the idea of a joint conference quickly captured the energy and support of the Canadian Society for Spirituality and Social Work. The First North American Conference on Spirituality and Social Work at Renison College in 2006 was a direct result of Brian's reaching out to our American colleagues.

He was a faculty member in the Department of Social Work at St. Thomas University where, in 1994, he developed and offered the very first course in Canada that focused on spirituality and social work. After that, Brian offered the course virtually every year, and for many years his was the only course on spirituality and social work offered in a Canadian university. Over the years Brian provided assistance not only to many students, but also to many faculty members interested in furthering their own work in the area of spirituality; in 2005 Brian facilitated a workshop for faculty interested in developing courses on spirituality and social work.

In addition to his contribution in the area of spirituality, Brian was a much loved, highly regarded faculty member in the Department of Social Work at St. Thomas, where he taught since 1983. Brian graduated from St. Thomas with a Bachelor of Arts in 1973 and received his Master of Social Work degree from the Maritime School of Social Work, Dalhousie University, in 1975. Brian was one of the very few graduates of St. Thomas who returned as a professor. Prior to becoming a full-time faculty member in the Department of Social Work at St. Thomas in 1985, Brian worked in the areas of mental health and hospital social work. Those who met Brian, even once, remembered him because they felt better; talking with Brian about anything made a person feel better.

Brian was known as an excellent teacher and was awarded the University's Excellence in Teaching Award in 1998 and the Faculty Merit Award for effective teaching in 2005. He thoroughly enjoyed his work, and this joy was contagious. Students of all ages valued his courses, as Brian had a wonderful ability to connect with students and to nurture their learning and development. Brian's skills lay as much in what he shared as with his ability to bring out the potential in each student. There are numerous "Brian stories" that describe his antics as a teacher—singing, introducing physical exercises if students looked restless, or sharing humorous stories about his family. We will miss Brian's stories and the enthusiasm with which he approached life. Our sympathy goes out to Brian's wife, Anne, and their four children, Denis, Rachel, Phillippe, and Eric.

While Brian was highly regarded as a teacher, he was also very involved in a host of other activities at St. Thomas, and as one student stated, "He was one of the few professors who students knew about and liked even if they did not take social work." Brian taught more than 15 different courses and was involved in many areas of university life. For example, Brian had served as chair of the Department of Social Work and served on numerous university committees and activities. In particular, Brian was a long-standing and key player in developing university policies, programs, and courses relating to HIV/AIDS. Nationally, his contributions included serving, for several years, on the editorial board of the *Canadian Social Work* journal, where he was appointed editor in 2005.

In the professional social work community Brian was very active locally and provincially in the New Brunswick Association of Social Workers, and for his efforts he was awarded the Canadian Association of Social Workers Distinguished Social Worker Award in 1996. As well, Brian facilitated numerous workshops every year (one or two each month on average) in areas such as crisis intervention, suicide, AIDS, spirituality, and sexuality, among others. Brian played a significant role in the development of AIDS New Brunswick, served on a number of local organizations, and was also deeply involved in his faith communities as a catechist for many years.

Brian will be remembered as a good friend, a wonderful human being, as a significant contributor to social work education and practice, and for his exemplary leadership in the area of spirituality and social work in Canada. A scholarship fund has been established in his honour at St. Thomas University.

ACKNOWLEDGEMENT

The majority of the chapters in this book are based on presentations made at annual conferences of the Canadian Society for Spirituality and Social Work. The editors wish to acknowledge the conference support received from the Social Sciences and Humanities Research Council of Canada and from the Social Work programs at St. Thomas University, University of Calgary, Renison College (University of Waterloo), University of Toronto, Dalhousie University, University of Manitoba, King's University College (Western University) and University of British Columbia.

CONTRIBUTORS

David W. Adams, MSW, RSW, CDE, CGT, Professor Emeritus, Department of Psychiatry and Behavioural Neurosciences, Faculty of Health Sciences, McMaster University, Hamilton, Ontario

Alean Al-Krenawi, PhD, Associate Professor and Chair, Department of Social Work, Ben Gurion University of the Negev, Beer-Sheva, Israel.

Cyndy Baskin, PhD, Associate Professor, School of Social Work, Faculty of Community Services, Ryerson University, Toronto, Ontario

Sarah Bowman, graduate student, Wilfrid Laurier University

Gord Bruyere, PhD, Associate, Bachelor of Social Work Program, Nicola Valley Institute of Technology, Merritt, British Columbia.

Michèle Butot, MSW, RSW, Social Worker, Palliative Response Team Victoria Hospice, Victoria, British Columbia

Susan Cadell, PhD, Associate Professor, Lyle S. Hallman Faculty of Social Work, Wilfrid Laurier University, Waterloo, Ontario

John Coates, PhD, Professor, Department of Social Work, St. Thomas University, Fredericton, New Brunswick

Diana Coholic, PhD, Associate Professor, School of Social Work, Laurentian University, Sudbury, Ontario

Rick Csiernik, PhD, RSW, Professor, School of Social Work, King's University College, University of Western Ontario, London, Ontario

David Este, PhD, Professor, Faculty of Social Work, University of Calgary, Calgary, Alberta

The Rev. Fr. Shaun Govenlock was Assistant Director, and after 1962 Director of l'École de Service Social, l'Université de Montreal; he retired in the early 1980s as Associate Professor, Faculty of Social Work, Wilfrid Laurier University

John R. Graham, PhD, RSW Murray Fraser Professor of Community Economic Development and Professor, Faculty of Social Work, University of Calgary, Calgary, Alberta

Dennis J. Haubrich, PhD, Professor, School of Social Work, Faculty of Community Services, Ryerson University, Toronto, Ontario

Linda Janzen, PhD, RSW, Executive Director, Northumberland Services for Women, Cobourg, Ontario

Michael McKernan, MSW, Director of Operations, Catholic Family Service of Calgary, Alberta, Canada

Brian Ouellette (1951–2005), MSW, was Assistant Professor, Department of Social Work, St. Thomas University, Fredericton, New Brunswick

Linda Snyder, PhD, Associate Professor, Department of Social Work, Renison College, University of Waterloo

Barbara Swartzentruber, MSW, Lecturer, Social Development Studies, Renison College, University of Waterloo, Waterloo, Ontario

Sarah Todd, Ed.D, Assistant Professor, School of Social Work, Carleton, University, Ottawa

Wanda Wagler-Martin, MSW, RSW, Executive Director, Shalom Counselling Services Waterloo. Part-time Faculty, Faculty of Social Work, Wilfred Laurier University, Waterloo, Ontario.

E.J. Urwick (1867–1945) was Professor of Political Economy and Professor of Social Work, University of Toronto, and was Director of the School of Social Work, University of Toronto between 1927 and 1937

Michael Kim Zapf, PhD, RSW, Professor, Faculty of Social Work, University of Calgary, Calgary, Alberta

INTRODUCTION

JOHN COATES

The study of spirituality in the social sciences, by clinicians and researchers, has been increasing since the early 1980s when scholars began to pursue an understanding of the multi-dimensional factors consistent with spirituality and religiosity, and identified that these factors have a strong influence on individuals (Egbert, Mickley, & Coeling, 2004; Smith, 2001; Zinnbauer, Pargament, & Scott, 1999). Recent literature supports this relationship between spirituality and social science academic pursuit.

In regards to social work, the area of spirituality is undergoing a resurgence of interest in Canadian social work literature and practice. While this increased interest has been stimulated by demands from some students and practitioners, many others have undervalued spirituality in social work practice, and, until quite recently, the field in Canada had limited scholarly work and publications. In fact, the editors of this book heard from several researchers and practitioners that their attention to the issue of spirituality had been severely limited and somewhat marginalized by the lack of scholarship in this area. Similarly, scholars in adult education (Hood, 2006; Young, 1997) have noted the absence of attention to spirituality in the academy as it struggled "to be sectarian and politically correct" (Hood, 2006, p. 1). So great was this marginalization that some social work PhD students were actively discouraged from pursuing research in the area of spirituality. This book is an attempt to begin to address the need for increased scholarly attention to spirituality in social work theory and practice. It is our hope that this book of selected Canadian readings will make a significant contribution to this important area of research and practice, and will encourage continuing scholarship on spirituality and social work.

In North America the historical connection between religion, spirituality, and social work is well established (see chapter 1; Wills, 1995). There is little doubt that the emergence of social work in Canada at the turn of the twentieth century, as in the USA and Britain, was heavily influenced by the Social Gospel movement, charity organizations, and settlement house movement, which had strong religious (specifically Christian) and spiritual affiliations. As social work sought professional status and credibility, however, it became increasingly secularized and distanced "itself from its Christian charitable foundations" (Holloway, 2006, p. 4). The obvious religious connections faded as secularism, humanism, and individualistic orientations prevailed and a "deep-rooted, historical antipathy towards religion amongst social work in Western societies" developed (Holloway, 2006, p. 4). While Canadian social work writers continued to be influenced by religious and spiritual values, as discussed in chapter 1, the secularization was so complete that through the 1970s, 80s, and 90s spirituality and religion were sparse in social work education, and not widely discussed as an area of practice. There was also little attention to spirituality in the social work literature. This reflected the growing secularism in Canada and abroad, as evidenced, with rare exception, by a decline in church attendance (Bibby, 1987; Henerey, 2003). Canadian social work scholarship at this time seemed preoccupied with services to specific populations, as well as theory development, notably concerning poverty, gender, and structural sources of social problems (Carniol, 1984, 1987; Mullaly, 1997).

Compounding secularization was bias against spiritual and religious perspectives, together with fears about proselytizing and the imposition of religious beliefs (Canda & Furman, 1999; Drouin, 2002). Such fears fuelled debates about the inclusion of spirituality in a social work curriculum (see Sheridan & Amato-von Hemert, 1999; Sheridan, Wilmer, & Atcheson, 1994), along with concerns about inadequate theoretical development and the lack of practice guidelines (Holloway, 2006). Even as social work focused on diversity (for example, cross-cultural and culturally sensitive practice), issues of religion and spiritual diversity were frequently left out in favour of culture. This presented a simmering challenge for mainstream social work; separating culture from religious beliefs and practices can be most difficult, as religion plays a prominent role in the lives of many immigrants and refugees. The separation of church and state is very "Western," though recent political realities in both the United States and Canada, notably the emergence of the "religious right," have brought this into question.

❖ THE RE-EMERGENCE OF SPIRITUALITY

In academic disciplines such as psychology, there exists a plethora of research that identifies spirituality as a variable. Great emphasis is being placed on the relationship between spirituality and the human psyche and is being operationalized in ways that seek to incorporate spiritual belief systems in methods of psychiatric treatment and management (Mohr, 2006; O'Hanlon, 2006; Chattopadhyay, 2005; Griffin, Bowen, & Marcoux, 2004). Further to this, recent literature has investigated how spirituality relates to how people cope in specific situations. A specific example includes Gall's study (2006), which identifies how positive and negative spiritual coping relates to the distress of adult survivors of childhood sexual abuse (for further examples see Frances-Fisher, 2006; Good & Willoughby, 2006). This connection between spirituality and the stress and well-being of individuals has also been presented in other psychological literature relating to the physical and mental health of people (see Giovagnoli, Meneses, & da Silva, 2006; Heszen, 2006; van Heck & van Uden, 2005; van der Stel, 2005). In relation to an individual's mental health, research has pursued how spirituality, or the lack of spirituality, contributes to mental illnesses such as depression (Johnson-Migalski, 2006; Larson, Vickers, Sampson, Netzel, & Hayes, 2006) and post-traumatic stress disorder (Sornborger 2006). Research has also demonstrated the connections between spirituality and addictions (see Drerup, 2006; Galanter, 2006; Grodzicki & Galanter, 2005). This discussion of spirituality has resulted in research identifying the need for psychiatric and psychological practitioners to be aware of the spiritual and cultural backgrounds of their patients, and to incorporate spirituality in training programs for this sector of employees (Hage, 2006; Mcaninch, 2006; Russell & Yarhouse, 2006).

The growing body of work on spirituality in the discipline of psychology is extensive and could be explored further than what has been presented herewith. Research involving the variable of religion and spirituality has also been on the rise, to a lesser extent, in the disciplines of sociology and anthropology. Sociologists have emphasized a "New Age spirituality," identifying the rise of "self-spirituality" as an important characteristic that challenges current sociological thinking (Aupers & Hautman, 2006; Lambert, 1999; Laubach, 2004). For example, recent literature highlights how the role of spirituality has been re-emerging (potentially in a different form) in places such as work (Grant, O'Neil, & Stephens, 2004). The understanding of religion and spirituality is taking a new form in anthropology, in a pattern similar to that in sociology. For example, challenges are being made to the established notion that ethnographers only relate to their subjects through social interactions; some anthropologists argue that a spiritual and emotional relationship also exists (Ganiel, 2006; Bowie, 2003). Spirituality has also been viewed, in recent literature, as a factor in how communities relate to and revolt against modernity in relation to environmental aspects of their particular cultural grouping (Hornborg, 1994). This move to understanding spirituality within the cultural and social fabric of a community seeks to move beyond understanding only the religious values and beliefs, to describing how the community is spiritually held together; as such it requires a deeper understanding of the spiritual and religious underpinnings of the community (Bates, 2001; Pratt, 2000).

The re-emergence of attention to spirituality in social work is also consistent with changes in North American and Canadian societies. This rise in public attention to spirituality is reflected in international best sellers such as *The Road Less Traveled, Care of the Soul,* and *Chicken Soup for the Soul*; frequent articles in popular magazines; references in business, social development, and health literature; and the prominence of writers such as Mathew Fox and Ken Wilber. This media attention reflects a prevalent craving for new ways to define spirituality so that it transcends the limitations of what has been traditionally called religion.

Research by Robert Forman led him to label this phenomenon as *Grassroots Spirituality* (2004), while David Tacey called it *The Spirituality Revolution* (2004). Both labels refer to the rise of a subjective and personal spirituality as distinct from more objective and authoritative religion, and represent a "shift away from a life lived according to other's expectations to one lived according to one's own inner experience" (Lorimer, 2004). The spiritual life has come to be understood as available to everyone, and spirituality has come to be seen not only as an important feature of human development, but also as an essential aspect of human nature (Vaughn, 2002).

What accounts for this re-emergence? Why are so many people referring to themselves as spiritual but not religious? Why has fundamentalism risen in popularity? Is spirituality an extension of modernity or is it a counter to the ills of modern society? What role can spirituality play in addressing individual and social problems? In what ways can spirituality be incorporated into the various levels of social work practice? These and more are important issues that warrant exploration.

Forman (2004) suggests that this re-emergence of spirituality is a consequence of many varied factors, including demographic shifts from rural to urban living, the loosening of family ties, the shift in gender roles, the rise of the feminine, disenchantment with church and science, and

the aging of baby boomers. Also of significance is the lack of fulfillment
from employment and disillusionment with the failure of modern society
to provide for everyone and to adequately cope with severe social justice
issues. Forman also identifies a hidden cause—"the death of God," the loss
of a "plausible overarching theological model" (p. 205). The dissolution
of belief in a mechanistic universe, the discoveries concerning evolution
and the birth of our solar system (see Coates, 2003), challenges to literal
interpretations of scriptures, and differences between personal beliefs
and religious orthodoxy are a few of the forces that have contributed to
the demise of a personified and "judgemental God-figure" in favour of
"imminent panentheistic presence" (Forman, 2004, p. 208). In a similar
way Leaves (2004), referring to the work of Cupitt, sees this as the loss
of the "realist idea of an all-powerful God 'out there' who sustains and
creates the universe" (p. 2).

Gray (in press) provides a solid analysis of why spirituality has re-
emerged in social work and in society overall. Building on the work of
Beck (1992), Giddens (1991), and others, Gray traces this re-emergence and
argues that it is a direct outcome of modernity, insofar as it is a product
of the weakening of tradition, the secularization of society, and the rise
of individualism. "Increasingly, religion has moved to the private sphere
where it became more and more about the individual's relationship with
God," where the "privatization of belief" leads one to construct one's
own religious identity, and where the "autonomous individual" is largely
responsible for his or her own life choices (p. 7). Gray continues:

> Ironically, the rise of individualism as a result of the weakening of
> tradition and the secularization of society provided the very conditions
> for the rise of professionalism, for with these events came our faith in
> scientific rationality and the need for knowledge to replace previously
> accepted sources of authority. Science and the professions have further
> entrenched humanistic and individualistic stances and created a world in
> which human beings feel alienated and at risk.... The alienation ... gives
> rise to the renewed search for meaning and purpose in life and a rekindled
> awareness of the importance of our spiritual dimension. (p. 8)

Nagler (2005) sees modern society currently in a state of spiritual
crisis—a state of distress in which the existing belief system or "paradigm"
is "becoming obviously unworkable but the new one has not yet, at least
for most people, appeared over the horizon to replace it" (p. 6). Nagler sees
such a crisis occurring when a culture "finds itself trapped in an outmoded,

suffocating network of values and conceptions, in a world view, a 'creed outworn,' that has become too small to allow people to get on with their cultural evolution" (p. 5). Many people think that established religion is inadequate, yet they continue to believe in the transcendent or remain "loosely coupled" to many religious values.

Several writers argue that the emergence of spirituality in modern society is a response to the spiritual emptiness and search for meaning that arise from the values, beliefs, and lifestyles essential for the continuation of modern society—materialism, consumerism, dualism, and individualism, to name a few (Coates, 2003; Gray, in press; Henerey, 2003; Laurence, 2000; Nagler, 2005). Nagler sees overconsumption as a problem of "modern industrial civilization" (p. 3) in which consumption is equated with happiness and fulfillment. Bauman (1997) shares this interpretation. Materialism and scientism reinforce what Toynbee (in Nagler 2005) called "sensate civilization"—a society in which the purpose of existence and even human identity are defined by sense experience. Commercialism's incessant advertising in favour of buying more and more, with the message that what you have is not enough, leads to an endless and ultimately vacuous search that leaves the majority of the population stuck without an alternative.

This search, however, can be a never-ending struggle when identity has become attached to possessions—when "Net worth equals self-worth" (Kroeger qtd. in Durning, 1991, p. 162)—as identity and consumption are self-reinforcing. Henerey (2003), referring to Bauman (1997), points out that "the possession of products allows an individual to acquire a lifestyle" through which he/she "acquires a sense of achievement and relief from anxiety" (p. 1107). But materialism is so prominent in modern culture that one must always be adapting and changing just to stay in the game. Many people have begun to face the reality that the emptiness they feel cannot be overcome with a seductive, consumption-oriented lifestyle. A spiritually empty existence can never be filled by anything that we try to consume.

This modern existential anxiety has contributed to renewed interest in spirituality and religion, as some people seek a moral foundation (guidance) or the certainty and direction found in authoritative solutions. Just as many students look to their professors (experts) for the answer, many people seek out fundamentalism, as it offers solace through its interpretation of the authority of God (see Bauman 1997) and a supportive community. Still others look to gurus and lifestyle consultants, personal development magazines and self-help books, all of which proliferate as people seek self-expression and fulfillment through such lifestyle indicators as clothing, possessions, and home renovations. By modern consumerist standards those who are not able to "play the game" (in youthful parlance, those who are not cool) are outsiders and often led to feel personally inadequate. Bauman (1997) sees this reliance on the "culture of expertise" and "regimens of consumption" as characteristic of modern society.

However, many people reject religion for the very stability and security it offers. Henerey (2003) points out that religion can take people out of the consumer game because its "truths are static and unchanging and therefore incompatible with a continually revisable environment" (p. 1108). This is where spirituality comes in for many people, as it seemingly avoids dogma and traditions, and, as the Global Alliance for Transforming Education (2000) points out, provides people the opportunity "to set off on their own spiritual adventure of discovery" in an effort to "transform our ordinary lives into an extraordinary journey of awakening" (p. 8). This is reminiscent of both the individual spiritual journey/quest/pilgrimage of mythology and the vision quests of many Indigenous spiritualities, which seem to be becoming more popular and are being incorporated in psychological and sociological theory. Here we see spirituality offering what religion has traditionally provided—legitimation and meaning. In this view religion is reduced to a resource and spirituality is seen to be about individual self-expression and uniquely personal experiences. This consumerist model of spirituality, in which there is a great deal of sampling and trying on, and in which many people opt for a "smorgasbord of therapeutic spiritualities" (Leaves, 2004), is very much a reflection of modern times. While this is but one understanding of spirituality, it is common among "New Age" adherents, as it emphasizes subjectivity, personal experience, and self-expression in the absence of self-transcendence.

Gray (in press), in discussing the work of Eckersley (2004), points out that reflexive individualism can lead to "a preoccupation with satisfying personal wants and needs, an entitlement mentality, an abrogation of social responsibilities, and a decline in collective effort" (p. 11). Such a self-centred, egoistic individual is the epitome of the downside of modern individualism. However, this isolation is countered, Gray argues, by the work of Beck and Jordan, where "subpolitics" (Beck, 1998; Jordan, 2004) describes bottom-up, self-organizing processes through which people organize around common interests and concerns quite independently of govern-ment and religion (Gray, in press, p. 13). Spirituality, particularly that which advocates interdependence and connectedness, while not providing a moral foundation, can satisfy the search for meaning by providing a sense of being part of a community.

O

On the other hand, one advantage of religion is that it allows those without resources a legitimate place, adding complexity to our understanding of spirituality in modern life. This is not to imply that all religious people lack resources, but it recognizes an important role played by religion—offering a sense of community, a place of refuge in a stormy world. Spirituality outside of a religious tradition does not, of itself, offer community and acceptance when it is practised individually. This is one of the factors that leads spiritually oriented people to form, or seek the support of, small groups or communities of like-minded people who gather periodically for prayer and mutual support. The need for "belonging" (Vanier, 1998) poses a hurdle for many spiritual seekers, as the outcome of their private practice—a sense of unity, interdependence, and connectedness with all things—leads many to seek guidance and community. In fact, Gray (in press) refers to New Age as a religion because its rituals and commonalities of belief and practice draw small groups together.

❖ RELIGION AND SPIRITUALITY

In contemporary usage, the words "religion" and "spirituality" have taken on distinct meanings. Religion has come to be seen as "a framework for beliefs, values, traditions, doctrine, conduct, and rituals … whereas spirituality is a much more encompassing term." Spirituality is seen as "the search for meaning, purpose, and morally fulfilling relations with self, other people, the encompassing universe, and ultimate reality, however a person understands it" (Furman, 2005, p. 1). "Spiritual relationships are defined as relationships to self, others, a higher power, or the environment that bring forth a sense of inner strength, peace, harmonious interconnectedness, and meaning in life" (Walton, quoted in Laurence, 2000, p. 233). A spiritual individual may or may not be religious. In fact, many individuals are not able to identify with traditional religions as a source of meaning and have rejected religion altogether, while others pick and choose from different religions and in this process create multiple forms of religiosity. Yet large numbers of these people are deeply committed to developing a spiritual life. A 1997 article stated that 93% of North Americans believe that a spiritual life is important (Grant, 1997).

Spirituality is a complex topic and has many definitions. Robert Forman (in Laurence, 1999) has identified some common elements in many people's understanding of spirituality:

- It is characterized by a sense of connectedness and being in relationship with "the Divine," other people, the Earth, the Cosmos, or some other reality that is greater than the self and can act as a source of comfort and guidance.
- It is inclusive and holistic: we see ourselves and all of reality as part of a larger spiritual reality.
- It deals with inner experience.
- It is subjective, non-rational, and non-linear, appealing to the intuitive, meditative side of ourselves.

Forman (2004) concludes that "spirituality seems to point to the intuitive, non-rational meditative side of ourselves, the side that strives for inner and outer connection and a sense of wholeness" (p. 48). The Global Alliance for Transforming Education (1993) sees spirituality as manifested in "a deep connection to self and others, a sense of meaning and purpose in daily life, an experience of the wholeness and interdependence of life, a respite from the frenetic activity, pressure and overstimulation of contemporary life, the fullness of creative experience, and a profound respect for the numinous mystery of life" (pp. 8–9). Spirituality can be seen as a force that moves us beyond seeing ourselves as exclusively isolated and independent individuals in an uncaring and competitive world; spirituality involves the human quest for connectedness with something larger and more trustworthy than ourselves.

Many professions have developed an interest in spirituality—nursing, psychology, medicine, business, occupational therapy, and counselling, to name a few. Some writers (Spayde, 1998; Teasdale, 1991, 1997) see spirituality as having the potential not only to change people's individual behaviour, but also to make us more responsible for the Earth and each other; in this view spirituality is a resource for building a more enlightened civilization. Laurence (1999) sees that spirituality can assist people in developing a sense of pluralism, which can open them to building a more stable and inclusive society.

What appears to be occurring is a response to the anxiety of modernity that is leading some toward a very subjective, uniquely personal, and experiential perspective of spirituality, others toward self-transcendence, and still others toward more traditional, religious, and indigenous perspectives in a search for direction through the uncertainties and perplexities of modern life. Gray (in press) points out that these three views exist among social workers, as they are consistent with the questioning of the dominance of secularization, rationalism, individualism, and universalism of modern social work, which struggles with diversity (see also Gray, 2005; Coates, Gray, & Hetherington, 2006).

Spurred largely by demands from clients and social work practitioners, attention to spirituality in Canadian social work has grown substantially, as indicated by references in scholarly articles, the first course on spirituality and social work in 1994 at St. Thomas University, and the emergence of the Canadian Society for Spirituality and Social Work in 2001.

Todd and Coholic (in press) point out that in social work most of the literature on spirituality prefers a more inclusive and non-sectarian understanding of spirituality, as this is consistent with social work values. However, as Canda and Furman (1999) and Laurence (1999) note, we must be proactive in encouraging movement beyond acceptance and tolerance (which often retain a sense of personal correctness and superiority) to an active engagement and proactive dialogue—what Laurence (1999) refers to as pluralism and what Gray (in press) sees as a revival of "social work's early aspirations and potential for social change" (p. 19). The re-emergence of spirituality has resulted in a plethora of spiritual practices and many consultants, coaches, and directors that give meaning (linking people to something larger than the self) and legitimacy (giving people the feeling that their lives are sanctioned by what they consider to be sacred). Ken Wilber (2007) refers to this as "translative" rather than transformative spirituality, as it identifies something bigger but does not transcend the self. Many spiritualities provide emotional expression, meaning, social cohesion, sanction, and promise, but the question arises whether spirituality consists primarily of intense feelings and making people feel good, or whether it actually leads to a spiritual maturation (Leaves 2004, p. 7).

What we are posing here is the need to understand that spirituality can be a force for social change, not just inward change. Canda (1998) refers to this as "transcultural spirituality" and Forman (2004, p. 173) calls it "trans-traditional spirituality." Korten (2006) refers to people with such a view as "spiritual creatives," whose personal world view leads them to act differently in the world—to remove them from supporting or engaging in behaviours that support inequalities and toward actions that support social justice and social transformation.

❖ CHALLENGES

The re-emergence of spirituality in social work is, overall, in response to the search for meaning in peoples' lives. In some cases it is limited to self-serving ideals, but in others it can be seen as a retrieving of communitarian ideals as people become more involved and conscious human agents who strive to be more active participants in the development of society. Spirituality is a significant element in the process of cultural evolution as postmodern society deals with the contradictions of modernity.

A major challenge for social work practice and education will be to develop methods that lead to social workers enacting anti-oppressive interventions. This includes practices that encourage self-reflection on how systems of privilege or penalty have shaped people's lives (Campbell, 2002, 2003), while also creating a culture in the classroom that addresses homophobia, sexism, and racism without marginalizing fundamentalist religious voices that may hold views antithetical to social work values (see Coholic, 2003; Todd & Coholic, in press). Todd and Coholic (in press) argue that efforts "not to reproduce harm to oppressed groups" may require outside-of-classroom discussions with some students to reduce the potential for harm in the classroom.

The chapters chosen for inclusion in this collection were selected not only for the quality of scholarship, but also because they represent a cross-section of the diverse areas in which spirituality is being addressed in social work practice and/or explored through research. Some chapters are based on exceptional papers or workshops presented at recent Canadian Conferences on Spirituality and Social Work; others are high quality articles published in respected social work journals. In terms of framework, the book is a "reader," with the chapters covering a spectrum of emerging scholarship in this field. Areas covered include history, practice, education, and research. When taken together, these readings provide a solid overview of this important field of study and practice.

REFERENCES

Aupers, S., & Houtman, D. (2006). Beyond the spiritual supermarket: The social and public significance of new-age spirituality. *Journal of Contemporary Religion, 21*(2), 201–222.

Bates, A. (2001). Saving soul: Lesbian anthropology, ethics, and spirituality in a post-world theology and sexuality. *The Journal of the Institute for the Study Of Christianity and Sexuality, 14*, 97–106.

Bauman, Z. (1997). *Post-modernity and its discontents*. Cambridge: Polity Press.

Beck, U. (1992). *Risk society: Towards a new modernity*. London: Sage.

Beck, U. (1998). *Democracy without enemies*. Cambridge: Polity Press.

Bibby, R. (1987). *Fragmented gods: The poverty and potential of religion in Canada*. Toronto: Irwin.

Bowie, F. (2003). An anthropology of religious experience: Spirituality, gender, and cultural transmission in the focolare movement. *Ethnos, 68*(1), 49–72.

Campbell, C. (2002). The search for congruency: Developing strategies for anti-oppressive social work pedagogy. *Canadian Social Work Review, 19*(1): 25–42.

Campbell, C. (2003). Anti-oppressive theory and practice as the organizing theme for social work education: The case in favour. *Canadian Social Work Review, 20*(1), 121–27 and 133–135.

Canda, E. (1998). *Spirituality and social work: New directions*. New York: Haworth Press. Published simultaneously in *Social Thought 18*(2).

Canda, E., & Furman, L. (Eds.). (1999). *Spiritual diversity in social work practice: The heart of helping*. New York: The Free Press.

Carniol, B. (1984). Clash of ideologies in social work education. *Canadian Social Work Review 2*, 184–199.

Carniol, B. (1987). *Case critical: Challenging social work in Canada*. Toronto: Between the Lines.

Chattopadhyay, S. (2005). Integrating religious and spiritual themes in psychiatric management. *Internet Journal of Mental Health, 2*(2), n.p.

Coates, J. (2003). *Ecology and social work: Toward a new paradigm*. Halifax, NS: Fernwood Publishing.

Coates, J., Gray, M., & Hetherington, T. (2006). Ecology and spirituality: Finally, a place for Indigenous social work. *British Journal of Social Work, 36*, 381–399.

Coholic, D. (2003). Incorporating spirituality in feminist social work practice. *Affilia, 18*(1), 49–67.

Drerup, M.L. (2006). Religion, spirituality, and motives for drinking in an adult community sample. *Dissertation Abstracts International: Section B: The Sciences and Engineering, 66*(12-B), 6918.

Drouin, H. (2002). Spirituality in social work practice. In F.J. Turner (Ed.), *Social work practice: A Canadian perspective* (2nd ed., pp. 33–45). Toronto: Prentice-Hall.

Durning, A. (1991). Asking how much is enough. In Lester Brown et al. (Eds.), *State of the world 1991* (pp. 153–169). New York: W.W. Norton.

Eckersley, R. (2004, May 30). The science of self. [Radio episode.] In *Ockham's Razor*. Sydney: ABC Radio National.

Egbert, N., Mickley, J., & Coeling, H. (2004). A review and application of social scientific measures of religiosity and spirituality: Assessing a missing component in health communication research. *Health Communications, 16*(1), 7–27.

Forman, R. (2004) *Grassroots spirituality*. Thorverton, Devon: Imprint Academic.

Frances-Fisher, J.E. (2006). The meaning and experience of spirituality for infertile women who have been through medical treatment in their efforts to produce a child: A phenomenological investigation. *Dissertation Abstracts International: Section B: The Sciences and Engineering, 66*(12-B), 6919.

Furman, R., Benson, P., Canda, E., & Grimwood, C. (2005). A comparative international analysis of religion and spirituality in social work: A survey of UK and US social workers. *Social Work Education, 24*(8), 813–839.

Galanter, M. (2006). Spirituality and addiction: A research and clinical perspective. *The American Journal on Addictions, 15*(4), 286–292.

Gall, T.L. (2006). Spirituality and coping with life stress among adult survivors of childhood sexual abuse. *Child Abuse & Neglect, 30*(7), 829–844.

Ganiel, G. (2006). Turning the categories inside-out: Complex identifications and multiple interactions in religious ethnography. *Sociology of Religion, 67*(1), 333–321.

Giddens, A. (1991). *Modernity and self-identity.* Palo Alto, CA: Stanford University Press.

Giovagnoli, A.R., Meneses, R.F., & da Silva, A.M. (2006). The contribution of spirituality to quality of life in focal epilepsy. *Epilepsy and Behavior, 9*(1), 133–139.

Global Alliance for Transforming Education. (1993). Education 2000: A holistic perspective. Retrieved 30 October 2006 from http://members.iinet.net.au/~rstack1/gate.htm#preamble.

Good, M., & Willoughby, T. (2006). The role of spirituality versus religiosity in adolescent psychosocial adjustment. *Journal of Youth and Adolescence, 35*(1), 41–55.

Grant, D., O'Neil, K., & Stephens, L. (2004). Spirituality in the work place: New empirical directions in the study of the sacred. *Sociology of Religion, 65*(3), 265–283.

Grant, P. (1997, December). How spiritual are you? *Self,* 132–135.

Gray, M. (2005). Dilemmas of international social work: Paradoxical processes in indigenisation, imperialism, and universalism. *International Journal of Social Welfare, 14*(2), 230–237.

Gray, M. (in press). Viewing spirituality in social work through the lens of contemporary theory. *British Journal of Social Work.* Advance Access, 31 July 2006.

Griffin, R., Bowen, R., & Marcoux, G. (2004). Spirituality and psychiatry in Canada: Psychiatric practice compared to patient expectations. *Canadian Journal of Psychiatry, 49*(4), 265–271.

Grodzicki, J., & Galanter, M. (2005). Spirituality and addiction. *Substance Abuse, 26*(2), 1–4.

Hage, S. (2006). A closer look at the role of spirituality in psychology training programs. *Professional Psychology: Research and Practice, 31*(3), 303–310.

Henerey. N. (2003). The reality of visions: Contemporary theories of spirituality in social work. *British Journal of Social Work, 33,* 1105–1113.

Heszen, I. (2006). Spiritual resources and physical health. *Polish Psychological Bulletin, 37*(2), 84–93.

Holloway, M. (2006). Spiritual need and the core business of social work. *British Journal of Social Work.* Advance Access, 20 March 2006.

Hood, G.K. (2006). The notion of spirituality in adult and higher education. *Higher Education Perspectives, 2*(1). Retrieved 15 August, 2006 from http://aries.oise.utoronto.ca/highered/viewarticle.php?id=90&layout=html.

Hornborg, A. (1994). Environmentalism, ethnicity and sacred places: Reflections on modernity, discourse, and power. *Canadian Review of Sociology and Anthropology, 31*(3), 245–267.

Johnson-Migalski, L. (2006). Levels and correlations of sense of coherence, depression, and spirituality/religiousness in the medically stable and unstable elderly. *Dissertation Abstracts International: Section B: The Sciences and Engineering, 66*(12-B), 6925.

Jordan, B. (2004). Emancipatory social work: Opportunity or oxymoron. *British Journal of Social Work, 34,* 5–9.

Korten, D. (2006). *The great turning: From empire to Earth community.* Bloomfield, CT: Kumarian Press; San Francisco, CA: Berrett-Kohler.

Lambert, Y. (1999). Religion in modernity as a new axial age: Secularization or new religious forms. *Sociology of Religion, 60*(3), 303–333.

Larsen, K., Vickers, K., Sampson, S., Netzel, P., & Hayes, S. (2006). Depression in women with heart disease: The importance of social role performance and spirituality. *Journal of Clinical Psychology in Medical Settings, 13*(1), 39–48.

Laubach, M. (2004). The social effects of psychism: Spiritual experience and the construction of privatized religion. *Sociology of Religion, 65*(3), 239–263.

Laurence, P. (1999, November–December). Can religion and spirituality find a place in higher education? *About Campus 4*(5). Retrieved 30 October 2006 from http://www.wellesley.edu/RelLife/transformation/pub-articles.html.

Laurence. P. (2000). Exploring spirituality. In J. Beversluis (Ed.), *Sourcebook of the world's religions: An interfaith guide to religion and spirituality* (pp. 232-235). Novato, CA: New World Library.

Leaves, N. (2004). Twenty years on: Christianity reformed or a smorgasborg of therapeutic spiritualities? Sea of Faith Network UK. Retrieved 30 August 2006 from www.sofn.org.uk/Conferences/twenty_years_on%20leaves%202004.htm.

Lloyd, M. (1997). Dying and bereavement, spirituality and social work in a market economy of welfare. *British Journal of Social Work, 27*(2), 175–190.

Lorimer, D. (2004). [Review of R. Forman, *Grassroots spirituality,* and P. Heelas and L. Woodhead, *The spiritual revolution.*] *Science and Medical Network.* Retrieved 15 July 2006 from http://www.scimednet.org/library/reviewsN86+N87Forman_grass.htm.

Mcaninch, J. (2006). Religion and spirituality multi-cultural training guide for mental health professionals. *Dissertation Abstracts International: Section B: The Sciences and Engineering, 66*(11-B), 6255.

Mohr, W. (2006). Spiritual issues in psychiatric care. *Perspectives on Psychiatric Care, 42*(3), 174–183.

Mullaly, B. (1997). *Structural social work: Ideology, theory, and practice* (2nd ed). Toronto: Oxford University Press.

Nagler, M. (2005). *Our spiritual crisis: Recovering human wisdom in a time of violence.* Peru, IL: Open Court.

O'Hanlon, B. (2006). *Pathways to spirituality: Connections, wholeness, and possibility for therapist and client.* New York: W.W. Norton.

Pratt, M. (2000). Building an ideological fortress: The role of spirituality, encapsulation, and sensemaking. *Studies in Cultures, Organizations, and Societies, 6*(1), 35-51.

Russell, S., & Yarhouse, M. (2006). Training in religion/spirituality within APA-accredited psychology pre-doctoral internships. *Professional Psychology: Research and Practice, 37*(4), 430–436.

Sheridan, M.J., & Amato-von Hemert, K. (1999). The role of religion and spirituality in social work education and practice: A survey of student views and experiences. *Journal of Social Work Education, 35*(1), 125–141.

Sheridan, M.J., Wilmer, C.M., & Atcheson, L. (1994). Inclusion of content on religion and spirituality in the social work curriculum: A study of faculty views. *Journal of Social Work Education, 30*(3), 363–376.

Smith, T.W. (2001). Religion and spirituality in the science and practice of health psychology. In Plante, T.G., & Sherman, A.C. (Eds.). *Faith and Health: Psychological Perspectives* (pp. 355–380). New York: Guilford.

Sornborger, J.A. (2006). Member workbook: A spirituality group intervention protocol for combat veterans with posttraumatic stress disorder. *Dissertation Abstracts International: Section B: The Sciences and Engineering, 66*(12-B), 6937.

Spayde, J. (1998, January–February). The new renaissance. *Utne Reader, 85*, 42–47.

Tacey, D. (2004). *The spirituality revolution: The emergence of contemporary spirituality.* New York: Brunner-Routledge.

Teasdale, W. (1991). Nature-mysticism as the basis for eco-spirituality. *Studies in Formative Spirituality, 12*, 215–231.

Teasdale, W. (1997). The interspiritual age: Practical mysticism for the third millennium. *Journal of Ecumenical Studies 34*(1), 74–92.

Todd, S., & Coholic, D. (in press). Christian fundamentalism and anti-oppressive social work pedagogy. *Journal of Teaching in Social Work.*

van der Stel, J. (2005). Spirituality and religion: The association with mental and physical health. *Gedrag & Gezondheid: Tijdschrift voor Psychologie en Gezondheid, 33*(3), 102–121.

van Heck, G.L., & van Uden, M. (2005). Religion, spirituality, and coping with health related stress. *Gedrag & Gezondheid: Tijdschrift voor Psychologie en Gezondheid, 33*(3), 133–143.

Vanier, J. (1998). *Becoming human.* Toronto: House of Anansi.

Vaughn, F. (2002). What is spiritual intelligence? *Journal of Humanistic Psychology, 42*(2), 16–33

Wilber, K. (2007). *A spirituality that transforms.* Retrieved 20 January 2007 from http://wilber.shambhala.com/html/misc/spthtr.cfm/.

Wills, G. (1995). *A marriage of convenience: Business and social work in Toronto, 1918–1957.* Toronto: University of Toronto Press.

Young, R. (1997). *No neutral ground: Standing by the values we prize in higher education.* San Francisco: Jossey-Bass Publishers.

Zinnbauer, B.J., Pargament, K.I., & Scott, A.B. (1999). The emerging meanings of religiousness and spirituality: Problems and prospects. *Journal of Personality, 67*, 889–919.

SECTION 1

HISTORY

INTRODUCTION

JOHN R. GRAHAM

This section considers the history of Canadian social work, and the profound impact that religion and spirituality have had in that trajectory. The first chapter surveys the Canadian social work literature in three stages. In each stage, spirituality has had a strong influence in shaping practice, research, and pedagogical discourses. First, the chapter emphasizes the overwhelming significance of spirituality to the early history of social work, prior to its emergence as a secular, professional discipline taught in university contexts. Second, it examines how spirituality continued to have a place within the writings of several major social work scholars in Canada up to 1970, at which point spirituality seems to fade from scholarly social work literature. Third, it looks at the re-emergence of spirituality as a Canadian topic for research in the 1990s. At the beginning of the third millennium, the literature on spirituality and social work has accentuated three major themes: social justice work and community organizing, social work pedagogy, and social work practice.

The next chapter examines The Haven, a Toronto charity for women, in the years 1878 to 1930. By considering one such institution in detail, broader inferences about Canadian social work may be garnered. Like many philanthropic organizations, The Haven was established with profound religious orientation in service programming; religion, likewise, significantly motivated its volunteers and fundraisers to undertake charitable work. By the 1890s these religious impulses had started to wane, and by 1930 The Haven had made the transition to a secular, professional institution. This case study highlights the religious origins of Canadian social work, and the relationship between the secular social work of today and its historic pre-professional origins.

Social development is also a core theme in the third chapter. The Social Gospel movement in Canada, like its counterparts in the United States and the United Kingdom, was a theological and social movement devoted to social development and change. Historian Richard Allen describes it as "an attempt to apply Christianity to the collective ills of an industrializing society" (Allen, 1988, p. 2026). Protestant clergy and laity were instrumental in promoting a new consciousness in Canadian society, particularly during the period 1880 to 1930, when the Social Gospel was at its zenith. The 1912 establishment of the Social Service Council of Canada, the encouragement of scientific studies of social problems, and the advocacy of increasingly comprehensive social policy legislation were important forerunners to the emergence of social work. All were intricately associated with the Social Gospel.

Canada's oldest school of social work, at the University of Toronto, was established in 1914. One of its most gifted scholars was E.J. Urwick (1867– 1945), an Oxford-trained philosopher who had extensive experience in London's East End settlement houses. Excerpts from his 1948 posthumous book, *Values of Life*, are based on lecture notes for a course he taught in the School of Social Work. As this chapter aptly demonstrates, his was a deep spirituality that embraced the world and others, in a unity that was highly indebted to Eastern mysticism, Plato, and the insistence on right living.

The final chapter in this section is by the Reverend Shaun Govenlock, a Roman Catholic priest and an important person in the history of Quebec social work training. Like so many social work scholars of his day, Govenlock's conception of vocation was true to that word's etymology: it was deeply religious in nature.

Three out of these five chapters concentrate on one faith, Christianity, as an important part of Canadian social work's spiritual origins. There were other traditions, including those associated with Aboriginal peoples, Buddhists, Hindus, Jews, Muslims, members of other faith communities beyond these, and people whose spirituality did not explicitly relate to a faith tradition. These included diverse groups of people based on ethnoracial identity, sexual orientation, and other parameters. For example, Dave Este's chapter in a subsequent section of this book deals with black Canadians; chapters in other sections also cover faith traditions other than Christianity. Yet a lot of further research needs to be done, rendering deeper and more representative insight into the history of spirituality and social work in Canada. Faith and spirituality may be quiet and understated, but are nonetheless germane to motivating professional life. A good example is a 1959 book edited by the late Albert Rose, professor of social work at the University of Toronto and a distinguished scholar of social policy and housing policy. *A People and Its Faith* is a wonderful document celebrating the Jewish synagogue in which Rose and his family worshiped, Holy Blossom Temple, in Toronto. But little has been written about Rose's spirituality. Indeed, historical research in Canada is only beginning to consider the profound diversity represented within Canadian social work's spiritual history; much good work can and should be undertaken.

REFERENCE

Allen, R. (1988). "Social Gospel." In Marsh, J. (Ed.) *The Canadian encyclopedia*, 2nd ed. Edmonton: Hurtig, p. 2026.

Rose, A. (Ed.). (1959). *A people and its faith.* Toronto: University of Toronto Press.

CHAPTER 1

SPIRITUALITY AS A GUIDING CONSTRUCT
IN THE DEVELOPMENT OF CANADIAN SOCIAL WORK:
PAST AND PRESENT CONSIDERATIONS

JOHN R. GRAHAM, DIANA COHOLIC, AND JOHN COATES

Personal and professional values are integral to social work teaching and practice—for social work, perhaps more than many other professions. *Caring and Curing* (1980), *Knowing and Caring* (1982), *The Moral Purposes of Social Work* (1992), *Values and Ethics in Social Work* (2005): these and other books provide ample evidence of the importance of values that underlie our profession. As Antle (2005, p. 3) argued, the social work profession in Canada is "founded on a set of long-standing core ethical principles rooted in the humanitarian values that all people are intrinsically worthy and should share in the benefits and burdens of society." However, the Canadian literature has only recently started to reconsider a historically important source of social work values—spirituality—as a vital source of scholarship and practice. We argue that spirituality has been a foundation and philosophical underpinning in the development of Canadian social work, and certainly poses challenges in the continued development of the profession. Indeed, the past 14 years have seen an emerging Canadian literature (Al-Krenawi & Graham, 1996, 1999abc, 2000ab; Coates, 2003a; Coates & Graham, 2003a, 2004; Coates & McKay, 1995; Coholic, 2002, 2003ab; Csiernik & Adams, 2002; Graham, 1992; Graham & Bradshaw, 2000; Graham & Coates, 2005), which complements a more long-standing presence in American circles (Canda, 1988; Canda & Furman, 1999). However, no comprehensive assessment has ever been made of Canadian research on social work and spirituality, or of the factors involved in the re-emergence of spirituality within Canadian social work scholarly and professional communities.

As a corrective, the present manuscript discusses first an historical overview of the origins of Canadian social work in the pre-1970 period. This analysis emphasizes the overwhelming significance of spirituality to the early history of social work, prior to its emergence as a secular, professional discipline taught in university contexts. In comparison to its nineteenth-century, non-professional predecessor, spirituality in twentieth-century social work was less overtly part of the discursive landscape. However, it nonetheless continued to have a place within the writings of several major Canadian social work scholars prior to 1970. The two decades spanning the 1970s and 1980s saw little attention paid to spirituality and religion within helping discourses, which mirrored societal trends at large. One of these trends was a decline in attendance at Christian churches, which sociologist Reginald Bibby (1987, 2002) reported successively, and which is used by some as evidence of a growing secularization during this period. The two decades spanning the 1970s and 1980s are not addressed because this was a period in which little substantive writing occurred in the area of spirituality.[1] Undoubtedly, American social work scholar Edward Canda's seminal work from the mid-1980s to the present has provided a renewed interest in spirituality and social work, and within Canada in the early 1990s the Canadian field began to experience a renaissance. Second, the chapter describes Canadian scholarship on social work and spirituality since 1992, and the 2001 emergence of the Canadian Society for Spirituality and Social Work, a major venue for the encouragement and dissemination of spiritually grounded social work scholarship and practice. This chapter is both analytical and critical. It is analytical, in that it is the first writing to provide intellectual coherence to the emergence, and present status, of spirituality in Canadian social work scholarship. It is critical, in that it celebrates both the recent emergence of spirituality in social work writing, and points out time periods when this fundamentally important area of concern bore little attention in mainstream social work scholarship, and outlines future challenges and directions. The overview approach that the present literature review takes is entirely in the tradition of social scientific and humanities scholarship as seen in historiographic articles (Berger, 1987; Graham, 1996), or in literature reviews appearing in such venues as *Annual Review of Anthropology* (Cf. Jackson & Warren, 2005).

❖ THE INFLUENCE OF SPIRITUALITY IN CANADIAN SOCIAL WORK'S ORIGINS

The conventional interpretation of the rise of social work emphasizes a narrative of transformation from a nineteenth and earlier century tradition of sacred, non-professional volunteerism, low technique, and little established research, to the early twentieth-century emergence of a profession that was secular, scientific, technical, and orientated to higher learning. This transition is said to have occurred in Canada, the United States, the United Kingdom, and other, now Organisation for Economic Co-operation and Development (OECD) nations, where the social work profession first took root (Woodroffe, 1962; Lubove, 1965). Social work, like many disciplines of the early twentieth century, was thought to be part of the triumphant march of secular, technical progress and human rationality. American social work pioneer Mary Richmond is proclaimed an exemplar of this emerging tradition. Her *Social Diagnosis* (1917) and *What is Social Casework?* (1922) are seen as important markers in the discipline's earliest transition to secular, technical prowess. However, all is not as it first seems. Richmond, like virtually all of her contemporaries, interacted with clergy on a regular basis, and had a strong intellectual indebtedness to sacred, in her case, Protestant reference points. As Canadian scholar Joel Majonis (2004) convincingly argued, Richmond's theory cannot be understood apart from the thinking of the Reverend Thomas Chalmers, a nineteenth-century Presbyterian thinker, who was an intellectual anchor to one of Richmond's English charity organization mentors, Charles Stewart Loch.

Canadian experiences were, in this sense, in close keeping with Richmond's, but also were unique to our context. For instance, in Canada there was a long tradition of responding to social need amongst Indigenous communities prior to European contact. That tradition, like the traditions that occurred on and after European contact, would have had groundings that we now understand to be "spiritual" in their relationship to self, a Higher Power(s), community, and, for some helpers too, the physical eco-logy (Miller, 2004). Religion intersects with other areas of human relations, and was a tragic facet of colonialism from the time of European contact in the New World. Religion and spirituality have not always had a positive impact as religion played a significant role carrying out the government policy of the enfranchisement of Indigenous people. Largely through their function in operating residential schools, churches of various Christian denominations, played a role in the destruction of culture and individual abuse that were a consequence of the enfranchisement policies (Miller, 2005, 2004, 1996). Regrettably, church- and state-sponsored institutions attempted to inculcate predominantly Christian values and principles, and to encourage Aboriginal youth to turn away from Indigenous ways of knowing.

Also, during the early period of New France, the seventeenth-century nun Margeurite Bourgeois laid an institutional framework of

Roman Catholic social concern that continued into our present century (Danylewycz, 1987). Finally, and with growing significance after 1850, there emerged a loose constituency of social work personnel, affiliated with religious traditions that were primarily Protestant, Roman Catholic, and Jewish, along with people committed to an emerging trade union movement, the emerging women's movement, and immigrants. Thus, a diverse collection of actors laid the foundation of an emerging structure of institutional social care. Furthermore, depending on the province, this foundation was first established among sectors most of which were either voluntary, attached to churches, industry or trade unions, or affiliated with a poor law tradition (Graham, Swift, & Delaney, 2003; Graham, 1995). As Graham contended, Canadian charitable personnel prior to 1900 had an orientation that could be highly oriented to religious traditions, were steeped in religious nomenclature and theology, and understood its mission in predominantly sacred terms. Into the twentieth century, a secular orientation predominated—but never entirely.

The welfare state, and social concern in Canada, was similarly influenced by religious conviction. The Women's Christian Temperance Union and the Young Women's Christian Association were international Protestant organizations, founded in Canada in the latter half of the nineteenth century to assert women's rights. The Social Gospel Movement, a loose coalition of Protestant clerics and laity, emerged in Canada in the 1890s to apply social democratic Christian principles to prevailing public policy. In Quebec, the *Semaines Sociales* was a forum in which Roman Catholic clergy and laity likewise discussed social issues. The Social Services Council of Canada (established under a different name in 1907, renamed 1912) was the creation of a number of diverse representatives from the trade union movement, Anglican, Methodist, Presbyterian, and Baptist churches, and others. Historians Michael Gauvreau and Nancy Christie (1996) see the rise of a twentieth-century welfare state as the ultimate ascendance of a United Church theology. The welfare state itself was highly indebted to a Canadian social democratic tradition, and here again, several Protestant clergy were important in the establishment and leadership of the Cooperative Commonwealth Federation (renamed the New Democratic Party in 1961), a social democratic political party elected to national and provincial legislatures: Methodist cleric and party founder J.S. Woodsworth (1874–1942) and Baptist minister Tommy Douglas (1904–1986). Woodsworth's famous 1911 *My Neighbor: A Study of City Conditions, a Plea for Social Service* captures a Social Gospel tradition perhaps as well as any other Canadian source. It is possible to argue that the welfare state owes much to faith traditions and that many of the country's oldest social service institutions have roots that are in some way associated with religious institutions or with personnel who were motivated by faith.

❖ FOUR CANADIAN SOCIAL WORK THINKERS TO 1970

Turning to Canadian social work itself, we see striking evidence of a persistence of spiritual grounding amongst major social work thinkers (Graham, 2002). Limits of space preclude a thorough analysis, but we will briefly examine four Canadian social work scholars who especially capture the enduring presence of spirituality in the twentieth century, prior to 1970. A rejoinder bears emphasis. These four are described because of their thoughtful writing and enduring significance to social work scholarship; they capture major examples of Canadian social work scholars who were interested in spirituality. We note that each writer is male and white, which is not to suggest that people of other positionalities were not important. Indeed, future research and discourse merits greater insight into other writers of diverse social locations, which would include the voices of women, members of visible minority communities, and others that deserve further, more comprehensive treatment beyond the parameters of the present chapter. The same comments apply to the faith orientation of three of the four writers: other faiths, and people, like Urwick, who did not align to one specific faith, were all important undercurrents that future research could explore.

The first is E.J. Urwick (1867–1945), director of the Department of Social Service at the University of Toronto (1927–1937). Born and raised in England, and with training in philosophy from Oxford University, Urwick was deeply influenced by Plato, the spiritual philosophy of the Vedanta, and a number of Indian writers and teachers, among them Vivekanananda, Sri Ramanathan, and Ananda Acharya. A prolific author, major works included *Luxury and Waste of Life* (1906), *A Philosophy of Social Progress* (1912), *The Message of Plato* (1920), *The Social Good* (1927), and the posthumous *The Values of Life* (1948); the latter-most work was based on lecture notes from undergraduate courses in social philosophy, in which social work students at the University of Toronto were enrolled (Graham, 2005a; Moffatt, 2001). His was a deep spirituality that embraced the world and others, in a unity that was highly indebted to Eastern mysticism, Plato, and the insistence on right living.

Our next thinker, Charles Eric "Chick" Hendry (1903–1979) was entirely different from Urwick. A Canadian by birth, Hendry spent twenty years of his career in the United States, providing leadership in research, community organization, and senior management in a succession of jobs of increasing responsibility—all somehow linked to his earliest experiences with the Young Men's Christian Association (YMCA) in Canada. He held two master's degrees from Columbia University: one in religious education from Union Theological Seminary and the other in educational sociology from Teacher's College, Columbia University. Recruited to the School of Social Work, University of Toronto, in 1946, Hendry succeeded Harry Morris Cassidy as Director of the School from 1951 until his 1969 retirement. Moreover, he spent much of his boys' work career, and to a lesser extent the social work career that followed, preaching to Protestant congregations. Hendry was also an active member of the United Church of Canada throughout his adult life in this country (Graham, 1994). He considered professional life a sort of religious vocation anyway, and commented at age 70 that while never ordained, he also had "never left the ministry" (Hendry, 1974, p. 2).

Finally, the two scholars completing our narrative are both Roman Catholic priests and social work educators. The Reverend Shaun Govenlock (1916–) was born in Montreal where his mother administered the Welfare Bureau within the Montreal Catholic Charities system. Educated at l'Université de Montréal, where he learned French, and ordained in 1943, Govenlock was targeted to follow his mother as a welfare administrator. However, after graduate training in social work at the Catholic University of America (MSc in social work, 1947), he was assigned to the assistant directorship of l'école de service social, which was laterally affiliated with l'Université de Montréal (where Govenlock became Director of the school in 1962 and full professor in 1965). The Reverend Frank Swithun Bowers (1908–1992) was an English-born, Roman Catholic priest who completed social work training at Columbia University in 1948, and the following year opened the first class at St. Patrick's College, Ottawa where he was St. Patrick's director until 1971. In 1967 the school became affiliated with Carleton University and in 1972 moved to the Carleton campus. By the early 1950s, St. Patrick's quickly had become one of Canada's leading casework faculties (Gripton & Valentich, 2005). The author of over 30 journal articles, Bowers published several on religion and spirituality, and these merit particular attention. A 1954 treatise on human values and public welfare, expressed a commitment to holistic social work. "The religious and spiritual aspects of the human condition," to Bowers,

> cannot be overlooked. If you ignore an aspect that has meaning to him, and which because of his wholeness must, therefore, enter into his total

pattern of functioning, you are no longer dealing with the human person who has sought your service, but a truncated creature of your own fashioning." (1954, p. 6)

Like his counterpart in Holy Orders, Father Shaun Govenlock, Bowers was committed to an inclusive social work that did not lose its sense of tradition (Bowers, 1954, 1955, 1956, 1959, 1960; Govenlock, 1958, 1966). Indeed, as Bowers accurately asserted, "Religion and social work once walked very closely together." There was much that could be done "to close the gap between them" and here, in "trying to bear active witness to the idea of a university which John Henry Newman envisaged," Bowers hoped to "reunite things which were in the beginning joined together by God, and have been put asunder by man" (1956, p. 4). Or as Govenlock wrote, "Among those for whom social work is more than a mere job ... there is a disquieting perception ... that the best skills, techniques, and resources of our profession fall short, somewhere, of reaching the ultimate sources of man's temporal distress and needfulness" (1958, p. 21).

Bower's impact, like that of Govenlock, Urwick, and Hendry, is resonant. Compared to Bowers and Govenlock, Urwick and Hendry had a less explicitly religious and institutional frame of spirituality in their respective approaches to social work. But all four scholars were very important leaders of Canadian social work. Each was director of a major school for over a decade; each was well published and well regarded; and together, they represent a period in social work's history from the 1930s to the early 1970s. Together, too, they represented major Canadian social work educators who would have appreciated the spiritual preconditions of social work, its historical record, and each, in their own way, personified a spirituality that had been long nurtured in their interior depths, and had been sustained in the profession.

❖ SOCIAL WORK SCHOLARSHIP, 1990s TO THE PRESENT

Much changed in social work between the early 1970s and today. In the 1970s and 1980s there was little attention in the social work literature to spirituality. This reflected a growing secularism in Canada as witnessed by a decline in church attendance (Bibby, 1987). Canadian social work scholarship at this time seemed preoccupied with theory development, notably poverty and other structural sources of social problems, and services to specific populations (Carniol, 1984, 1987; Moreau, 1979; Mishra, 1984; Turner, 1979). The early 1990s saw a re-emergence of spirituality and social work, and the growing consolidation, after 2001, of a group of scholars and practitioners committed to spirituality and the profession. Where the pre-1970 period provides evidence of some very high profile, high ranking leaders in social work scholarship with interests in religion and spirituality, or both, the post-1990 period sees an equally promising collection of scholars and practitioners committed to newer approaches to spirituality and social work. This more recent focus on spirituality reflects shifts in the scientific and academic communities, as well as global demographic and socio-cultural transitions that stress the importance of exploring spirituality in people's lives (Ai, 2002; Monk-Turner, 2003).

The 1990s saw the gradual emergence of this topic amongst a small cadre of scholars, while the appearance of a critical mass of explicit discussions about spirituality in social work within Canadian publications and by Canadian authors has been a phenomenon of the post-2000 period. Graham's work, with international collaborator Alean Al-Krenawi, represents one of the 1990s' earliest interests in spirituality—exploring social work knowledge related to Islamic theology and prayer, and spiritually grounded social service and mental health work with Arab and Bedouin-Arab communities in the Middle East (Al-Krenawi & Graham, 1997a, 1997b, 1999a, 1999b, 1999c, 2000a, 2000b; Graham & Al-Krenawi, 1996; Graham, 2007). Graham was also among a small group of social work scholars delving into the historical origins of spiritually or religiously based social work practice (Graham, 1992; Wills, 1994) and scholarship (Moffatt, 1994; Graham, 1994). Coates and McKay (1995) provided insight into the relationship among practitioners between spirituality and sympathy toward progressive social services. Also in the 1990s, culture started to be explored as an element of practice in which the spiritual dimension should be recognized (Matsuoka & Sorenson, 1991; Saldov, 1991; Schwager, Mawhiney, & Lewko, 1991). Indeed, some clients' cultures are strongly linked with spiritual and religious world views, and this has consistently been a rationale for the inclusion of spirituality in social work. Other examples of Canadian contributions in this area include Dei's (1998) critique of development in Africa, Gold's (1993) discussion of Jewish women, and examinations of social work with Aboriginal cultures in Canada (de Mello, 1992; Mandamin, 1994; Morrissette, McKenzie, & Morrissette, 1993; Tester, 1994a).

A theoretical base that may have obvious links with the work in spirituality and social work is Aboriginal theory and practice (Nabigon & Mawhiney, 1996). In fact, a study regarding social work education in some Ontario universities uncovered the importance of courses in Native

Studies for students who were interested in spirituality (Coholic, 2006). Also, it was reported that both students and educators believed that there was consistent demand for Aboriginal perspectives to be included in social work programs, and that courses in Native Studies had a strong impact on students' learning about spirituality, including their openness to incorporating it in their practice. This is an interesting finding and a unique one compared with much of the research in this area that has primarily been conducted in American universities (Kamya, 2000; Russel, 1998; Sheridan & Amato-von Hemert, 1999). Much more could be done to elaborate the relationship between social work and Aboriginal spiritualities, especially since spirituality plays a central role in the lives of many Indigenous people and their communities (see for example Graveline, 1998; Hart, 2002). Some have argued that theoretical attention to spirituality and ecology have created a more welcoming context in which Indigenous voices can be heard (Coates, Gray, & Hetherington, 2006; Gray, Coates, & Hetherington, 2007), keeping in mind of course, how social work has worked to oppress Aboriginal peoples in Canada.

A 1990s review of *The Social Worker* (now *Canadian Social Work*) and *Canadian Social Work Review* demonstrates that although spirituality was not often the primary focus of discussion, it did infuse other various topics for discussion. *The Social Worker* published a special issue in 1996 on HIV/AIDS, which included several articles that incorporated spirituality as a relevant issue for both clients and caregivers (see Cadell, 1996 for one example). The topics of serious illness, death, and dying are often inextricably linked with issues of spirituality for many clients and workers, given the subject matter and the need for people to make meaning of suffering. With regards to the process of making meaning, spirituality can be an integral aspect of how people make sense of events. Thus, if we ignore the spiritual dimension of people's lives, we may be missing an opportunity to help people construct holistic narratives that accurately fit their experiences. Other Canadian contributions included new and more holistic practice paradigms (Gallant, Holosko, Gorey, & Lesiuk, 1998; Hodge, 1998; Kruger, 1999; Meier, 1997; Turner, 1983). Finally, a few Canadian texts such as Frank Turner's *Social Work Treatment* also contained theoretical chapters that can be linked with spirituality; for instance, Aboriginal theory, existential social work, meditation, and transpersonal theory, to name a few examples (1996). *Social Work Practice: A Canadian Perspective* (Turner, 2002) included the first book chapter in a Canadian textbook (Drouin, 2002) to focus exclusively on spirituality. Drouin (2002), while citing mostly American sources, reviewed the growing interest in spirituality in social work, and presented an overview of some of the issues surfacing as spirituality began its re-emergence in social work practice.

❖ THE NEW MILLENNIUM AND SPIRITUALITY

The new millennium saw discussions about spirituality by Canadian practitioners and academics really begin to emerge in an overt and burgeoning fashion. A major catalyst for this development was the 2001 creation of the Canadian Association for Spirituality and Social Work (now known as the Canadian Society for Spirituality and Social Work). Barbara Swartzentruber, an instructor of social work at Renison College, University of Waterloo, had contacted noted American scholar Edward Canda, inquiring about Canadian scholars who had interests in spirituality. Canda referred Swartzentruber to Professor John Graham of the University of Calgary. Graham knew of the work of two scholars at St. Thomas University, professors Brian Ouellette, the instructor of the first Canadian course on spirituality and social work, and John Coates, a researcher with interests in physical ecology. Together, the four co-founded the Canadian Society for Spirituality and Social Work (CSSSW), and secured funding from the Social Sciences and Humanities Research Council for a two-day conference, which was held at the Faculty of Social Work, University of Toronto in conjunction with the annual conference of the Canadian Association of Schools of Social Work (CASSW). Along with the more than expected attendance of over 100 participants, the quality of the workshops and papers was high. Graham and Coates secured publication of a special edition based on this first conference, and this appeared as the inaugural edition of the University of Calgary's recently launched online journal, *Currents: New Scholarship in the Human Services* (www.fsw.ucalgary.ca/currents).

Subsequent years' conferences were held in conjunction with the CASSW in Winnipeg, Halifax, and London, precipitating the publication of special issues, co-edited by John Coates and John Graham (Coates & Graham, 2003a, 2004; Graham & Coates, 2005) and appearing in the peer-reviewed online journals, *Currents: New Scholarship in the Human Services,* which is a Canadian journal, and *Critical Social Work* (www.criticalsocialwork.com/), an international journal located in Canada since 2003. *Currents'* 2002 special theme edition, titled "Spiritual Diversity in Social Work," featured an invited paper by Edward Canda (2002), one of the most prolific American writers in this field, who discussed the American experience and examined the issue of internationalization. The 2003 and 2004 publication of the second special theme issue in *Currents*, "Spiritual Diversity in Social Work II," saw contributions written exclusively by writers situated in Canada. A similar pattern is evident in the special edition of *Critical Social Work* (2005, vol. 6, no. 2), which included six Canadian articles, two international contributions, and one American paper. Of note is that four of the six Canadian papers were written by practitioners, which demonstrates the influence that practice issues and practitioners have in developing this emergent body of knowledge. The Canadian Society for Spirituality and Social Work's annual conferences have also had papers in French. A most encouraging further development is the 2006 special theme issue (not associated with the conference) of *Reflets*, a French language journal based at Laurentian University. The scholarly contributions arising from the CASSW conferences are unique compared to the American experience. For example, while the Society for Spirituality and Social Work in the United States publishes the peer-reviewed *Spirituality and Social Work Forum*, their conferences have tended to focus more on experiential workshops than on research and theoretical developments.[2]

From 2000 onwards, the topics examined by Canadian contributors can be grouped into three broad themes: social justice work and community organizing, social work pedagogy, and social work practice that includes historical analyses of the profession and early workers. To turn to the first area, social justice, the ability to conduct and sustain social justice work was discussed by Nash and Stewart (2005) as being strengthened by spiritual awareness. Social justice work has also been inextricably linked with ecological movements and specifically deep ecology by Coates (2003b, 2004), and Ungar (2003). This latter article also has a direct connection with practice in that the author used the concept of deep ecology to explain how at-risk populations taking part in outdoor programming can be best helped to develop in their own environments.

One area of social justice meriting particular attention is physical ecology (Coates, 2003a, 2004; Tester, 1994b; Zapf, 2005). *Critical Social Work* featured a special edition (2003, vol. 4, no. 1) on ecological concerns, reflecting social work's slow but growing awareness of environmental concerns. Spirituality and ecology emphasize alternative world views based upon an expanded understanding of person-in-environment, which assume interdependence, relatedness with each other and the Earth, the essentialness of place, and the importance of the sacred in our lives. This broader framework enables social work to more easily embrace a focus on well-being, as opposed to exclusively problem solving, and to discuss the more ultimate sources of meaning in people's lives. Furthermore, the beliefs of an eco-spiritual perspective are more open to traditional and Indigenous forms of helping, and have created a welcoming and inclusive context enabling the celebration of diversity, and the sharing of knowledge (Coates, et al., 2006; Gray, et al., 2007); culture may become an essential aspect of professional education and practice. As Coates (2003a) argued, this trend can have a significant impact in shifting foundational beliefs and values away from their embeddedness in modern, Western systems of belief.

Certainly, social justice activities can be in strong harmony with community organizing. Todd's (2004) contribution examined how feminist community organizers' narratives about their secular work were actually intertwined with spiritual and religious stories. Thus, a commitment to social justice and organizing practices may be informed by religious affiliation and/or spiritualities. The concept of spirituality is sometimes criticized as being too focused on individualistic concerns. Clearly, these contributions demonstrate that spirituality does permeate social justice work and the narratives of practitioners and organizers in this field. Indeed, spirituality can help sustain social justice activity by giving a higher purpose to work that often comes into conflict with dominant and mainstream paradigms and ideologies.

Social work pedagogy has been another area targeted by Canadian social workers. Coholic (2003b) wrote about how student desires and needs, coupled with the issues clients bring to practice, encourage us to make room for discussions about spirituality in social work education. While some educators remain wary of the underdeveloped knowledge in this area, others recognize the importance of integrating spirituality into teaching practices. For example, Clews (2004) presented examples of assignments that could be used to help integrate spirituality into an undergraduate curriculum. As an Aboriginal woman, Baskin (2002) questioned how the spiritual dimension of life can even be separated from the activities of social work practice and education, as spirituality is equated with human existence. Csiernik and Adams (2002, 2003) found that social work education in general had an impact on students' spiritual development, and that spirituality was identified as more important for social work students compared to a control group of liberal arts students. Finally, Wong (2004), focusing on a critical social work pedagogy, described the use of mindfulness as a way of assisting students to learn through their feelings of discomfort. These studies, along with numerous American publications concerning social work education, point to the importance of making room for spiritually influenced discussions because many students will face these matters in the field, and spirituality can be an important aspect of a student's growth and development as a practitioner.

It makes sense that discussions concerning practice methods should constitute a large segment of the literature on spirituality and social work, given that the impetus to include spirituality in the profession derives from, in large part, social work's practitioner base and client demands. This mirrors developments within the medical field and the increase in studies examining alternative health care practices, which are often based on spiritual world views (Gaylord, 1999). Researchers at major universities in North America are studying connections between the mind, body, and spirit due in part to the popularity and increased use of these practices (Clark, 1999; Koenig, George, Titus, & Meador, 2004; Palmer, Katerndahl, & Morgan-Kidd, 2004).

Canadian contributions are numerous and varied. Coholic's (2002, 2003a, 2005) publications included the development of practice principles, spiritually influenced feminist practice, and investigations into the helpfulness of spiritually influenced group work. Butot (2005) and Fardella (2005) examined the interplay between a critical social work practice and spirituality, while others explored the spiritual dimension of practice more generally (McKernan, 2005; Wagler-Martin, 2005), and within a postmodern context (Damianakis, 2001; Moules, 2000). Zapf's (2005) work discussed the interconnections between spiritual transformation and people's environments. Suicide was also a matter that begged an examination of spiritual concerns (Morin, 2004), as was clients' cultures and religious perspectives (Al-Krenawi & Graham, 2003; Graham & Bradshaw, 2000)—a prominent theme in the 1990s literature, which was in line with social work's developing emphasis on diversity and inclusivity. Related to these discussions about practice is work that considers the self-development of social workers and their opportunities for professional transformation within postmodern contexts; using interreligious dialogue (Baum, 2003; Beres, 2004; Gallant, Holosko, & Gallant, 2005); as well as how social workers cope with and grow from their practice (Cadell, Regehr, & Hemsworth, 2003; Coholic & Blackford, 2003). Finally, as with the 1990s period, historical analysis of spiritually influenced helping and social work continued to be discussed (Graham, 2005b; Majonis, 2004; Moffatt & Irving, 2002).

These practice-oriented papers represent a unique contribution on the global scene, and they are also consistent with the broader literature in this area; that is, much of the work examining the inclusion of spirituality in practice has relied on personal experiences, case studies, and survey research. However, there is a dearth of empirical practice research that investigates spiritually influenced intervention methods and their influence on client change. To acknowledge the newness and limits of the current literature is not a criticism of it, or the type of knowledge it represents. Rather, this overview reflects the state of development in this field. We are at the point where more systematic investigation needs to occur regarding whether, in what situations, and to what extent, attending to spirituality actually improves client outcomes (Ai, 2002), not just in social work but across helping professions.

❖ CONCLUSION

Although the emergent scholarship in this field, and the demands of clients and practitioners, is moving us closer into mainstream social work, many researchers, students, and practitioners continue to worry that "their interest in spirituality has been ignored, marginalized, and at times actively discouraged" (Coates & Graham 2003b). The marginalization of spiritually influenced helping continues for various reasons. For instance, some helping professionals are concerned with blurring professional and personal boundaries with clients. A lack of clarity surrounding definitions of spirituality and religion creates confusion and can lead to fears of proselytizing. Others are concerned about colleagues' opinions regarding their work and worry that they will be viewed as unprofessional. Also, the lack of empirical knowledge in this emergent field and the reality that it is a new area of practice discourages professionals from integrating a spiritual dimension in their work—many are not aware of the burgeoning literature and developments in this area. Finally, the abstract and experiential nature of spirituality makes it difficult to study spiritually influenced processes from the dominant positivist research paradigm. Graham (2002) has described spirituality as our profession's last, and perhaps greatest, taboo. However, a sustained and developing research agenda seems probable within contemporary social work given the continued growth of interest in this field, and the drive to include spirituality in social work by many practitioners and clients, whose spirituality and religion are essential aspects of their identity and are frequently reflected in their work and life experiences. Indeed, the attention to diversity that postmodernism has brought encourages social work to be able to effectively attend to multiple belief systems, including spirituality, culture, and religion.

Social work has been at the forefront of this shift towards more holistic ways of working with people—recently, even the business community

(Wilber, 2000; Williams, 2003; Zsolnai, 2004) and health and medical researchers (Gilbert, 2002; Orchard, 2001; Shea, 2000) have turned their attention to studying spiritually influenced practices. However, the complexities inherent in attending to a diversity of belief systems have not been adequately addressed within the spirituality and social work literature. We are at the beginning, for example, of analyzing how an anti-oppressive pedagogical approach can have the effect of silencing, marginalizing, and even excluding those whose values and beliefs do not fit within secular, anti-oppressive social work pedagogy, such as students with fundamentalist religious beliefs. At the same time, fundamentalist views can harm students and educators, and perpetuate patriarchal and heterosexist belief systems. Is this a reasonable limit on inclusivity? The prospect of negotiating fundamentalism raises questions that require a critical reflection on our own belief systems, a rethinking of social work anti-oppressive values and ethics, and a consideration of our role as educators within the academy (Todd & Coholic, in press).

Certainly, given the emergent nature of this field, the options for future study and discussion are vast. And, as noted above, the inclusion of spirituality inevitably raises many queries and concerns that require debate. Other examples include the possible dangers of proselytizing when the realm of religion and spirituality is intentionally broached, and the possible ethical implications in the use of alternative therapies (such as meditation, yoga, body work, massage, and natural medicines) in social work practice. We believe that as Canadian society becomes increasingly diverse and the profession more sensitive and open to practising social work in alternative ways and utilizing knowledge and interventions more consistent with local and Indigenous cultures, we will be expected to work with various expressions of spirituality and spirituality's significance in the lives of people and communities. Thus, we will likely also need to examine the boundaries of our practices, especially when we work with other professions who already attend to the spiritual dimension of people's lives: clergy, chaplains, and pastoral care and bereavement counsellors.

Furthermore, there are also client populations that very much need to be addressed via empirical study in this field. For instance, spiritually influenced practice with children has received little attention in the practice literature. This being said, some studies reported that spirituality was a resiliency factor in helping children cope with childhood abuse and homelessness (Kidd, 2003; Lindsey, Kurtz, Jarvis, Williams, & Nackerud, 2000; Valentine & Feinauer, 1993), and that spiritual growth is significantly related to an adolescent's initiative and responsibility for self-care

(Callaghan, 2005). Findings such as these provide impetus for research in this area: if spirituality is an important factor in helping children cope with adverse life circumstances, it makes sense to study spiritually sensitive helping with this client group. As Graham recently insisted, one of the best ways for the social work profession in North America to respond properly to a spiritual imperative is to move beyond its own geographically bound anchors and to understand spirituality in international terms. Indeed, spirituality is a viable source of engaging with a recently rejuvenated movement to render social work relevant to the international communities in which it occurs in the effort to indigenize or localize social work's knowledge base. Social work journals in the global north, therefore, could usefully move beyond the topic of spirituality in strictly northern terms, and encourage scholars in the global south to publish in northern journals on spirituality topics from a global south perspective. There may be instances where scholars in the global north could be invited to collaborate in that dissemination (Graham, 2006). Canadian scholars could play an important role in this imperative.

This chapter has demonstrated that Canadian social workers have made a unique contribution in the construction of knowledge in this emergent field. We must move to find further ways to appropriately re-connect the personal and professional domains (Loewenberg, 1988) in order to expand our understanding of the complexities of modern life; to be more inclusive of varying perspectives; and be more open to helping people explore what provides meaning in their lives by way of narratives that best fit their experiences. The integration of spirituality into our contemporary knowledge base is vital as it assists us in working with increasingly diverse clients and communities.

NOTES

1. Lyndall Demere, PhD, in a personal communication (May 7, 2006), referred to her conversations at the First International Family Therapy Conference (Washington, DC, 1983/1984). Virginia Satir was asked to speak about the role of spirituality in her work, but she declined: "She told me, 'No,' saying Milton Erickson started to tell these truths in his later years and was not well received. She feared her work would be seen as less valuable."

2. The Canadian and American societies cooperated in planning the First North American Conference on Spirituality and Social Work on May 25–27, 2006, at Renison College, University of Waterloo.

REFERENCES

Ai, A. (2002). Integrating spirituality into professional education: A challenging but feasible task. *Journal of Teaching in Social Work, 22*(1/2), 103–130.

Al-Krenawi, A., & Graham, J.R. (1996). Social work practice and traditional healing rituals among the Bedouin of the Negev, Israel. *International Social Work, 39*(2), 88–111.

Al-Krenawi, A., & Graham, J.R. (1997a). Nebi-musa: A therapeutic community for drug addicts in a Muslim context. *Transcultural Psychiatry, 34*(3), 377–391.

Al-Krenawi, A., & Graham,J.R. (1997b). Spirit possession and exorcism in the treatment of a Bedouin psychiatric patient. *Clinical Social Work Journal, 25*(2), 211–222.

Al-Krenawi, A., & Graham, J.R. (1999a). Gender and biomedical/traditional mental health utilization among the Bedouin-Arabs of the Negev. *Culture, Medicine, and Psychiatry, 23*(2), 219–243.

Al-Krenawi, A., & Graham, J.R. (1999b). Conflict resolution through a traditional ritual among the Bedouin-Arabs of the Negev. *Ethnology: An International Journal of Cultural and Social Anthropology, 38*(2), 163–174.

Al-Krenawi, A., & Graham, J.R. (1999c). Social work and Koranic mental healers. *International Social Work, 42*(1), 53–65.

Al-Krenawi, A., & Graham, J.R. (2000a). Culturally sensitive social work practice with Arab clients in mental health settings. *Health and Social Work, 25*(1), 9–22.

Al-Krenawi, A., & Graham, J.R. (2000b). Islamic theology and prayer, relevance for social work practice. *International Social Work, 43*(3), 289–304.

Al-Krenawi, A., & Graham, J.R. (2003). Principles of social work practice in the Muslim Arab world. *ASQ, 25*(4), 75–91.

Al-Krenawi, A., Graham, J.R., & Maoz, B. (1996). The healing significance of the Negev's Bedouin Dervish. *Social Science and Medicine, 43*(1), 13–21.

Antle, B.J. (2005). Ethics and contemporary social work practice: Highlights from the new CASW Code of Ethics. *OASW Newsmagazine, 32*(1), 2–4.

Baskin, C. (2002). Circles of resistance: Spirituality in social work practice, education, and transformative change. *Currents: New Scholarship in the Human Services, 1*(1). Retrieved 12 December 2005 from fsw.ucalgary.ca/currents/articles/baskin_v1_n1.htm.

Baum, G. (2003). Interreligious dialogue as an exercise in renewal. *Currents: New Scholarship in the Human Services, 2*(2). Retrieved 12 December 2005 from fsw.ucalgary.ca/currents/articles/baum_v2_n2.htm.

Becket, C. (2005). *Values and ethics in social work: An introduction.* Thousand Oaks, CA: Sage.

Beres, L. (2004). A reflective journey: Spirituality and postmodern practice. *Currents: New Scholarship in the Human Services, 3*(1). Retrieved 12 December 2005 from fsw.ucalgary.ca/currents/articles/beres_v3_n1.htm.

Berger, C. (Ed.). (1987). *Contemporary approaches to Canadian history.* Toronto: Copp Clark Pitman.

Bibby, R. (1987). *Fragmented gods: The poverty and potential of religion in Canada.* Toronto: Irwin.

Bibby, R. (2002). *Restless gods: The renaissance of religion in Canada.* Ottawa and Toronto: Stoddart.

Bowers, S. (1954). Human values and public welfare. *The Social Worker, 23*(2), 1–7.

Bowers, S. (1955). *What is Catholic in Catholic social work?* San Francisco: Catholic Conference of Social Work of California.

Bowers, S. (1956). The place of religion in social work practice. *Council on Social Work Education's Social Work Education: Bimonthly News Publication, 4*(6), 1-4.

Bowers, S. (1959). Religion and social welfare. In *Facing This Hour* (pp. 22–26). Toronto: Board of Evangelism and Social Service of the United Church of Canada.

Bowers, S. (1960). The church and social welfare. *Social Order, 10,* 25–29.

Butot, M. (2005). Reframing spirituality, reconceptualizing change: Possibilities for critical social work. *Critical Social Work, 6*(2). Retrieved 15 December 2005 from www. criticalsocialwork.com/units/socialwork/critical.nsf/EditDoNotShowInTOC/BF3C 294588412BE785257017004CBDDA.

Cadell, S. (1996). Posttraumatic growth in HIV/AIDS caregivers in Quebec. *The Social Worker, 64*(4).

Cadell, S., Regehr, C., & Hemsworth, D. (2003). Factors contributing to posttraumatic growth: A proposed structural equation model. *American Journal of Orthopsychiatry, 73*(3), 279–288.

Callaghan, D. (2005). The influence of spiritual growth on adolescents' initiative and responsibility for self-care. *Pediatric Nursing, 31*(2), 91–99.

Canda, E.R. (1988). Spirituality, religious diversity, and social work practice. *Social Casework, 69*(4): 238-47.

Canda, E.R. (2002). A world wide view on spirituality and social work: Reflections from the USA, experience and suggestions for internationalization. *Currents: New Scholarship in the Human Services, 1*(1). Retrieved 15 December 2005 from fsw. ucalgary.ca/currents/articles/canda1_v1_n1.htm.

Canda, E.R., & Furman, L.D. (1999). *Spiritual diversity in social work practice: The heart of helping.* New York: Free Press.

Carniol, B. (1984). Clash of ideologies in social work education. *Canadian Social Work Review* 184-199.

Carniol, B. (1987). *Case critical: Challenging social work in Canada.* Toronto: Between the Lines.

Clark, P. (1999). To treat or not to treat: The ethical dilemma of alternative medicine therapies. *AIDS and Public Policy Journal, 14*(3), 117–131.

Clews, R. (2004). Spirituality in an undergraduate social work curriculum: Reflective assignments at the beginning and end of a programme. *Currents: New Scholarship in the Human Services, 3*(1). Retrieved 15 October 2005 from fsw.ucalgary.ca/currents/ articles/clews_v3_n1.htm.

Coates, J. (2003a). *Ecology and social work: Toward a new paradigm.* Halifax: Fernwood Publishing.

Coates, J. (2003b). Exploring the roots of the environmental crisis: Opportunity for social transformation. *Critical Social Work, 4*(1). Retrieved 15 October 2005 from www.

criticalsocialwork.com/units/socialwork/critical.nsf/982f0e5f06b5c9a285256d6e 006cff78/d8b8aa070b431afb85256f0400513e74?OpenDocument.

Coates, J. (2004). From ecology to spirituality and social justice. *Currents: New Scholarship in the Human Services, 3*(1). Retrieved 15 October 2005 from fsw.ucalgary.ca/ currents/articles/coates_v3_n1.htm.

Coates, J., & Graham, J.R. (Eds.). (2003a). Spiritual diversity and social work I. *Currents: New Scholarship in the Human Services, 2*(2).

Coates. J. and Graham, J.R. (2003b). Introduction to the special edition on spirituality. *Currents: New Scholarship in the Human Services, 2*(2).

Coates, J., & Graham, J.R. (Eds.). (2004). Spiritual diversity and social work II. *Currents: New Scholarship in the Human Services, 3*(1).

Coates, J., Gray, M, & Hetherington, T. (2006). An "Ecospiritual" perspective: Finally, a place for Indigenous voices. *British Journal of Social Work, 36*, 1–19.

Coates, J., & McKay, S. (1995). Toward a new pedagogy for social transformation. *Journal of Progressive Human Services, 6*(1), 27–43.

Coholic, D. (2002). Practice principles for social work and spirituality: A focus on practice methods and relationships. *Currents: New Scholarship in the Human Services, 1*(1). Retrieved 15 October 2005 from fsw.ucalgary.ca/currents/articles/coholic_v1_n1.htm.

Coholic, D. (2003a). Incorporating spirituality in feminist social work perspectives. *Affilia, 18*(1), 49–67.

Coholic, D. (2003b). Student and educator viewpoints on incorporating spirituality in social work pedagogy: An overview and discussion of research findings. *Currents: New Scholarship in the Human Services, 2*(2). Retrieved 15 October 2005 from fsw. ucalgary.ca/currents/articles/coholic_v2_n2.htm.

Coholic, D. (2005). The helpfulness of spiritually influenced group work in developing self-awareness and self-esteem: A preliminary investigation. *The Scientific World Journal, 5*, 789–802.

Coholic, D. (2006). Spirituality in social work pedagogy, a Canadian perspective. *Journal of Teaching in Social Work, 26*(3–4), 197–217.

Coholic, D., & Blackford, K. (2003). Exploring secondary trauma in sexual assault workers in northern Ontario locations: The challenges of working in the northern Ontario context. *Canadian Social Work, 5*(1), 43–58.

Csiernik, R., & Adams, D.W. (2002). The impact of social work education on students' spirituality *Currents: New Scholarship in the Human Services, 1*(1). Retrieved 15 October 2005 from fsw.ucalgary.ca/currents/articles/csiernik1_v1_n1.htm.

Csiernik, R., & Adams, D.W. (2003). Social work students and spirituality: An initial exploration. *Canadian Social Work, 5*(1), 65–79.

Damianakis, T. (2001). Postmodernism, spirituality, and the creative writing process: Implications for social work practice. *Families in Society, 82*(1), 23–35.

Danylewycz, M. (1987). *Taking the veil: An alternative to marriage, motherhood, and spinsterhood in Quebec, 1840–1920.* Toronto: McClelland and Stewart.

de Mello, S. (1992). Canada's first nations and rural Thaïs: Comparative issues for community development education. *Canadian Social Work Review, 9*(2), 168–182.

Dei, G.J.S. (1998). Interrogating "African development" and the diasporan reality. *Journal of Black Studies, 29*(2), 141–153.

Downie, R.S. (1980). *Caring and curing: A philosophy of medicine and social work.* London: Methuen.

Drouin, H. (2002). Spirituality in social work practice. In F.J. Turner (Ed.), *Social work practice: A Canadian perspective* (2nd ed., pp. 33–45). Toronto: Prentice Hall.

Fardella, J. (2005). Spiritual identity and transformation: Christian theory, public discourse and critical social work practice. *Critical Social Work, 6*(2). Retrieved 15 October 2006 from www.criticalsocialwork.com/units/socialwork/critical.nsf/ EditDoNotShowInTOC/D7D942F3D015850E8525701700616A47.

Gallant, W., Holosko, M., & Gallant, M. (2005). Using bio-spiritual music focused energetics for social workers to enhance personal identity and professional transformation: The power of self-reflective empathy. *Critical Social Work, 6*(2). Retrieved 15 October 2006 from www.criticalsocialwork.com/units/socialwork/ critical.nsf/EditDoNotShowInTOC/2DB5D44C083AE67885257018000F1125.

Gallant, W., Holosko, M., Gorey, K.M., & Lesiuk, T. (1998). The role of spiritually-oriented music as a form of intervention with alcoholic couples. *Social Work and Christianity, 25*(2), 115–129.

Gauvreau, M., & Christie, N. (1996). *A full-orbed Christianity: The Protestant churches and social welfare in Canada, 1900-1940.* Montreal and Kingston: McGill-Queen's University Press.

Gaylord, S. (1999). Alternative therapies and empowerment of older women. *Journal of Women and Aging, 11*(2/3), 29–47.

Gilbert, R.V. (Ed.). (2002). *Health care & spirituality: Listening, assessing, caring.* Amityvillle, NY: Baywood Publishing.

Gold, N. (1993). On diversity, Jewish women, and social work. *Canadian Social Work Review, 10*(2), 240–255.

Govenlock, S. (1958). Moral and spiritual values in social work. *The Social Worker, 26*(3), 21–30.

Govenlock, S. (1966). Ecole de service social: Perspectives d'avenir. *The Social Worker, 34*(1), 12–15.

Graham, J.R. (1992). The Haven, 1878–1930: A Toronto charity's transition from a religious to a professional ethos. *Histoire Sociale/Social History, 25*(50), 283–306.

Graham, J.R. (1994). Charles Eric Hendry (1903–1979): The pre-war formational origins of leader of post-World War II Canadian social work education. *Canadian Social Work Review, 11*(2), 150–167.

Graham, J.R. (1995). Lessons for today: Canadian municipalities and unemployment relief during the 1930s great depression. *Canadian Review of Social Policy, 35*, 1–18.

Graham, J.R. (1996). An analysis of Canadian social welfare historical writing. *Social Service Review, 70*(1), 140–58.

Graham, J.R. (2002, May). R.M. MacIver, E.J. Urwick, and Charles Eric "Chick" Hendry: Three directors of the University of Toronto school of social work walking along the road of secularism, 1918–1970. Paper presented at the First Annual Canadian Conference on Spirituality and Social Work, the Learneds, Toronto, Canada.

Graham, J.R. (2005a). E.J. Urwick. In J. Herrick and P. Stuart (Eds.), *Encyclopedia of social welfare history in North America* (pp. 411–412). Thousand Oaks, CA: Sage. Canadian entries edited by J.R. Graham.

Graham, J.R. (2005b). Religion. In F.J. Turner (Ed.), *Encyclopedia of Canadian social work*. Waterloo: Wilfrid Laurier University Press.

Graham, J.R. (2006). Spirituality and social work: A call for an international focus of research. *Arete: A Professional Journal Devoted to Excellence in Social Work, 30*(1), 63–77.

Graham, J.R. (2007). Helping processes in New York City: Insight into social services for Muslim peoples. *Muslims in New York Project*. New York: Columbia University.

Graham, J.R., & Al-Krenawi, A. (1996). A comparison study of traditional helpers in a late nineteenth-century Canadian (Christian) society and in a late twentieth-century Bedouin (Muslim) society in the Negev, Israel. *Journal of Multicultural Social Work, 4*(2), 31–45.

Graham, J.R., & Bradshaw, C. (2000). A forgiving state of heart: Narrative reflections on social work practice from a Christian perspective. *Social Work and Christianity, 27*(1), 40–48.

Graham, J.R., & Coates, J. (Eds.). (2005). Spirituality and social work. *Critical Social Work, 6*(2).

Graham, J.R., Swift, K., & Delaney, R. (2003). *Canadian social policy: An introduction* (2nd ed.). Toronto: Prentice Hall.

Graveline, F. (1998). *Circle works: Transforming Eurocentric consciousness*. Halifax, NS: Fernwood Publishing.

Gray, M., Coates, J., and Hetherington, T. (2007). Hearing Indigenous voices in mainstream social work. *Families in Society, 88(1), 55–66*.

Gripton, J., & Valentich, M. (2005). Bowers, Frank Swithun Barrington. In J. Herrick & P. Stuart (Eds.), *Encyclopedia of social welfare history in North America* (pp. 40-41). Thousand Oaks, CA: Sage. Canadian entries edited by J.R. Graham.

Hart, M.A. (2002). *Seeking mino-pimatisiwin: An aboriginal approach to helping*. Halifax, NS: Fernwood Publishing.

Hendry, C.E. (1974, October). "Towards renewal and the rediscovery of oneness: An overview and summary of the consultation." Unpublished Speech to the Western Economical Consultation, Banff, AB. University of Toronto Archives, Charles Hendry Collection. B80-0013, Box 16.

Hodge, D. (1998). Welfare reform and religious providers: An examination of the new paradigm. *Social Work and Christianity, 25*(1), 24–48.

Imre, R.W. (1982). *Knowing and caring: Philosophical issues in social work*. Washington, DC: University Press of America.

Jackson, J.E., & Warren, K.B.(2005). Indigenous movements in Latin America, 1992–2004: Controversies, ironies, new directions. *Annual Review of Anthropology, 34*(1), 549–573.

Kamya, H. (2000). Hardiness and spiritual well-being among social work students: Implications for social work education. *Journal of Social Work Education, 36*(2), 231–240.

Kidd, S. (2003). Street youth: Coping interventions. *Child and Adolescent Social Work Journal, 20*(4), 235–262.

Koenig, H., George, L., Titus, P., & Meador, K. (2004). Religion, spirituality, and acute care hospitalization and long-term care use by older patients. *Archives of Internal Medicine, 164*(14), 1579–1585.

Kruger, A. (1999). A personal reflection: The social gospel and the Canadian social work code of ethics. *Canadian Social Work, 1*(1), 25–29.

Lindsey, E.W., Kurtz, D., Jarvis, S., Williams, N., & Nackerud, L. (2000). How runaway and homeless youth navigate troubled waters: Personal strengths and resources. *Child and Adolescent Social Work Journal, 17*(2), 115–141.

Loewenberg, F. (1988). *Religion and social work practice in contemporary American society.* New York: Columbia University Press.

Lubove, R. (1965). *The professional altruist: The emergence of social work as a career, 1880–1930.* Cambridge: Harvard University Press.

Majonis, J. (2004). T. Chalmers, C.S. Loch and M.E. Richmond's development of increasingly secular, interpersonal, and purposeful helping methods. *Currents: New Scholarship in the Human Services, 3*(1). Retrieved 30 November 2005 from fsw.ucalgary.ca/currents/articles/majonis_v3_n1.htm.

Mandamin, J. (1994). Breaking free, the viewpoint of Aboriginal women. *The Social Worker, 62*(3), 137–139.

Matsuoka, A., & Sorenson, J. (1991). Ethnic identity and social service delivery: Some models examined in relation to immigrants and refugees from Ethiopia. *Canadian Social Work Review, 8*(2), 255–268.

McKernan, M. (2005). Exploring the spiritual dimension of social work. *Critical Social Work, 6*(2). Retrieved 15 December 2006 from www.criticalsocialwork.com/units/socialwork/critical.nsf/EditDoNotShowInTOC/BFD468E710F8AB58852570190012 3F32

Meier, A. (1997). The treatment of a major depressive episode using a pastoral counselling approach: A phenomenological study. *American Journal of Pastoral Counselling, 1*(1), 3–35.

Miller, J.R. (1996). *Shingwauk's vision: Canada's Native residential schools.* Toronto: University of Toronto Press.

Miller, J.R. (2004). *Lethal legacy: Current Native controversies in Canada.* Toronto: McClelland and Stewart.

Miller, J.R. (2005). Aboriginal people and policy in Canada. In J. Herrick & P. Stuart (Eds.), *Encyclopedia of social welfare history in North America* (pp. 5–7). Thousand Oaks, CA: Sage. Canadian entries edited by J.R. Graham.

Mishra, R. (1984). *Society and social policy.* London: Macmillan.

Moffat, K. (1994). Social work practice informed by philosophy: The social thought of Edward Johns Urwick. *Canadian Social Work Review, 11*(2), 133–149.

Moffatt, K. (2001). *A poetics of social work: Personal agency and social transformation in Canada, 1920–1939.* Toronto: University of Toronto Press.

Moffatt, K., & Irving, A. (2002). "Living for the brethren": Idealism, social work's lost enlightenment strain. *British Journal of Social Work, 32*(4), 415–428.

Monk-Turner, E. (2003). The benefits of meditation: Experimental findings. *The Social Science Journal, 40*, 465–470.

Moreau, M. (1979). A structural approach to social work practice. *Canadian Journal of Social Work Education, 5*(1), 78–94.

Morin, M.-L. (2004). Le suicide chez les jeunes et la quête de sens et de spiritualité. *Canadian Social Work, 6*(1), 63-89.

Morrissette, V., McKenzie, B., & Morrissette, L. (1993). Towards an Aboriginal model of social work practice: Cultural knowledge and traditional practices. *Canadian Social Work Review, 10*(1), 91–108.

Moules, N. (2000). Postmodernism and the sacred: Reclaiming connection in our greater-than-human worlds. *Journal of Marital & Family Therapy, 26*(2), 229–241.

Nabigon, H., & Mawhiney, A. (1996). Aboriginal theory: A Cree medicine wheel guide for healing first nations. In F.J. Turner (Ed.), *Social work treatment* (4th ed., pp.18-38). New York: The Free Press.

Nash, M., & Stewart, B. (2005). Spirituality and hope in social work for social justice. *Currents: New Scholarship in the Human Services, 4*(1). Retrieved 15 November 2006 from fsw.ucalgary.ca/currents/articles/nash_v4_n1.htm.

Orchard, H.C. (Ed.). (2001). *Spirituality in health care contexts.* Philadelphia, PA: J. Kingsley.

Palmer, R., Katerndahl, D., & Morgan-Kidd, J. (2004). A randomized trial of the effects of remote intercessory prayer: Interactions with personal beliefs on problem-specific outcomes and functional status. *Journal of Alternative & Complementary Medicine, 10*(3), 438–448.

Reid, P.N., & Popple, P. (Eds.) (1992). *The moral purposes of social work: The character and intentions of a profession.* Chicago: Nelson Hall.

Richmond, M.E. (1917). *Social diagnosis.* New York: Russell Sage.

Richmond, M. (1922). *What is social casework?* New York: Russell Sage.

Russel, R. (1998). Spirituality and religion in graduate social work education. *Social Thought, 18*(2), 15–29.

Saldov, M. (1991). The ethnic elderly, communication barriers to health care. *Canadian Social Work Review, 8*(2), 269–277.

Schwager, K.W., Mawhiney, A., & Lewko, J. (1991). Cultural aspects of prevention programs. *Canadian Social Work Review, 8*(2), 246–254.

Shea, J. (2000). *Spirituality & health care: Reaching toward a holistic future.* Chicago: Park Ridge Center for the Study of Health, Faith, and Ethics.

Sheridan, M.J., & Amato-von Hemert, K. (1999). The role of religion and spirituality in social work education and practice: A survey of student views and experiences. *Journal of Social Work Education, 35*(1), 125–141.

Tester, F.J. (1994a). Integrating the Inuit: Social work practice in the eastern arctic, 1955–1963. *Canadian Social Work Review, 11*(2), 168–183.

Tester, F.J. (1994b). In an age of ecology: Limits to voluntarism and traditional theory in social work practice. In M. Hoff and J. McNutt (Eds.), *The global environmental crisis: Implications for social welfare and social work* (pp. 53-74). Brookfield, VT: Ashgate.

Todd, S. (2004). Feminist community organizing: The spectre of the sacred and the secular. *Currents: New Scholarship in the Human Services, 3*(1). Retrieved 15 November 2005 from fsw.ucalgary.ca/currents/articles/todd_v3_n1.htm.

Todd, S., & Coholic, D. (in press). Christian fundamentalism and anti-oppressive social work pedagogy. *Journal of Teaching in Social Work.*

Turner, F. (Ed). (1979). *Social work treatment: Interlocking theoretical approaches*. New York: The Free Press.

Turner, F. (1983). Competence: A key to healing in a broken world. *Social Work and Christianity, 10*(2), 42–53.

Turner, F. (1996). *Social work treatment: Interlocking theoretical approaches* (4th ed.). New York: The Free Press.

Turner, F. (Ed). (2002). *Social work practice: A Canadian perspective* (2nd ed.) Toronto: Prentice Hall.

Ungar, M. (2003). Deep ecology and the roots of resilience: The importance of setting in outdoor experienced-based programming for at-risk children. *Critical Social Work, 4*(1). Retrieved 15 November 2005 from www.criticalsocialwork. com/units/socialwork/critical.nsf/982f0e5f06b5c9a285256d6e006cff78/ 0bcd7e76cc12b74885256f02004f3df1?OpenDocument.

Urwick, E.J. (1906). *Luxury and waste of life*. London: Dent.

Urwick, E.J. (1912). *A philosophy of social progress*. London: Methuen.

Urwick, E.J. (1920). *The message of Plato*. London: Methuen.

Urwick, E.J. (1927). *The social good*. London: Methuen.

Urwick, E.J. (1948). *The values of life*. Toronto: University of Toronto Press.

Valentine, L., & Feinauer, L. (1993). Resilience factors associated with female survivors of childhood sexual abuse. *American Journal of Family Therapy, 21*(3), 216–224.

Wagler-Martin, W. (2005). Listening to our stillness: Giving voice to our spirituality (spirituality & clinical practice). *Critical Social Work, (6)*2. Retrieved 20 December 2005 from www.criticalsocialwork.com/units/socialwork/critical.nsf/ EditDoNotShowInTOC/6A8878B500586CF685257019001C306F.

Wilber, K. (2000). A theory of everything: An integral vision for business, politics, science, and spirituality. Boston, MA: Shambhala.

Williams, O.F. (2003). *Business, religion, & spirituality: A new synthesis*. Notre Dame, IN: University of Notre Dame Press.

Wills, G. (1994). *A marriage of convenience: Business and social work in Toronto, 1918–1957*. Toronto: University of Toronto Press.

Wong, Y.-L.R. (2004). Knowing through discomfort: A mindfulness-based critical social work pedagogy. *Critical Social Work, 5*(1). Retrieved 20 November 2005 from www.criticalsocialwork.com/units/socialwork/critical.nsf/8c20dad9f1c4be3a 85256d6e006d1089/dd7c350ba0866ae785256ec20063c090?OpenDocument.

Woodroffe, K. (1962). *From charity to social work in England and the United States*. Toronto: University of Toronto Press.

Woodsworth, J.S. (1911). *My neighbor: A study of city conditions, a plea for social service. Textbook No. 7*. Toronto: The Missionary Society of the Methodist Church.

Zapf, M.K. (2005). Profound connections between person and place: Exploring location, spirituality, and social work. *Critical Social Work, 6*(2). Retrieved 25 November 2005 from www.criticalsocialwork.com/units/socialwork/critical.nsf/ EditDoNotShowInTOC/62C3C075C4133F288525701900280CFB.

Zsolnai, L. (2004). *Spirituality and ethics in management*. Amsterdam: Kluwer Academic.

CHAPTER 2

THE HAVEN, 1878–1930:

A TORONTO CHARITY'S TRANSITION FROM A

RELIGIOUS TO A PROFESSIONAL SOCIAL WORK ETHOS

JOHN R. GRAHAM

Other chapters in this section examine Canadian social work scholars' interest in different expressions of spirituality. It so happens that several of the more important Canadian writers were men. This chapter concentrates on the experiences of women, both as clients and providers of social welfare. It also highlights the spiritual basis of Canadian social work's charitable origins, prior to the profession's transformation into a secular, university-based profession. Social work first emerged in Canada, the United States, and Western Europe, in the early twentieth century, and out of a series of influences. A wide spectrum of individuals and groups, often overlapping, were involved: politicians, members of the media, volunteers, women's organizations, labour organizations, religious organizations, among others. The present chapter highlights one charitable institution, The Haven, which was established in 1878 in Toronto. By the 1890s the organization had started to display more secular, professional tenets in service delivery, and by 1930, a secular, professional social work ethos had replaced the organization's original religious foundation. In examining one such case study in considerable detail, insight is rendered into the Canadian profession's spiritual and religious origins.

In Canada, the broader forces of urbanization, industrialization, and democratization undoubtedly came to play, as did a vast network of charitable institutions that gradually emerged after European contact, but that gained greater momentum during the last half of the nineteenth century, when urban and industrial growth took off. Numerous charities had been founded to respond to the city of Toronto's growing social needs, including the Protestant Orphans' Home in 1851, the Working Boys' Home (1867), the Newsboys' Home (1868), the Infants' Home for unwed mothers

(1877), and the Nursing-at-Home Mission and Dispensary for women (1885) (Speisman, 1973, pp. 41–43). The Haven's mandate was broader than many, providing shelter, emotional support, counselling, or employment training to any woman who required it. Most admissions were either self-referrals or came by way of the courts, clergy, concerned friends or families, or other charities. Using terminology of the day, those staying at The Haven included the so-called "feebleminded," mothers and their children, unmarried expectant women, prostitutes, so-called "drunkards,"[1] the elderly, the unemployed, and infirm women. The extension of its services corresponded with a significant growth in facilities and resources. When it opened its doors on Berkeley Street, between Dundas and Queen in 1878, The Haven had a capacity of about eight beds, an annual revenue of $271.80, and provided assistance to a total of 178 women. By the late 1880s it had moved into new facilities at 320 Seaton Street, where it remained for over 40 years. The construction of a new wing in 1893 increased overall capacity to close to 75 beds, and a record number of 741 inmates were admitted into residence over the course of the following year (Toronto Women's Christian Association, 1878, pp. 17–23; The Haven, 1893, p. 3; Ontario Sessional Papers, 1895, pp. 83–84). Later, in 1907, the addition of a new section to one of the building's wings further increased The Haven's capacity to a little fewer than 100 residents (The Haven, 1907–1908, pp. 8–9). It should be noted that annual numbers of total admissions gradually decreased after the mid-1890s reaching an all-time low of 176 in 1930, reflecting the tendency to admit residents for longer periods of time. Furthermore, revenues increased during these years, jumping from $1,390 in 1880 to $8,000 in 1900, to over $18,000 in 1916, and to about $33,000 in 1929–1930 (see Graham, 1990).

The Haven was an off-shoot of the Toronto branch of the Women's Christian Association (WCA, later changing its name to the YWCA in 1889 [Pedersen, 1987]), having been established as part of the WCA's Gaol Committee. It should be noted that several of The Haven's founding members may not have been affiliated with the WCA. According to a Canadian Church of England evangelical periodical (*The Evangelical Churchman*), for example, The Haven was established by members of the WCA as well as "other benevolent ladies and gentlemen" who were presumably not associated with the WCA (Canadian Church of England, 1878, p. 616). This connection between some of the founders of The Haven and the WCA should not imply complete harmony; however, from the very beginning, WCA-Haven relations were not what they might have been. The Haven's mandate to help so-called "degenerate" women was carefully contrasted with the work of its parent organization.[1] As the 1890 Toronto YWCA *Annual Report* noted, in order to avoid offending "some of the older ladies of the [WCA] Board of Directresses," the WCA publicly and explicitly distinguished its different programmes, noting that rescue and relief initiatives at The Haven and elsewhere were run under different boards of management and were "entirely separate" from the WCA's work "for respectable young women who are earning a living for themselves in Toronto"(p. 9). The final break came in 1891, when The Haven officially severed its connection with the Young Women's Christian Association (YWCA), as it was henceforth known, and set out on its own.

It seems surprising, at first glance, that The Haven's organizing committee members should become a renegade splinter group within the WCA. They were, after all, men and women who were more revered for their success in Canadian business and politics and their prominence in Toronto high society than for pioneering charitable activities for some of Toronto's most marginalized citizens, but this was not an unusual phenomenon. In late nineteenth-century America, for example, wealthy urban residents turned their attention to the salvation of needy women (Magnuson, 1977, pp. 20–21). The Haven's male founding members included Clarke Gamble, a railway promoter and former city solicitor; John Macdonald, proprietor of a large wholesale importing house and reputedly one of the wealthiest men in Toronto; Samuel Hume Blake, a prominent Toronto barrister and vice-chancellor of the province of Ontario (whose brother Edward had been the province's premier, and was later the national leader of the Liberal Party); and W.H. Howland, lawyer, insurance executive, former president of the Toronto Board of Trade, Toronto's reformist mayor in 1886 and 1887, and the son of wealthy grain trader and "Father of Confederation" Sir William Pierce Howland (Armstrong, 1966, p. 365; Morgan, 1912, p. 111; Rose, 1888, pp. 579–581; Russell, 1982, pp. 113–114).

Women dominated the Administrative Committee from its inception, accounting for 24 of the 32 founding members. Like their male counterparts, women members belonged to prominent Toronto families that were closely linked by family ties, friendships, and business and political connections (see Cook, 1987, p. 70). These included Harriet (Mrs. Clarke) Gamble, Lady Susanna Julia (Mrs. William Pierce) Howland, her daughter-in-law Matilda Howland, Anne Margaret Kerr (sister of Samuel Hume Blake and wife of J.K. Kerr, a prominent Toronto lawyer and later a Canadian Senator), Mary Louise Gooderham (daughter-in-law of William Gooderham, founder of Gooderham and Worts Distilling Company and one of the city's most successful nineteenth-century merchants), and Georgiana McMurrich (wife of William B., who was a prominent lawyer, railway promoter, and mayor of Toronto in 1881 and 1882) (Chadwick, 1972; Lee, 1912; Middleton, 1923; Morgan, 1912; Newell, 1982; Russell, 1982; Schull, 1975).

What prompted people to establish and run such organizations? Like many but not all Victorian-era charities (see Fingard, 1975; Houston, 1975, 1982; Noble, 1979) the influence of socioeconomic class was particularly profound at The Haven. Historians have likewise emphasized the emergence of professional accreditation (see Bator, 1979; MacDougall, 1990; Pitsula, 1979) and gender (see Cook, 1989; Rooke & Schnell, 1982) in the helping process; the latter was important to The Haven several decades after its establishment, the former to its initial and emergent mandates. But there was more to it than this. The present analysis argues that evangelical Protestantism was the principal driving force during the organization's formative years, from its establishment in 1878 until the early 1890s. Thereafter, religious impulses waned and were replaced, in the post–World War I era, by an ethos of professional social work practice. And so, like many charities of its day, The Haven had an important spiritual component that was essential to its establishment and early years. As the following pages also point out, this spirituality was expressed in particularistic ways, reflecting the religious backgrounds of key members. More broadly, Canadian social work owes its existence to numerous charities in the pre–World War I period, such as The Haven, and the spiritually minded personnel with which these charities were associated.

Several of The Haven volunteers epitomize religiously inspired service to church and community that was anchored to time and place. W.H. Howland, for instance, was a fervent evangelical Anglican who undertook several personal crusades on behalf of the temperance movement, establishing coffee houses to keep working men from strong drink, conducting house-to-house visits in St. John's Ward (then one of the city's most destitute areas), and providing direct relief in the form of cash and kind. As one tribute noted, Howland "made practical philanthropy his chief business in life…. He was loyal to what he believed to be the truth of God's Word, and the will of Christ, and carrying out in everyday life the teachings of Christianity" (*Jubilee Volume of Wycliffe College*, 1927, p. 71). Another Committee member, Elizabeth J. Harvie, was associated with The Haven from its inception until her death in 1929, and was its president for 17 years. Her involvement with the Presbyterian Church's foreign missionary work was well known. As Secretary to the Women's Board of Missions for a 20-year period, she had travelled overseas to observe missionary activity.

A founding member of the Ontario Women's Christian Temperance Union and of the Women's Medical College in Toronto, Harvie was also a one-time president of the Ladies' Committee at the Hospital for Sick Children, and in 1896, she assisted J.J. Kelso in his work with the Children's Aid Societies in Ontario, Canada (Morgan, 1912, pp. 511–512).

Although never a formal Committee member, William Lyon Mackenzie King, future prime minister of Canada was, as an undergraduate student in political economy at the University of Toronto in the early 1890s, a volunteer associated with The Haven, taking a personal interest in saving so-called "fallen" women. Much, of course, has been written on King's charitable undertakings (see Stacey, 1976). His personal diary provided fairly conclusive evidence that King was a religiously inspired Presbyterian whose activities were part of a short-lived interest in entering the ministry. As noted in *The Mackenzie King Diary* (*MKD*) entries before, during, and after his association with The Haven, there are numerous references to his earnest desire to love and serve God, as highlighted by this passage and in other later passages:

> I am going to seek to know more of Christ and to live a better life.... I want to give my whole life to Him.... I am learning more of our Saviour every day.... I must become more earnest in my work for the Master, it will not do to be half-hearted. I hope I can do more and more every day to lift up the fallen, I hope that my life may be a pure and holy one devoted to Christ alone. (King, October 15, 1893; see also King, November 5, 1893, November 7, 1893, December 1, 1893, December 13, 1893, December 16, 1893, January 11, 1984)

Furthermore, in late 1893, Mackenzie King wrote that he had "made up [his] mind decidedly to go into the ministry" (King, December 15, 1893). Earlier, he had "thoughts of entering the ministry" (King, November 7, 1893) and soon became "fully determined" to do the same (November 12, 1893). This determination did not last, however, and by December 31,1895, he had decided that he wanted "to be connected with a university as a professor of Political Economy, or Social Science." Suffice it to say that The Haven Committee members such as Harvie and Howland, and occasional volunteers such as King, were not afraid to involve themselves directly in helping some of the city's most needy people. They had (to use William James' words) "knowledge about" the city's marginalized population based upon the concrete experience of helping rather than simply abstract "acquaintance with" social problems (Graham, 1999).

As such activity was motivated by personal beliefs, religious enthusiasm was the natural and central premise behind The Haven's work. Most of its volunteers were Protestant, evangelical laypeople, and members of a variety of sects. A considerable number predictably belonged to the Church of England, which was Toronto's largest denomination throughout the nineteenth century; among them were the evangelicals S.M. Blake, W.H. Howland, the Gambles, and the Reverend and Mrs. Richard Greene (*Jubilee Volume of Wycliffe College*, 1927, p. 14; Masters, 1947, p. 157; Morgan, 1912, p. 111). Other Protestant denominations, however, were also represented. Mary Agnes Hoskin was married to a leading Plymouth Brethren (Morgan, 1912, p. 548). Elizabeth J. Harvie was the daughter of a Methodist minister and the wife of a prominent Presbyterian (Morgan, 1912, pp. 511–512). Other Presbyterians, as well as at least one Baptist, had also joined the Committee by 1881. These included Mrs. William B. McMurrich, who joined the board in 1881, and was married to a prominent Elder at Knox Presbyterian Church (Russell, 1982). Mrs. R.W. Laird was with The Haven from its inception. She and her husband were long-time members of the Jarvis Street Baptist Church; her husband would eventually be appointed a deacon of the congregation (Canada Baptist Archives, 1856–1899).

The evangelical impulse was manifest in almost every aspect of work from the late 1870s to the early 1890s. Even the social conditions which the organization sought to improve were conceived in religious terms. The 1879 *WCA Annual Report*, for example, recognized the unprecedented proportion of social and spiritual problems that were brought about by massive urbanization. An "undercurrent of vice" rushed "madly through every large centre of population." "Never in the world's history," the report continued, "was such a glamour thrown around sin; never was vice presented in such a multitudinous of forms" (Toronto Women's Christian Association, 1879, pp. 18–19).

Religious terminology was often used to describe a resident's plight. In 1878, for example, The Haven volunteer Harriet Gamble urged young women to "avoid evil" lest they "be swallowed up in the vortex of sin" (Canadian Church of England, August 15, 1878, p. 219). The organization's services were also conceptualized in religious terms. As the 1878 Toronto *WCA Annual Report* noted, all work undertaken by its volunteers was meant to glorify God, as well as to save sinners:

> The Divine Master has taught us that one soul exceeds in the value [of] the whole world, and we know that within the casket of these sin-stained, sin-marred bodies, there lives, dwarfed and depraved though it may be,

an immortal and redeemed spirit, and we are willing to labour a lifetime that, even one of these priceless gems may be laid at the feet of Jesus (p. 21).

Moreover, The Haven's personnel, and indeed, any followers of Christ — working with The Haven, with other organizations, or by themselves — had the moral imperative to "bring deliverance" to those held "captive" by sin and to "forgive" them and "restore" them "to righteousness and peace … in the name of Christ … and to the eternal joy in earth and Heaven" (Canadian Church of England, February 7, 1878, p. 616; December 9, 1880, p. 488; Toronto Women's Christian Association, 1879, p. 19).

Evangelization was a major, if not the most important, underlying justification for the organization's existence in its early years. The Haven's ministries to the community, for instance, were entirely inspired by the Christian imperative to rescue sinful women. As the 1879 Toronto *WCA Annual Report* proclaimed,

> Followers of Christ must seek out the wanderers; must pursue them with fleet footsteps over the dark mountains of sin; must watch for them at the midnight hour, under the glare of the gas-light, or at the early dawn; and when one has been found she must be taken up rejoicingly — joy in earth and Heaven — in the strong arms of love and faith and carried to a place of safety. (p. 19)

Conversions at The Haven, or at other places visited by its volunteers where would-be residents could be found, such as the Toronto Jail, the Mercer Reformatory, the General Hospital, or downtown brothels, were a *sine qua non*. An example of the evangelization efforts of one of The Haven's volunteers visiting the General Hospital was cited in the 1881 *Annual Report*:

> The visitor, while engaged in reading the Scriptures to the unfortunate girls under treatment in his ward [the locked ward] observed a young woman who seemed particularly attentive, and, as the reading proceeded, apparently much affected. The visitor spoke very kindly to her, and before leaving urged her to come to The Haven; the girl did so, remained some few weeks, and was eventually placed in a good situation in the family of an earnest Christian lady. (The Haven, 1881, p. 15)

This religious approach to helping had other implications as well. Because programmes at The Haven were rooted so deeply in the Christian sensitivity to human need, the organization operated with enormous breadth and consistency. Rather than being preoccupied with one type of resident group (as they would once the organization became secular and professional), The Haven personnel, in the 1880s and 1890s, responded to a religious imperative that required them to embrace disadvantaged persons of all types. As one of its annual reports put it, The Haven admitted "the odds and ends of humanity": meaning anyone who required shelter, which frequently included those who had been refused admission to other charitable institutions (The Haven, 1885, p. 14). Indeed, in 1881, as referenced herewith from the 1881 *Annual Report*, a heterogeneous clientele became an explicitly declared hallmark of The Haven's services:

> No other institution in the city makes provision for all classes and grades of fallen women.... The doors of The Haven always stand open to receive any poor, homeless, friendless, miserable wanderer, the only difficulty being limited accommodation. No question is asked save the simple one: "Do you wish to do better?," and when the answer is in the affirmative, the Lady Superintendent admits until the house is full. (The Haven, 1881, p. 11)

In the process, as the 1881 *Annual Report* noted, the organization had become "not a permanent, but a transferring home." Its "main design," the report continued, was "to supplement the work of existing charities" (The Haven, 1881, pp. 10, 12). The Haven, then, acted as a clearinghouse for many women in Toronto, providing temporary accommodation while they waited to be admitted to other institutions, to the care of friends or relatives, or to the homes of families who provided employment. The women who ran and provided services within The Haven were no strangers to controversy. They were the city's only organization providing services to women with venereal disease (The Haven, 1885, p. 14), and—until other organizations with specialization removed the need—were among the few to provide shelter to women with substance abuse problems. It was not until the 1914–1915 *Annual Report* that mention was made of other services for women with substance abuse problems. In that report it was noted that "the inebriates like to go to the 'Women's Industrial Farm,' as they enjoy a certain amount of freedom there" (p. 7).

As the city's charitable services became more robust and specialized, The Haven gradually began to identify a niche: working with what was then termed "the feebleminded." The *Annual Report* of 1919–1920 noted that over one-half of inmates staying at The Haven were "feebleminded" (p. 9), and the 1925–1926 *Annual Report* confirmed that "the work of The Haven" was "gradually changing to specialized work with the mental defectives needing special care" (p. 10). This commitment to the "feebleminded" was a thread that connected the evangelical period of the nineteenth century to the emergent professional ethos of the 1920s and the decades that followed, until 1987, when the organization ceased operation at Lorimer Lodge (Graham, 1990).

By the 1890s, The Haven Committee was in a state of transition, as old guard evangelically inspired members were passing away or otherwise terminating formal connection with the organization. In 1895, for example, only two of twenty-three Committee members had served since the foundation stage (1878–1881). Like The Haven's founders, many new members belonged to the city's socioeconomic elite. In its early years, The Haven relied heavily upon personal donations canvassed by voluntary Committee members. In 1890, for the first time in the organization's history, personal donations constituted less than 50% of total income; within ten years this figure was down to 15%, and the decline continued to less than 1% in the 1920s. Municipal and provincial government grants increased markedly during this period, reaching a little over 40% of total revenues by 1900 (up from 18% in 1880). Another 40% of the organization's funding in 1900 came from its industrial services. As a result of the growing importance of so-called industrial activity, increasing numbers of paid personnel were hired to assist the Superintendent, a position that had been created in the organization's second year of operation (Toronto Women's Christian Association, 1879, p. 21). By the early 1890s, there were several new employees: a housekeeper, a Sewing Room Matron, an Assistant Superintendent, and a Nursery Matron. Committee members increasingly delegated responsibilities to paid staff, and the Superintendent became the most important individual in The Haven's daily and ongoing operations. As the *Annual Report* of 1901 noted, she was to "take charge of the household ... receiving visitors wishing to inspect the institution, interview[ing] all applicants for admission and friends of inmates ... and control[ling] the behaviour of the inmates," as well as being the person to whom all paid personnel were answerable (p. 17).

Consequential to the rise of industrial services and the departure of the founding Committee membership, the daily interactions between inmates and The Haven staff did not convey the evangelical enthusiasm of the 1870s and 1880s. The organization's Superintendent, Camilla Sanderson, noted in a private letter in 1898 that "the womanly, Christian influence in the daily performance of duty" still characterized paid staff.

Yet even if they were considered "earnest Christians," personnel were no longer religious "extremists along any line," a suggestive reference to past evangelical practices (Sanderson, May 25, 1898, p. 428). Sanderson was implicitly criticizing the religious enthusiasm of the organization's former members. In like manner, The Haven was no longer closely connected to the churches to which its Protestant founders had belonged. A passage from the 1903–1904 *Annual Report* captured this transition. The organization's Superintendent, the *Report* noted, had been asked to speak to several church groups about the work of The Haven. Having long since lost their direct links with the organization, "the City churches," it was hoped, would "become better acquainted with our work" (p. 7).

Not surprisingly, The Haven's annual reports increasingly made reference to secular and more systematic ways of helping. Borrowing from developments in other institutions, the organization for the first time referred to classification in 1885; inmates were separated on the basis of identified problems (for discussion on corrections classification see Wetherell, 1979). "Special attention will be given," the 1885 *Annual Report* noted, "to classification, our more youthful cases being kept as far as possible separate, except when attending the religious services," from the bad influences of the older, "more hardened and depraved" inmates (p. 14). Ten years later, further separation of The Haven residents took place. A maternity wing was established entirely removed from other parts of the facility, presumably so that the babies would not be disturbed by the industrial work and vice versa. A distinct prison gate wing was also added (The Haven, 1895, p. 18). The rationale was similar to the principles of classification introduced 10 years earlier. As the Ontario government's Inspector of Prisons and Charities noted approvingly in 1891, The Haven's inmates were "divided into two classes, the more degraded and shameless ones being kept in the old building, and the others in the new building" (*Ontario Sessional Papers*, 1891, p. 57).

The increasing number of professionally trained personnel may have helped to spur on this more refined, secular approach to helping. The first of the professions to be introduced to The Haven was nursing. Reference to the new position of Nursery Matron was made in late 1898, and for the next 30 years, until the organization's infant care services were terminated in late 1931, a professionally trained nurse was on staff (Sanderson, May 25, 1898, p. 428; May 28, 1898, p. 430; July 8, 1898, p. 442). The 1911 *Annual Report* made first mention of another professional, "a public school teacher," who instructed Haven inmates "once a week ... in elementary English" (p. 6).

The appointment of Lucy Brooking as Superintendent in 1907 reflected the organization's growing specialization. An authority on the purportedly growing white slave trade in the city of Toronto, she argued in Bell's edited book, *Fighting the Traffic in Young Girls, Or the War on the White Slave Trade* (1910), that white slavery was invariably connected with the problem of feeblemindedness. An important symbol of an emerging sense of professionalism, Brooking left The Haven in 1911 and eventually became a part-time lecturer at the University of Toronto's Department of Social Service, later named the School of Social Work (Hurl, 1983, p. 20).

The emergence of social casework greatly influenced The Haven's services. In 1914 the Department of Social Service had been established at the University of Toronto, which supplied a growing number of prospective graduates whom organizations such as The Haven could employ (Hurl, 1983, pp. 51–52, 54). At the same time, there appeared an emergent body of professional theory; for instance, the American social work pioneer Mary Richmond published *Social Diagnosis* in 1917 and *What Is Social Casework?* in 1922.

But The Haven's greatest incentive to accept social work's ultimate ascendancy came from the Federation for Community Services, a formal associative arrangement of Toronto charities, to which The Haven belonged after 1918. The Federation, which strongly encouraged the hiring of a professionally trained social worker, influenced every aspect of The Haven's operation. It had relieved Haven volunteers of the burden, which they had had since the organization was founded, of "general collecting" door-to-door (The Haven, 1918–1919, p. 7). More importantly, it provided an increasing proportion of the organization's overall revenues, accounting for over 40 percent of The Haven's total income by 1930. With increasing financial clout, the Federation was able to encourage considerable modifications to The Haven's programmes.

Much of this change was foreshadowed by cryptic references, in the *Annual Reports* of 1918–1920, to the length of residence of some of The Haven inmates (The Haven, 1918–1919, pp. 6–7; 1919–1920, p. 6; 1920–1921, p. 6). Revenues garnered from inmates comprised almost 25% of all income by 1918 (the laundry accounted for almost 50%, and board payments for 25%). There can be little doubt of the primacy of industrial and housework in The Haven's programmes for its residents. In the *Annual Report*, 1918–1919, it is noted that in a typical month, all residents were engaged in one form of in-house work. Forty did the laundry, 16 helped the nurse with caring for the resident infants, 8 were in the kitchen and dining room, 10 did the "sweeping, dusting, and cleaning" of the house, and the remainder worked in the sewing room (p. 6). As the 1919–1920 *Annual Report* stated, however, Committee members absolutely rejected any accusation that "the Board keeps some inmates longer than is necessary because they need their help in the workroom or in the Home." The interest "of the individual and the community outside The Haven," the 1919–1920 *Annual Report* continued, were "always considered first." Those inmates in question had to be deemed "mentally fit" by "the Hospital Clinic." "If the Board and staff thinks she can be trusted morally, she is given the chance" to go out on her own in the community (The Haven, 1919–1920, p. 6). (It was "a real grief to all connected with The Haven," the 1918 *Annual Report* noted, "that more cannot be trusted in this way" [p. 7].) Every effort was made, the 1919–1920 *Report* assured its readers, to see to it that the homes to which released inmates were sent (presumably as domestics) would "help the girls in every way." After release, moreover, "the careers of the girls" were "closely followed." Former inmates were "always encouraged to come to The Haven as Home," and were "always welcome on Sunday" and on such holidays as Christmas (The Haven, 1919–1920, p. 6).

Although it is unclear whether The Haven was responding to the concerns of the Federation, the Toronto public, or both, these were still serious insinuations. A 1924 survey of all of the Federation's member organizations proposed fundamental changes to The Haven's programmes. One was "to at once engage a suitably trained social service worker, so that each case admitted should be thoroughly investigated." In addition, The Haven's present population was to be "studied and trained," presumably so that programmes could be tailored to their needs. All cases were to be carefully monitored, and "full records" were to be prepared of all residents (The Haven, 1924–1925, p. 5). The organization's first social service worker, a Mrs. Abbott, left after four months of employment in 1925 (The Haven, 1924–1925, p. 6). The Federation for Community Services, however, managed to secure a new worker, Miss Effie Chesnut. "Since then," The Haven's 1926 *Annual Report* noted, "she has accomplished an enormous amount … and has given the Board the joy of realizing how we can cooperate more fully with other institutions and charitable organizations of the city" (The Haven, 1925–1926, p. 5).

The Federation proposed four principles of social work practice to be incorporated into The Haven's programmes. First, as recommended in the Federation's 1924 survey, the helping process was divided into several stages, all of which were standardized following the precepts of social casework. This included "social investigations" to determine applicants' eligibility for residence, and the nature of helping strategies. Each inmate had "a separate folder," which was "to contain a report of their physical condition, their mental condition, their social history, and a record of the case work done" while they were in residence (The Haven, 1925–1926, p. 12). Follow-up work for released inmates was equally systematic. "Plans [were] made," according to the 1925–1926 *Annual Report*, "while the girl is in The Haven and either the social worker of The Haven or the social worker of another organization" helped the inmate "to carry out the plans" and to "keep in touch with her" (p. 11).

The second principle stressed, according to the 1927 *Annual Report*, "re-education for community life and helping our girls to find out what kind of work they can do"(p. 8). No longer were inmates to be treated primarily as employees in the various industrial facilities within the organization. Indeed, in June 1931, the laundry facilities were permanently closed (The Haven, 1930–1931, p. 11). The interests of individual inmates instead were to take precedence over the financial needs of the organization. Corresponding with the concept of re-education for community life were classes in occupational therapy, given twice weekly by "a teacher supplied by the Department" (The Haven, 1927–1928, pp. 10–11). There is no direct mention of which department this quote refers to; in all likelihood, it is the city's Department of Public Health. Furthermore, similar classes in Home Nursing were arranged by the Red Cross (The Haven, 1927–1928). Recreational programmes, which were intended to foster residents' self-confidence and autonomy, were also initiated; for example, a Talent Club that was mentioned in the *Annual Report*, 1927–1928 (p. 11), and a dance class and seminar given by the Girl Guides were discussed in the *Annual Report*, 1929–1930 (p. 12). A weekly "Well Babies Clinic," run at The Haven by the city Department of Health, was introduced in 1925. Mothers were taught basic methods of childcare, and children routinely were examined (The Haven, 1925–1926, p. 7).

The third principle, the classification of inmates according to their mental age, was introduced in 1925. Psychiatrists employed by the city of Toronto's Department of Health diagnosed The Haven's "feebleminded" residents, thereby helping The Haven's social worker to "know what kind of work they are capable of doing to succeed" (The Haven, 1925–1926, p. 11). Although annual reports made no explicit references to improved psychiatric assessments, psychiatrists visiting the organization probably made use of the remarkable advances, in the World War I era, in the diagnosis and treatment of mental retardation (see Simmons, 1982).

The fourth principle was keeping abreast of current developments in the field of social work and in work with the "feebleminded." In 1927, The

Haven's Superintendent, Mrs. Effie Chesnut, who was appointed in 1926 and was herself a professionally-trained social worker, attended the first Social Service Conference of Canada, which was held in Montreal (The Haven, 1927–1928, p. 16). Two years later she visited "several institutions of the feebleminded in the United States," and took note of the way in which inmates were placed "in colonies [small homes] in the country" (The Haven, 1929–1930, p. 17). It should be noted that the colony house approach would be adopted by The Haven in the 1930s, and refined in the mid-1940s (see The Haven, 1930–1931, 1936; Jeffrey, 1943; Lewis and Jeffrey, 1945).

Professional social work, therefore, had been firmly instilled at The Haven and the last vestiges of the benevolent philanthropy of the nineteenth century were abandoned. Lubove (1965) made the argument that a growing sense of professional identity moreover demanded a strict delineation between the social worker and the social agency volunteer (p. 20). Differentiating the former from the latter was a scientific knowledge base and specialized skills that were the social worker's alone. The Haven volunteer, whose importance to the organization's programmes had started to wane with the declining numbers of evangelical Committee members in the 1890s, began to be relegated further to relative insignificance by the forces of professionalism.

The organization's entire administrative structure was reorganized in 1926 to include three distinct divisions under the supervision of the Superintendent. The first, financial work, was performed by a bookkeeper. The daily running of the house, or institutional work, was the second division. Under the House Supervisor were five matrons in charge of the following departments: the sewing room, the nursery, the laundry room, the kitchen, and housekeeping. The third division, social work, was the responsibility of a trained professional (The Haven, 1926–1927, p. 7). There continued to be other professionals, a day nurse and a night nurse who were in charge of the infants, a teacher who conducted evening classes and another in charge of young pre-school children, but it was not stated in the 1926 or subsequent annual reports to which division they belonged (The Haven, 1926–1927).

Further modifications took place at the onset of the Great Depression. The laundry facilities were closed in June 1931 and the nursery three months later (The Haven, 1930–1931, p. 11). The organization also moved out of its 320 Seaton Street location and opened two new facilities. The reason given for this move was that the Toronto Fire Department had insisted that the organization's fire escapes were unsafe (The Haven, 1930–1931, pp. 5, 7). There had been plans, in 1927, to move the facilities to the outskirts of town "with several acres of land suitable for recreation and for growing fruit and vegetables" (The Haven, 1927–1928, p. 5). With the advent of the Great Depression, however, these plans were abandoned, and for the remainder of The Haven's history, it would continue to be located in downtown Toronto. Whether the organization moved out of the 320 Seaton Street for financial reasons is unknown, although it is known that the building's mortgage had been paid off by 1914 (The Haven, 1913–1914, p. 6). The first new facility, Lorimer Lodge (named after a recently deceased long-time committee member), located at 137 Havelock Street, was a residence for so-called "mental defectives" released from the Ontario Hospital at Orillia, Ontario. The second new facility, at 614 Church Street, provided temporary shelter and, as the 1930 *Annual Report* noted, was "really [intended for] the same class of girls that we had been admitting at 320 Seaton Street" (pp. 8–9); that is, women who needed to be rescued from the pitfalls of the street.

These changes consolidated, according to the 1930 *Annual Report*, the trend toward specialization that had been taking place over the past several decades. The old practice of "handling eight distinct types of problems besides running an industry from which they [Haven officials] were supposed to acquire part of their funds" had ended. "In reality," The Haven had been "running eight different institutions in one building," an arrangement that a growing number of people perceived as "unfair to the girls admitted, and also to the staff and executive" (The Haven, 1930, p. 8). The number "eight" is somewhat arbitrary and is likely used for rhetorical purposes, demonstrating that there had been a wide variety of residents. Annual reports had not and would not explicitly identify the number of resident classes as eight. Furthermore, The Haven made the final break from its religious past in 1937 when it decided to confine its mandate to working exclusively with the so-called "mentally retarded." As the 1937 *Annual Report* noted, the organization's two objectives were

> to care and supervise mentally retarded girls and women with a view to fitting them for life in the community; and to study the problem presented by the mentally retarded in the community, the way in which it is being met, and by experiment, to demonstrate possible improvement. (p. 1)

It subsequently became, in every sense, a specialized, professional social work agency.

As American historian James Leiby (1978) has commented, the Christian tradition was most important in the development of nineteenth-century institutions of charity and corrections. Above all else, it "furnished a cosmic drama—the story of creation, sin, judgement, and salvation—in which human suffering had meaning, [as did] efforts to relieve it" (p. 21). The personal interaction between those providing help and those receiving it "counted for a great deal in the structure of the universe" (p. 21). This was salvation, an imperative which, in the realm of charity, went hand in glove with charismatic leadership, individual incentive, benevolent spontaneity, and village neighbourliness. The social agencies of a modem urban-industrial society, however, demanded the secular initiative of the professional social caseworker. Whereas charity had been a humanitarian crusade to bring salvation and comfort to society's less fortunate individuals, social work was a systematic approach to a complex web of social problems, among them what came to be known as mental retardation.

There was a great deal that was troubling to The Haven's earlier, religious mandate. Particularly by the standards of our day, The Haven's services were class-based, frequently pejorative to clients, and reproduced prevailing and troubling notions of gender. And its emphasis on religious conversion, and insistence that clients adhere to particular notions of religion, are deeply problematic to most readers. But in its transformation from a religiously/spiritually motivated agency responding to social need to a professional and secular social service agency, were there also losses in vision or mandate? Were the roles of volunteers at The Haven, as at other organizations across the country, gradually supplanted by the trained professional, and if so, what were the consequences for Canadian society?

NOTE

1.   Nomenclature from the historical period will be used throughout this chapter. The author obviously intends no offence by using such terminology.

REFERENCES

Armstrong, F.H. (Ed.). (1966). *Toronto of old by Henry Scadding*. Toronto: Oxford University Press.

Bator, P.A. (1979). "The struggle to raise the lower classes": Public health reform and the problem of poverty in Toronto, 1910–1921. *Journal of Canadian Studies, 14*(1), 43–49.

Brooking, L.W. (1910). Conditions in Toronto. In E.A Bell (Ed.), *Fighting the traffic in young girls, Or the war on the white slave trade*. Chicago: G.S. Ball.

Canada Baptist Archives. (1856–1899). *Directories of the Jarvis Street Baptist Church*. Hamilton, ON: McMaster University.

Canadian Church of England. (February 7, 1878). *The evangelical churchman*, 616.

Canadian Church of England. (August 15, 1878). *The evangelical churchman*, 616.

Canadian Church of England. (December 9, 1880). *The evangelical churchman*, 488.

Chadwick, E.M. (1972 reprint). *Ontario families: Genealogies of united empire loyalist and other pioneer families of Upper Canada* (Vol. 1). Belleville, ON: Mika Silk Screening Limited.

Cook, S.A. (1987). "A Helping Hand and Shelter": Anglo protestant social service agencies in Ottawa, 1880–1910. Unpublished MA thesis, Carleton University, Ottawa.

Cook, S.A. (1989). A quiet place ... to die: Ottawa's first Protestant old age homes for women and men. *Ontario History, 81*(1), 25–40.

Fingard, J. (1975). The relief of the unemployed poor in Saint John, Halifax, and St. John's, 1815–1860. *Acadiensis, 5*(1), 32–53.

Graham, J.R. (1990). *The Haven: A Toronto charity for women, 1878–1930*. Unpublished MA thesis, Queen's University, Kingston, ON.

Graham, J.R. (1999). William Lyon Mackenzie King, Elizabeth Harvie, and Edna: A prostitute rescuing initiative in late Victorian Toronto. *Canadian Journal of Human Sexuality, 8*(1), 47–60.

The Haven (1881–1885). *Annual report*. Toronto: Author. Retrieved from the Collection of the Metropolitan Association for Community Living.

The Haven (1895–1930). *Annual report*. Toronto: Author. Collection of the Toronto Reference Library.

Houston, S. (1975). Victorian origins of juvenile delinquency: A Canadian experience. In M.B. Katz & P. H. Mattingly (Eds.), *Education and social change: Themes from Ontario's past*. New York: New York University Press.

Houston, S.E. (1982). The "waifs and strays" of a late Victorian city: Juvenile delinquents in Toronto. In J. Parr (Ed.), *Childhood and family in Canadian history*. Toronto: McClelland and Stewart.

Hurl, L.F. (1983). *Building a profession: The origin and development of the department of social service in the University of Toronto, 1914–1928* (Working Papers on Social Welfare in Canada Series). Toronto: Faculty of Social Work, University of Toronto.

Jeffrey, A.M. (1943). A follow-up study on the re-establishment of mentally defective girls in domestic science in an urban centre under colony house supervision. *American Journal of Mental Deficiency, 48*(1), 96–100.

Jubilee Volume of Wycliffe College. (1927). Toronto: Wycliffe College.

King, W.L.M. (1893–1895). *Mackenzie King diary*. Public Archives of Canada, MG 26 J13.

Lee, S. (Ed.). (1912). *Dictionary of national biography, second supplement* (Vol. 2). London: Smith, Elder, and Company.

Leiby, J. (1978). *A history of social welfare and social work in the United States*. New York: Columbia University Press.

Lewis, E.P., & Jeffrey, A.M. (1945). Ross cottage: A special foster home. *American Journal of Mental Deficiency, 49*(3), 377–382.

Lubove, R. (1965). *The professional altruist: The emergence of social work as a career, 1880–1930.* Cambridge, MA: Harvard University Press.

MacDougall, H. (1990). *Activists and advocates: Toronto's health department, 1883–1983.* Toronto: Dundurn Press.

Magnuson, N. (1977). *Salvation in the slums.* Meetuchen, NJ: Scarecrow Press.

Masters, D.C. (1947). *The rise of Toronto.* Toronto: University of Toronto Press.

Middleton, J.E. (Ed.). (1923). *The municipality of Toronto, Vol. 2, Part 4: Biographical sketches.* Toronto: Dominion Publishing Company.

Morgan, H.J. (1912). *The Canadian men and women of the time.* Toronto: William Briggs.

Newell, D. (1982). William Gooderham. In *Dictionary of Canadian biography* (Vol. 11). Toronto: University of Toronto Press.

Noble, J. (1979). Classifying the poor: Toronto charities, 1850–1880. *Studies in Political Economy, 2*(1), 109–128.

Ontario Sessional Papers (1895), 27(3,12), 83–84.

Ontario Sessional Papers (1891), 23(3,11), 57.

Pedersen, D. (1987). The Young Women's Christian Association in Canada, 1870–1920: A movement to meet a spiritual, civic, and national need. PhD Dissertation, Carleton University, Ottawa.

Pitsula, J. (1979). The emergence of social work in Toronto. *Journal of Canadian Studies, 14*(1), 35–42.

Richmond, M. (1917). *Social diagnosis.* New York: Russell Sage Foundation.

Richmond, M. (1922). *What is social case work?* New York: Russell Sage Foundation.

Rooke, P.T. & Schnell, R.L. (1982). The rise and decline of British North American Protestant orphans' homes as woman's domain, 1850–1930. *Atlantis, 7*(2), 21–35.

Rose, G.M. (Ed.). (1888). *A Cyclopaedia of Canadian biography* (Vol. 2). Toronto: Rose Publishing.

Russell, V. (1982). *Mayors of Toronto* (Vol. 1). Erindale, ON: Boston Mills Press.

Sanderson, C. (1895–1899). *Letterbook.* Collection of the Metropolitan Toronto Association for Community Living, Toronto.

Schull, J. (1975). *Edward Blake.* Toronto: Macmillan.

Simmons, H.G. (1982). *From asylum to welfare.* Downsview, ON: National Institute on Mental Retardation.

Speisman, S.A. (1973). Munificent parsons and municipal parsimony: Voluntary vs. public poor relief in nineteenth-century Toronto. *Ontario History, 65*(1), 41–43.

Stacey, C.P. (1976). *A very double life.* Toronto: MacMillan.

Toronto Women's Christian Association (1878–1890). *Annual Report.* Ontario Public Archives, Add. MS 561.

Wetherell, D.G. (1979). To discipline and train: Adult rehabilitation programs in Ontario prisons, 1874–1900. *Histoire sociale — Social History, 12*(3), 145–165.

CHAPTER 3

THE SOCIAL GOSPEL

RICHARD ALLEN

The Social Gospel was an attempt to apply Christianity to the collective ills of an industrializing society, and was a major force in Canadian religious, social, and political life from the 1890s through the 1930s. It drew its unusual strength from the remarkable expansion of Protestant, especially Evangelical churches, in the latter part of the 19th century. For several decades the prevalent expression of evangelical nationalism, the Social Gospel was equally a secularizing force in its readiness to adopt such contemporary ideas as liberal progressivism, reform Darwinism, biblical criticism, and philosophical idealism as vehicles for its message of social salvation. It developed, however, a distinctive spirituality elevating social involvement to a religious significance expressed in prayers, hymns, poems, and novels of "social awakening." Its central belief was that God was at work in social change, creating moral order and social justice. It held an optimistic view of human nature and entertained high prospects for social reform. Leaders reworked such traditional Christian doctrines as sin, atonement, salvation, and the Kingdom of God to emphasize a social content relevant to an increasingly collective society. The Social Gospel at large gave birth to the new academic discipline of social ethics and in Canada contributed most of the impetus to the first sociology programs.

It appeared in Canada in the 1880s, a decade of materialism, political corruption, economic distress, and a growing sense of urban disorder. Moved by the difficulties of the time, by Protestant negativism and otherworldliness, and enthused by such social prophets as Carlyle, Ruskin, Tolstoy, and Henry George, and by young Protestants such as J.W. Bengough and Salem Bland, together with idealist philosophers such as John Watson at Queen's, precipitated a movement that by the mid-1890s had become the stuff of church journalism, ministerial institutes, college alumni conferences, and youth movements. Early evidence of the church's expanding role came with the founding of city missions and institutional churches such as the St. Andrew's Institute (Toronto, 1890) and the Fred Victor Mission (Toronto, 1894), followed by a chain of church settlement houses (1901–1919). Whereas Methodism probably fielded the Social Gospel most easily, between 1894 and 1910 all the major Protestant denominations created board structures to handle its mushrooming concerns. Older moral causes—temperance, Sabbath observance, and social purity (against prostitution)—were reinterpreted, reinvigorated, and incorporated into the progressive reforms.

Joined nationally and provincially in 1908 under Presbyterian J.G. Shearer in the Moral and Social Reform Council, the churches readily aligned these concerns with others: the child, health, housing, and urban reform.

In 1912 the council was reorganized as the Social Service Council of Canada, and the churches began sponsoring comprehensive surveys of urban conditions. In 1914 the council sponsored the first national congress on social problems. With notable exceptions, the male leadership did not give a high place to women's suffrage, but many women of the National Council of Women, the Woman's Christian Temperance Union, and the suffrage organizations found in the Social Gospel a convenient vehicle for articulating the needed reforms based on their maternal feminist creed.

Although the Social Gospel is often categorized as an urban middle-class phenomenon, it did attract agrarian and labour reformers. W.C. Good of the United Farmers of Ontario, R.C. Henders of the Manitoba Grain Growers' Association, E.A. Partridge of the Saskatchewan Grain Growers' Association, and H.W. Wood of the United Farmers of Alberta were all enthusiasts, as were labour leaders, including James Simpson in Ontario, A.W. Puttee in Manitoba, and Elmer Roper in Alberta. By World War I it had become a primary informing principle of social reform. The increase in social purpose occasioned by the war brought the movement to a height of influence as reforms it espoused—direct legislation, prohibition, women's suffrage, civil service reform, bureaus of social research, expansion of co-operatives, the decline of party government, and, for some, state direction of the economy for national efficiency—all made immense strides.

Postwar unrest gave the Social Gospel further prominence through association with the Winnipeg General Strike of 1919 and the Progressive Party campaign, 1919–1921. Radical Social Gospellers, such as J.S.

Woodsworth and William Irvine, became increasingly alienated from the church-based Social Gospel. In turn, its hopes and accomplishments were compromised by economic decline, the secularizing of social work, and the backlash against prohibition, while labour and agrarian factional strife undermined the basis of radical Social Gospel action. The formation of the United Church in 1925, itself in part a product of the Social Gospel, did not stem the growing crises in the movement, whose fortunes plummeted.

The reasons for decline in the 1920s were manifold: the accomplishment of many reforms, a delayed disillusionment with the war, a weariness with doing good, a general abandonment of moral earnestness for a new hedonism, and the decline of idealism as a reigning philosophy. The Social Gospel, ideologically bound to the primacy of reason in a being vitally attuned to a benevolent God, could hardly survive in a world apparently animated by power and unreason on the one hand and frivolity on the other.

However, under the impact of the Great Depression, a new younger generation combined the insights of Alfred North Whitehead, Reinhold Niebuhr, and Karl Marx to fashion what some termed a new Social Gospel, others a form of "radical Christianity," which recognized the need for personal as well as social renewal, accepted the importance of class struggle, and sought a society of "mutuality."

Associated in the Fellowship for a Christian Social Order (later complemented by the Anglican Fellowship for Social Action), most of this younger leadership (J.W.A. Nicholson in the Maritimes, King Gordon and Eugene Forsey in central Canada, T.C. Douglas and J.H. Horricks on the Prairies, and Harold Allen in BC) contributed to the creation of the Co-operative Commonwealth Federation (1932).

A broadly diffused older Social Gospel played a less obvious role in the creation of the Social Credit and reconstruction parties, and in the Depression attempts to transform the Conservative and Liberal parties. After World War II the Social Gospel could be given much credit for public readiness to maintain Canada's new welfare state and its international posture as a peacekeeping nation. Sons and daughters of the Social Gospel could be found critically placed throughout both enterprises. That an almost apocalyptic age of the later 1960s and 1970s has overtaken the grandly progressive, if somewhat vaguely entertained, social hopes of a residual social gospel is evident in the limited objectives of church-based coalitions on Native rights, corporate responsibility, and the environment. Nonetheless, Third World Christianity, Marxist-Christian dialogue, and

Catholic liberation theology have had some effect in regenerating a body of Canadian Christian social thought and action reminiscent of the radical Social Gospel.

CHAPTER 4

EXCERPTS FROM *THE VALUES OF LIFE*

(ORIGINALLY PUBLISHED 1948)

E.J. URWICK

[...] But the principle of disinterest also appears in an extreme form in the ethic of some Eastern religions, particularly in the purest doctrines of Hinduism and Buddhism. In these it is exalted into complete dispassion, aloofness from all desires, even annihilation of the desiring self. [...]

There is further reason why the ideal of dispassion exalted in the Eastern religions cannot serve us in the West as an ideal of goodness. Not only do we insist upon regarding our present life as an adventure in and for a social world, which we intend to make better if we can, but also we are, as the psychologists would say, conditioned to a different concept of life. The Christian ethic, to which we are at least nominally wedded, is emphatically an ethic for neighbours living together on earth.[...]

[...] But to those of us who believe in the reality of beauty or the eternal existence of goodness, the scientific intellect neither gives nor refuses justification of our faith. Indeed, a very little thought will convince us that the scientific mind is not concerned at all with good or bad conduct or good or bad aims. Its great virtue is that it is always impartial. For science and for scientific thought there is no such thing as quality in the sense of quality of beauty or quality of goodness. Its sole interest is in truth, and its sole test of truth is conformity with all observed facts. Nor is it at all interested in purpose, at any rate the purposes of human endeavour. For purpose is always related to ideal ends, to imagined future conditions; and the only facts which exist for science are past facts; the only evidence upon which scientific logic can work is the evidence of what has already happened. All its premises, all its causal conditions, are behind us; they are not even in the present, for the present is only a point dividing past and future, and the moment we try to use a present fact as evidence it has already become a past fact. But human conduct, when it is really significant, is always anchored to the future. Its causal purposes are ideal conditions yet to be realized. Whether we call it desire or aspiration, the force that leads us on is the thought of some better state which does not yet exist, has indeed no real existence except in our imagination. In other words, our significant conduct is determined from the front, and not from behind; by ideas, and not by facts. [...]

[*After speaking of King Solomon and the death of Socrates*]
    [...] But it is still the case that a man who shows his conformity by ostentatious church membership may live a thoroughly anti-social life with very little criticism from his fellow churchmen. And it is still true that religious dogma is the one thing in the world which pious people, in the teeth of all evidence, insist upon regarding as unchangeable. [...]
    [...] Preachers in every sect have for centuries proclaimed the deceitfulness of riches, the folly of vanity, and the worthlessness of most worldly pursuits, with conspicuous lack of success. But this of course would be an unfair criticism of religion, for a very significant reason. The religious teachers are in competition with much more powerful, persistent, and ubiquitous teachers; that is, with the worldly desires of worldly men and women. We are all inheritors of the original sin of desiring intensely all sorts of pleasures, satisfaction, comforts, and luxuries. The desire for power, privilege, distinction, and security is hardly less intense. Not only so: we live in a world in which golden calves are permanently exalted and universally admired. With few exceptions, our elders and contemporaries, backed by the obvious facts of modern life, are forever urging us, tacitly and by example, to avoid the supreme folly of being poor, or meek, or humble, or self-sacrificing, or anything except sensible seekers after a secure and comfortable life. Religion is hardly to be blamed because it develops only an occasional Saint Francis. [...]
    [...] In all practical matters we belong to groups or sects or parties, each with its own special tenets, beliefs, and accepted dogmas. Obviously, if one group is right, the others must be wrong. If Christians are right, Muslims and Hindus are wrong; if Roman Catholics are right, Protestants are wrong; if Conservatives are right, Socialists are wrong. And in each case the wrongness applies to a very large body of detailed beliefs and dogmas. This means in all practical matters—in the general conduct of life, in short—the only test of truth is the rightness of the actions which follow from the dogmas. [...]
    [...] It is true that in religion and morality most of us adopt the attitude— let sleeping absurdities lie, for by waking them you will only disturb the

basic good which religion and morality uphold; just as in science we adopt the attitude—do not raise awkward questions about absolute truth, but fix your attention upon the tested agreements between all discovered laws and the phenomena to which they relate. At the same time, we are not going to let anybody or anything rob us of our bug truth; and if attacks upon the "little lies" or fallible details of doctrine imperil the big truth we will repel them with all our might. Every political and social creed is of course vulnerable at many points, and ethical doctrines are far from infallible in detail. […]

[…] If a man really loves God or liberty or justice—or power or pleasure or gain—if he really believes in the ultimate value of these things, then you may understand you cannot alter his multitudinous ideas about this human world and our life in it. Argument will lay bare this bedrock; but it will not change it. […]

[…] But what really matters is whether we love the law and love our neighbours. And that lesson is not easily taught in classroom or lecture hall. It does not depend upon any intellectual process. Example counts for infinitely more than precept. The world we live in is our teacher, and most of all the little world of family and closest associates. […]

[…] Millions of people have loved God and have let that love purge their souls, without knowing in the least how to define God. All they have needed is the firm conviction that God is good, and God is love—by no means the kind of concept which a scientist could approve. But our ideals are the jumping-off ground for new adventures in living, not for new discoveries of science. And for that purpose it is enough that we should grasp just a little of the reality which the ideal embraces. […]

[…] Plato makes it very clear that his concept of love in its highest form is that of a passion for absolute beauty, goodness, and wisdom, and therefore the inspirer of all the best souls in their great search for the great reality which men call God. […]

Now the degradation of charity is of course an old thing. Long before the Christian era rich people were bestowing their gifts to be seen of man in order to lend ostentation to the conspicuous virtue. Long before the Reformation pious Christians were using their gifts as an easy key to heaven. Their benefactions were made less to benefit the poor than to benefit themselves. The poor were a necessary part of society because they were such useful stepping stones to salvation for the rich. […]

[…] Progress only takes place when there is movement or change towards a condition which is better than the existing condition—better in reality as well as better in our estimation. While the change is in process we call it progressive only by an act of faith; but the validity of the faith is sometimes so robust as to amount to certainty, as (to take very simple examples) when a drunkard or a libertine changes in the direction of sobriety or chastity. In the matter of truth and knowledge the tests are much simpler and easier to apply. Few would deny that human history displays a very marked if intermittent advance in that kind of knowledge called scientific, that is to say, in knowledge of the facts and processes of the phenomenological universe. The goal here is greater power in the use of natural processes of all sorts; and the test of experience confirms our belief that we are constantly approaching nearer to our goal. [...]

[...] We need an attitude of our psyche which shall impel us to embrace every real thing, in its humblest manifestation, not only with those faculties of the mind which are rational or logical or analytical, but with all faculties of the soul which enable us to reverence and to love as well as to recognize whatever is beautiful and real. For the famous triad—beauty, truth, and goodness—describes a single reality. Truth cannot be separated from beauty nor either from goodness. And whoever would know reality must search for all three with every power his soul possesses. [...]

[...] In many families and larger circles the Bible, like church-going, has passed out of fashion. This need not mean that religion has disappeared from such circles, nor that lower standards of morality have been accepted. The lives of many rationalists refute any such suggestion. But what has been called a mythical religion has certainly lost its hold on very many young people. The texts embodying a very fine morality, the verse throbbing with a passion for righteousness, are no longer instilled into their minds as a matter of course. [...] It may be that the values instilled by texts and collects and sermons had rather shallow roots. It may be that these failed to make an indelible impression because the teachers and other professed believers have not been conspicuous for any passion for righteousness. It may be that for most of us older people the religion of conviction has degenerated into a religion of habit. But no one can question the danger of the change. Freedom and free choice are good; but will this freedom be justified by its fruits? [...]

[...] It is probable that in the great majority of cases the principles which they accept, and their firm loyalty to them, are directly derived from religion, and the authority behind them is therefore unquestioned. It is probable also that in other cases, where adherence to orthodox religion no longer exists, the source to the accepted moral principles is still a religious source. Materialists and atheists never free themselves from the all-pervading atmosphere of beliefs and attitudes which many centuries of religious faith have created for them. That is their heritage, whether they like it or not. Only the permanent can change, say philosophers. Certainly change is meaningless unless it grows out of firmly planted and vital roots. The new thought of the freest of freethinkers is never his own creation. It grows in the soil prepared for him by all his orthodox ancestors. [...] I think it is Bergson who has suggested that moral progress involves moral creators who see with their mind's eye a new social horizon—a better world, so much better that, if we tried it, we should refuse to go back to the old one. [...]

For all of us the conclusion is plain. We needs must strive for progress, else we begin to die. We needs must believe in progress, else we lose all our goals. And by all means let us plume ourselves on our progress, so long as we are very sure about the value of the goals we are nearing. It is a fine thing to advance in learning, in strength, in the confident handling of difficulties, or in any chosen line of worthwhile achievement. It is a fine thing—if only because our self-respect demands it. But it is a poor thing if it means that we are content to ask "How am I getting on in life?" And forgetting to ask "How is life getting on in me?" It is a poor thing, both for individuals and for society, if our principal achievement is the amassing of stuff to feed our vanity or the increase of power to feed our greed. [...]

[...] If religion includes the firm acceptance of truths revealed by God and made accessible to us by a Bible or a Church, the new have here a final authority for the values which we call good. Difficulties of interpretation will of course remain; but if you are not only a believer but also honest, the tests of value will be clear enough for you. [...]

[...] I have implied a sharp distinction between dogmatic religion and intuition as sources of our knowledge or moral values. If, as we are often compelled to do, we emphasize the word "dogmatic," then this distinction must be accepted. But if we understand by religion the striving for closer harmony with God, or Reality, or the Good, then it is clear that no such distinction can stand. All great seers are religious, and are our guides in the road to religion. Their intuitions are the light on our path. They all seem to give substantially the same message, of the truth they see. And they stand out from the greater crowd of spectators or guessers or would-be teachers by the sheer force that their direct knowledge impacts to their words. [...]

CHAPTER 5

MORAL AND SPIRITUAL VALUES IN SOCIAL WORK

(ORIGINALLY PUBLISHED 1958)

REV. SHAUN GOVENLOCK

1 THE SCOPE OF THE TOPIC

Evidence of soul-searching on part of the profession

There is undoubtedly some deep meaning in the fact that meetings of
professional social workers tend more and more frequently to include in
their programmes questions related to moral and spiritual values. There
must be something significant, too, in the tendency of discussions among
small groups of thoughtful practitioners to gravitate towards inquiry into
our *deeper* and *more far reaching responsibilities* towards the clientele we
serve. Among those for whom social work is more than a mere job, there is
a more insistent concern about the ultimate effectiveness of much that we
do—as if the alleviation of material stress or the untangling of disabling
relationships, however worthy and necessary this be, were somehow an
unfinished thing. Perhaps there is a disquieting perception among some—
or many—that the best skills, techniques, and resources of our profession
fall short, somewhere, of reaching the ultimate sources of man's temporal
distress and needfulness.

These and similar questions *do* preoccupy many social workers
today. It would admittedly be an exaggeration to suggest that such soul-
searching is becoming anything like an epidemic within our ranks—but
there are unmistakable symptoms of its presence at every level of social
work practice.

More than a desire to bridge a gap which has grown

A superficial diagnosis of the condition might conclude that what is really
being experienced is no more than a regressive homesickness for the

simpler times when social work was mainly the form of the Church's official corporal works of mercy—when whatever efforts at alleviating community ills and personal misery were the traditional monopoly of religious congregations and authorities. While we today may have no particular affection for the nineteenth century stereotype of the "lady bountiful" or the proselytizing dispensers of moral indignation, we may dimly suspect that these prototypes of modern social work had access to certain strengths, which have somehow been filtered out of our mid-twentieth century formulae. We fully appreciate that the advances of sociological and psychological understanding have immeasurably enriched our ability to deal with social pathology. We feel no compelling urge to forego any of these gains in favour of casework by precept or community organization by sacred eloquence.

But with all our scientific assurances and skills, many of us cannot escape the impression that there is a further dimension of our work, which we no longer fully command and which nevertheless is decisively related to the success of its eventual outcomes. This feeling, I suggest, is much more than a simple nostalgia for the days of "social uplift" under ecclesiastical patronage.

More than a pragmatic wish to exploit a community resource

I choose to think that it is more, too, than an artfully motivated desire to draw maximum advantage from a long-recognized institution for community influence. Whenever I listen to an address or read a paper on the church as a partner in social welfare, I am alert to discover whether the objective is purely to remind workers that good public relations and wise exploitation of all community resources urge that we should not neglect this strategic source of collaboration. Such a principle of operation is undoubtedly a valid one in our professional philosophy but it misses the *real* point almost as widely as that which painstakingly reckons with religious values only as one cultural component, admittedly important, in diagnosis and treatment planning.

If the roots of our self-examination go no deeper than this, then the profits to be derived from the exercise may be real—but they will be meagre indeed. Because it will leave quite intact the essential question of the *intrinsic* significance of the moral and spiritual dynamics in the shaping of personal and social destinies.

2 THE ROLE OF SOCIAL WORK IN THE CONTEMPORARY SCENE

The problem of defining the purpose of social work

Now, this line of reasoning brings us rather abruptly up against an enormously difficult and basic question—i.e., what, indeed, is the real and legitimate function of social work as a professional discipline? Even though I wear a Roman collar and find myself discussing a religiously connected topic, it must not be anticipated that I shall perform a miracle by successfully answering this fundamental and persistent query. But if we are not yet able to answer it definitively, we are at least obliged to continue *asking* it, and finding whatever partial and provisional responses our wisdom and experience may dictate.

There are those who refuse on principle to attempt a definition of social work or its function, on the premise that we are dealing here with an essentially dynamic, evolving thing. Any definition would be a limiting, paralysing impertinence. When I am told this, I always find myself slipping back with Lewis Carroll and Alice to behold the Cheshire Cat gradually disappearing from the branch of the tree, until only the *grin* remains. A pure grin is a very impalpable thing. Accident without substance is a very unnatural thing. Movement without direction is a very idle thing. Direction without intention is a very pointless thing. Intention without understanding is a very irresponsible thing.

Somewhere along the line we must arrive at a tentative agreement on what social work properly proposes to undertake, at least here and now. And as with many other similar questions it is perhaps easier to begin by negation than by affirmation.

Social work cannot be "all things to all men"

First of all we might perhaps agree that social work should rid itself of any Messianic complex. It cannot successfully undertake to be "all things to all men." This way lies frustration—and ulcers of the stomach! Yet there are not few among us who are disposed to assume such global responsibilities—from the reconstructing of international harmony, to the elimination of the last vestigial complex in the individual psyche. It is both a tribute to the earnest dedication of the social work professions, and a commentary on its relative immaturity, that so many of us feel that all of man's needs must somehow find their satisfaction under our auspices. To resist this notion is not, of course, to deny that social work *has* a valuable contribution to make at every level of human interchange. But it remains a *contribution*, and does not become a monopoly.

The crucial point, therefore, becomes the question of what *is* this specific *contribution*, and *how* shall we make it. This, I believe, is the most urgent issue confronting our profession at the present moment. Within its answer will be contained the secret of how we shall appropriately relate to other established agencies of human betterment, to other human service professions, and to the infinitely varied children of Adam who turn to us for aid.

The integrative function in a divisive social economy

If, at the risk of oversimplifying a very complex matter, I should say that the principal task of professional social work today is that of *putting* together or *keeping* together the human person in the midst of a *social* process which seems more and more designed to divide and subdivide his personal unity and integrity, I would have identified what appears to me to be the essential function of our discipline.

It is paradoxical indeed that at the very time when we are hearing proclaimed most insistently the twentieth century gospel of the rights of man, man himself is finding it increasingly difficult to maintain and even to discover his feeling of significance and personal control in a society which imposes ever more artificialities upon the business of living.

This is neither the time nor the place to analyse the innumerable consequences which industrialization and urbanization have brought upon the individual in terms of radical dislocations of primary human institutions. Man's relationship to his mate and his children, to his intimate neighbour group, to his altar of worship, to the products of his labour and craft, to the larger society of compatriots—all these and many other pivots of personal security which have served him well since the dawn of history, have—by and large—been undermined by the inevitable logic of a technological age. And we have only begun to see, as in a glass, darkly, what further challenges will emerge from the nucleus of the atom. If there is a any justification whatever for the familiar designation: "This Age of Anxiety," it is to be found in the anguished cry of so many: "Who am I?", "Why am I?"

It is precisely here that I see the providential relevance of the social work profession. Not, surely, to supply the *ultimate* and *final* answers to these questions. This is clearly the province of the philosopher and the theologian. But it *is* the province of social work to help man to rediscover and secure that priceless sense of purpose, value, and meaning in what he is and does amid these ever more numerous and ever more conflicting pressures in the specifically temporal and social order. The social worker, it would seem, has the vocation of being a generalist of human nature in a society which has surrendered to the specialists. I wonder indeed whether this may not be the unconscious substrate of the current emphasis on the generic as against the specific in technical social work theory.

Social order and human values

Viewed from a slightly different perspective, it may be said that the overall moral responsibility of social work is to stand and act as a witness, in the community, for the principle that society is for man—and against the principle that man is for society. This is why social work as we conceive it is basically incompatible with a totalitarian ideology such as communism. It is, in the last analysis, a moral concept of the value of man which must justify our professional idea—an ideal which insists that however complex become the patterns of living, the institutions of society must be kept in harmony with the genuine interests of the human personality, that the rights and essential prerogatives of the person shall not be sacrificed to the tyranny of technological efficiency, legalistic convenience, economic advantage, or authoritarian whim.

If social work has a distinct reason for being, it will be found in this dedication to the notion that man's relationships with his personal and social environment shall remain in harmony with the fundamental dignity and aspirations of his human nature.

3 THE SPIRITUAL AND MORAL FOUNDATIONS OF SOCIAL WORK

The ideological assumptions of the profession

Having said this much—and it is admittedly quite a mouthful—it becomes necessary to look very closely at those slogans which have become the common coin of our profession—that perpetual insistence on "the value of the human person," "the essential dignity of man," "the non-condemnatory approach," and so on. These, we like to believe, are the axioms of our discipline. What we have not perhaps sufficiently realized, is that not one of these first principles of professional practice can long be successfully sustained apart from the spiritual and religious philosophy of life. A thoroughgoing materialism, whether frankly declared or disguised under the mask of sociological, psychological, or historical determinism can go only so far in justifying the position that the interests of the human person have inviolable priority over other temporal and social goals. Beyond this point, the materialist must become more dogmatic than the believer.

The theology of social work principles

I would go much further than this, and suggest that these very principles which we acknowledge as axiomatic in our practice are in fact little more than direct implementations, in the social and behavioural order, of Christian doctrinal teachings by which our occidental political and social philosophy was shaped and inspired. It would be too far from our immediate subject to examine how the very theory of a *democratic* society must have its roots in a spiritual and moral definition of man (though I consider this to be rigorously so, and not unrelated to our theme).

Let us rather consider what profound new insights are obtained when we connect some of our day-to-day professional assumptions, with the religious and moral compass points from which I believe they ultimately derive.

We speak, for example, of "the inviolable worth of the individual person." This is a noble ideal indeed—and one *in the absence of which* we have seen and are seeing in our own generation the most ghastly outrages perpetrated in the name of social progress. But upon what foundation does such an ideal rest? If man is no more than the sum total of his chemical components, then we are the sentimentalists and the others are the social realists. If, on the other hand, man is infinitely more than this, if he has a destiny beyond this span of years, if he has within him a spiritual principle, a soul, for whose final well-being an infinite price has been paid—then we may truly speak of his inviolable worth.

Or we speak of "the non-condemnatory attitude." This, strangely enough, is frequently viewed with alarm by otherwise knowledgeable religious people, who suspect it is a cloak for moral indifferentism or a crude surrender to the Id. And yet, among all our principles I find none which echoes more searchingly the truest dictates of our moral and religious tradition. It begins with the truth that I am not my client's better—that we are both the heirs of our original parents' fall—that we each bear within ourselves that proclivity to error and unreason. It proclaims also our religious conviction that no man can be coerced into virtue or manipulated into paradise. And it denies the social worker the luxury of playing God, by acknowledging that rectitude of life is the fruit of divine grace, to be given when God finds the soul prepared. Sanctity is not something which can be ensured by edict or censure, but rather something that takes possession of a man when the dispositions of nature have paved the way. It is the social worker's role to take away, by art and understanding and *acceptance*, the material, the emotional, the interpersonal, and the social stumbling blocks which clutter the human being's pilgrimage through this life toward better things. There is no better authority for our principle of acceptance of the client as he comes to us, than the words of Him who, when the last scornful accuser had slipped away, raised up the woman taken in adultery: "Daughter, are there none left to accuse thee? Neither do I accuse thee. Go in peace."

There *is* such a higher rationale for *each one* of the basic laws about which our professional ethic and skill are cast. It would be burdensome to consider in detail why our belief in the right of every individual to the means of decency is eventually inseparable from a theology which teaches that redemption is for the weak and strong alike; why our conviction in the necessity of social justice and mutual aid is bound up, not with a devious pursuit of indirect self-interest, but with the vastly more sublime precept of spiritual brotherhood which in my theology I would call the Mystical Body of Christ.

The futility of rootless philanthropism

The foregoing remarks are certainly open to commentary from many quarters. To some they may seem no more than a quasi-poetic essay in plausibilities. To others they may seem an elaborate attempt at rationalization in favour of vested interests. To others they may seem no more than an eruption of metaphysics in an area which has been adequately taken over by scientific positivism.

I must insist that they are more than any of these. It will always strike me as more than somewhat strange that we should have to remind social workers, of all people, of the essential spiritual component in their profession. And yet, in a somewhat larger context, it is worthy of note, that at the present time it is the *physical* sciences—the nuclear physicists, the biochemists, and the rest—who are more and more frequently voicing the necessity of a rediscovery of moral and religious values, while the *human* and *behavioural* sciences seem to be sinking ever deeper into the strata of factorial analysis, cybernetics, and logical empiricism. I do not believe that social work, for all its present and future need of richer scientific certitude, can rightly allow itself to be seduced into this latter direction.

Social work must maintain its commitment to the integral human person, and to whatever dimensions of that human whole may have an effect upon the individual's capacity to deal more successfully with the challenges of living in this uncertain and complex social era. We have long since agreed that this eventually becomes a matter of revitalizing the interpersonal relationships which sustain personal security and social well-being. But as Father Swithun Bowers said very pertinently in an address delivered in Boston last year, if religion is essentially man's relationship with the divinity from which he springs and towards which he moves, and if this, as seems inevitable, influences profoundly his relationships with all else which surrounds him, it would seem a dereliction of professional responsibility for social workers not to be at least mindful of this direct and indirect area of the client's relationship needs.

The fact, however—and I might say the tragic fact—is that this intimate connection between religious and spiritual values on the one hand, and the content of day-by-day activities and relationships on the other, has largely been lost sight of in contemporary scientific, political, and social thinking.

It is not merely that religion has become a compartmentalized aspect of living. It is rather that we, without fully realizing it, are living on borrowed spiritual and religious capital. The most alarming symptom of modern man's crisis is that, while engaged in a death struggle for the defence of certain human values, he has too often lost faith and confidence in the theological principles upon which these values are founded. In fact, we have, more often than not, actually *forgotten* these principles, while suspecting more or less consciously the weakness of the latter-day ideologies which have preyed upon them like parasites (see Maritain, 1952, pp. 189–199). It is not surprising, therefore, that we speak of "This age of anxiety"—but I firmly believe that, before all else, it is an age of *metaphysical* anxiety.

The implications of our duty to the integral man
Thanks be to God that it is not the specific task of the social work profession to take upon its young shoulders this cosmic burden. But the fact that it *exists* cannot be excluded from our attention if we honestly claim to approach community problems and personal social ills with a comprehensive focus. It may, to be sure, pose delicate and difficult questions for us when we come to decide *how* in the course of our professional practice, due weight and importance shall be given to the religious and spiritual needs and interests of individuals and groups—and to the moral issues which are the intrinsic by-product of man's communication with God.

But we cannot act as if the problem did not exist—and we must equip ourselves with the understandings, the attitudes, and the skills required to deal *appropriately* with the religious and moral, no less than with the psychosexual, biophysical, and socioeconomic dimensions of our client's difficulty. To heed these latter but ignore the first suggests one of three things:

1. that matters of religion and morals are a potato too hot for us to handle, or

2. that for some reason religion and morals are in no sense our business, or
3. that the less said about religion and morals the better, because they are an impertinent anachronism in this scientific age.

The first attitude, I would say, is a sad commentary upon the worker's professional maturity; the second is best an arbitrary narrowing of the profession's field of vision; the third is a counsel of despair, for it annihilates the significance of man.

Personal ideology of the professional person

Here, precisely, is the nub of the entire question in so far as it concerns the worker on the job. It would be idle to expect that *every* practitioner will bring a positive and conscious religious ideology to his professional tasks. To the extent that he fails to do so, of course, his scope for adequate empathy with his client—whether individual, family, or group—is proportionately diminished. But we have a right to hope that at the very least, he shall not systematically disregard the religious and moral preoccupations or needs of his case, or harbour a persistent blind-spot in their regard. On the other hand, the practitioner who has mature and enlightened convictions about the powerful spiritual potentialities in his own and his client's lives vastly expands his range of deep identification and at the same time finds access to new reserves of confidence and worthwhileness in his labours.

4 THE RELATIONSHIPS OF PROFESSION TO CHURCH

Essential differences with unique interdependencies

The danger in all that I have been saying may lie in supposing that, *if these things be true*, then professional social work somehow becomes a branch of evangelism—that the social worker, in his *role* of *social worker*, becomes something of a religious counsellor. Nothing I can think of would do a greater disservice to both religion and the social work profession than this confusion of roles. Despite their unique interdependencies, their proper and specific functions remain fundamentally distinct.

As a professional discipline, social work assumes responsibility for *man* in his earthly *estate*, using methods and resources proportionate to earthly effects, for the purpose of insuring *earthly* benefits for the individual and for the community.

In its primary role, the Church assumes responsibility for man's *soul* in its earthly *state*, using methods and resources proportionate to *supernatural* effects, for the purpose of insuring *eternal* benefits for the individual and for mankind.

If *social work* recognizes that moral and spiritual factors enter deeply into *earth-bound* problems, it must so deal with these factors as to permit the achievement of desired *social* outcomes.

If *the Church* recognizes that material and social factors enter deeply into *spiritual* problems, it must so deal with these factors as to permit the achievement of desired *supernatural* outcomes.

Social work, *as a professional discipline*, is not called upon to save souls. This is not its competence. But *its practitioners, as believing people*, will not be oblivious to the eternal destiny of those they serve.

The Church, *as an agency of supernatural life*, is not called upon to reconstruct the city of man. This is not its competence. But *its representatives, as socially minded people*, will not be indifferent to the earthly condition of those to whom they minister.

The problem of collaboration
The net conclusion of all the foregoing is surely that social work and the church should be working together in a relationship of utmost harmony born of reciprocal need. Let us not be so naïve as to pretend that this is typically the situation. All too often, if there is not an elegantly disguised mutual suspicion, there is not much more than a casual nodding acquaintance. Far too seldom indeed does there exist that truly dynamic teamwork which would be required to make what I have said anything more than pious philosophizing.

Without attempting to give you any gimmicks or trick formulae to get the church and social work working hand in hand, may I merely suggest a few of the basic prerequisites for fruitful collaboration:

First of all it would seem to me, we have to do something about the problem of simple verbal communication. If social work has sometimes been rightly characterized as a "culture within a culture," the same can be said with due modifications about the world of ecclesiastical affairs. Each has developed a technical terminology (which some would call a "jargon") that effectively renders intelligible dialogue an almost lost cause. Perhaps social workers are the greatest offenders in this regard, but they are surely not the only culprits. When we patiently advise the local clergyman that Mrs. McGillicudy has not yet established a sufficiently meaningful relationship with the Worker to permit us to move in on her latent hostility towards Junior, it is not to be wondered that our clerical listener reacts with a somewhat incredulous "hum!" On the other hand when the Rev.

Pastor advises us that Mr. Fogerty "needs a good talking to" to correct his unwholesome devotion to the local bookmaker, or that the Grogan family is a particularly "deserving case," it is forgivable, if not commendable, that the worker wishes the thing might be put a little more "diagnostically."

Terminology, of course, is really no more than symptomatic. Even if the schools of social work and theological seminaries added a course in comparative semantics to their already overcrowded curricula, we would not automatically overcome all the stumbling blocks in our common pathway. What is perhaps more needed is a relatively better *understanding* on either side of what the other is *really trying to achieve*. Only thus will the occasional spasms of scepticism cease to encumber our collaboration. Only thus will the mechanisms of defence intrude less frequently into our dealings with one another. Only thus will the profession be less likely to reproach the Church for unwarranted insistence upon moral technicalities; only thus will the Church be less likely to censure the profession for arbitrary secularism.

How this quality of improved mutual understanding can be brought into being is probably too large an issue to be dealt with adequately here. In summary, I believe it must await a spiritual maturation on the part of the social work profession and on the part of social work practitioners, no less than it must await a scientific-social maturation on the part of those who formally speak for the spiritual and moral values in modern life. This undoubtedly has implications for the educational programmes on either side—and I have the impression that the challenge will be and is being met.

The fruit of such efforts will be not only better *understanding*, leading to more effective *communication*, but a heightened respect for one another between these two agencies of human betterment. I cannot think of an outcome more ardently to be hoped for—because it can only result in advantages to the individuals, the families, the groups, and the communities which, each in our own way, we have assumed the mission to serve.

REFERENCE

Maritain, J. (1952). *The range of reason.* New York: Scribners.

SECTION 2

SPIRITUALITY IN SOCIAL WORK PRACTICE

INTRODUCTION

BRIAN OUELLETTE

Even though the social work profession's history is replete with many examples of religious/spiritual influences, there has been a long and simmering discomfort with these issues as they apply to social work practice (Marshall, 1990). Holland has argued that "the oft-noted Flexner Report (1915) prompted our own profession to abandon the old parent figure, the priest or minister, and redirect professional loyalty to the freshly esteemed older sibling, the physician" (1989, p. 32). In its efforts to be a credible and scientific profession, social work distanced itself from religious/spiritual issues, emphasized objectivity, techniques, and interventions, while neglecting the subjective, intuitive, reflective, and creative part of the person. As Canda observed, "we threw the baby of spirituality out with the bathwater of sectarianism" (1988, p. 30).

Despite the significant increase, in recent years, of Canadian writers exploring the concept of spirituality and social work, many authors maintain that empirical research on spirituality and social work is in its very early stages (Coholic, 2002; Okundaye & Gray, 1999) and that there is a dearth of literature providing guidelines, practice principles, or descriptions of how social workers could incorporate the spiritual dimension into their practice (Baskin, 2002; Coholic, 2003; Cowley & Derozotes, 1994; Gotterer, 2001). While the literature on the integration of spirituality and practice is still emerging, social work practitioners have been provided with some direction in the area of assessment (Bullis, 1996; Hodge, 2001, 2003) and intervention (Abels, 2000; Becvar, 1997; Canda & Smith, 2001; Cascio, 1998; Gotterer, 2001; Okundaye & Gray, 1999). However, a distinctly Canadian voice with a strong emphasis on multiculturalism and critical thought has yet to be fully developed.

Fortunately, efforts in Canada to increase "scholarly attention to spirituality from both theoretical and practice perspectives" (Coates & Graham, 2003) are bearing fruit, and Canadian scholars and practitioners are beginning to write about their experiences with the integration of spirituality into social work practice. In this section of the book we hear from Canadian social work practitioners and educators who provide distinct perspectives on their efforts to examine and incorporate spirituality into practice.

In this section's first chapter, Michael McKernan argues that the profession is challenged to create a bridge between the wisdom of social work and the wisdom of spirituality. He posits that as social workers are increasingly asked to honour spiritual issues in practice, the integration of spirituality can occur on two levels—information about the client's experience and the subjective experience that includes the experience of the worker. McKernan explores several key questions that arise once one begins this dialogue, and he identifies several specific implications for social work practice that aims to integrate the spiritual dimension.

In chapter 7, Diana Coholic provides an exploratory study of the application of spiritually influenced group practice with women. The group work included non-traditional or alternative approaches such as meditation, mindfulness practice, dream work, and other arts-based processes. Among other outcomes, the participants found the spiritual-related aspects of the group work to be helpful with increasing self-awareness and self-esteem. This study begins to build important knowledge in understanding the helpfulness and applicability of spirituality to group work practice and lays out promising directions for the future.

In chapter 8, Wanda Wagler-Martin provides a glimpse into the evolution of her practice from one initially influenced by Freudian thought to one influenced by existential/humanistic thought. She describes how her incorporation of the spiritual dimension has altered her therapeutic practices, and she suggests several key questions that are helpful in recognizing the spiritual component of people's lives. Wagler-Martin encourages social work clinicians to be "purveyors of hope."

Michèle Butot engages the reader in a dialogue on how social work might view spirituality through a critical lens in chapter 9. She explores themes gleaned from "participant dialogues" with individuals she describes as "spiritually informed critical practitioners." She further describes the participants as practitioners who took a spiritual stance of loving commitment to emancipation that appeared to be based in an understanding of the coexistence of diversity and unity. She contends that such critical conceptualizations of spirituality have the potential to revitalize and increase the sustainability of social work.

In chapter 10, Sarah Todd explores the connections between feminist community organizing and personal stories of religion and spirituality. While researching the experiences of nine feminist community organizers, she discovered that stories of religion (institutionalized faith and worship) and spirituality (informal, non-institutional faith in spirits and/or the divine) influenced their secular practices. She concludes that it is possible to "read feminism and/or community organizing as a type of faith, a mission, and a value-system."

In chapter 11, Susan Cadell, Linda Janzen, and Dennis Haubrich expand on a qualitative study focusing on grief and HIV/AIDS and noted that there has been little research focusing on the role of spirituality in the lives of those bereaved by HIV/AIDS. Examining material collected through surveys and interviews with 15 individuals who had experienced at least one AIDS-related bereavement, and using grounded-theory data analysis, they identify the overarching theme of engagement as a broad expression of spirituality. The authors conclude that spirituality is expressed through various forms of engagement experienced by the participants and that spirituality is a key factor in moving forward in an adaptive fashion.

Finally, in chapter 12, Cyndy Baskin describes the significant influence that Aboriginal spirituality has had on her life and practice, and she provides suggestions on how social work practitioners can support Indigenous ways of knowing and helping. She also argues that spirituality cannot be seen only as an inward journey; rather, it is our responsibility to use our spirituality in creating a better world. Baskin advocates a "spirituality of resistance" that links individual and community spirituality to social change.

Each of these authors opens new paths for exploring practice innovations, related opportunities for further research, and critical reflection on the application of spirituality to practice.

REFERENCES

Abels, S. (Ed.). (2000). *Spirituality in social work practice: Narratives for professional helping.* Denver, CO: Love Publishing.

Baskin, C. (2002). Circles of resistance: Spirituality in social work practice, education, and transformative change. *Currents: New Scholarship in the Human Services, 1*(1). Retrieved 25 October 2006 from fsw.ucalgary.ca/currents/articles/documents/Currents_baskin_v1_n1.pdf.

Becvar, D. (1997). *The family, spirituality, and social work*. Binghamton, NY: Haworth Press.

Bellamy, D., & Irving, A. (2001). Pioneers. In J. Turner & F. Turner (Eds.), *Canadian social welfare*. (4th ed.) Don Mills, ON: Collier MacMillan, pp. 96-117.

Bullis, R. (1996). *Spirituality in social work practice*. Washington, DC: Taylor and Francis.

Canda, E. (1988). Conceptualizing spirituality for social work: Insights from diverse perspectives. *Social Thought, 14*(1), 30-46.

Canda, E. (2002). A world wide view on spirituality and social work: Reflections from the USA experience and suggestions for internationalization. *Currents: New Scholarship in the Human Services, 1*(1). Retrieved 26 October 2006 from 207.34.118.41/fsw/currents/articles/index.

Canda, E., Nakashima, M., Burgess, V., & Russel, R. (1999). *Spiritual diversity and social work: A comprehensive bibliography with annotations*. Alexandria, VA: Council on Social Work Education, Inc.

Canda, E., & Smith, E. (2001). *Transpersonal perspectives on spirituality in social work*. Binghamton, NY: Haworth Press.

Cascio, T. (1998). Incorporating spirituality into social work practice: A review of what to do. *Families in Society: The Journal of Contemporary Human Services, 79*(5), 523–531.

Coates, J., & Graham, J. (2003). Introduction to the second special edition on spirituality. *Currents: New Scholarship in the Human Services, 2*(2). Retrieved 16 October 2006 from fsw.ucalgary.ca/currents/toc.htm#SpecialTheme2.

Coholic, D. (2002). Practice principles for social work and spirituality: A focus on practice methods and relationships. *Currents: New Scholarship in the Human Services, 1*(1). Retrieved 25 October 2006 from fsw.ucalgary.ca/currents/articles/coholic_v1_n1.htm.

Coholic, D. (2003). Incorporating spirituality in feminist social work practice. *Affilia, 18*(1), 49–67.

Cowley, A.S., & Derozotes, D. (1994). Transpersonal psychology and social work education. *Journal of Social Work Education, 30*(1), 32–41.

Gotterer, R. (2001). The spiritual dimension in clinical social work practice: A client perspective. *Families in Society: The Journal of Contemporary Human Services, 82*(2), 187–193.

Hodge, D. (2001). Spiritual genograms: A generational approach to assessing spirituality. *Families in Society: The Journal of Contemporary Human Service, 82*(1), 35–48.

Hodge, D. (2003). *Spiritual assessment: Handbook for helping professionals*. Botsford, CT: North American Association of Christians in Social Work.

Holland, T.P. (1989). Values, faith, and professional practice. *Social Thought, 15*(1), 28–40.

Leiby, J. (1985). The moral foundations of social welfare and social work. *Social Work, 30*(4), 323–330.

Marshall, J. (1990). *Social work thoughts on spirituality*. Master's thesis, Smith College School of Social Work, Northampton, MA.

Okundaye, J., & Gray, C. (1999). Reimaging field instruction from a spiritually sensitive perspective: An alternative approach. *Social Work, 44*(4), 371–383.

CHAPTER 6

EXPLORING THE SPIRITUAL DIMENSION
OF SOCIAL WORK

MICHAEL McKERNAN

Social work's response to the rising levels of public and professional interest in spirituality poses some important questions:

1. Why is this important to social work practice?
2. What do we mean by spirituality?
3. What are the obstacles posed by religious and spiritual traditions that must be overcome to honour social work values and wisdom?
4. What research is available to help us understand the value of spirituality to clients?
5. How can spirituality help us to serve our clients?

Based on research conducted as a Muttart Fellow, the writer uses these questions as a framework for exploring the role and significance of spirituality in social work. The chapter ends with specific, applied benefits that a credible spiritual perspective brings to social work practice.

❖ EXPLORING THE SPIRITUAL DIMENSION OF SOCIAL WORK

> To be human means to be spiritual. Human beings have longings and aspirations that can be honoured only when the person's spiritual capacity is taken seriously. (Gratton, 1995)

Popular interest in spirituality has experienced a rapid growth in recent years. This subject has occupied the top of the bestseller lists in bookstores, become a common theme of entertainment media, and is featured in many professional conferences and training programs for human service workers. Notice of this trend prompted well-known journalist Bill Moyers to comment, "Any journalist worth his salt knows that the real story today is to define what it means to be spiritual. This is the biggest story—not only of the decade but of the century" (Keen, 1994, p. 22).

The demographics of this popular interest in spirituality is revealing as well. A 1996 survey by the Fetzer Institute and the Institute of Noetic Sciences leads to the conclusion that there were 20 million Americans referred to as "cultural creatives" concerned with psychology, spiritual life, and self-actualization (Simpkinson & Simpkinson, 1998). Research conducted by Reg Bibby (2002) found that while the vast majority of Canadians believe in God (86%), a very small number actually attend church regularly (17%).[1] These figures represent a sharp drop in the past 40 years, prompting Bibby to observe: "Something is wrong. Canadians are asking religious questions at a time when the nation's churches have never been emptier" (Bibby, 1995, p. xviii).

The figures above show that many of our social work clients have spiritual beliefs of great importance to them. It is not much of a leap, then, to suggest that human services, including social work, psychology, and psychiatry have become the place most commonly turned to in times of crisis—we have inherited a role that was once reserved for priests and ministers. Like it or not, social workers are being challenged to honour the spiritual issues woven into the concerns clients bring to us. Yet, it is my impression that we currently lack the credible and accessible means of integrating spirituality into social work practice. This has implications for client engagement as well as access to the resources that a client's spiritual beliefs and experience can offer.

This chapter summarizes findings from a one-year fellowship that explored the spiritual dimension of family service work (McKernan, 2004).[2] The discussion that follows identifies the challenges that current spiritual trends present to social work, the task of building a bridge joining the wisdom of social work and spirituality, and a list of some advantages for spiritually integrated social work.

What we understand as the "modern helping professions" are relative newcomers to the business of serving human needs. While social work and psychology have been reckoning with human experience for a little over a century, spiritual traditions (including major organized religions, shamanic, esoteric, or hidden and mystical traditions) have been refining their grasp of the cosmos and human healing for millennia. We cannot ignore the potential richness that this can add to current social work practice. For example, while modern social work presses for empirical validation, the scope of our inquiry into human experience is limited to what is rational, logical, and empirical. This fails to do justice to the full human experience in the same way that dogmatic religion rejects empirical and rational inquiry. In recent years, the work of many writers and practitioners of healing has sought to create a credible connection between spiritual experience and empirical research.[3]

There are three important factors that I believe are allowing spirituality to become more accessible to the business of social work today. First, our connection to spirituality is changing. In addition to the information about spiritual practice being more accessible in many different forms, we are discovering new words and metaphors for speaking of the transcendent and mystical. Spiritual perspectives arising in science (quantum physics, chaos theory, creativity studies, biology, ecology) and other bodies of learning including art and alternative healing, are enriching our understanding of the spiritual dimension outside of traditional religious formulas. We need no longer to see spirituality as an arbitrary set of beliefs held by a select group.

A second factor helping spirituality to be more accessible to social work is that we are living in times of pervasive anxiety that is calling for a new vision of life. The dominant current myth of "scientific progress" and control is simply not adequate to the challenges of terrorism, the ecology crisis, and astounding levels of strife including genocide and global poverty. In our local communities we observe the crisis of housing shortages, loneliness, and high rates of relationship breakdown, loss of confidence in institutional leadership, and crippling poverty that exist in the midst of very wealthy communities. The ethic of individualism, with its claims for freedom and privacy, has lost its counterbalancing principle of connection that joins people to each other, to the earth, and to the cosmos as a whole. Joseph Campbell puts it as follows:

> The psychological dangers through which earlier generations were guided by symbols and spiritual exercises of their mythological and religious inheritance, we today … must face alone.… This is our problem as modern "enlightened" individuals for whom all gods and devils have been rationalized out of existence. (1968, p. 82)

These unstable times are calling for a new world view, a new paradigm that can assist us. Marilyn Ferguson argues that this new paradigm must include the "insights of breakthrough science and the insights of earliest recorded thought" (1980, p. 68). William Harman, President of the Institute of Noetic Sciences contends that this shift includes the creation of

> a body of knowledge, empirically based and publicly validated, about the realm of subjective experience. For the first time in history we are beginning to create a growing, progressively funded body of established experience about humanity's inner life—and particularly about the perennial wisdom of the great religious traditions and Gnostic groups. For the first time there is a hope that this knowledge can become—not a secret repeatedly lost in dogmatization and institutionalization, or degenerating into manifold varieties of cultism and occultism—but rather the living heritage of all humankind. (as cited in Ferguson, 1980, p. 27)

A third factor that makes spirituality more accessible to social work is found in its origins. Social work's roots in the Christian and Jewish charity movements of the 19th century remind us that the bridge to spirituality/ religion is part of its foundations (Barker, 1998). For social work, it will not be enough to merely introduce greater and greater levels of regulation of practice or greater levels of results-oriented research. If I were to speculate about how this new paradigm were to arise in social work, I believe it will not come from official leadership (universities, professional associations, major employers of social workers) but rather from a progressive consensus of social workers invested in the spiritual perspective. This may be particularly true amongst those in the private practice community and marginal organizations that embrace a spiritual mission. This will create a new path joining spirit to social work that will eventually become a well-travelled road (Ferguson, 1980).[4] There will come a time, I believe, when the spiritual dimension of social work will seem a self-evident truth and excluding it from practice will seem unprofessional and even unethical.

❖ TWO LEVELS OF INTEGRATING SPIRITUALITY IN SOCIAL WORK

Addressing spirituality in social work can happen on two levels. The first order of integration sees spirituality as a more superficial issue of information about client experience. When a client speaks about their relationship with God or wonders about life after death following the loss of a parent or spouse, we are faced with questions about how we understand and respond to this issue. This level of spiritual work does not require the worker to have a spiritual perspective for him/herself. Instead it requires that they view spirituality as an important factor of client experience in the same way that we would see gender, race, or culture. Through understanding, we can use language, employ strategies, and adjust our approach to the way that spirituality is presented. It encourages us to ask questions about how spirituality matters to our clients and how it is a resource for their success. Again, it does not imply a "buy in" on the part of the therapist. Instead, a professional may adopt a "politically correct" stance that is sensitive to the client's spiritual perspective.

The second order of integration assumes that spirituality is a subjective experience that includes the experience of the worker. Like attending to the process of a client interview, it is subtler because it is focused not merely on content but on the experience itself. The social worker is not separate or neutral about what is taking place. The insights of quantum physics tell us that we cannot measure things in absolutely objective ways—the act of measuring changes what we measure. In this sense, the initiative for addressing spirituality in social work practice is shaped by the worker's beliefs and experience. This is a much more challenging, subjective, and controversial area, yet it is also the richest place of inquiry; it requires that we bring our fullest and deepest grasp of ourselves into the work we do— no holds barred.

❖ WORKING WITH SPIRITUALITY ON THE CONTENT LEVEL

On the content level, issues of spirituality applied to social work can include 1) the use of prayer and meditation with clients; 2) reckoning with research that highlights the power of prayer for healing, and the health effects of spiritual practice; 3) the implications of non-local healing (from a distance), energy work, explorations of consciousness including transcendent experiences, dissociative phenomena, mystical experience, altered states of consciousness; and 4) viewing agencies and communities as fields of creativity imbued with spiritual purpose.

Until recently, these areas of attention were a marginal aspect of social work practice. This is not to say that many social workers have not held their own personal spiritual perspective—simply that professional associations and schools of social work have not officially addressed it.[5] This is changing. The questions are being shared more overtly, the information and research more pervasive and compelling, the spiritual ideas more informed. There is a call to acknowledge these issues so that we can bridge the rigours of good social work practice with the enriching dimension of spirit. It is also true that as we explore spiritual matters more freely, our confidence and vocabulary for dealing with such matters grows.

❖ CREATING A BRIDGE BETWEEN SPIRITUALITY AND SOCIAL WORK

The challenge of creating this bridge between the wisdom of social work and the wisdom of spirituality brings up certain basic questions:

1. What do we mean by spirituality?
2. What are the obstacles posed by spiritual traditions that must be overcome to honour social work values and wisdom?
3. What are the important factors necessary for spirituality to be accessible to well-grounded social work?
4. What research is available to help us understand the value of spirituality to clients?
5. How can spirituality help us to serve our clients?

The remainder of this chapter will use these questions as the guiding structure for exploring the spiritual dimension of social work.

Defining Spirituality

A broad definition of spirituality arising from this writer's research is "Searching for a trustworthy wisdom that will connect us with the larger purposes and meaning of everyday life" (Gratton, 1995, p. 6). This definition does not specify a particular belief but rather focuses on the action of seeking and experience. It addresses the bridge joining our particular experience with "the larger purposes of everyday life." This definition supports an expansive notion of spirituality that is not limited to a particular creed or institution. This more general sense of spirituality implies less concern with regulation, tradition, or dogma, and a much greater attention to experience. Spirituality may draw from more than one tradition or from no tradition at all. The weakness of this approach is in its lack of built-in self-criticism—the absence of a specific belief reference allows for "beliefs of convenience," "smorgasbord religion," or, as singer Tom Cochrane mentions in his liner notes to *Songs of a Circling Spirit*, "fast food religion" (Cochrane, 1998). Spiritual ideas are not all equally valid and, like other perspectives to social work, must stand up to the scrutiny of the most informed thinking we can bring to the topic in addition to our intuition and experience. Wilber defines credible spiritual truth as something that touches on three vital criteria: subjective experience, objective study, and community/reference group discernment (Wilber, 1996, p. 120). To ignore any of these three is risking distortion.

Organized religion has been the dominant carrier for spirituality in the West but it has not been the only one, and not necessarily the dominant source of spirituality and spiritual practice today. Besides organized religion, spirituality is also informed by mystical traditions from the East and West, shamanic traditions, Aboriginal spiritual practice, art, various yogic practices, scientifically based explorations of quantum physics, New Age literature, poetry, and esoteric spiritual traditions (such as mystery schools, theosophy, and the Masonic movement). These examples cite a wide range of spiritual practices, some that qualify as religion in the sense of their degree of organization and exclusive adherence to core beliefs. It is more realistic to see a continuum between less formalized and more individualistic practices of spirituality, and the more formal and communal ones of religion. It is possible to see how spirituality is more "bendable" to the values and practices of social work.

The following table helps to define the difference between spirituality and religion as adapted from the work of Jack Hawley:

Table 6.1 Differences between religion and spirituality

Religion	Spirituality
Product of a certain time or place	Broadly inclusive of many eras and traditions
Meant for a group	More private, personal
Focus more on prescribed beliefs	Contains elements common to all religions
Codes of conduct	Methods of practice
A system of thought	A body of practice
A set of beliefs, to move along the path	A state beyond the senses (beyond even thought)
Institutions and organizations	Networks of like-minded seekers
A way of life	A practice

Source: Hawley, 1993, p. 4.

What Are the Obstacles Posed by Spiritual Traditions That Must Be Overcome to Honour Social Work Values and Wisdom?

The obstacles to incorporating spirituality in social work practice are many. Some arise from irrational prejudice within social work that is based on ignorance or fear. For example, I have spoken with work groups expressing concerns about exploring spirituality based on the assumption that speaking of spirituality would require them to join a particular religion. Unsubstantiated biases against the spiritual perspective deserve to be challenged in the same way that our profession felt free to challenge workers reluctant to screen for domestic violence issues in their practice. It is no more acceptable for professional social work to tolerate fear-based, irrational perspectives about spirituality than it has been for many religious traditions to defy good science.

There are, on the other hand, substantial concerns about admitting the spiritual perspective into social work arising from personal and historical experience: the devastating abuse of power by ministers and leaders of different churches including physical and sexual abuse; injustice to Aboriginal cultures, women, and gays; sectarianism; fear-based teaching; rigid dogma that prohibits intelligent discussion; and judgements and rules that seem at times more important than the love they proclaim.

Contrary to the notion that spirituality and psychology oppose one another, an integrated perspective on spirituality views them as complementary aspects of health. The professional grasp of the dynamics of relationships (both community and personal) and our understanding of psychological functioning is vital to healthy spirituality. Without this, spirituality can be corrupted by a lack of psychological integrity. Jack Kornfield, a leader in the Buddhist Vipassana movement in the United States, cites examples of spiritual leaders from the East who have fallen prey to addictions and sexual acting out because they failed to come to terms with their own psychological and relationship issues. Others have used meditation as an escape from facing the practical issues of their lives.[6]

It is crucial here to not get swept up in the trend to see religion as negative and spirituality as positive. Both have risks of abuse, distortion, hypocrisy, etc. Huston Smith contends, "Religion shows an ugly face to many contemporary eyes"; however, "these crude surfaces often blind us to the liberating wisdom that courses far below" (as cited in Novak, 1994, p. xiv).

What Are the Important Factors Necessary for Spirituality to Be Integrated into Well-Grounded Social Work?

Productive professional explorations of spirituality work best, I believe, when certain factors are present:

- Tolerance based on core values of respect for difference, the conviction that we can learn from one another's experience
- That there is a serious commitment to make spiritual beliefs accountable to the standards employed in best practice social work including intellectual and research integrity
- That any belief is open to challenge when it contradicts the professional ethical codes of social work
- Beliefs, rituals, and interpretations—regardless if we are dealing with social work research or sacred text—are best understood in tentative terms. Just as in all aspects of social work, this attitude to beliefs keeps social workers open to others and to new and different ideas.[7]
- The greatest part of professional effectiveness lies with the ability to be authentic within ourselves and therefore authentically present to clients.[8] Quality spirituality exhorts us to the kinds of discipline and lifestyle that supports openness and authentic presence. In fact, this is a crucial factor distinguishing effective social work and spiritual practice from bogus and unethical practice. This can be seen in cultism and dogmatism (in social work as in spirituality) where compulsive belief replaces authentic presence.
- It should be as appropriate to ask about a worker's spiritual practice, as it is to ask about their theory base.

What Research Evidence Is There about the Value of Spirituality to Clients?

Research about the health benefits of spiritual practice draws from studies of religious groups as well as surveys that focus on the broader phenomena of spirituality. In a recent survey, Jeff Levin found more than 200 "peer-reviewed articles reporting the statistical findings on the impact of religious[9] involvement on health and illness" (2001, p. 6). Some of these findings include work from leading universities, such as Michigan, Yale, Duke, Berkeley, Rutgers, and Texas. These findings are summarized as follows:

- People who regularly attend religious services have lower rates of illness and death than do infrequent or non-attenders.
- For each of the three leading causes of death in the United States—heart disease, cancer, and hypertension—people who report a religious affiliation have lower rates of illness.
- Older adults who participate in private and congregational religious activities have fewer symptoms, less disability, and lower rates of depression, chronic anxiety, and dementia.
- Religious participation is the strongest determination of psychological well-being in African Americans—even more important than health or financial wealth.
- Actively religious people live longer, on average, than the non-religious. This holds true even controlling for the fact that religious folks tend to avoid such behaviours as smoking and drinking that increase the risk of disease and death.

According to a team of British scientists who researched the topic closely, religious and spiritual beliefs "may be at least as important as the more traditional psychological and secular social factors in the illness process" (Levin, 2001, p. 102). Dr. David Larson, National Institute of Health Research president, contends that

> While medical professionals have been privately assuming and publicly stating for years that religion is detrimental to mental health, when I actually looked at the available empirical research on the relationship between religion and health, the findings were overwhelmingly positive. (2001, p. vii)

Larry Dossey adds a final conviction arising from his research that "future historians of medicine will describe the 20th century as a period in which spirituality, after a long absence, began to return to healing" (Levin, 2001, p. vii).

How Does Spirituality Help Us to Serve Our Social Work Clients?
This question asks about the way that spirituality alters the world, client experience, and the social worker. Here we begin to bridge the spiritual dimension with social work in a more applied way. It is my sense that the rising interest in spirituality is connected to an increased awareness of the essential energies that inform our being but lie beneath the radar of an "objective, professional" perspective. Hameed Ali asserts, "The effectiveness of psychotherapy has been limited by its ignorance of essential

states, so that resolutions occur on the levels of ego and emotions, which are not the level on which we are ultimately satisfied" (cited in Schwartz, 1996, p. 412).

The insights of quantum physics, the perceptions of subtle energies shaping our experience discerned by alternative medicine, chaos and field theories, and the wisdom of Eastern and Western mystical traditions have pressed for a richer appreciation of healing. In fact, Carl Jung writes in *Modern Man in Search of a Soul* that it is our spiritual needs that produced the discovery of psychology in our time (1955). Social work's access to credible spiritual exploration is being made remarkably easier by the work of pioneers in many fields of inquiry.[10]

❖ EIGHT APPLICATIONS FROM THE SPIRITUAL DIMENSION OF SOCIAL WORK

Let me jump to some specific implications for social work practice that arise from this richer perspective. It is important to recognize, as these points are offered, that many already have a place in the practice of some social workers. There are many spiritually attuned social workers—with or without a specific religious affiliation or practice.

1. It is not the worker but the conscious facilitation of life energy that leads to healing

Gerald May, psychiatrist and long-standing pioneer in integrating spiritual perspectives into his work, suggests that "with progressive appreciation for the spiritual dimension, we move from working on the client to working with the client to facilitating the spiritual energies or expressions of grace for each other" (1992, p. 8). This role of facilitation moves away from technique and focuses on the quality of presence a worker brings to the healing relationship. Eckhart Tolle describes this as "a state of intense conscious presence" that helps to "accelerate things" (Tolle, 1997).

Social work can utilize the techniques of many spiritual traditions, which offer practices for cultivation of greater maturity of self-management or mindfulness that enables individuals to become more fully present to others and ourselves. This can be a powerful social work tool. This point is echoed in the research on therapy effectiveness (Lebow, 2001).

2. Moving from ego to soul

While psychology and social work tend to focus on support of ego (our particular self), spiritual attention enriches the perspectives of social work by inviting us to see the soul (in transpersonal psychology "Self" is an alternative term)—a deeper, more connected dimension of human experience. This calls attention to the abiding mystery of our essential natures and innate reverence warranted for each human being. Just as important, though, is the attention to a notion of foundational energies that shape our experience. This perspective is echoed in the words of a desert hermit, Monoimus, a fourth century Gnostic teacher:

> Abandon the search for God and the creation and other matters of similar sort. Look for him by taking yourself as a starting point. Learn who it is within you who makes everything his own and says, "My God, my mind, my thought, my soul, my body." Learn the sources of sorrow, joy, and love, hate.... If you carefully investigate these matters you will find him in yourself. (quoted in Keen, 1995, p. 2)

The soul's divine calling and its connection to a larger purpose reminds us of a larger system of energy that is shaping both the client's vital core and the context for social work interventions.

3. Ritual and myth as guides for managing life transitions

The work of Freud and others (see Bakan, 1975), Jung (1955), Joseph Campbell (1968), Mircea Eliade (1959), have shown how religious and spiritual traditions contain a storehouse of symbols, myth, and ritual enactments that have served as guides through life's developmental transitions. Certain schools within psychology and social work have worked with this wisdom to great value (work with dreams, explorations of the unconscious, ritual practices in family therapy, and narrative therapy to name a few) for they contribute a vital piece to our work with individuals, families, and communities. When social workers facilitate community celebrations, or support couples to ritualize their time together to get past conflict, we are drawing upon wisdom from our spiritual traditions. Social workers need only to read sympathetically the stories of different mythic traditions without the prejudice of modernity, to see the rich teachings on love, facing death and loss, coping with despair, and transformation. These are gifts to all of us seeking our own richest path.

Myth and ritual, properly understood, cultivate reverence and connection that combats loneliness and nihilism. Joining our sense of who we are with the stories and rituals invites us to discover how our life and its tribulations are part of the story of all life. In this we find instruction and solace.

4. Expanding the social work toolbox to include energy work

Spirituality challenges us to value all aspects of experience and to realize that we are not mere physical beings; we are not merely the product of our minds and intentions. The medium for work that includes the spiritual realm is one of energy—the non-visible life force that is foundational to thoughts, feelings, and physical form. Social workers are challenged, in direct practice, to engage in the experience of creative mystery that exceeds understanding yet also is accessible to subtle intuitions. As demonstrated with such approaches as Integrative Body Psychotherapy (IBP) (Rosenberg, Rand, & Asay, 1985) and Eye Movement, Desensitization and Reprocessing (EMDR) (Shapiro, 2001), dream work, and altered consciousness work, the subtleties of energy work reach beneath words addressing the formative influence shaping thoughts, feelings, and behaviours. Work with energy includes clearing of energy blockages and thought forms as well as the cultivation of higher levels of energy associated with psychological and physical health. Known variously as spirit, chi, Qui, baraka, hosero, morphogenic field, implicate order, light, prana, soul, and so forth, this field of energy is held to form the foundation of being, more fundamental than physical being—a powerful intervention to help our clients.[11]

5. Prayer has power to heal

Spiritual traditions such as Buddhism and Christianity teach us to revere the power of thoughts and intentions. On the more subtle levels of consciousness, thoughts and intentions are seen to affect others and ourselves in ways that exceed notions of perception and "self-fulfilling prophesy." How might we include a careful and reverent attitude to the intentions we bring to our work with clients? How might prayers become a powerful means of clearing intentions and introducing another kind of healing force to our work?

> It never occurred to me that religious practices such as prayer could be assessed like a new drug. At the time, I did not pray for my patients, and soon I found myself facing an ethical dilemma. If this study was reliable, how could I justify not praying for my patients? (Dossey, as cited in Levin, 2001, p. 9)

6. The powerful examples of spiritual leaders

These examples offer encouragement and vision of life's possibilities. The lives of holy persons, saints, avatars, shaman, revered leaders, and great teachers from all traditions offer much to teach and inspire us in our work (Schwartz, 1996, and Yancey, 2001, are wonderful summaries of great spiritual leaders). More than mere devotion, attention to the stories of great leaders brings to light the struggles, achievements, and the acts of courage implicit in inspired lives. The encouraging examples of these leaders demonstrate the great potential available to human beings.

7. Understanding spirituality as a quality of our outlook rather than the content of our beliefs

It is a common misunderstanding that spirituality is a set of particular beliefs. However, it is my impression that spirituality is defined more by the quality and degree of awareness or consciousness than by the content of belief. This insight helps get past the idea that integrating spirituality into social work practice involves adopting specific beliefs—this can be a real problem for individual and professional sensitivities.

Spirituality offers a perspective on human consciousness that is not merely a function of our conscious thoughts or even our unconscious ones. It includes experience that is drawn from what has been called transcendent states or non-ordinary states of consciousness, such as those common to clients facing distressing life situations.[12] A spiritual perspective in social work invites us to discover the hope and power of endurance that arises when life is faced with an expanded sense of what we see our life to be. This includes understanding healing on a soul level (Targ & Katra, 1999).[13]

The understanding of extraordinary consciousness and its role in healing is found particularly in the mystical traditions of East and West, and in Shamanism. While consciousness studies are certainly found in psychology and psychiatry, much of this is tentative, limited, and relegated to the less well-accepted realm of parapsychology.

8. Moving from power based on mastery to power based on "dynamic connectedness"

Spiritual consciousness employs paradox as a way of linking the contradictions of life. Our professional schools teach us to think in terms of "right outcome," mastery of technique, and being a case manager. Spiritual awareness sees beyond assumptions about mastery based on control. Erich Jantsch, a neuroscientist says it this way: "In life, the issue is not control but dynamic connectedness" (1980, p. 196). This is not a great reach for the profession of social work—so intricately familiar with systems theory.

W.N. Murray, a member of a Scottish Himalayan expedition offers this testimony regarding this kind of openness to the "dynamic connectedness" that defines spiritual consciousness. When we take great risks for things we believe in, "all sorts of things occur to help one that would otherwise never have occurred. A whole stream of events issues from the decision raising in one's favour all manner of unforeseen incidents and meetings and material assistance, which no man could have dreamed would have come his way" (quoted in Jaworski, 1998, p. 137). My sense is that many seasoned social workers have been witness to such synchronicity in the factors that lead to change for clients. In more traditional spiritual terms we might call this "grace," "the Tao," or the "hand of God."

❖ FINAL COMMENTS

In a creative dialogue amongst social work professionals, there is much we can learn from each other's experience in matters of spirituality. I encourage the reader to do their own research with colleagues, with the literature, in their work with clients, and in their personal growth work. The rigours of social work, the noble goal of service and the wisdom that clients bring with them make social work a privileged opportunity for this exploration.

I believe that reckoning with the spiritual dimension of social work is a necessary stage of growth for social workers as professionals and for the profession as a whole. Not everyone will agree, but many do. We live in a world of rapidly changing paradigms. Recognizing the dimension of spirituality in social work, I believe, is moving rapidly from being regarded as a completely outlandish and even offensive notion, to one that is a self-evident truth. For both the well-being of clients and the creative health of the profession, social workers must be willing to engage the spiritual dimension of our work.

NOTES

1.   Alberta sociologist Reg Bibby reports that 86% of all Canadians surveyed report that they believe in God, that 74% believe in miracle cures, that 61% believe in angels, and, surprisingly, 25% believe in reincarnation. This same survey notes that only about 17% of Canadians attend any formal religious gathering on a regular basis (Bibby, 2002). These figures are echoed in the work of George Gallup and Michael Lindsay (Gallup and Lindsay, 1999).

2.   This was research conducted as a Muttart Fellow. It involved extensive interviewing, literature review, workshops, and time spent in monasteries, ashrams, and

spiritual centres in North America and Asia. This research is presented in *Radical Relatedness: Exploring the Spiritual Dimension of Family Service Work* (available through the Muttart Foundation and Volunteer Calgary).

3. See note 9 (below) for a listing of these integrative researchers.

4. Thomas Kuhn, *The Structure of Scientific Revolutions* (1996), also discusses this notion of change in this highly regarded work.

5. There are exceptions to this including two organizations in the United States and one in Canada: the Society for Spirituality and Social Work, the North American Association of Christians in Social Work (NAACSW), and the Canadian Society for Spirituality and Social Work (CSSSW).

6. For a well-grounded and sensible exploration of spiritual practice used for neurotic avoidance, I recommend Kornfield, 2001.

7. I refer the reader to the work of Eckhart Tolle, Ken Wilber, and to the great poets such as Rumi, Rilke, and D.H. Lawrence. They offer a fuller exploration of spiritual experience distinct from the ideas of spiritual experience offered herewith. I wish to add here that what I am sharing here is not spirituality but information *about* spirituality. This is a crucial distinction for, as I will point out later, these ideas are merely abstractions pointing to what is ultimately an experience beyond information and thinking. Gregory of Nyssa, a Cappadocian monk of the fourth century says it elegantly: "Concepts create idols; only wonder comprehends anything. People kill one another over idols. Wonder makes us fall to our knees."

8. An excellent article summarizing research on psychotherapy effectiveness is found in Lebow, 2001.

9. In this context, the use of the term "religious" is generally referring to church-based activities, which is not the same as "spiritual" (not necessarily involving a church). The importance of these findings is the recognition that there are important overlaps between spirituality and religion in the realm of practice and its impact on the health of the individual.

10. I would refer the reader to some of the real pioneers of re-integrating the spiritual perspective in their respective fields. Besides those cited elsewhere, I recommend William James's classic work, *Varieties of Religious Experience*; David Bohm (a renowned quantum physicist's perspective outlined in *Wholeness and the Implicate Order*); explorations in chaos theory by David Peet (*Seven Life Lessons in Chaos Theory*); work on leadership and spirituality by Margaret Wheatley (*Leadership and the New Science*) and Joseph Jaworski (*Synchronicity: The Inner Path of Leadership*); alternative health perspectives and research (Deepak Chopra); Marilyn Ferguson (a brilliant overview of social change arising from her work on brain research); Rupert Sheldrake (exploring the biology from a spiritual perspective); Matthew Fox (a prolific theologian and teacher responsible for remarkably integrative perspectives on spirituality and science and the arts); Greg Braden (scientist with remarkable insights into the science of spirituality); psychiatrist Gerald May's integration of spirituality in the treatment of addictions; Carolyn Myss (combining her skills as an intuitive healer with her studies in theology); the work of David Whyte (poet); Joseph Campbell (the great mythologist); Jean Houston (psychologist); Sam Keen (philosopher, psychologist); Huston Smith (world religions expert). We are now

beginning to also see writers bridging spirituality and the helping professions such as Ann and Charles Simpkinson, Froma Walsh, James Hillman, and Otto Rank.

11. I learned to appreciate this through study with Robert Detzler (Spiritual Response Therapy), training in cranial sacral energy work, and meditation practice.

12. In my research, reported in *Radical Relatedness*, I have spoken of three broad levels of consciousness: physical (world defined by the information of the five senses), psychosocial (awareness based on insights about perception, insight and relationship context), and spiritual (transcendent awareness, innate connection) (McKernan, 2004, pp. 99–132). Transcendent consciousness refers to the experience, usually temporary, when one encounters the spiritual level of consciousness. Trauma and falling in love are two examples of temporary states of transcendent consciousness. The spiritual traditions offer direction and discipline to support a more conscious and sustained encounter with this quality of consciousness. In addition to my discussions about qualities of consciousness in *Radical Relatedness*, I refer the reader to the incisive exploration of these different levels of consciousness in the work of Ken Wilber (particularly Wilber, 1996) and William James (1982) and the elegant work of Pima Chodren, Buddhist nun (*When Things Fall Apart*) and Jose Hobday, Seneca healer and Franciscan nun (1999). Larry Dossey provides a description of these three levels applied to the practice of medicine (materialistic medicine, mind/body medicine, and mind/body/spirit medicine) (cited in Levin, 2001, p. 206).

13. See also the work of Norm Shealy (1999). For some scientific explorations about prayer see Braden, 2000.

REFERENCES

Bakan, D. (1975). *Sigmund Freud and the Jewish mystical tradition*. Toronto: Beacon Press.

Barker, B. (1998). Spiritually sensitive social work. In A. Simpkinson & C. Simpkinson (Eds.). *Soul work: A field guide for spiritual seekers* (pp. 66–68). New York: Harper Collins.

Bibby, R. (1995). *The Bibby report: Social trends Canadian style*. Toronto: Stoddart Publishing Company.

Bibby, R. (2002). *Restless Gods: The renaissance of religion in Canada*. Toronto: Stoddart Publishing Company.

Braden, G. (2000). *The Isaiah effect: Decoding the lost science of prayer and prophecy*. New York: Harmony Books.

Campbell, J. (1968). *The hero with a thousand faces*. Princeton: Princeton University Press.

Cochrane, T. (1998). *Songs of the circling spirit*. Capitol Records, catalogue #59612.

Elaide, M. (1959). *The sacred and the profane: The nature of religion*. Orlando, FL: Harcourt.

Ferguson, M. (1980). *The Aquarian conspiracy: Personal and social transformation in the 1980s*. Los Angeles: J.P. Tarcher.

Gallup, G. & Lindsay, M. (1999). *Surveying the religious landscape*. Moorehouse Publishing.

Gratton, C. (1995). *The art of spiritual guidance*. New York: Crossroads.

Harman, W. (1998, Winter). What are noetic sciences? *Noetic Sciences Review, 47*, 32.

Hawley, J. (1993). *Reawakening the spirit in work: The power of dharmic management*. San Francisco, CA: Berrett-Koehler Publishers.

Hobday, J. (1999). *Simple living: The Path to joy and freedom*. New York: Continuum.

James, W. (1982). *Varieties of religious experience*. New York: Penguin Books.

Jantsch, E. (1980). *The self-organizing universe*. Oxford: Pergamon Press.

Jaworski, J. (1998). *Synchronicity: The inner path of leadership*. San Francisco: Berrett-Kohler Publications.

Jung, C. (1955). *Modern man in search of a soul*. New York: Harvest Books.

Keen, S. (1995). *Hymns to an unknown God: Awakening the spirit in everyday life*. New York: Bantam Books.

Kornfield, J. (2001) Psychotherapy, meditation, and spirituality: Even the best meditators have wounds to heal. Retrieved from www.buddhanet.net/psymed1.htm.

Kuhn, T. *The structure of scientific revolutions* (3rd ed.). Chicago: University of Chicago Press.

Lebow, J. (2001). From Research to Practice: Therapy by the Numbers? *Psychotherapy Networker, 25*(2), 73-75.

Levin, J. (2001). *God, faith, and health: Exploring the spirituality healing connection*. New York: John Wiley and Sons.

May, G. (1992). *Care of mind, care of spirit*. New York: Harper Collins.

McKernan, M. (2004). *Radical relatedness: Exploring the spiritual dimension of family service work*. Edmonton: Muttart Foundation.

Novak, P. (1994). *The world's wisdom: Sacred texts of the world's religions*. San Francisco: Harper.

Rosenberg, J., Rand, M., & Asay, D. (1985). *Body, self, and soul: Sustaining integration*. Lake Worth, FL: Humanics Publishing.

Schwartz, T. (1996). *What really matters: Searching for wisdom in America*. New York: Bantam.

Shapiro, F. (2001). *Eye movement, desensitization, and reprocessing* (2nd ed.). New York: Guilford.

Shealy, C.N. (1999). *Sacred healing: The curing power of energy and spirituality*. Boston: Element.

Simpkinson, A., & Simpkinson, G. (1998). *Soul work: A field guide for spiritual seekers*. New York: Harper Collins.

Targ, R. & Katra, J. (1999). *Miracles of mind: Exploring non-local consciousness and spiritual healing*. Novato, CA: New World Library.

Tolle, E. (1997). *The Power of Now: A Guide to Spiritual Enlightenment*. Vancouver: Namaste Publishing.

Wilber, K. (1996). *A brief history of everything*. Boston: Shambala.

Yancey, P. (2001). *Soul survivor*. New York: Doubleday Press.

CHAPTER 7

THE HELPFULNESS OF SPIRITUALLY INFLUENCED GROUP WORK IN DEVELOPING SELF-AWARENESS AND SELF-ESTEEM: A PRELIMINARY INVESTIGATION

DIANA COHOLIC

This chapter discusses an exploratory study that investigated the helpfulness of spiritually influenced group work with eight adult women who shared a history of substance abuse. The overall purpose of the group was to help participants develop their self-awareness and self-esteem. The group, which was contextualized in transpersonal theory, was organized around the following themes and experiential exercises: meditation, mindfulness practice, dream-work, stream-of-consciousness writing, the shadow self, and other arts-based processes. Grounded-theory analysis of group sessions and individual interviews with the participants found that the participants perceived the group to be helpful in developing their self-awareness and self-esteem. While the participants identified different aspects of the group as spiritual, making-meaning was one practice that was consistently described as a spiritually sensitive process. The results of this study in this emergent field are promising and suggestions are provided for future research.

❖ INTRODUCTION

A transition is occurring within the scientific and academic community in that a spiritual dimension is increasingly being considered (Ai, 2002; Clark, 1999). Indeed, researchers at major universities in North America are studying connections between the mind, body, and spirit (Koenig, George, Titus, & Meador, 2004; Lo, Kates, Ruston, Arnold, Cohen, Puchalski, et al., 2003; Luskin, Newell, Griffith, Holmes, Telles, DiNucci, et al., 2000; McCaffrey, Eisenberg, Legedza, Davis, & Phillips, 2004;

Palmer, Katerndahl, & Morgan-Kidd, 2004). Within social work, there has been a burgeoning development of literature (particularly in the past decade) that discusses the incorporation of spirituality in helping (Abels, 2000; Canda & Smith, 2001b; Coates, 2003; Nash & Stewart, 2002). This literature generally refers to spirituality as a universal aspect of human life that encompasses experiences that transcend the self; it is a feature of human life and development that is accessible to all. The rationales for incorporating spirituality into social work practice include issues raised by clients, cultural diversities, coping resources and resiliency factors, social work's holistic approach, the need for knowledge development, and the effectiveness of spiritually influenced interventions (Bewley, 1995; Bullis, 1996; Kamya, 2000; Lloyd, 1997; Robbins, Chatterjee, & Canda, 1999; Roberts, 1999; Ballou, 1995; Barrett, 1999; Berliner, 1992; Coholic, 2002; Edwards, 2002; Hagon, 1998; Hartman, 1996; Kimmel & Kazanis, 1995; Pearlman & Saakvitne, 1995; Schwartz, 1999; Sermabeikian, 1994; Wilner, 2001).

   We are especially interested in the latter idea that spiritually influenced practice is effective. Presently, this belief is evidenced in the literature by way of case studies, survey research, practice wisdom, and personal experiences (Derezotes, 2001; Leight, 2001; Smith, 2001). Although there is great merit in practice wisdom and in constructing knowledge from practice, especially when considering an experiential construct such as spirituality, the accuracy of these beliefs must be explored. Social workers have not yet investigated whether attending to spirituality actually improves client outcomes or not (Ai, 2002). At the same time, the belief in spirituality's helpfulness underpins many of the arguments for the inclusion of spirituality in practice and education. For example, it has been contended that when spirituality is ignored, the fulfillment of people's potential for wholeness, their right to fully express their experience, and creative transformation are all restricted (Russel, 1998; Walker, 1998). Processes such as meditation, prayer, and ritual have all been described as effective (Bewley, 1995; Russel, 1998). Also, practitioners have described the more rapid progress of clients when spirituality was addressed, and even social work students with little experience or knowledge of the social work and spirituality literature believed in spirituality's effectiveness (Coholic, 2001, 2003b). Studies that aim to learn more about how spiritually influenced helping occurs and studies that examine its helpfulness constitute one of the next important steps in the development of this body of knowledge, and it is these goals that our research has attempted to explore.

Consequently, this chapter describes a pilot study that investigated the helpfulness of a spiritually influenced group program that had as its overall goal the improvement of participants' self-esteem by way of developing their self-awareness. Trying to improve people's self-esteem and self-awareness is a basic aspect of most helping approaches (Heinonen & Spearman, 2001), and a high level of self-esteem is linked with resiliency and the ability to cope (Walsh, 1998); they are key elements underpinning healthy human development (Sharf, 2004). The uniqueness of our group program is its focus on spiritually influenced practices, and the connections between these practices and the development of self-awareness and self-esteem. Specifically, the chapter discusses what the participants found helpful and spiritual about the group. For instance, we found that the group participants experienced different practices as spiritual, except for the process of making-meaning, which they all expressed to be linked with their spiritual beliefs. Other group processes that were identified as helpful and as spiritual experiences were dream-work, meditations and mindfulness practice, and feelings of connectedness among group members.

❖ AN OVERVIEW OF THE STUDY AND GROUP PROGRAM

The pilot study was completed in May 2004, with the support of the Northern Regional Recovery Continuum (NRRC), a community agency that works with women and addictions (see www.lakesidecentre.ca). The group program consisted of six sessions in total, each of which was 2 h in length. The group sessions utilized various experiential and arts-based exercises that are integral in other spiritually sensitive approaches for the purposes of building self-awareness and self-esteem such as stream-of-consciousness writing, relaxation, walking meditation and mindfulness practice, and dream-work (Wilner, 2001; France, 2002; Kabat-Zinn, 1990). Initially, the group was facilitated with 10 participants affiliated with the NRRC, but one woman dropped out of the group for reasons unknown to us, while another woman was asked to leave by the NRRC due to a relapse—thus we ended the group with eight participants. The study explored how spirituality is discussed in group practice and experienced by group participants, examined the group participants' perceptions about the group processes and its helpfulness (or not), and collected self-reports of self-esteem before and after participation in the group as another measure of the group's influence or perceived helpfulness (or lack thereof). We used the Multi-dimensional Self-Esteem Inventory to collect these self-reports (O'Brien & Epstein, 1988).

Transpersonal theory offered a useful theoretical base for the development of this group, as there are very few psychological or social work theories that specifically address the spiritual dimension in life. Transpersonal theory offers a way of making sense of and discussing spiritually influenced practice. Transpersonal simply means beyond the person or ego—there is a higher or inner self distinct from the personal ego. For example, transpersonal approaches focus on an expanded theory of human consciousness. Transpersonal theory builds on the work of Jung, Assagioli, Maslow, Rogers, Wilber, Walsh, Vaughn, and others (Cowley, 1996). It has been called the "fourth force" in psychology because it challenges and moves beyond the theoretical influence of the first three movements: psychoanalytic, behaviourism, and humanistic psychology (Scotton, Chinen, & Battista, 1996). In general, transpersonal theorists advocate for methodological pluralism and multidisciplinary helping methods, a cross-cultural approach to building knowledge, a belief that spiritual experience is universal, and that an appropriate stance is one that includes a component of curiosity and openness to mystery. In terms of practice, transpersonal theory is described as a modality that seeks to establish a growth-producing link between a person and transpersonal experience, and has an interest in the spiritual, which includes intuition, meditation, relaxation, visualization, and dream-work (Scotton, et al., 1996). Canda and Smith (2001a) pointed out that transpersonal theory has only recently begun to influence mainstream social work although it has been growing steadily within psychology and philosophy since the 1960s. In particular, *Nexus: Transpersonal Approach to Groups* was a good source of information for us in developing the group program (France, 2002).

The six group sessions were organized around the following themes: an introduction to the importance of process and the nature of the group work, stream-of-consciousness writing, the shadow self, mindfulness meditation, dream analysis, and ending and evaluating the group experience. Session one was an introduction to the group. The nature of the group was explained to the participants and exercises were used to help establish a context in which participants would feel comfortable with their diversity, and learn to focus on the importance of the process of learning about themselves and improving their self-esteem. A short introductory relaxation/meditative exercise was conducted (meditations were used in every session). Discussion also occurred regarding their feelings about creativity and art. At the end of every session, books were made available to the participants to borrow (Batchelor, 2001; Hart, 2003; Hazen-Hammond, 1999; Rozman, 1975; Sams, 1998; Starhawk, 1987; Tanner, 1988).

In session two, the facilitator explained stream-of-consciousness writing. The goal of stream-of-consciousness writing is to become more aware of the constant dialogue in our minds, that is, the process helps us to connect with inner thoughts and feelings, strengthening self-awareness. Importantly, it was stressed that there is no evaluation attached to the writing and that judgements should not be made about the process, especially while engaged with it. Clay work followed the writing exercises. One participant explained that if she had not engaged in the stream-of-consciousness writing first, she would not have been able to sculpt a beautiful flower. She explained:

> Because by writing this down and just letting our minds flow and stuff, I ended up in a positive space and then I made my flower … it's like I brought myself inside and it stayed there and then I made my stuff. Because if I would have done this just before, then I wouldn't be focused on the positive and I was just feeling like, I was a mess you know … so I wouldn't have made it, anything pretty, I would have just made a flower … I wasn't feeling unique and individual, I was feeling lonely.

The shadow self was the theme in session three and it was discussed as encompassing those things that we hide from ourselves and the world such as feelings like shame and anger—essentially, qualities and feelings that are held in our unconscious because they are unacceptable to our conscious mind. The shadow is a term coined by Carl Jung (Pascal, 1992; Ventegodt, Andersen, & Merrick, 2003a). Simply, the idea is that we need to acknowledge the parts of ourselves that we hide, deny, and repress in order to know and understand ourselves fully. However, the process of doing so is much more complex, because it involves developing self-awareness of aspects of ourselves that we would rather not acknowledge.

To begin session four, an exercise of mindful eating was conducted with small bits of food such as raisins and cereal pieces. Discussion included the idea that mindful moments help us to become aware of what is transpiring in our environment, of our inner workings, and our reactions to situations. The idea of interconnection was also raised, for example, contemplating all the people that it took to create one raisin. The participants also engaged in a walking mindfulness meditation outside at a running track located very close to where the group was being held.

Session five began with constructing dream collages. The participants were instructed to scan through the provided magazines and to extract anything that seemed associated with their dream images (a type of free association exercise). The facilitator explained that dreams are often multi-layered and have meanings on many different levels, so the layering of the pictures in a collage is completely appropriate. As well, dreams use both language and images, which can be represented in the collage. Participants were encouraged to interpret symbols and images according to their own experiences and viewpoints—developing their own meaning was important. Group discussion and analysis of the dream collages was conducted.

The final group session began with a guided imagery exercise focused on interconnections. One of the group's goodbye rituals included discussion about both the challenges and highlights of the group, and their future goals.

The Process of the Research Study

Potential participants were recruited from the NRRC (Northern Regional Recovery Continuum) using Participant Information Statements, which provided them with a brief description of the group program's structure and goals. After women indicated an interest in participating, they met individually with the principal investigator (PI) prior to beginning the group so that the goals of the group could be discussed, questions could be answered, the consent form signed, the demographic form completed, and the Multi-dimensional Self-Esteem Inventory (MSEI) administered. A research assistant (an experienced practitioner) assisted in developing the group and facilitated the group sessions. The PI and the facilitator met after each session to discuss the group process and to address any issues that arose. On completion of the group, the PI met individually with the eight group participants in order to conduct a semi-structured interview that explored their experiences of the group, and their viewpoints on the helpfulness (or not) of the process. This was also an opportunity to discuss the results of the MSEI, which was administered again at the end of the last group session. The group sessions and the postgroup individual interviews were all audio-recorded for the purposes of grounded theory analysis.

Brief Description of the Research Participants

The participants ranged in age from 20–53 years. All had been previously involved with the NRRC, either through the 21-day inpatient program or in aftercare groups. A few were still actively involved with the agency and lived in the agency's aftercare program and/or attended other agency groups. With regard to their spiritual and/or religious affiliations, one participant identified as First Nation (Aboriginal). Two identified as Catholic, another stated that she was raised Catholic and sometimes attended church. A fifth participant said that she was raised Catholic, but does not practise anymore. One participant reported that she was raised Baptist/Pentecostal and that she currently attended a Pentecostal church. One participant was raised Protestant. One woman was raised in the Mormon religion, but stated that she does not practise anymore. One participant stated that she was affiliated with the Rosicrucians, Billy Graham, and bible studies, such as "A Course in Miracles." Finally, one participant reported that she was raised Catholic, but now attended a Pentecostal church.

Research Design

While both quantitative and qualitative methods are utilized in practice-based research, qualitative methods such as grounded theory approaches were better suited for this study for several reasons. First, grounded theory methods are inductive approaches that aim to generate theory. This research was exploratory with the goal of discovering new knowledge because this is a developing field. Indeed, a widely accepted practice framework for spiritually sensitive work has yet to be developed. At this stage, we need to better understand how spiritually influenced practice actually transpires in the real world with real people and all the complexities they bring to the helping process. Second, practice professions such as social work and nursing have made considerable use of grounded theory methods in their quest to conduct research that is relevant for practice (Swigonski, 1994). Indeed, the demand for solid links between practice and research has consistently been a strong theme in social work (Gilgun, 1994). Grounded theory methods enable the discovery of knowledge from the world of practice, which in turn produces frameworks that are useful for practitioners and consumers. Third, a grounded theory approach allows an investigation of spiritually influenced practice with the ability to respond to unexpected events that often occur when conducting psychotherapy with people, that is, we can improvise to meet participant needs (Gingerich, 2000; Seligman, 1995).

Grounded Theory Methodology and Analysis

A grounded theory method helped us construct knowledge from the analysis of group sessions and research interviews with participants. Research data (transcribed group sessions and individual interviews) was converted into systematic schema for examining its meaning, discovering themes and patterns, and making connections among concepts—making links between themes is a means of putting conceptual order on the mass of data. Final integration of research data follows this process, but done at a higher, more abstract analytical level (Glaser & Strauss, 1967). For example, all of the participant interviews were coded and sorted into relevant categories. As new data emerged, they were either clustered into already existing categories saturating those groupings or, particularly in the preliminary stages of analysis, they were sorted into a new category. As the analysis continued, the categories were continuously compared with one another and with new emerging data in order to discover links among the groups. Any categories that are related are combined and once again compared to incoming data to assess their relationships to hypotheses that emerged from the comparisons among groupings. Refinement of the categories that have emerged from the analysis comes from the continued connection and reduction of concepts that leads to increased abstraction (Corbin, 1986; Stern, 1986). Grounded theory analysis allowed us to identify the intricacies of how spirituality is actually discussed in group practice, how it shapes practice processes, and how participants perceived the helpfulness of the spiritually influenced work.

The Multi-dimensional Self-Esteem Inventory (MSEI)
The use of the MSEI in this study adds another layer of data collection and analysis of self-reports of self-esteem. The MSEI is an objective self-report inventory that provides measures of the multi-dimensional components of self-esteem (O'Brien & Epstein, 1988). Respondents complete the MSEI by entering their responses on a rating sheet: for section 1 they are directed to use a 5-point Likert scale to report how accurately the 61 items describe them, and for section 2 they are instructed to use a 5-point Likert scale to report how often they experience the thoughts and feelings described in the 55 items. The MSEI takes approximately 15–30 min to complete. In operationalizing theory into concrete measures, the MSEI uses the following 11 scales: global self-esteem, eight component scales (competence, lovability, likeability, self-control, personal power, moral self-approval, body appearance, and body functioning), identity integration as a measure of global self-concept, and defensive self-enhancement as a validity measure to provide information on the degree to which a person is defensively inflating her self-presentation. The MSEI has undergone extensive conceptual and psychometric development over a 10-year period (O'Brien & Epstein, 1988).

❖ ANALYSIS AND DISCUSSION

The following discussion specifically focuses on how spirituality was discussed in the group and experienced by the participants, particularly as this relates to their development of self-awareness and self-esteem. The presentation of the research findings is meant to be an overview. It is beyond the scope of this chapter to examine each topic, such as mindfulness, thoroughly. However, the discussion demonstrates how spirituality can enter into group helping processes and provides direction for future study in this emergent area. Although spirituality was deemed to be a really important part of the group, the participants experienced different aspects of the group as spiritually sensitive; this should be expected given the diversity of their backgrounds and the complex nature of spirituality. However, it can be noted that two of the participants reported that the entire group experience felt spiritual for them.

Working with Dreams

Although many practitioners feel unprepared to attend to their clients' dreams, the usefulness of dream analysis is increasingly being considered across helping approaches and its connection with spirituality is evident in the literature (Pesant & Zadra, 2004). Krippner, Jaeger, and Faith (2001) explained how dreams are intimately connected with major religious and spiritual traditions throughout the world. France (2002, p. 129) made the point that since the beginning of time, all cultures regarded dreams as having some special power that transcended the past, present, and future, and that many cultures believed that dream messages are the vehicle through which God can speak. In group work, dream exploration can allow participants to go beyond the physical world into the spiritual realm. Indeed, dream exploration constitutes an important part of the psychotherapeutic work in transpersonal approaches (France, 2002; Scotton, Chinen, & Battista, 1996; Pascal, 1992).

Along the same lines, for some of the group participants, dream-work was connected with spirituality. For example, one participant reported that a lot of her dreams guided her to action. She stated, "God was letting me know this all along, that my addiction had to quit, so I went into rehab after [having the dream]." One participant discussed how a recurring dream was actually representative of a past-life experience. She used the dream to make-meaning of her current life situation and family dynamics. Yet another participant explained that further reading about dreams elicited a spiritual experience. She described:

> It came to me [understanding] … it popped out of the book. That doesn't
> usually happen, so for me that's more of a spiritual thing because usually
> if I start reading, I'll ask my higher power to let me grasp what I really

need to grasp. So that means ... if I don't understand, it's not made for me to actually get it today.

In the individual interviews, six of the participants described how working with their dreams was helpful, while one woman stated that she had difficulty making connections between the dream collage and her life experiences. They also identified that there was not enough time to analyze their dream collages fully in the group. However, several women reported that they brought the collages home and continued to work with them either on their own or in individual counselling. One participant described her group highlight as constructing the dream collage. She found the analysis that occurred in group helpful to developing her understanding of the dream's meaning for her. We agree that self-analysis or the "dreamer as authority" is essential (Zichi Cohen & Bumbaugh, 2004), and the relevance of the participants' self-analysis of their dreams was emphasized. Another participant explained that working with dreams increased her self-awareness by helping her connect with unconscious messages. Several women reported that they would continue to use dream-work for self-discovery and healing.

Similarly, within the research literature, dream-work has been reported to be useful. Moss (2002) argued that dream-work can help people access deep unconscious feelings in order to facilitate a more complete mourning process. Barrett (2002) stated that dreams represent a powerful metaphor for irrational beliefs that might not otherwise be articulated. In group counselling, the analysis of dreams has been reported to help with understanding other group members, promoting group cohesiveness, and stimulating therapeutic group interactions (Clark, 1994). Even cognitive therapists have begun to examine the usefulness of dream-work and devoted a special issue of the *Journal of Cognitive Psychotherapy* to this topic (see Vol. 16[1], 2002). Dream analysis and the other exercises utilized in the group do not have to be classified as spiritual experiences. However, as is evident in the participants' comments above, these processes make sense to some people as spiritual experiences, and the discussion of dreams may naturally lead to considering spiritual viewpoints. If helping practitioners remain uncomfortable with considering the spiritual dimension of people's lives, they may miss the opportunity to help the client construct a holistic narrative that best fits their experience.

Meditations and Mindfulness Practice
The facilitator introduced the participants to a variety of meditative exercises in order to address different preferences. Each session began

with a meditation or meditative exercises were incorporated later in the session in order to help ground and connect the participants to the work of the group. Meditating before engaging in experiential exercises and other psychotherapeutic work can help to quiet the mind and open up the possibility for a stronger connection with feelings and/or unconscious processes. Self-awareness and insight arise from an ability to pay attention to and experience one's anxieties, fears, and other feelings that often reside in the unconscious mind. Frattaroli (2001, p. 194) contended that you can think of this process as simply getting in touch with a feeling or, more profoundly, as listening to the soul.

For some participants, the meditations felt spiritual because they were taking the time to connect with their higher self, while for others it was an opportunity to feel their energy and other people's energy, or to connect with their higher power. One woman believed that the meditations allowed conversations about participants' higher powers and spirituality because everybody had something to contribute. On the other hand, one participant explained that while the meditations were relaxing, they did not feel spiritual to her because they were not long enough or in-depth enough. This participant experienced the stream-of-consciousness writing as the most spiritual exercise, because for her, it was directed by God. She stated, "it continued to flow and I know it was from within me and it wasn't me. And how God, in my writing, came out."

For some of the participants, the meditations were difficult at first because this was a new experience for them, and one's ability to meditate and relax generally becomes easier and more effective with practice (Kabat-Zinn, 1990). However, several participants discussed how the meditative exercises were particularly helpful in developing their self-awareness. One woman explained how through the use of meditation and guided imagery (with the help of her sponsor) she was able to visualize rescuing her "inner child" and so felt for the first time in 20 years that she could protect herself from abuse. She stated that meditation is a gift, "is like wow, it really is and I just can't get over what I've accomplished, what I've achieved through meditation ... I found my heart ... It's like I found my soul-mate, and it's in me!" Another participant also explained how learning meditation has helped her to feel less congested than normal with thoughts racing through her mind. Some women stated that they liked meditating at night because it helped them sleep, while others preferred to do it in the morning because it helped them deal with the day ahead.

Mindfulness practice is a specific form of meditation. Jon Kabat-Zinn (1994) explained that the key to mindfulness meditation is an appreciation of the present moment and the cultivation of an intimate relationship with it through a continual attending to it with care and discernment. While mindfulness lies at the root of Buddhism, Taoism, and yoga, it is also found in the works of Emerson, Thoreau, and Whitman, and in Native American wisdom. Kabat-Zinn (2003) further proposed that an operational working definition is the awareness that emerges through paying attention on purpose, in the present moment, and nonjudgementally to the unfolding of experience moment by moment. Recently, mindfulness has been adopted as an approach in contemporary psychology for increasing awareness and responding skillfully to mental processes that contribute to emotional distress and maladaptive behaviour (Bishop, Lau, Shapiro, Carlson, Anderson, Carmody, et al., 2004). Indeed, mindfulness practice is increasingly being studied in various fields with a myriad of client populations and problems, with research results indicating its effectiveness. For example, researchers have found that mindfulness is effective in helping chronic pain patients deal with grief (Sagula & Rice, 2004), in helping a broad range of individuals cope with problems (Grossman, Niemann, Schmidt, & Walach, 2004; Ventegodt, Merrick, & Andersen, 2003a), in fostering health benefits (Ventegodt, et al., 2003b, 2003c; Harvard Women's Health Watch, 2004), in decreasing mood disturbance and stress (Brown & Ryan, 2003), in treating negative body images (Stewart, 2004), and it has been proposed as a core common factor in psychotherapy (Martin, 1997), to name just a few examples. In harmony with these results, most of the group participants reported that learning mindfulness was helpful in assisting them to better appreciate life's moments and themselves, and in understanding themselves more fully.

For example, one participant reported that the mindful eating exercise helped her to actually taste the food, which was a different experience for her "because I don't really taste my food, really." Another participant discovered that normally she would have swallowed a handful of the raisins before learning that she really thought they were gross. This was affirmed by another participant who stated that "I thought I liked the little squares ... and I started tasting it and you were right, I don't really like them." The mindful walking exercise was also a new experience for most of the participants. One woman reported on her new-found awareness:

> The awareness is great, when it overcomes you, when you become very aware how big the world is. I know that sounds weird but I'm thinking of myself and feeling like my body walking, and then I'm seeing everything around me and it's like "wow, it's just me here walking on this huge big world."

Three participants identified that learning about and being more mindful facilitated feelings of gratefulness. One woman explained that she can now appreciate more the small details that we all take for granted. Importantly, she reported "that it's making things more worthwhile ... it fills my day with healthy things ... I don't feel like I'm wasting my time," which in turn helped her to feel better about herself. Another participant summed up her experience by reporting that mindfulness has encouraged her to feel happier, calmer, and more confident. For her, the mindfulness practice was "the last of the steps that I needed ... the program that we're putting together here, what I'm planning incorporating in my life, it seems to be just the thing to complete it [her healing]." Mindfulness is a good example of a helpful process that is rooted in spirituality, but that can be learned by many people with both diverse spiritual beliefs or even no spiritual standpoints. Perhaps this accounts, in part, for the current interest in mindfulness across helping approaches and disciplines. However, we should contemplate the complexities involved in divorcing mindfulness from its spiritual roots. As Kabat-Zinn (2003, p. 145) argued, it is important that we recognize the unique qualities of mindfulness meditation practice so that it is not "simply seized upon as the next promising cognitive behavioural technique or exercise, decontextualized, and plugged into a behaviourist paradigm with the aim of driving desirable change, or of fixing what is broken."

Connectedness

The idea of connectedness and helping to foster connections is a concept found in the spirituality and social work literature; it has been identified as a spiritually influenced helping process. For example, feminist social workers have discussed the process of helping clients to foster connections with community, in groups, and with their feelings as spiritually influenced practice. They have also described the spiritual connections they sometimes form with clients (Coholic, 2003a). Ballou (1995) argued that feminist spirituality is grounded in community, connection, and relationship, while Kimmel and Kazanis (1995) described the deep spiritual connections that can occur in counselling groups. These "deep connections" can be conceptualized as spirit-spirit connections. Zukav (2000) described this by arguing that we are all souls wearing Earth suits (our gender, colour, etc.), and that people are increasingly coming to recognize each other as a fellow soul who is part of a universal family, rather than focusing on the particular Earth suit they have donned for this lifetime.

The connectedness experienced between the group members was discussed as feeling spiritual and a spiritual experience by some of the participants. For example, one participant stated that "just the way everybody … got so involved … it felt (pause) it was really good … I found everyone was at ease … more relaxed and at peace in that group than a lot of the other groups you can go into." Another woman found it hard to put into words her experience of this connectedness, but said that the group was about being at peace "like nobody judged what you said … And now I see how much confidence everybody had in one another." For another participant, the experience of spiritual connection felt inspiring and encouraging even after the group was completed. Articulating experiences that are based in feeling and that feel spiritual can be difficult. We lack the language to describe and capture these processes fully. However, based on these and other experiences reported to us by the group participants, it would seem that a spiritual connectedness among the participants accounted, in part, for the group's camaraderie and respect for one other, which was evidenced throughout all of the group sessions.

The Importance of Making-Meaning
The process of making-meaning has been identified in the literature as a practice principle for spiritually sensitive practice, and has been described as a spiritual practice because spirituality itself is often defined as a process of making-meaning (Coholic, 2002). Barrett (1999) described healing from trauma as a quest for spirituality that reflects a deep need for meaning. Anderson (1999) stated that spirituality is the experience of making-meaning informed by a relationship with the transcendent in life. Thus, therapy from a spiritual perspective aims to help people fashion narratives that weave together human and Divine realities, enabling people to hear their own stories retold with clarity and new possibilities, transforming their lives in the process.

Certainly for the participants in this group, spirituality helped them make-meaning of their struggles with addiction. In the first group session, one participant stated that she always "felt I was here for a reason … I definitely do believe I'm here at this moment for a reason." Another woman agreed and discussed her belief that people have different troubles in their lives for certain reasons that they need to figure out. She stated:

> I know about my disease but now I have to find what else I was put on this Earth [for] … right now it's to learn about myself … this is one of the processes of life, a journey that we have to attend to. That's the way I see it in a spiritual way.

Similarly, a third participant explained that the path she is on was meant for her, even though some of it has been bad. She stated that "everything

I've done in my past makes me a better person for today and will help me in the future." Another participant stated that she agreed that everyone has a purpose, although she was not sure who made up that purpose. She raised the question: "Is it possible to reach a spiritual peak in life?" In response to this query, another participant reported that if she does not finish her life journey the right way that she's going to come back [in another lifetime]. Yet another woman asserted that "no one reaches their spiritual limit until they die and go on to the spiritual world … we're on a journey and we have to go through these experiences for us to look at ourselves … I don't believe in coincidences … because our paths were meant to cross."

These are just a few examples of how the process of making-meaning feels spiritual to some people or gets interpreted in a spiritual way. Making-meaning is the one process that stands out in the analysis because it was discussed in all of the group sessions. Also, it entered into the discourse on different layers. For example, as noted above, spirituality permeated the participants' more global understandings of why they had problems and what they needed to do to heal. But spirituality also helped them to make sense of the specific exercises and processes they engaged with during the group. As the participants noted, God or their higher power communicated with them via their writing, reading, and dreams. The participants' comments illustrate the importance of making-meaning of experiences as part of the process of healing, integrating one's life experiences, and continuing to grow and develop as a person. Because assisting people to make sense of or make-meaning of their life events is such a basic element of many helping perspectives, practitioners should be open to integrating people's spiritual viewpoints into this process. When we create the space or grant permission for spirituality to enter into peoples' stories, they will raise it and incorporate it when required. We can then engage in meaningful and helpful discussion with them in order to cocreate more complete and healthy life narratives that make sense for them.

Self-Esteem Measures
We analyzed the test scores from the MSEI as follows: first the data were tested for normality. Because none of the data were normal (they were more evenly distributed across a range, which is not unusual for these types of data), we used paired Wilcoxon tests (a nonparametric test that is the equivalent of a t-test for non-normal data) on all 11 scales for pre- and postgroup scores. For each scale, the postgroup scores were significantly higher. All of the scores were at least $p < 0.05$. Due to uncontrolled variables, we cannot assume that this increase in self-esteem scores can

be attributed solely to the women's participation in the group program. However, it was still a useful process to discuss the improvement in scores with the participants in the individual interviews. They were pleased with the documented increase in scores and the areas in which they continued to score low provided material for their consideration. Interestingly, the participants attributed their increase in self-esteem scores in part to their participation in the group and their increased self-awareness. For example one participant stated: "I'm feeling more positive now than before. I put everything I had into the group, like everything that was required of me to do, I did the best that I could … like this really helped plus I've taken a course on Monday for relapse prevention. So between the two of them … it's really keeping me focused and on track."

A second participant said that "the group helped me to deal with issues … I'm now able to sit down with myself through meditation or whatever … I can just focus on stuff that I've learned … I've achieved something … I've grown so that I don't have to feel less than." A third participant explained that she would attribute over half of the change in her self-esteem to the group, with the rest of the change coming from engagement with individual counselling. A fourth participant who reported that the group processes were right up her alley reported that she feels better about herself in that she is surer about herself and what she needs to do to keep developing; her expectations of herself are much more realistic now and positive. She argued that 70–75% of her change was due to her group participation. A fifth participant spoke about how the spirituality of the group and specifically the dream-work was important in developing her self-esteem. She explained that the change in her scores was very much all about the group because the group helped her to amalgamate all of her previous learning and further develop her healing—to actually go there and [resolve previously identified issues]. A sixth participant reported that the group helped her to develop her self-esteem by encouraging her to identify her strengths and confidence in her own abilities. A seventh participant explained that the group helped develop her self-esteem by "putting balance into my life. Also, having fun through recovery makes you even more open in sharing because it doesn't have to hurt this time. I can sit here and laugh and I'm still being open. So I guess it teaches us another level of intimacy." Finally, the eighth participant explained how the creativity of the group was relaxing and life-changing. She was able to become more creative at home with her children so that they saw a part of their mother that they had not previously experienced. She reconnected with her children on their level, and "the kids, I think, noticed something different … I mean the kids are my life, so that's really had an effect."

Thus, for some participants, the group was a profound experience in itself that was significant in helping them to develop their self-awareness and self-esteem, while for others it was a helpful adjunct to other strategies for change such as individual and other group counselling.

The Group's Purpose and the Idea of "Fun"

One final point can be made concerning the nature of the group. We did not realize how different this group would be for most of the participants. Although a few did have previous experience with meditation and experiential therapeutic tools such as journaling, for most of the women, the techniques used in the group constituted a very different experience particularly in relation to building self-awareness and self-esteem. Six of the participants discussed the group difference in the individual interviews. One woman stated, "I found it really different. Just the hands on ... at first I wasn't sure about the group because to me it felt like a little kid playing with play-dough." Another participant explained "that the group program was different in that we didn't have to be as deep and talk deeply [about] ... our sobriety and things. And we didn't have to cry." Similarly, another participant stated "that it was a very different group ... I was thinking, well I'm not getting anywhere with this group because I didn't melt-down today, I didn't cry today ... because we were having fun through it all. And I think that's something that I know that I was missing and that all women were saying that they were missing. Because ever since getting into recovery everything has been so serious, so intense ... it doesn't have to hurt, at the moment, for you to be able to grow."

Along these lines, another participant described the group as "refreshing ... I don't know how else to explain it, because it felt good. It was fun ... and we laughed a lot I think." One other participant discussed how this group fostered balance in her overall process of recovery. The concept that the participants were having fun while they were learning about themselves and new ways of addressing issues without feeling like they had to "pull out your wisdom tooth or something" is interesting, as it can help us expand our notions of the helping process as including both pain-filled experiences with other more joyful processes. Another woman summarized this sentiment well: "I was longing for a group where I [could] deal with my issues in a positive way ... I think in the first two sessions I was thinking ... if I'm not sitting there and having a hard time and crying, I am not dealing with anything ... But this group ... allowed me that connection with my inner child ... it's brought up a lot of past issues, stuff that I didn't want to remember but gave me the opportunity to deal with it."

The principal investigator did meet with each participant before the beginning of the group to explain the nature and purpose of the group, but this was clearly not enough. In the future, we will spend more time in the first session building an understanding of how experiential techniques and processes can be helpful in developing self-awareness and self-esteem. Otherwise there could be a risk that people will drop out or not utilize the group experiences to their fullest potential.

❖ CONCLUSIONS

This chapter discussed how spiritually influenced group work was useful in helping participants strengthen their self-awareness and self-esteem. One of the goals of this study was to learn more about how spirituality is actually discussed in group practice and how it can shape the helping process. It was evident in the first session that the participants felt comfortable raising their spiritual viewpoints, which affirms for us the importance of making room for the discussion of spirituality and the willingness of people to raise it, when this space is created. Because the participants were informed that the group included the spiritual dimension in their self-discovery process, discussions that took place naturally involved this facet of people's lives. One aspect of how the participants discussed spirituality stands out in this group. For instance, most of the participants talked about their spiritual beliefs as a way of helping them to make-meaning of their life circumstances. This is interesting to contemplate with regard to social work and other helping perspectives, because we are often involved in helping people to make sense of life events. For this group of women, spirituality was an integral part of this process.

One can make room for spirituality to enter into healing spaces, but participants will find and experience spirituality differently. For instance, for a couple of the participants, the whole group felt spiritual. For other women the meditations were the most spiritual experience, while for others the dream-work and/or mindfulness elicited spiritual connections. So, for some people, meditation is a chance to connect with a higher power, while for others it is simply a means to becoming grounded, calm, and focused. The important point here is that in a group that incorporates the spiritual realm, participants are encouraged to bring their spirituality to the process and to make sense of their experiences in a holistic manner if they so wish and if they deem this to be important for them. And for some people, spirituality is how they make sense of a particular process; for example, one participant described stream-of-consciousness writing as a way that

God can speak to her. While the experiential exercises conducted in this group do not have to be classified as spiritually influenced practices, we should keep in mind that they are experienced as spiritual experiences for some people.

We were also interested in learning more about the helpfulness (or not) of incorporating spirituality into group practice. According to the participants, the group was helpful in a myriad of ways including helping to create a shift in self-esteem. The participants found that the meditations assisted them to become more self-aware by helping them to visualize therapeutic processes, or by helping them connect more strongly with their thoughts and feelings by providing focus. Mindfulness practice helped some women change their self-perceptions and fostered feelings of gratefulness. They learned that healing can be "fun" and creative, and that creativity could help them build relationships with their children, others, and themselves. For some, the group was the missing link in their recovery. For others it enabled them to expand their healing to another level or helped them to understand and amalgamate previous work they had completed. The group also served as a useful adjunct to other therapeutic work they were already engaged in.

There is much more work required in continuing to build knowledge about spiritually influenced helping. It can be noted that the group goals and its processes are generic enough to be applicable with various clientele. It will be important to study how spiritually influenced practice works with different client populations and problems because social work practice is so diverse. Also, as knowledge continues to be built in this field, future studies may explore the helpfulness of spiritually oriented practice compared with other approaches and control groups. The possibility of bringing people from different backgrounds together to discuss spirituality was also reaffirmed. However, this is something that future studies may want to explore in greater depth. Although the women in our group held different belief systems, the differences were not as radical as they could be. Specific processes such as dream-work and mindfulness, two exercises identified as particularly helpful in this study, could also be investigated further. Although several of the participants stated that they used the group exercises outside of group, we do not know how long this learning and practice was sustained. Also, it would be interesting to conduct a spiritually influenced group with participants who have knowledge and more experience of some of the processes used in group: How would their experiences differ? In conclusion, the results of this current study are promising in terms of learning about how spiritually influenced group practice takes place and is experienced as helpful, and they provide impetus for future study in this emergent field.

ACKNOWLEDGEMENTS

The Northern Regional Recovery Continuum funded and supported this study. I would like to acknowledge the work of Julie LeBreton, BSW, who helped to develop and facilitate the group program.

REFERENCES

Abels, S.L. (Ed.). (2000). *Spirituality in social work practice: Narratives for professional helping*. Denver: Love Publishing.

Ai, A. (2002). Integrating spirituality into professional education: A challenging but feasible task. *Journal of Teaching in Social Work, 22*(1/2), 103–130.

Anderson, H. (1999). Feet planted firmly in midair: A spirituality for family living. In F. Walsh (Ed.), *Spiritual resources in family therapy* (pp. 157–176). New York: The Guilford Press.

Ballou, M. (1995). Women and spirit: Two nonfits in psychology. *Women and Therapy, 16*(2/3), 9–20.

Barrett, M. (1999). Healing from trauma: The quest for spirituality. In F. Walsh, (Ed.), *Spiritual resources in family therapy* (pp. 193–208). New York: The Guilford Press.

Barrett, D. (2002). The "royal road" becomes a shrewd shortcut: The use of dreams in focused treatment. *Journal of Cognitive Psychotherapy, 16*(1), 55–64.

Batchelor, M. (2001). *Meditation for life*. Boston: Wisdom Publications.

Berliner, P.M. (1992). Soul healing: A model of feminist therapy. *Counselling and Values, 37*(1), 2–14.

Bewley, A. (1995). Re-membering spirituality: Use of sacred ritual in psychotherapy. *Women and Therapy, 16*(2/3), 201–213.

Bishop, S., Lau, M., Shapiro, S., Carlson, L., Anderson, N.D., Carmody, J., et al. (2004). Mindfulness: A proposed operational definition. *Clinical Psychology and Scientific Practice, 11*(3), 230–241.

Brown, K.W., & Ryan, R.M. (2003). The benefits of being present: Mindfulness and its role in psychological well-being. *Journal of Personal and Social Psychology, 84*(4), 822–849.

Bullis, R.K. (1996). *Spirituality in social work practice*. New York: Taylor and Francis.

Canda, E.R., & Smith, E. (2001a). Introduction. *Social Thought, 20*(1/2), 1–3.

Canda, E.R., & Smith, E. (Eds.). (2001b). *Transpersonal perspectives on spirituality in social work*. New York: The Haworth Press.

Clark, A. (1994) Working with dreams in group counselling: Advantages and challenges. *Journal of Counselling and Development, 73*(2), 141–144.

Clark, P. (1999). To treat or not to treat: The ethical dilemma of alternative medicine therapies. *AIDS Public Policy Journal, 14*(3), 117–131.

Coates, J. (2003). *Ecology and social work: Toward a new paradigm.* Halifax: Fernwood Publishing.

Coholic, D. (2001). *Exploring spirituality in feminist practices: Emerging knowledge for social work.* Unpublished doctoral dissertation, University of New South Wales, Sydney, Australia.

Coholic, D. (2002). Practice principles for social work and spirituality: A focus on practice methods and relationships. *Currents: New Scholarship the Human Services, 1*(1). Available online at http://fsw.ucalgary.ca/currents.

Coholic, D. (2003a). Incorporating spirituality in feminist social work perspectives. *Affilia, 18*(1), 49–67.

Coholic, D. (2003b). Student and educator viewpoints on incorporating spirituality in social work pedagogy: An overview and discussion of research findings. *Currents: New Scholarship in the Human Services, 2*(2). Available online at http://fsw.ucalgary.ca/currents/articles/articles/Coholic2/coholic2_index.htm.

Corbin, J. (1986). Qualitative data analysis for grounded theory. In W.C. Chenitz & J.M. Swanson (Eds.), *From practice to grounded theory* (pp. 91–101). Menlo Park, CA.: Addison-Wesley.

Cowley, A.-D. (1996). Transpersonal social work. In F. Turner (Ed.), *Social work treatment* (4th ed., pp. 663–698). New York: The Free Press.

Derezotes, D.S. (2001). Transpersonal social work with couples: A compatibility-intimacy model. *Social Thought, 20*(1/2), 163–174.

Edwards, P. (2002). Spiritual themes in social work counselling: Facilitating the search for meaning. *Australian Social Work, 55*(1), 78–87.

France, H. (2002). *Nexus: Transpersonal approach to groups.* Calgary: Detselig Enterprises Ltd.

Frattaroli, E. (2001). *Healing the soul in the age of the brain: Becoming conscious in an unconscious world.* New York: Viking.

Gilgun, J.F. (1994). Hand into glove: The grounded theory approach and social work practice research. In E. Sherman & W.J. Reid (Eds.), *Qualitative research in social work* (pp. 115–125). New York: Columbia University Press.

Gingerich, W. (2000). Solution-focused brief therapy: A review of the outcome research. *Family Process, 39*(4), 477–499.

Glaser, B.G., & Strauss, A. (1967). *The discovery of grounded theory.* New York: Aldine.

Grossman, P., Niemann, L., Schmidt, S., & Walach, H. (2004). Mindfulness-based stress reduction and health benefits: A meta-analysis. *Journal of Psychosomatic Research, 57*(1), 35–44.

Hagon, Z. (1998). Spirituality and trauma therapy. *AASW Queensland Branch Newsletter, 4*, 30–35.

Hart, T. (2003). *The secret spiritual world of children.* Maui: Inner Ocean Publishing.

Hartman, P.M. (1996). *Finding meaning in crisis: A link between spirituality and social work practice.* Unpublished doctoral dissertation, University of Denver.

Harvard Women's Health Watch. (2004). The benefits of mindfulness. *Harvard Women's Health Watch, 11*, 1–3.

Hazen-Hammond, S. (1999). *Spider woman's web: Traditional Native American tales about women's power.* New York: Perigee.

Heinonen, T., & Spearman, L. (2001). *Social work practice: Problem solving and beyond.* Toronto: Irwin Publishing.

Kabat-Zinn, J. (1990). *Full catastrophe living: Using the wisdom of your body and mind to face stress, pain, and illness.* New York: Delta.

Kabat-Zinn, J. (1994). *Wherever you go, there you are: Mindfulness meditation in everyday life.* New York: Hyperion.

Kabat-Zinn, J. (2003). Mindfulness-based interventions in context: Past, present, and future. *Clinical Psychology and Scientific Practice, 10*(2), 144–156.

Kamya, H. (2000). Hardiness and spiritual well-being among social work students: Implications for social work education. *Journal of Social Work Education, 36*(2), 231–240.

Kimmel, E.B., & Kazanis, B.W. (1995). Explorations of the unrecognized spirituality of women's communion. *Women and Therapy, 16*(2/3), 215–227.

Koenig, H., George, L., Titus, P., & Meador, K. (2004). Religion, spirituality, and acute care hospitalization and long-term care use by older patients. *Archives of Internal Medicine, 164*(14), 1579–1585.

Krippner, S., Jaeger, C., & Faith, L. (2001). Identifying and utilizing spiritual content in dream reports. *Dreaming, 11*(3), 127–147.

Leight, A. (2001). Transpersonalism and social work practice: Awakening to new dimensions for client self-determination, empowerment, and growth. *Social Thought, 20*(1/2), 63–76.

Lloyd, M. (1997). Dying and bereavement, spirituality and social work in a market economy of welfare. *British Journal of Social Work, 27*, 175–190.

Lo, B., Kates, L., Ruston, D., Arnold, R., Cohen, C., Puchalski, C., et al. (2003). Responding to requests regarding prayer and religious ceremonies by patients near the end of life and their families. *Journal of Palliative Medicine, 6*(3), 409–415.

Luskin, F.M., Newell, K., Griffith, M., Holmes, M., Telles, S., DiNucci, E., et al. (2000). A review of mind/body therapies in the treatment of musculoskeletal disorders with implications for the elderly. *Alternative Therapies Health Medicine, 6*(2), 46-56.

Martin, J. (1997). Mindfulness: A proposed common factor. *Journal of Psychotherapeutic Integration, 7*(4), 291–312.

McCaffrey, A., Eisenberg, D., Legedza, A., Davis, R., & Phillips, R. (2004). Prayer for health concerns: Results of a national survey on prevalence and patterns of use. *Archives of Internal Medicine, 164*(8), 858–862.

Moss, E. (2002). Working with dreams in a bereavement therapy group. *International Journal of Group Psychotherapy, 52*(2), 151–170.

Nash, M., & Stewart, B. (Eds.). (2002). *Spirituality and social care: Contributing to personal and community well-being.* London: Jessica Kingsley Publishers.

O'Brien, E., & Epstein, S. (1988). *MSEI The multi-dimensional self-esteem inventory, professional manual.* Odessa, FL: Psychological Assessment Resources.

Palmer, R., Katerndahl, D., & Morgan-Kidd, J. (2004). A randomized trial of the effects of remote intercessory prayer: Interactions with personal beliefs on problem-specific outcomes and functional status. *Journal of Alternative Complementary Medicine,* *10*(3), 438–448.

Pascal, E. (1992). *Jung to live by.* New York: Warner Books.

Pearlman, L.A., & Saakvitne, K.W. (1995). Vicarious traumatization: How trauma therapy affects the therapist. In L.A. Pearlman & K.W. Saakvitne (Eds.), *Trauma and the therapist* (pp. 279–294). New York: W.W. Norton.

Pesant, N., & Zadra, A. (2004). Working with dreams in therapy: What do we know and what should we do? *Clinical Psychological Review, 24,* 489–512.

Robbins, S., Chatterjee, P., & Canda, E.R. (1999). Ideology, scientific theory, and social work practice. *Families in Society: The Journal of Contemporary Human Services, 80*(4), 374–384.

Roberts, J. (1999). Heart and soul: Spirituality, religion, and rituals in family therapy training. In F. Walsh (Ed.), *Spiritual resources in family therapy* (pp. 256–271). New York: The Guilford Press.

Rozman, D. (1975). *Meditating with children: The art of concentration and centering.* Boulder Creek, CA: University of the Trees Press.

Russel, R. (1998). Spirituality and religion in graduate social work education. *Social Thought, 18*(2), 15–29.

Sagula, D., & Rice, K.G. (2004). The effectiveness of mindfulness training on the grieving process and emotional well-being of chronic pain patients. *Journal of Clinical Psychology in Medical Settings, 11*(4), 333–343.

Sams, J. (1998). *Dancing the dream: The seven sacred paths of human transformation.* San Francisco: Harper.

Schwartz, R.C. (1999). Releasing the soul: Psychotherapy as a spiritual practice. In F. Walsh (Ed.), *Spiritual Resources in Family Therapy* (pp. 223–239). New York: The Guilford Press.

Scotton, B., Chinen, A., & Battista, J. (Eds.). (1996). *Textbook of transpersonal psychiatry and psychology.* New York: Basic Books.

Seligman, M. (1995). The effectiveness of psychotherapy: The Consumer Reports Study. *American Psychologist, 50*(12), 965–974.

Sermabeikian, P. (1994). Our clients, ourselves: The spiritual perspective and social work practice. *Social Work, 39*(2), 178–183.

Sharf, R. (2004). *Theories of psychotherapy and counselling* (3rd ed.). Boston: Thomson.

Smith, E. (2001). Alleviating suffering in the face of death: Insights from constructivism and a transpersonal narrative approach. *Social Thought, 20*(1/2), 45–61.

Starhawk. (1987). *Truth or dare: Encounters with power, authority, and mystery.* San Francisco: HarperCollins.

Stern, P. (1986). Conflicting family culture: An impediment to integration in stepfather families. In W.C. Chenitz & J.M. Swanson (Eds.), *From practice to grounded theory* (pp. 168–180). Menlo Park, CA: Addison-Wesley.

Stewart, T. (2004). Light on body image treatment, acceptance through mindfulness. *Behaviour Modification, 28*(6), 783–811.

Swigonski, M.E. (1994). The logic of feminist standpoint theory for social work research. *Social Work, 39*(4), 387–393.

Tanner, B.W. (1988). *The mystical magical marvelous world of dreams*. Tahlequah, OK: Sparrow Hawk Press.

Ventegodt, S., Andersen, N.J., & Merrick, J. (2003a). The life mission theory V: Theory of the anti-self (the shadow) or the evil side of man. *TheScientificWorldJOURNAL, 3*, 1302–1313.

Ventegodt, S., Merrick, J., & Andersen, N.J. (2003b). Quality of life as medicine: A pilot study of patients with chronic illness and pain. *TheScientificWorldJOURNAL, 3*, 520–532.

Ventogodt, S., Merrick, J., & Andersen, N.J. (2003c). Quality of life as medicine II: A pilot study of a five-day "quality of life and health" cure for patients with alcoholism. *TheScientificWorldJOURNAL, 3*, 842–852.

Walker, P. (1998). Sharing the stories: Spirituality in practice. *AASW Queensland Branch Newsletter, 4*, 15–18.

Walsh, F. (1998). *Strengthening family resilience*. New York: The Guilford Press.

Wilner, K. (2001). Core energetic couples therapy: An integrated approach. *Journal of Couples Therapy, 10*(2), 25–34.

Zichi Cohen, M., & Bumbaugh, M. (2004). Group dream work: A holistic resource for oncology nurses. *Oncology Nursing Forum, 31*(4), 817–824.

Zukav, G. (2000). *Soul stories*. New York: Simon & Schuster.

CHAPTER 8

LISTENING TO OUR STILLNESS:
GIVING VOICE TO OUR SPIRITUALITY
(SPIRITUALITY AND CLINICAL PRACTICE)

WANDA WAGLER-MARTIN

This chapter explores the integration of spirituality in clinical social work practice. Social work's history with respect to spirituality and practice, and the tensions that have existed, are reviewed. Further, the chapter outlines a rationale for the importance of this integration, while also looking at obstacles to including spirituality in practice that some social workers encounter. Interventions are posed as a possible means to facilitate the integration of spirituality and clinical social work practice.

Over 18 years of clinical practice, I have found that traditional social work education and the profession of social work have not fully validated the spiritual dimension of the clients with whom we work. As a beginning practitioner I would have leaned toward Freud's view that the soul and the psyche are separate spheres in clinical practice. Perhaps this was a reflection of the need to define my professional self, my life stage, and my own process of reconsidering early beliefs. Undoubtedly it is no coincidence that as I have moved into mid-life, I have increasingly accepted that both the spiritual and the psychological are inextricable dimensions of being human, and are thus core components of clinical social work.

The spiritual component can be a significant variable for people in terms of re-awakening to meaning in their lives, particularly in the context of difficult times. It can be an important anchor for them at a time when they are likely to feel adrift. We miss out on a valid therapeutic variable if we ignore or discount this component of people's experience.

My reconsidering of the spiritual dimension has been prompted by the wisdom of the many fine people with whom I have walked in the context of therapy. Often I have used the image of "sacred ground" to capture the richness of the therapeutic experience and my awed respect for those clients who have invited me to enter into their most vulnerable space. In the process of work with clients, I have observed that when recognition of the spiritual dimension is included there is potential for increased wholeness in the healing process.

I was rooted in a faith tradition that validated the importance of the spiritual dimension and gave encouragement for nurturing inner stillness—this being accomplished primarily in the context of prayer and reflection. However, throughout my social work education and at the beginning of my career I sensed disconnect between those who valued the spiritual dimension and the values upheld in clinical practice. The language of spirituality was not part of the conversation in either the academic or the clinical settings that I participated in. Yet in spite of this, I have come to more fully appreciate the importance of the spiritual dimension in the lives of clients, and have sought to integrate the spiritual and psychological in ways that reflect clinical competence, and respect belief systems and expressions of spirituality that may be different from my own.

Edward Canda (2002), a well-known voice on spirituality and social work, underscores the importance of this need to respect divergent beliefs systems. He stresses the necessity of social work's commitment to "an inclusive approach to spirituality that is grounded in professional social work purposes and values, respecting diverse religious and non-religious spiritual perspectives" (p. 6).

It seems paramount to define spirituality as it is used here. Essentially spirituality is about meaning-making. Spirituality is what grounds us. It frames our view of the world and our deepest beliefs. It includes our sense of order and chaos, our understanding of good and evil, and our belief in a form of a higher power. It finds expression in the way that we choose to live our lives. Spirituality takes the form of religious expression for some, but not for others. Geri Miller (2003) offers a helpful distinction between spirituality and religion in that "both share a sense of transcendence, of other. They differ in that spirituality is a personal connection with the universe, and religion involves a creed, institution, and rituals connected with a world religion" (p. 6). James L. Griffith and Melissa Elliott Griffith in *Encountering the Sacred in Psychotherapy* (2002) would caution, however, that, "although spirituality and religion are not synonymous, the division between them is not so clean as the prospirituality/antireligion position in recent cultural politics often presents it" (p. 21).

Social work as a profession has gone through several stages in terms of recognizing the importance of spirituality. Canda (2002) reminds us that by the 1970s social work had become separated from the religious connections in which it was rooted and there was much "professional skepticism" about the integration of social work and spirituality. He points out that through the 1980s and 1990s there was an increased call for the profession to reconnect with its "roots in spiritual perspectives" (p. 2).

A certain tension or ambivalence between spirituality and social work has seemingly informed a generation of practitioners, whereby the spiritual dimension has not been fully validated in a social work context. In my part-time teaching role in a social work program, I have had rich conversation and reflection with students on the spiritual component of social work practice. While I have been encouraged by the comfort that today's students bring to discussions about spirituality, spirituality is a less discussed dimension for many experienced practitioners. When social workers experience uncertainty regarding this dimension of their own lives it may complicate the recognition of spirituality as an intrinsic piece of the human experience. It can be all too easy to ignore or pathologize the spiritual beliefs of our clients, if we are not clear regarding our own. Henri Nouwen (1996) underscores the importance of this clarity by noting, "when, however, we can define where we stand we can also draw a map of where we want to go. Every professional is responsible for his or her own definition" (p. 61).

A client will pick up cues from a social worker regarding their openness to the spiritual dimension. Clients may be quite subtle in their references to their beliefs or religious experience. For example, you might hear it in comments about going to church as a child, positive or negative, or in statements like "I really believe that." We have a choice in those moments whether we follow up with these phrases or not. I would surmise that the more comfortable we are with our own sense of spirituality, the more likely we are to notice these passing comments as areas for important inquiry.

In his article, "Therapy Without Walls: Addressing Religion in the Consulting Room," George Simon (2003), an experienced therapist, concludes that "the best clinicians are those who don't check their political, philosophical, and religious convictions at the door when they enter the consulting room. Without engaging in proselytizing, these therapists find a way in their therapy to embody their beliefs about what it means to be human" (p. 21). It is important to underscore Simon's point about not proselytizing. Clients do not need to hear a soliloquy of a social worker's beliefs, nor should a social worker ever attempt to impose personal beliefs on clients. To do so would undermine a core social work value of respecting the unique experience of each client and their self-determination. However, we cannot be so benign in our responses or inquiries that we give the message that spirituality is not important, and prevent people from fully exploring their own spirituality.

Geri Miller (2003) adds to this caution: "When determining when to incorporate a spiritual dimension in counselling, counsellors need to examine their own motivation and possible bias to avoid attempting to convert their clients to their own spiritual views or ignoring a client's spirituality altogether" (p. 5). We also need to avoid assumptions that lead us to certain conclusions just because a person is part of a particular spiritual or religious group. You cannot assume anything about a person's beliefs based on their affiliation. The same principles of therapeutic intervention apply in the understanding of a person's spirituality, as when attempting to assess emotional or relational concerns. You have to seek to listen to and understand their experience and the meaning they take from it.

Social workers also have to monitor countertransference to be clear that we are not projecting our own sense of what we would need if we were "in the client's shoes." This is always important in clinical social work. When seeking to understand a client's deepest beliefs and what gives them meaning, we have to be aware of the danger of missing our client's story because of our own lens on life.

In seeking to understand the spiritual component, the key lies in openness and attentive interest. One does not have to be a spiritual or religious expert to consider the spiritual, but one does have to be willing to explore it and seek to understand it. It is helpful for social workers to understand, as Bo Lozoff (2000) notes, that commonalities exist between what he calls "every great religion or wisdom tradition" (p. 5). Lozoff underscores that each revolves around "two main principles, one dealing with internal spirituality and the other dealing with external spirituality" (p. 5). He concludes that our internal and external work are interdependent and never fully separate; "If we search outside ourselves for the meaning of life, we tend never to find it. But if we centre ourselves and look for meaning in life, it's always waiting for us, right here in the present moment" (p. 3). As clinical social workers, an essential task is to help people find meaning in the midst of struggle, pain, and challenge.

Lozoff (2000) points out that "spiritual practice helps us handle what Zorba the Greek called the 'full catastrophe'" (p. 19–20). Jon Kabat-Zinn (1990, 1994) promotes mindfulness as an avenue to manage the catastrophe of life. Kabat-Zinn (1994) describes mindfulness as an ancient Buddhist practice with relevance for us today. He reminds us that it is not about becoming Buddhist, and that mindfulness does not contradict or conflict with beliefs or religious traditions. Rather, it is about living in harmony with self and the world. He further adds that mindfulness is one way to help us get in touch with our own wisdom, our deepest nature, through fostering "the art of conscious living" (p. 6). Mindfulness is really about paying attention. It is about living fully in any given moment. It is about being, not doing. Thinking about mindfulness highlights how we spend considerable time rehashing the past or anticipating the future, thus missing out on "the now." The discipline of mindfulness centres on meditative breathing as a means to quiet oneself and to focus on the present. In essence, breathing serves as a reminder of what ultimately gives us life.

I use mindfulness techniques in clinical work as I appreciate the simple wisdom of helping people to slow themselves down in a very tactile way through attentiveness to breathing. In modern society people function at such a pace that much of the anxiety people feel in life results from trying to avoid our quiet centre. Kenneth Leech (1985) says:

> The protest of the solitary is not against human companionship as such, but against the evasion of self which can easily occur when involvement with people obscures and prevents any real encounter with one's own identity. Only in stillness can the truth be seen. (pp. 139–140)

When social workers encourage clients to find a ritual for creating quiet time it helps them to slow themselves internally so that what is important to them will surface. Whether someone finds that stillness through breathing, sitting in silence, prayer, meditation, journaling, reflective reading, or in other ways is immaterial. What is most important is that it fits for them, and that they create time for it. However, this can be difficult for people to do.

Robert J. Wicks (1992) underscores the challenge of welcoming quiet time through his reflections on prayer:

> [Q]uiet honest prayer is often unnerving. So, unconsciously knowing this leads many of us to develop a schedule in which we become too active to slow down and too full to make room for God. In an effort to run from our own sense of emptiness and utter dependence on God, our minds become filled with anxieties and worries, our lives and spirits weighed down with angers, hurt, and a sense that no one really understands. (p. 41)

Whether we avoid prayer as a chosen ritual, or evade other forms of quieting, Wicks is getting at the reality of the many obstacles that stand in the way of creating this space for ourselves. When clients show up at my office they are generally in significant enough distress that they are acutely aware of the need to do something different. I often use the language that anxiety, depression, or stress is getting their attention. Their feelings are making them uncomfortable enough to start to pay attention. Thomas Moore (1992), in his book *Care of the Soul*, has a chapter entitled "The Gifts of Depression." Moore asks, "What is it [the depression] doing here? Does it have some necessary role to play?" (p. 137). These are relevant questions because they normalize that uncomfortable feelings push people to question, to take action to make needed change; this change often taps into people's core beliefs and constructs of deepest meaning.

Exploring spirituality in the context of clinical work reminds social workers that most, if not all, people have beliefs about the nature of the world, humanity, and how they themselves personally find a place. This is true regardless of whether or not they have ever participated in organized religion. People struggling with anxiety, depression, stress, burnout, or other forms of emotional or relational upheaval, often find themselves facing questions of intense meaning. In a context of crisis, the spiritual component is often seen as an important component of re-evaluating and moving forward. However, when working with clients in difficulty it is important to stress that social work intervention must always be rooted in a thorough, broad-based clinical assessment, the involvement of other professionals and review of the need for medication as appropriate, and solid practice principles. I have found over the years that cognitive-behavioural therapy, existential concepts, aspects of narrative therapy, and some solution-focused techniques have informed my practice.

I suppose one could consider me, and others who value the spiritual component of people's lives, to be existential thinkers. Corey (1992) says the following about existentialism, which underscores the overlap with social work and spirituality:

> It [the existential tradition] grew out of a desire to help people engage the dilemmas of contemporary life, such as isolation, alienation, and meaninglessness.... Rather than trying to develop rules for therapy, it strove to understand these deep human experiences.... Existential therapy is best considered as an invitation to clients to recognize the ways in which they are not living fully authentic lives and to make choices that will lead to their becoming what they are capable of being. (p. 257)

Bugental (1986) notes that humanistic-existential psychotherapy's task is to "evoke the latent aliveness in our clients. We do not seek to teach them something so much as to call on them to listen better to what they already know, but to which they do not attend, owing to lack of presence. This view contrasts with the perception of therapy as the repair of an ailing or broken being" (p. 223). Bugental's statement, "help them listen better to what they already know," underscores a great deal of my belief about therapy and the need for social workers to avoid imposing our constructs and solutions, but to help our clients discover ones that are core for them.

Corey (1992) notes that the goal of existential therapy is "to expand self-awareness and thus increase the potential for choice" (p. 259). He refers to Paul Tillich's book *The Courage to Be* (1952), and states that this title "convey[s] the essence of the spirit it takes to affirm ourselves and to live from the inside" (p. 271). Mary Pipher (1996) echoes this by noting that "we can encourage people to tell the truth and be themselves. We can help people define themselves from within, rather than allowing the larger culture to define them" (pp. 142–143). I value Corey's (1992) reminder that "living authentically also entails knowing and accepting our limits" (p. 271). This, too, is an important component of wise, respectful therapy.

In my practice I have found several key questions helpful in recognizing the spiritual component of people's lives. These questions include the following:

1. Are there any spiritual beliefs that give your life meaning? (Or that you subscribe to?) If so, could you tell me about them?
2. Are there specific practices or rituals that are important to you? (Or that enhance your sense of being true to your beliefs?)
3. What has contributed to or informed your beliefs?
4. How do you find ways to honour these beliefs in your life?
5. What gets in the way?
6. What do you think might be different for you if you honoured these beliefs more fully?

These questions can be phrased in many different ways, depending on the language choices you are comfortable with, and those that fit for your client. These questions, like any technique, cannot simply be sprung on the client; timing is crucial. A well-timed question, even one that is not eloquently phrased, that reflects that you have been listening closely to a client's process, will have a much greater impact than the most profound question uttered just because you think it is a great question.

Bo Lozoff (2000, p. 27) poses two questions that are additionally relevant in a counselling context:

1. What is my biggest view of life and my place in it?
2. What steps or behaviour are necessary to bring my daily existence into harmony with my views?

I concur with Mary Pipher's (1996) encouragement that as clinicians we are to be "purveyors of hope" (a phrase she notes was coined by Donald Meichenbaum). This is my "biggest view" of myself as a social worker. My role is to help clients find hope out of despair in a way that transforms their experience from depletion to life-giving. I do this by seeking to understand the spiritual experience of my clients, and assisting them to listen to themselves as they find the meaning they desire. This is how, over 18 years, I have brought my daily work as a social worker into harmony with my belief in the importance of spirituality.

REFERENCES

Bugental, J.F.T. (1986). Existential-humanistic psychotherapy. In I.L. Kutash & A. Wolf (Eds.), *Psychotherapist's casebook* (pp. 222–236). San Francisco: Jossey-Bass.

Canda, E.R. (2002). A world wide view on spirituality and social work: Reflections from the USA experience and suggestions for internationalization. *Currents: New Scholarship in Human Services, 1*(1). Retrieved from fsw.ucalgary.ca/currents/Canda1/canda_main.htm.

Corey, G. (1992). *The existential approach to groups: Theory and practice of group counselling.* Boston: Brooks Cole Publishing Company.

Griffith, J.L., & Griffith, E. (2002). *Encountering the sacred in psychotherapy: How to talk with people about their spiritual lives.* New York: The Guilford Press.

Kabat-Zinn, J. (1990). *Full catastrophe living.* New York: Bantam Doubleday Dell.

Kabat-Zinn, J. (1994). *Wherever you go, there you are.* New York: Hyperion.

Leech, K. (1985). *Experiencing God.* San Francisco: Harper & Row.

Lozoff, B. (2000). *It's a meaningful life: It just takes practice.* New York: Penguin.

Miller, G. (2003). *Incorporating spirituality in counselling and psychotherapy.* Hoboken, NJ: John Wiley & Sons.

Moore, T. (1992). *Care of the soul.* New York: Harper Collins.

Nouwen, H.J.M. (1996). *Ministry & spirituality.* New York: Continuum.

Pipher, M. (1996). *The shelter of each other: Rebuilding our families.* New York: G.P. Putnam's Sons.

Simon, G. (2003, March/April). Therapy without walls: Addressing religion in the consulting room. *Psychotherapy Networker,* 21–22.

Tillich, P. (1952). *The courage to be.* New Haven, CT: Yale University Press.

Wicks, R.J. (1992). *Touching the holy.* Notre Dame, IN: Ave Maria Press.

CHAPTER 9

REFRAMING SPIRITUALITY, RECONCEPTUALIZING CHANGE: POSSIBILITIES FOR CRITICAL SOCIAL WORK

MICHÈLE BUTOT

This chapter examines the possibilities and potential of spirituality in critical social work, both in relevant literature and in the views of participants in a research inquiry undertaken in urban centres in the three western provinces. My purpose is twofold: first, to explore how critical conceptualizations of spirituality might alter the ways in which social workers frame social and individual change; and second, to suggest that it is imperative for critical social work to address spiritual issues.

❖ INTRODUCTION

Spirituality has emerged as a theme in contemporary mainstream social work, leading to myriad writings, conferences, and opinions. However, the definition of spirituality presented is often confusing and problematic (Potts, 2003), either tending to be concerned with individuals' sense of personal well-being at the expense of commitments to social justice, or veering closely toward religious connotations with which many of us are uncomfortable.

Contrary to this trend in the dominant discourse, much critical practice writing, rightly concerned with the frequent appropriativeness of "New-Age" philosophies and with the attempts by White people to seek refuge from dealing with race (Jeffery, 2002), has maintained a canonical stance unwelcoming to spirituality because of fear of a "slippery slope." Social workers who do have a spiritual framework often feel we must keep our spirituality to ourselves lest we be ridiculed or marginalized by our colleagues (Lerner, 2004).

As critical practitioners we claim to value reflexivity, openness to change, and our ability to engage creatively in work for solidarity, empowerment, and social justice. Yet something is missing. With some notable exceptions,[1] our theorizing has not responded to what is occurring around and within us in regard to spirituality. I find myself deeply troubled by depoliticized notions of spirituality in mainstream social work. Equally, I feel compelled to engage in dialogue about how we might view spirituality through a critical lens.

During the past 20 years of involvement in progressive politics and practice, I have watched neo-liberal governments systematically strip away hard-won changes and have witnessed activist organizations crumble under the weight of judgement, self-righteousness, and despair. I have come to question whether radical[2] societal and individual transformation can be realized if it is not grounded in a loving stance toward others,[3] especially those considered "other" from ourselves. I wonder if deep and sustainable change towards social justice and individual well-being can arise, or even be fully conceived, if the context for the change process does not include recognition of unity and diversity as coexistent.

Not only do I contend that critical conceptualizations of spirituality have the potential to revitalize and increase the sustainability of our work, I also fear that if we, as critical practitioners, do not begin to conceptualize spirituality, it will be defined for us either by essentializing liberal voices or by those who are intent on social work remaining an instrument of governmentality and colonization.

The notion of critically informed spirituality I offer here is intended not as a prescription, but as an invitation to others to research, explore, and perhaps experience for themselves the generative possibilities of spiritual ways of perceiving, being, and doing in practice. My intention is to invite readers to consider a (re)insertion of spirituality into the discourse of critical theory and practice. I want to plant a seed of radical and liberatory possibility that might fill a gap in our theorizing and allow our work to become more holistic and more relevant.

There is danger that this work could be used in ways that decontextualize it from its grounding in a critical perspective. Given the complex nature of spirituality, as well as religion's complicated relation to social work, I ask readers to keep two things in mind. First, the participants in my research were all long-time anti-oppressive practitioners and activists; the critical stance was a key component of their practice and a crucial element in their ways of conceptualizing spirituality. Second, while those involved came from a wide range of social locations, a notable convergence arose in the dialogues. Participants all took a nondualistic and paradoxical stance not characteristic of critical social work's tendency towards "oppression versus anti-oppression, and bad versus good" (Wong, 2004); they acknowledged the reality of injustice and oppression and, *at the same time*, argued for a belief in the basic goodness of all beings.

❖ VOICES FROM THE LITERATURE

The structure of this chapter suggests my literature review preceded the participant dialogues. In fact, during the unfolding of my research inquiry, I undertook a second literature review based on participants' comments and recommendations. The views espoused in the dialogues, while rare in the written discourse of critical social work, are reflected in a variety of pertinent literatures. In the following section I explore some relevant writings by First Nations theorists and engaged Buddhists that might help expand the literature base for this discussion of spirituality in critical practice.

Baskin (2002) explores First Nations spiritual approaches to social work practice. In her argument for the inclusion of spirituality in social work education, she defines spirituality simply as "the connection to all that is in existence" (p. 2) and contends that our practice requires an infusion of "action-oriented spirituality." She understands Aboriginal spirituality as "an interconnectedness and interrelationship with all life. All (both 'animate' and 'inanimate') are seen as being equal and interdependent, part of the great whole and as having spirit ... a sacred expression of the Great Mystery" (p. 4, parentheses in original).

While her work draws heavily on structural social work, Baskin contends that structural analysis is an insufficient basis for practice in and of itself, because it "lacks any discussion of culture, values, and spirituality" (p. 17). In the realm of spirituality, she argues, structural social work is no different from conventional social work: "While [it] is anti-oppressive and focuses on social change ... it does not incorporate spirituality in any way and, therefore, is not a holistic approach" (pp. 17–18).

Baskin distinguishes between religion and spirituality, noting that religion is usually structured and group oriented, whereas spirituality "can include individual experiences with or without a structured belief system" (p. 3). However, she honours the positive *intent* in some historical social work practice based on what she describes as the "religious values" of love, justice, and mutual responsibility for all human beings (pp. 3–4).

Hart (1999), whose work was recommended to me by one of the research participants, also addresses the spiritual foundation of Aboriginal social work approaches.[4] Like Baskin, he focuses on interrelationship within a framework that recognizes the interconnection within and between all beings (pp. 93–94), with each being seen as "enmeshed" in the "inclusiveness" of the whole (Ermine, 1995, p. 103, cited in Hart, 1999, p. 101).

Hart begins with a definition of the medicine wheel common to many Aboriginal approaches that reflects five key and interrelated elements to helping: "wholeness, balance, connectedness or relationships, harmony, and growth and healing" (p. 92). These elements require that we explore each part in the whole and the relationships among the parts in order to understand the world (pp. 92–93).

Finding balance is seen as momentary, achieved when one is in harmony with other beings and nature. It is a condition that necessitates an awareness of "the existence and expression of bad attributes by people" but focuses on the positive, within a view of human nature as intrinsically good (Hart, 1999, pp. 97–98). This focus on the positive is understood to lead to the "natural death" of the negative (p. 97) and people are perceived as existing in a state of being, or being-in-becoming (p. 98).

The central goal of healing[5] in this approach is well-being and a good, full life for all.[6] In order to reach this goal, each being is offered unconditional respect because all are considered equally valuable and inherently *of* the Creator. This view of all as worthy leads naturally to sharing and democratic process (Hart, 1999).[7] Relationship is perceived as key, and "good conduct" is understood to include non-interference, non-judging, and non-directiveness; the alternative is seen to be coercive and limiting of autonomy and self-determination (pp. 99, 103).

Buddhism also figured prominently in participants' conversations on relationship with the other in my research. Chödrön (1996) is a prominent Buddhist author to whom one participant referred several times; she addresses interconnection and spirituality in the following way:

> What we might call … Sacred Outlook is the main thing. It actually doesn't have anything to do with religion or philosophy.… What people are ready for now—is compassion, the importance of our interconnectedness with each other. That would take care of all these rules (trying to be "good"). People need to see that if you hurt another person, you hurt yourself, and if you hurt yourself, you're hurting another person. And then we begin to see that we are not in this alone. We are in this together. For me, that's where the true morality comes from. (p. 300)

Chödrön does not suggest that we abandon our critical stance and stop speaking out about injustice; rather, she recommends a model for practice in which spiritual self-work is seen to precede and proceed with working with others, allowing us to act for justice without dehumanizing the other, even when the other is an oppressor or perpetrator.

In congruence with the notion of interconnection, Thich Nhat Hanh (1993) speaks of "interbeing" (pp. 67–68)[8] as a holistic approach to activism. The recognition of interbeing, he asserts, is a way towards sustainability of work for social and ecological justice (1993, p. 138). He contends that "mindfulness, insight, and altruistic love [are] the only sustainable bases for political action" (p. 155).

Thich Nhat Hanh sides with Baskin's (2002) critique of the absence of spirituality in structuralist practice, saying: "We know there is no place for spirituality in Marxism" (Thich Nhat Hanh, 1993, p. 57) and echoes Chödrön's (1996) view of the possibility of movements for social justice that do not dehumanize or demonize our oppressors and enemies. The tools required for social action, he suggests, are embodied deep listening, non-harming, loving-kindness, and discernment (Thich Nhat Hanh, 1993, pp. 68–71).[9]

Bai and Dhammika Mirisse (2000) also recommend loving-kindness as "the solution to the pandemic problems of rising violence, exploitation, and degradation" (p. 2), asserting a need to "distinguish love that is based in personal likes and dislikes" from a "more-than-personal," "moral and spiritual" love that, "like the sun … shines on all, regardless of the qualification of the particular beings receiving sunlight" (p. 3). They suggest that we do not lose our discernment and begin to *like* everything; instead, from a stance of spiritual awareness, we are called to *practise* love towards all (p. 11).

We can move towards this, Bai and Dhammika Mirisse (2000) suggest, by engaging in mindfulness[10] and *metta*—"universal, unconditional love towards all" (p. 9).[11] These practices can precipitate insights into the delusion of separate "ego selves" (p. 9) and lead to the "eradication" of greed, hatred, and anger. The authors contend such practices can create a "radical," "foundational and total" transformation of one's being, and how one perceives and interprets the world (p. 11).

❖ THE PARTICIPANT DIALOGUES

While literatures such as those explored above offer great insight into possibilities for spiritual ways of framing social work practice, there remains a relative absence of discussions of spirituality or love in the canonical critical practice literature. Consequently, I felt it imperative to speak to a range of practitioners, and conducted a study in which critical practitioners were offered the opportunity to reflect on, question, and theorize about their own experiences of "loving" practice (Butot, 2004).

I approached participants who a) self-identified, or were identified by others, as critical or anti-oppressive, that is, engaged in critical reflection, analysis and action (Brechin, 2000); and b) considered themselves, or were considered by others, to be engaged in loving practice. In keeping with a valuing of difference and multiple ways of knowing, I aimed for maximum diversity across gender, race, class background, age, and site of practice.

The participants included two men and five women, ages 30 through 57. There were three First Nations people, one woman of colour, and three White women. Participants were currently living in large urban centres in Western Canada; several had been raised between cultures or geographical locations. They were of several sexual orientations. Sites of practice included outreach to street youth, work with Ministry-involved families, Indigenous healing, drug and alcohol recovery, sexual abuse and trauma recovery, individual and family counselling, and teaching and research at the post-secondary level.[12]

All participants described themselves as spiritual, but none as religious. Of those who specifically referred to their spiritual beliefs, three came from Indigenous spiritual systems, one was Jewish culturally and a practitioner of Buddhism. I would describe two non-Aboriginal participants (one of colour and one White), who did not themselves specify, as Earth-based in their spirituality.

One to one-and-one-half hour interviews were scheduled with each person at a location of their choice. Participants were offered the opportunity to conceptualize love in practice for themselves; to question, comment on, and critique my initial conceptualization of love in practice; and to engage in conversation about how love manifested in their own practice. In some cases participants also commented on love's relevance to social work practices as a whole. Throughout the interview process I strove not to impose my own views, but to open myself to learning from participants and their ways of perceiving, being, and doing. My goal was to develop, through dialogue with the participants, a description of "love as emancipatory praxis."

❖ RESEARCH FINDINGS AND DISCUSSION

1 Spirituality

All participants agreed that love was relevant to their practice, except one. Les did not feel comfortable with the use of the word "love" in a professional context, but after several preliminary conversations stated that what I called love, he would describe as "spirituality" and that he was willing to participate: "I'd see all of that also as under the umbrella of spirituality. When you embrace some basic principles of spirituality, then all of these things would fall [into place]" (Les, p. 9).

While I was exploring "love" in practice specifically, it soon became clear that many participants were reframing this concept in a spiritual way. Over the months of analysis, I realized that Les's comment was indicative of a strong emergent theme in all the interviews. My own background in feminist spirituality, non-dual yoga philosophy, and social justice-oriented Judaism was implicit in how I presented my inquiry to participants, but participants' ways of perceiving and being brought spirituality to the foreground. I had been so stringent in my attempt not to lead participants toward my own views that several of them challenged me about why I was not including spirituality more overtly.

Participants referenced spirituality in two particular ways: First Nations participants referred to a practice foundation in Aboriginal spirituality; non-Aboriginal participants referred to Buddhist philosophy. In spite of a wide divergence in social location, participants' framing of spirituality was remarkably convergent—all participants conceptualized *spirituality* as a *recognition of the intrinsic interconnection of all beings* and a *recognition of, and respect and reverence for, one's own and others' intrinsic wholeness, sacredness, and value as an expression of the diversity of this interconnection* (Butot, 2004).

This critical conceptualization of spirituality is relevant in three ways. First, conceiving spirituality in this way may help to avert the conflation of spirituality and religion so common in current social work writing. Second, I would suggest it increases the possibility of our finding common ground across our differences in which we can begin to dialogue. Third, applying this interconnected perspective has the potential to dramatically change our experience of and relation to others and the world.

Like Bai and Dhamikka Mirisse (2000) who assert that spiritual views and practices can create a transformation in how one perceives and interprets the world and in one's way of being (p. 11), participants described spirituality as a way of perceiving, of being, and of doing. Erika, for example, referring to notions of interconnection across diverse spiritualities, stated: "we hear the same from the Elders here in Aboriginal traditions as from Eastern traditions, that 'we're all connected, and we're all one and all part of the same web'.... Love extends not just to other human beings but to all of Creation—it's a way of being totally" (Erika, p. 14).

Echoing Baskin's (2002) claim that structural analysis is non-holistic and an insufficient basis for practice if removed from spiritual perspectives on interconnection (pp. 17–18), participants were clear that for them spirituality was a key component of critical social work practice. Raven, for example, commented: "I sometimes struggle to think, well, I mean common sense, you know—if you're not balanced physically, emotionally, spiritually, or mentally ... then what do you expect?" (Raven, p. 14).

O   The interconnection of diversity and unity was understood by participants in a spiritual way, but it is not necessarily so. Even among those of us who consider ourselves spiritual, what we call Spirit/Creator/God might differ substantially—we might mean the interconnection of all things, the animating force of Life, or even an actual perceived entity. Regardless of whether we describe it as "spiritual," it is my contention that an understanding of everything as interconnected and everyone as intrinsically valuable has the potential to dramatically alter our relation to practice and how we view change.

2 Spirituality and Religion

While it is argued that some historical social work practice that took a stand for social justice may have been helpful in meeting individual and social needs (Baskin, 2002, pp. 3–4), I contend that intent notwithstanding, much of historical religious social work practice (based primarily on EuroChristian values) was in function oppressive and an extension of colonization.[13]

In stressing the importance of the spiritual, the practitioners I spoke to clearly distinguished spirituality from religion, by which they seemed to mean EuroChristianity[14] as experienced in colonial contexts. Raven, for example, commented: "I think lots of times people get [spirituality] confused with religion" (p. 14).

Several participants asserted that in attempting to distance themselves from a history of imposed religiosity and assumptions of EuroChristian normativeness, social workers have created a functional if not intentional lack of space for spirituality in relation to practice. Their observation is congruent with Canda's (2002) review of social work in North America, which suggests a movement away not just from religion but also from spirituality in social work during the period from the 1920s through the 1970s (p. 1).[15]

The participants saw this distancing as a positive step but cautioned that it might have inadvertently closed spaces in which critical spirituality might be explored. Les, for example, said: "I think the reluctance to include spirituality/religion [in] social work practice stems from some good intentions, from not wanting to impose beliefs or not wanting to change people, or having respect for people's own beliefs ... which is good. But I think that's stopped us ... because [spirituality] can be used if you use it in a respectful way, as defined, you know, by the people that you work with, not yourself" (Les, p. 17). Karen concurred: "Social work has spent a lot of time distancing itself from its roots ... the whole religious benevolence thing. I think in doing so [it's] lost some of the most profoundly healing and transformative aspects of spirituality" (Karen, p. 18). In spite of concerns about the conflation of spirituality and imposed religiosity, I side (as did all the participants) with Baskin's (2002) suggestion that "social work practice cannot be whole without including the spiritual dimension" (p. 6) and "cannot be truly effective without it" (p. 9).[16]

3 Spirituality in Practice — Wholeness, Non-Judgement, and Non-Interference

Similar to Hart's (1999) exploration of humans' inherent worthiness as "being-in-becoming" and insistence on recognizing harmful attributes while focusing attention toward the good, participants described relations with self and other as beginning from an assumption of inherent goodness, wholeness, perfection, and value.

Karen said she worked from "basic goodness ... [a] fundamental belief in people's goodness" (Karen, p. 23), as opposed to a problem-focused deficit model. Tom agreed: "not meaning they're deficient because there's something wrong with them but because they're missing what we call the wheel: the physical, mental, the emotional, the spiritual" (Tom, p. 3).

Les concurred: "We look at all individuals in that positive way. It's not a deficit model ... it's not something wrong with you ... you know, Elders would say that if you can't understand something it's only, *only* because your position on the wheel is preventing you from seeing everything clearly" (Les, p. 12).

Several participants stated that they meant we are *all* inherently good and whole, and described how this belief made a difference in practice. Raven, for example, stated: "People are whole just the way they are ... that doesn't translate into wrong or broken ... that is so crucial because we communicate everything ... if we go into something with the assumption that someone is broken and needs to be fixed at some level, they're going to hear that and see that" (Raven, p. 10). Like other participants, she encouraged recognition of inherent "wholeness and perfection ... that what is, *is*. I guess that's where the acceptance comes in, doesn't it." However, she and I went on to agree that this did not preclude analysis, critique, or "mak[ing] choices to do something about [current conditions]" (Raven, p. 12).

Along with acceptance and an assumption of wholeness, several people spoke of a concomitant necessity for non-judgement and non-interference in social work: "Well, you can't judge people. You're not there … and how can you judge somebody when you're not behind their eyes. You can say that someone is very bad or someone is a very irresponsible person, but we don't know what the pressures are" (Tom, p. 18).

Les agreed, talking about non-interference and the fact that we cannot know other people's truths: "it's deadly important for us not to lapse into judging anybody including perpetrators. I mean they have their stories too; [they've] had their heart broken … to me that's the spiritual component" (Les, p. 12).

Carol described not being attached to any particular outcome for those she worked with, even though she held her own feminist perspective and shared it as appropriate. Carol described caring very deeply for people's ability to live well, and at the same time acknowledging she didn't know how their path should unfold: "I don't know if they're going to leave their husband or not and I have no idea, you know, whether they should" (Carol, p. 13).

Processes of healing and change in these spiritual approaches seem to differ from mainstream Western models, including critical social work, which so often begin from a problem-focus. They are based on an assumption of wholeness rather than on something needing to be changed or fixed. Change is experienced as "an ongoing transitional process of balancing and connecting relationships within the individual and between individuals" (Hart, 1999, p. 102). The realization that participants' ways of relating spiritually had implications for the way they conceptualized change was one of the most interesting themes to emerge from the research.

4 Conceptualizing Change from a Spiritual Perspective

Non-judging and non-interference in these approaches did not imply non-engagement.[17] In an apparent paradox, participants seemed to frame acceptance, not-knowing, and non-interference within a critical analysis, *as* change:

> I don't think you can create change without [love/spirit]. I don't even want to say create change—we're not. We have to create an acceptance, in a sense … which is the ground for change. It's the ground for any kind of choicefulness. We have to start with accepting where things are. Our whole open heart thing and being fully present and opening to whatever is—that acceptance place—is the fertile ground for whatever's going to grow. (Carol, p. 6)

As Erika and I discussed action for social justice, we explored the tension ⟳ of acceptance on the one hand and desire for social change and justice on the other. In a clear example of the nondualistic stance participants took throughout the interviews, she wondered about this paradox as we talked about the racist politician against whom we had been protesting the day before. "How," she asked, might we "love him without any attachment to him changing? Do we? Can we?" (Erika, p. 11). "How do we reclaim our own power and have our sense of grounding in ourselves separate from the changes that we'd like to see in the external world?... It's a paradox always" (Erika, p. 12). She suggested that First Nations, Buddhist, and yogic notions of non-attachment and non-judgement were "so valuable for social work" (Erika, p. 11) in helping to balance these tensions.

Contrary to much critical theorizing, which suggests challenge as the "driving force" of critical practice (Burke & Harrison, 1997), participants in this study appeared to favour attending, supporting, and offering tools or ways of perceiving over attempting to "change" people or things. Challenge was seen not as the driving force of sustainable critical practice, but rather as a tool, grounded in a spiritual and loving approach.

Les questioned what might happen if social work, rather than focusing on what's wrong, focused on support and sharing as in Aboriginal approaches: "Social work [is] concerned with change, what we define as something wrong.... In Native social work practice we don't look at change because nobody can change anybody. We look at *support*, we look at *education*, we look at *connection*" (Les, pp. 13–14).[18]

He went on to refer to the absence of a word for "should" in the Blackfoot language, stating: "That's *massive* in its implications. As social workers—'you should do this,' 'you shouldn't do that'...can we operate [without should]? If you do, what would it look like? *That's* interesting." (Les, p. 15). It is an interesting question indeed.

Can critical social work function with this sense of acceptance, non-judgement and non-interference, without a sense of "should"? If so, how might that manifest in practice? How might we reconcile the apparent paradox of critical analysis and change with "as-is" acceptance and non-interference? The key for participants was the notion of "compassionate challenge."

5 Compassionate Challenge

Participants did not suggest that acceptance, non-attachment, and non-interference were passive states. In fact, truth-telling and challenging were consistent themes in the dialogues. Compassionate challenge was inextricably linked by all participants to notions of inherent goodness and acceptance of "what is," as it is.

Participants suggested that we needn't try to change people—and can't—but that we do have an obligation to tell our own truth(s) in practice. As Chödrön and hooks (1997) argue, it is possible to engage with discernment and truth-telling but without blame, to work to "de-escalate suffering" and move toward accountability without dehumanizing or "othering" ourselves or others (pp. 29-30).

While adopting a non-judging stance, participants "reframe[d] dissent as a positive force" (Karen, p. 28) for just such anti-oppressive purpose. In fact, Karen asserted that coming from a spiritual/loving stance made it more likely that we could be effective in our practice: "If people are confident in your care for them, in your love, your absolute unequivocal acceptance, it is way easier to [say], 'I'm calling bullshit on that', or ... 'I'm wondering if I could just challenge you a bit on something you said'" (Karen, p. 26).

Les offered another example of how this might sound in practice:

> I tell students, "It's none of my business who you or your parents vote for." However, we also need to know the interconnectedness between things. There's a reason why teachers are overloaded in [this province], why people working in the human or social services are leaving the province in droves—why doctors and social workers are vastly underpaid—why [we have] the lowest minimum wage in the entire country. It's because its attention is focused elsewhere and not on human being issues. (Les, p. 24)

Karen also referred to speaking truth without thinking she knew "the" answer: "I don't have to dismantle, even though I want to, his particular orientation in the world, but he knows a little bit more about mine" (Karen, p. 36).

Connecting compassionate challenge to the concept of not-knowing, Carol said she could speak from her own heart and analysis, but knew she couldn't know what was right for another: "I really worried about it and in my personal heart of hearts I thought, this really isn't good. I was really concerned. And I would say that sometimes, I would say my truth about it. But I knew she'd have to find her own way" (Carol, p. 38).

The people I interviewed framed their work as a spiritual and interconnected way of perceiving, being, and doing. They promoted the importance and possibility of emancipatory social and individual change, and they located this change within a supportive, accepting, non-judging, not-knowing, and non-interfering stance. At the same time, they advocated strongly for speaking one's own truth in compassionate challenge. All were passionate and deeply committed to their practice and to social justice. Their spiritual stance did not prevent them from being critically engaged, but rather appeared to impact strongly on how they theorized and practiced their work for change.

❖ CONCLUSION

Key contributions of critical social work include challenges to essentialism, the recognition and valuing of diversity, and the recognition and movement toward ending intersecting hierarchical oppressions. It is imperative that notions of universality not render diverse ways of knowing, being, and doing indistinct; we must continue, and even expand, our valuing of difference.

At the same time it is crucial to movements for social justice and community and individual healing that notions of difference do not erase underlying interconnection. In order for our work facilitating change to be meaningful and sustainable in the long-term, I argue that we must also reconnect with a sense of reverence for the interconnection of all the diverse manifestations of life.

When I began my research, I described the participants as critical practitioners. As I delved more deeply, I came to imagine that a more accurate description might be "spiritually informed critical practitioners." Like Munroe's gentile Holocaust resistors, whose only common characteristic was recognition of an underlying connection and "essence" among human beings combined with a belief in human rights (Chinnery & Bai, 2000, p. 92), the participants in my research took a spiritual stance of loving commitment to emancipation that appeared to be based in an understanding of diversity and unity as coexistent. They seemed to recognize both the impact of social construction *and* a belief in a deeper spiritual self.

In 1905, Bertha Reynolds, social worker and radical activist, wrote, "Practice is always shaped by the needs of the times, the problems they present, the fears they generate, the solutions that appeal, and the knowledge and skill available" (quoted in Ehrenreich, 1985, p. 13). I believe that our times desperately require an infusion of critically informed spirituality; we must begin to consider the possibilities that the spiritual might offer to the praxis of critical social work in this century. While causal connections cannot be drawn between values or ethics and behaviour, different beliefs and principles can and do inspire different ways of being and acting.

A challenge for critical social work is the realization that regardless of intent, we often reproduce the oppressive hierarchies we seek to address. How might we attempt to conceptualize a critical vision for practice that would acknowledge social work's complicated history under modernism, and still make room for potentially emancipatory narratives? Leonard (2001) suggests that such a vision can exist only if based on a constant dialectical tension between a belief in the interdependence of all human subjects and a deep valuing of difference (p. 6) such as that demonstrated by the participants in this inquiry.

Spirituality, if consistent with the principles of critical practice as described here, may be one such emancipatory narrative. Perhaps it is time for critical practitioners to stop dismissing spirituality out-of-hand and to reclaim notions of spirituality in practice from the exclusive purview of liberalism, neo-liberalism, and fundamentalism. Can we begin to create our own critical "politics of meaning" (Lerner, 1996, 2004) and join other social workers in exploring how this might manifest in our own lives and practice? I offer not a prescription nor a protocol, but rather an invitation to begin a dialogue about how the spiritual might inform our critical and emancipatory work.

NOTES

1. Notable exceptions to this gap in theorizing love and spirituality in critical social work are Brandon (1976), Morley & Ife (2002) and Wong (2004). See also Lerner's treatise on spirituality and social policy (Lerner, 2006).
2. I mean "radical" in the etymological sense of "to the root," rather than surface changes in policies, protocols, or governments, which may not address the deeper roots of hierarchical oppression that I understand to lie in our ways of perceiving the other as "other" from ourselves.
3. For an in-depth critical conceptualization of what "love" might mean in relation to social work, see (Butot, 2004).
4. Hart (1999) strongly emphasizes the impact of history and politics on spirituality, and recognizes the impact of colonization on Aboriginal spirituality and well-being both individually and collectively.
5. Healing is understood as a "shared experience of learning and growing" (Hart, 1999, p. 103) in which there is no inherent difference between the parties involved (p. 105). The "helper" is seen less as a reified and constant category, and more

as one "being helpful"—a supporter in interdependent relationship with the one receiving. As the participants in my inquiry suggested as well, this model of healing requires that those helping begin from themselves, engaging in personal practice that attends to all parts of self (physical, mental, emotional, spiritual), and living according to their principles in relationship with the world (p. 106).

6. *Pimatasiwin, minopimatasiwin* or *pimadaziwin* in various Aboriginal languages.

7. See similar notions of inherent worth and the practice of democracy in the work of Bai (2001), a Buddhist and critical philosopher.

8. See also Thich Nhat Hanh (1998, p. 134).

9. See also Thich Nhat Hanh (1998, p. 116) and Wong (2004).

10. For an exploration of mindfulness in relation to critical social work, see Wong (2004).

11. These two elements are common to all forms of Buddhism (Bai and Dhammika Mirisse, 2000, p. 4).

12. The participant quotations in this chapter are taken directly from Butot (2004); citations reference the page numbers in the original work. In keeping with their valuing of authenticity, the seven participants, Fiona, Tom, Les, Carol, Erika, Raven, and Karen, all chose to use their own names.

13. At the same time, we must also recognize that a critical religiosity that values difference and multiplicity, including critical and social justice oriented Christianity, is for some, a liberatory possibility. For example, see Amato-von Hemert's (1995) work on Niebuhr's critiques of liberal Christianity, and arguments for love and justice in social work from a Christian perspective.

14. Please note that I have chosen to use the term "EuroChristian" rather than the more familiar "Judeo-Christian" for three reasons: first, it was the term used by more than one participant in exploring this line of thinking; second, as a Jew, I find the latter term imprecise, in that it overlooks serious distinctions of meaning between supposedly common concepts in the two value systems (charity/justice, peace and sin, for example, which mean quite different in things in Hebrew and in English), and because it seems to suggest a "natural progression" from the one to the other. Third, the term suggests a link between European and Christian cultural practices and philosophies, which may differ considerably from the practice of Christianity in other cultural contexts.

15. While I perceive Canda as arguing for "inclusivity" and "spiritual sensitivity" in this article, rather than beginning as I would prefer, from full recognition and valuing of diverse spiritualities, I include the reference here as he has studied extensively in the area of spirituality and religion as related to social work and is widely considered a key expert in this area. I also note that I often find Canda to conflate spirituality and religiosity in his writings.

16. Herein lies one of the paradoxes of this work. The participants and I are speaking of spirituality and not religion per se; and several of us have specifically recognized social work's troubling history of governmentality and imposition in our dialogues and are very cautious about any opening for reinsertions of imposed colonialistic religiosity into social work. Spirituality, as participants discuss it, however, is

about a recognition of interconnection within a context that deeply values diverse ways of perceiving, being, and doing.

17. For example, see Chödrön's discussion with bell hooks about Buddhism and working to end racism and sexism. hooks, a critical feminist and race analyst, struggles to know how to begin where she is and how the world is, and still have a vision of how it might be different. Chödrön suggests it is less a situation of hoping for change (where there is too much hope, she contends, one often begins to have a "strong sense of enemy" or "other"), but of aspiring to an end to suffering for all beings. She says: "I give up both the hope that something is going to change and the fear that it isn't. We may long to end suffering but somehow it paralyzes us if we're too goal-oriented. Do you see the balance there?" (Chödrön & hooks, 1997, pp. 26-27). This is similar to the paradox I heard participants allude to, in hoping for change and speaking one's own truth, without trying to change the other and without being attached to how the change ought to unfold.

18. Carol and Tom also referred to this enacting of love/spirituality in practice as sharing—including sharing support, education, tools, and ways of perceiving (Tom, pp. 3, 7; Carol, p. 13).

REFERENCES

Amato-von Hemert, K. (1995). *Towards a social work imagination: Reinhold Niebuhr on social work, sin, love, and justice—a hermeneutic exploration.* Unpublished doctoral dissertation, University of Chicago.

Bai, H. (2001). Cultivating democratic citizenship: Towards intersubjectivity. In W. Hare & J. Portelli (Eds.), *Philosophy education: Introductory readings* (rev. 3rd ed., pp. 307–319). Calgary, AB: Detselig Enterprises.

Bai, H., & Venerable Dhammika Mirisse. (2000, May). The way of mindfulness and lovingkindness: A Buddhist approach to learning love. Unpublished paper presented at Learning Love Conference, University of British Columbia, Vancouver. Courtesy of the author.

Baskin, C. (2002). Circles of resistance: Spirituality in social work practice, education, and transformative change. *Currents: New Scholarship in the Human Services, 1*(1), 1–21. Retrieved from fsw.ucalgary.ca/currents/cyndy_baskin/baskin.htm 08/18/2003.

Brandon, D. (1976). *Zen in the art of helping.* London: Routledge & Kegan Paul.

Brechin, A. (2000). Introducing critical practice. In A. Brechin, H. Brown, & M. Eby (Eds.), *Critical practice in health and social care* (pp. 25–47). Thousand Oaks, CA: Sage.

Burke, B., & Harrison, P. (1997). Anti-oppressive practice. In L. Dominelli (Ed.), *Sociology for social work* (pp. 229–238). London: MacMillan.

Butot, M. (2004). Love as emancipatory praxis: Practitioners' conceptualizations of love in critical social work practice. Unpublished master's thesis, School of Social Work, University of Victoria, Victoria, British Columbia. Available from the author.

Canda, E. (2002). A world wide view on spirituality and social work: Reflections from the USA experience and suggestions for internationalization. *Currents: New Scholarship*

in the Human Services, 1(1), 1–4. Retrieved from fsw.ucalgary.ca/currents/canda1/
canda.htm 08/18/2003.

Chinnery, A., & Bai, H. (2000). Altering conceptions of subjectivity. In M. Leicester, C.
Modgil, & S. Modgil (Eds.), *Education, culture & values: Vol. 1: Systems of education—
theories, policies, and implicit values* (pp. 86–94). London: Falmer Press.

Chödrön, P. (1996). No right, no wrong. In M. Dresser (Ed.), *Buddhist women on the
edge: Contemporary perspectives from the western frontier* (pp. 293–303). Berkeley, CA:
North Atlantic Books.

Chödrön, P., & hooks, b. (1997). Cultivating openness when things fall apart. *Shambhala
Sun, 5*(4), 26-31.

Ehrenreich, J. (1985). *The altruistic imagination.* New York: Cornell University Press.

Hart, M. (1999). Seeking Mino-pimatasiwin (the good life): An Aboriginal approach to
social work practice. *Native Social Work Journal, 2*(1), 91–112.

hooks, b. (1996). Contemplation and transformation. In M. Dresser (Ed.), *Buddhist
women on the edge: Contemporary perspectives from the western frontier* (pp. 287–292).
Berkeley, CA: North Atlantic Books.

hooks, b. (2000). *All about love: New visions.* New York: William Morrow.

Jeffery, D. (2002). *A terrain of struggle: Reading race in social work education.* Unpublished
doctoral dissertation, Ontario Institute for Studies in Education, Toronto.

Leonard, P. (2001, Spring). The future of critical social work in uncertain conditions.
Critical Social Work Journal, 2(1), Retrieved from www.criticalsocialwork.com/01_
1_reinventing_healy.html 04/30/2002.

Lerner, M. (1996). *The politics of meaning: Restoring hope and possibility in an age of cynicism.*
New York: Addison-Wesley Publishing.

Lerner, M. (2004). The voice of radical hope and practical utopianism. *Tikkun: A critique
of politics, culture, and society, 19*(6), 33—38. (Also see regular editorials at www.
tikkun.org.)

Lerner, M. (2006). *The left hand of God: Taking back our country from the religious right.*
Berkeley, CA: HarperCollins.

Morley, L., & Ife, J. (2002). Social work and a love of humanity. *Australian social work,
55*(1), 69–77.

Potts, S. (2003). Review of "Spirituality and Social Care." *Journal of Social Work Practice,
17*(2), 191–192.

Thich Nhat Hanh (1993). *Love in action: Writings on non-violent social change.* Berkeley,
CA: Parallax Press.

Thich Nhat Hanh (1998). *Teachings on love.* Berkeley, CA: Parallax Press.

Wong, Y.L.R. (2004, Spring). Knowing through discomfort: A mindfulness-based
critical social work pedagogy. *Critical Social Work Journal, 4*(1). Retrieved from
www.criticalsocialwork.com/units/socialwork/critical.nsf 20/10/2004.

CHAPTER 10

FEMINIST COMMUNITY ORGANIZING:
THE SPECTRE OF THE SACRED AND THE SECULAR

SARAH TODD

In this chapter I explore the stories of nine white, middle-class feminist community organizers, told during a series of individual interviews and discussion groups. The women participating in this project did so following a number of years of us working together as feminists and community organizers. During our discussions it became clear that our secular work was entwined with personal stories of religion and spirituality. In addition, I argue that our stories are shaped by a broader social discourse about social work and community organizing, which similarly negotiates spaces between secularity, religiosity, and spirituality. Reflecting on these stories and the way we tell them, I suggest that a more integrated understanding of secular feminist organizing, as constituted through notions of the sacred, opens up new spaces for thinking about feminist community development.

❖ INTRODUCTION

At the beginning of her book *Ghostly Matters*, Avery Gordon states, ◯ "To study social life one must confront the ghostly aspects of it. This confrontation requires (or produces) a fundamental change in the way we know and make knowledge, in our mode of production" (1997, p. 7). This thought lingered in my head over the last year as I completed research into the experiences of nine white feminist organizers, a project that was intended to explore secular feminist community organizing. In conversation with these women, who were my colleagues and friends, I challenged them (and myself) to reflect on how we came to think of ourselves as feminists and community organizers and what meaning that had in our lives. In the weeks following the interviews and focus groups that I had organized for this research project, as I pored over the transcripts, I began to notice a pattern below the surface of our autobiographies. While all of us worked and were trained in secular settings, it became clear that stories of religion (institutionalized faith and worship) and spirituality (informal, non-institutional faith in spirits and/or the divine) shaped our secular practices and spaces. This slipping between the secular and sacred took me by surprise because our conversations occurred at the end of almost a decade of working and socializing together, during which I had imagined our work as an exclusively secular practice. However, as our stories unfolded it became clear that our contemporary practices of secular feminist organizing are, at times, intermingled with personal histories of religious and spiritual practices, and a social history of community work and social work.

This broader history, in the Canadian context, has roots in the Social Gospel and settlement house movements of the turn of the 20th century (Moffatt, 2001). As Gale Wills (1992) has noted, social work has often navigated a slippery terrain between secular and spiritually motivated practice. In this chapter, I suggest that our individual spiritual histories, even when absent from the frameworks through which we recognize feminist community organizing practices, shape the presence of contemporary secular practice. In addition, our contemporary conversations are shaped by the untidy lived experience of secularity and sacredness. By linking our personal and political histories of spirituality and secular practice, I believe that we can open up important spaces to discuss the possibilities and limitations of feminist community organizing.

Oftentimes, it seemed as though the women involved in this study had come to know themselves explicitly in opposition to this historical, religious social activism. Our conversations were without attention to any sacred motivation behind our practices. However, as I read through the transcripts of our conversations, I wondered whether secular mappings of our work are nonetheless "haunted" by sacred histories of feminist organizing. In considering this question, I was influenced by Avery Gordon's notion of "ghostly haunts," with which she problematizes "the reduction of individuals to a mere sequence of instantaneous experience, which leaves no trace, or rather whose trace is hated as irrational, superfluous, and 'overtaken'" (1997, p. 20). Thus, she argues, "[attention to] haunting and ghosts is a way of maintaining the salience of social analysis as bounded by its social context, as in history, which is anything but dead and over" (1997, p. 13). By mobilizing this spectral terminology in the context of feminist community organizing, I suggest that our past encounters with religion and spirituality leave marks on our secular practice. These marks, or traces, outline another way to get close to feminist organizing, not to know it, but to unsettle the binaries we have traditionally used to categorize feminist organizers.

The evidence upon which I rely here is by no means concrete or unequivocal. In the conversations among participants in this study, most of our references to spirituality seem fleeting, ambivalent, and even contradictory, as ghosts are wont to be. Indeed, my own assumption of a secular practice resulted in my avoidance of any specific interview questions that might have brought forth the spectres of spirituality. As a result, I am left exploring subtle narratives that seldom address specific dis/connections with the temporalities of spirituality, feminism, and community. I weave together shadows in the hope of offering a narrative possibility that makes sense of a feminist organizing while it also transgresses secular/ sacred divides. Imagining such a narrative is to unsettle our existing self-knowledge, offering a new set of dangers and possibilities, ones that might allow us to integrate religious histories and critically analyze how they shape our contemporary secular practices.

❖ SACRED/SECULAR BINARIES AS MADE THROUGH COMMUNITY DEVELOPMENT LITERATURE

As I began to explore writing that considers community organizing, feminism, and spirituality, I was surprised to discover how clearly the research literature, too, is organized around the assumed exclusivity of secular and sacred categories. There is an entire body of writing that investigates community organizing in religious communities and, in turn, community organizing as spirituality (see Grant, 1990; Lernoux, 1982; McRoberts, 1999; Shortell, 2001; Wood, 1999). Histories of modern Canadian community organizing often locate the beginnings of community practice in the social purity work of Protestants, Methodists, and the Salvation Army (see Moffatt, 2001; Valverde, 1991; Wills, 1992). In this context, community organizing was a means by which white, middle-class women could bring their spiritual and religious beliefs into broader society. These religious activities are frequently remembered as making room for social reformers, but contemporary social work is described as the "secularization of social gospel ideals," suggesting that religious heritages have been forgotten,

lost in the past, exorcised (see Wills, 1992). The ghosts of spirituality
and religiosity are seen as distant, in need of reclamation, instead of as a
continued haunting that can be felt in the present:

> Social work has lost its radical heritage and the critical question to be
> answered is whether it can, or should, be recovered. Do we care, or are we
> content to leave the dilemmas of poverty and injustice in other hands? If
> we do care, then the key to practice in the future may well lie in recovering
> a feminist community practice, rooted in values not unlike those of the
> radical social gospel. (Wills, 1992, p. 38)

A seemingly distinct body of literature relies upon a secularist
perspective of feminist organizing (Adamson, Briskin, & McPhail, 1988;
Naples, 1998; Wine and Ristock, 1991). When Adamson, et al. (1988, p. 257)
reflect on the history of feminist activism, they note as follows:

> The vibrancy of the movement came straight out of a very immediate
> awareness of women's oppression, and as women catalogued their
> experiences it seemed that the enormity of that oppression cried out
> for change. Feminists thought that simply exposing the extent of this
> oppression would itself create change. There were no insurmountable
> barriers to change: it seemed obvious that, once revealed, the oppression
> of women would no longer be tolerated.

While these categories are not always mutually exclusive, each still seems
to organize accounts that exist independently of the other. There is clearly
a historical telling of social work that suggests contemporary practices
are somehow removed from the religious structures that framed the very
beginnings of our profession.

In Canada, various churches have historically provided an opportunity
for white, middle-class women to work in a public sphere. At a time before
the state had taken a strong role in social reform work, churches provided
an acceptable context for white women to work, in diverse ways, for social
justice. Reform movements at the end of the nineteenth century ranged
from the explicitly civilizing work of the Protestant missionary societies
to the superficially non-denominational National Council of Women
(Mitchinson, 1987).

These histories of spirituality based community work are inscribed
onto secular feminist organizing. Our Western notions of "community"
are often heavily invested in Christianity and retain a redemptive narrative

as underlying the "promise" of community organizing. Edward Arnold (1982, p. vii) observes as follows:

> [The Western ideology of community] has a rich and important pre-history in the Christian concept of community: in the ideal of being brothers and sisters in Christ.... In the nineteenth century, as part of the great social changes first dramatized by the French Revolution and the Industrial Revolution, the concept of community acquired new content and a new urgency. It came increasingly to be contrasted, for better or for worse, with individualism, the atomization, and the alienation that accompanied the emphasis on private property, progress, enterprise, and the capacity for innovation and change characteristic of the new, industrial commercial society.

Feminist community development relies heavily upon these ideas, engaging in a practice that suggests that there is salvation from oppressive conditions and it is to be found in activist communities.

I contend, then, that these "sacred" ideas haunt secular feminist organizing despite our practices of forgetting the ways in which secular/ sacred histories have always mingled through the narratives we use to know ourselves and "others." When we try to forget these stories, they do not disappear. Rather, they linger as the spectres against which we define our selves. For as much as we imagine that feminist organizing is grounded in secular notions of community practice, spiritual ghosts float in the shadows shaping our daily practices.

❖ FEMINIST COMMUNITY ORGANIZING AND SPIRITUAL/SECULAR AMBIVALENCE

The individual and complex relationship that many feminist activists have with our religious backgrounds and/or ongoing understandings of spirituality is not without its own history. Jane Addams, for example, describes the centrality of her family's Quaker beliefs in her becoming involved in the Settlement House movement (Addams, 1935). Similarly, in her book about the women of Hull House, Eleanor Stebner (1997, pp. 2, 3) suggests that while the "formal religious life of their day did not provide an overriding and underlying meaning to their experiences and visions" the women of Hull House did "desire to transform evangelical Protestantism into a practical source of personal and political power." Martha Ackelsberg (1998, p. 135) notes that for all of Emma Goldman's anarchist commitments she also "drew deeply on Jewish religious themes in her speeches and found them extraordinarily effective in mobilizing predominantly Jewish garment workers." The Canadian feminist and labour activist Alice Chown grew up in a Methodist, philanthropic family. Though she railed against the religious practices of charity, her ideas of justice grew out of a long, religiously motivated, family tradition of taking care of the disadvantaged (Valverde, 1991, p. 155).

This reading of history provides marginal room for speaking a complex set of dis/connections between religion, spirituality, and activism. Indeed, the chronicles of feminist organizers' ambivalence and reconstruction of personal religious relationships resonate with the stories told in this study. In our discussions, spiritual narratives were often sidelined or taken up with varying degrees of ambivalence. Our ambivalence produced creative, contradictory stories of personal religious histories, present spiritual practices, and, at times, a notion of community organizing as spirituality. Some of us recognize religious institutions as sites where the relations of oppression that we were discovering in society were ever present. Nancy, a long time anti-poverty organizer, remembers her upbringing in a fundamentalist church as an example of the gender oppression she discovered as a child:

I grew up in a fundamentalist Church with all these things about men as the head of the Church and the household. As I got older I started to think what the hell is this? My parents, who articulated that they bought into that whole religious notion of the role of men and the role of women, actually don't have that in their marriage where they are very equal in their partnership. Actually, if anybody is in charge, it's my mother.

Nancy focuses upon religious narratives when exposing the contradictions between the gender equality that was modelled in her family and the inequality that was espoused by her church. Her analysis of her religious background was introduced into our discussion as a means to define the values against which her feminism was constituted. Claire has a similar critique of her family's religious community's values, but explores their direct impact on her mother:

[My mother] was a good Catholic woman and as such had a baby nine months after her honeymoon and then, fourteen months later, she had twins. I saw her raise five kids and have a job ... and its also very telling about the work I chose to do. Like work[ing] for Planned Parenthood ... duh, use birth control.

Claire's story suggests that her involvement in feminist activism was, in many ways, a direct resistance to the values, teachings, and subsequent effects of the church in which she was socialized. Generally, the stories told by Claire and Nancy suggest that some of our commitments to feminism are, in part, a response to the sexism that is present in many major religious institutions. As we began to know ourselves as resisters to general injustices, we also began to recognize ourselves as located outside of spiritual narratives.

Yet, the sacred/secular narratives we drew upon to make sense of ourselves were often significantly more intricate than this binary might suggest. At times, we resituated religious narratives to make sense of our involvement with progressive community practices. Sometimes we drew upon two, relatively separate, spiritual narratives, one evolving out of the religious practices of our childhoods and another that we "author" in our adulthood. Compare, for example, Claire's description of the effects of Catholicism on her family with her discussion of holding a house blessing as a strategy to bring her community together:

> I asked all my friends who came to bring a present for the blessing.... I had twenty people come to my house and when someone came early, I asked them to sweep the floor. I wanted people to be part of [the blessing] and that is why it was potluck ... people become part of it and are not just observers. And I think that is part of community organizing.

In contrast to "socialized" spiritual narratives, she uses "found" or "made" spiritual narratives to make sense of connections between the sacred and community organizing in her personal and professional life.

Our stories of oppressive religious practices or institutions could also function towards building the conceptual, moral, and practical foundations for our involvement with secular activism. From Lori's perspective, community development promised her an idealized Christianity that she had found missing in childhood religious teachings:

> I think community development meshed well with my Christian faith. I remember thinking community development is like Christianity or what I had hoped Christianity was, not necessarily my experience of it up until that point, but what I thought that Christ had intended ... you know, the story of Jesus living with people, being with people, helping them to be empowered and to change their lives. That vision of Christianity came from reading and fighting against the hell and damnation message—for

example, if you smoke and drink and swear you couldn't be a Christian.
So I think I wanted to believe in a different Christianity.

In this statement, Lori mobilizes her Christian ideals to support the promise
of community organizing; stories of Jesus's community practices suggested
to her that organizing could be understood as a "hopeful," spiritual practice.
She alludes to redemption here, "helping people to be empowered and to
change their lives," which is a powerful narrative in both Christianity and
organizing. The ideologies of "hope" and "redemption" provide a central
mechanism through which the fire-and-brimstone rhetoric of religion can
be rewritten to suggest a sense of entitlement to social justice, thereby
offering the moral terrain upon which organizing, and thus organizers,
rest.

Natalie also employs sacred narratives in a somewhat contradictory
fashion. At the beginning of the following quotation, she describes how
her childhood experiences within a religious community helped shape her
commitment to "help" others. At the same time she identifies how these
narratives and practices became oppressive, something from which she
withdrew:

In the Salvation Army, I grew up with the idea that you worked together
to help people. I don't think I necessarily grew up with a very good idea
of how to help. The job was to go out there and to save people's souls
but not only save their souls because I know that there is talk in there
about how to help people in their daily lives. So for me growing up, I
was learning what was important was "doing for other people."... The
definition of joy means Jesus first, others second, yourself last. So that was
a big thing growing up and the thing is, for me that was destructive. It
would be destructive for anyone. Not only did I not get the care I needed
or the love I needed growing up, but there was a lot of abuse. If I hadn't
somehow found a way to take care of myself first, in spite of getting that
message, I would either be dead or in some institution somewhere.

Natalie first describes what she understands as the positive, yet
problematic socialization practices of the Salvation Army. These are based
upon ideals of helping "others"—both materially and spiritually. Yet she
also perceives "helping" as dangerous, not necessarily for the people
who are "being helped," but for the "helpers" themselves. This danger
evolves from the community's continued focus on the practices and objects
of helping, ignoring whatever needs the "helper" has that cannot be met

inside this relationship. Natalie sets her critique of religious narratives against absent secular narratives that she seems to feel offer a professional promise of "a good idea of how to help." By situating the problem of "helping" on a religious practice that she has moved away from, it seems possible to invest more hope in the promise of her secular ideas about social change.

The contradictions of childhood religious communities may help to ensure the possibility of a feminist social worker subject. The tensions themselves form a subjective location, one marked by faith in a promised, better world, achievable in this world. Experience in religious communities familiarizes some of us with notions of faith and hope (Lernoux, 1982), while our disassociation from religion makes it possible to hope for something in the material, as opposed to the ethereal world. Faith in an ideal helps to make sense of our interventions with those who do not know "this promise," who cannot envision it, nor draw upon it to shape their daily practices. This subject location is both "self-aware" and "other-aware," suggesting a moral responsibility to intervene in the lives of "others."

❖ UNSETTLING THE BINARY

Though not critically or explicitly explored, the links between feminism and religion and/or spirituality also slipped into the conversations in my study. At times religion and/or spirituality was used as an approximation or as an analogy to explain the meanings of feminism in our work. Nancy hints at this when she attempts to describe feminism as something more than a political belief:

> So if I hadn't been paid to be at that women's march on the first sunny
> Saturday we had there's no way I would have been there. But this is stuff
> that's always been really important and it hooks into feminism, which is
> not just some political belief. It's how I want the world to be and how I
> want the world to be for my kids and that kind of stuff. It's hard because
> I feel like I have to take care of the world if I want that to happen and it
> becomes really hard.

Here, feminist narratives are posited as a promised future that Nancy has faith in and is working towards. The redemptive narratives of feminism and community organizing are made explicit, as perhaps are the ways in which feminist social work regulates bodies in the present towards an idealized, "better world." Relations of race and class are at work in our stories. Our narratives draw upon histories of "white women's burden," thus our claims to respectability are wound up in rescuing various racialized "others" (Heron, 1999). In these histories "the West" was the "better world" that feminists had faith in and offered as a promise to women of colour (see Roger, 1998).

Once we established some "faithful" similarities between feminism and religion, we utilized religious metaphors to understand the ways in which feminism is taken up as an identity and a practice of community organizing. We also began to rework community organizing as spirituality. While we drew on these religious narratives to understand our relationships with feminism, we simultaneously distanced ourselves from evangelical (or publicly spoken) religious practices.

Diane: "You know this may sound really weird, but I was thinking about this after Sarah and I talked and in some respects being a feminist can be like people being a Christian. It's not necessarily something that you have to talk about. To me its something that you are, that's inside you, that means you have certain values and certain principles that you live with and you bring that to the community work you do. So it means a respect for the women who you work with whether they are saying the most anti-feminist things around, which is often you know the case, right?"

Different voices: "Yes."

Nancy: "But you believe in their worth even if they don't. But it doesn't have to be exclusive."

Diane: "Yes, or … 'evangelical,' we don't have to go around talking about it all the time. Even if you don't state that your work is explicitly feminist, I think my feminism still informs it all the time so I still think it's really feminist community organizing."

Diane draws on religious metaphors in an attempt to secure a white feminist identity that is not publicly spoken. In fact, Nancy renders it publicly unspeakable: to not name a white, middle-class feminist organizing intervention or identity is to present oneself as more inclusive. At the same time, these silences seem to suggest a desire for innocence, to not be seen as coercive, or taking sides, while simultaneously engaging in politicized work towards a specific notion of social justice. I suggest that this contradiction exists because we only want to take sides when our complicity in relations of dominance can be obscured. Megan provides another example:

I think for me, in some ways it's almost like a religion. When I'm working with a group of people, I'm of course using my values that are strongly

> held, but I am not imposing my values on them. So, I wouldn't say something like, "well my religion is this." I don't say, "This is a value system." I don't impose it, but it's there—that talking about my values without labelling.

Megan tries to distance herself from labelling while maintaining a presence of feminist values. It is a contradictory strategy for recognizing oneself. We are at once innocent in relations of dominance, while engaging with practices that are coercive in their very attempt to promise a collective "justice" or "freedom." Razack and Fellows suggest that "to be unmarked or unnamed is also simply to embody the norm and not to have actively produced and sustained it. To be the norm, yet to have the norm unnamed, is to be innocent of the domination of others" (1998, p. 341). Thus, remaining silent about our feminism can be read as a strategy to allow us to have our values normalized, thereby making it easier to see our strategies and practices as not overladen with values. Therefore, our work seems not to involve imposing on others, but rather can be read as the norm into which all practices "naturally" fit. The coercive aspect of feminist organizing disappears.

❖ SECULARITY AS OBSCURING COERCION

Our disassociation from sacred narratives further shapes the subjectivity of feminist organizing because it relies on the possibility that one may make sense of interventions through ideologies that are inclusive, socially just, and not salvation oriented (at least when recognized in contrast to sacred interventions). The redemptive nature of our own narratives is obscured. As a result, a feminist organizer can be imagined as non-coercive, and non-judgemental. This "found" subject location, though imagined as distinct from sacred histories is, in fact, heavily invested with notions of morality (i.e., helping people through collective interventions is "good"). It is also bound within notions of "taking care" of those who we identify as disadvantaged, self-awareness (i.e., social work's reflexivity and feminism's consciousness raising), and an awareness of "others" as not self-aware and/or disorganized.

Our attempt to appear inclusive, neutral, and non-coercive, while engaging in progressive, collective work draws upon a long history of feminist and reform movements trying to negotiate their various locations in secular society. For example, at the close of the 19th century, the non-denominational National Council of Women insisted on a silent prayer at their meetings (Mitchinson, 1987). Likewise, the settlement houses at the turn of the century avoided religious preaching entirely and emphasized service to the community (Valverde, 1991, p. 142). While these may be admirable attempts at inclusivity, silence may render that which is present and normative into the invisible, an absent presence. This allows us the opportunity to deny the sometimes coercive, productive nature of our identities and practices. For instance, when Megan remains silent about her feminism, it becomes difficult for communities to interrogate her work as embedded in a social analysis that may or may not offer them a useful understanding of their situation. Despite our attempts to keep our values "under cover," they are "spoken" in the way we work, the kinds of consciousness we attempt to foster in the community members with whom we work, and the expectations of change that we work towards. During one conversation, Nancy observed, "the policies around ... how the coalition should behave and act and operate are shaped by my feminist philosophy. I don't know how successful it's been, though, in changing that group." Although we do not expect a complete, explicit commitment to feminism, or a declaration of faith in our value system from the people with whom we work, we do desire some conversion. We do impose our values on the groups of "others" we organize; in such moments our religious histories may appear closer than we had hoped.

As Nancy's statement suggests, the work of organizers is often about changing/raising consciousness. Part of coming to see oneself as a member of a community is linked with developing a class/race/gender consciousness. This involves developing a critical analysis of the ways in which power and resources move in society and linking them with notions of justice. I believe community organizing is vitally important to affecting social change, but it also rests on certain ideological underpinnings. Value-laden practices aimed toward raising people's social consciousness have been effective in achieving a significant amount of progressive change (for example, Wang, 1999). At the same time, these practices do have an element of coerciveness (see Cruikshank, 1999). The issue is whether we, as organizers, are able to explore the investments we have in certain social changes and the possibility that there may be other equally valid, maybe contradictory, visions of a just future and means of achieving such a justice.

❖ CONCLUSIONS

It is possible that our religious affiliation and/or spiritualities may shape our commitment to social justice and our ethical relations with others.

Out of this blend may come organizing practices and even (for some) feminism. Perhaps spiritual affinity seeps into the mix so as to "keep critically minded folks aware and interrogational of the 'something more' to which our present efforts point" (Lelwica, 1998, p. 123). It is possible to read feminism and/or community organizing as a type of faith, a mission and a value system. To do so, would be to recognize feminist social work consciousness as "an alternative way of seeing and acting in a broken world, a way that points beyond as it struggles to transform current realities" (Lelwica, 1998, p. 123), and that illuminates the plurality of truth, enabling us to take a stand "without resorting to the absolutizing strategies of classical Christian theology" (Sands, 1992, p. 30). Maybe the possibility of speaking religiosity outside of the dogmas of faith opens up an opportunity for merging the sacred into the secular feminisms of community organizing, or at least reusing the dualism in a reflexive manner that provides explicit consideration of the slippages. In so doing, we might be able to explore the ways in which our secular experiences shape our notions of transformation, help, and redemption, all of which remain integral to social work practice.

REFERENCES

Ackelsberg, M. (1998). Spirituality as a resource for activism. *Journal of Feminist Studies in Religion, 14*(2), 132–138.

Adamson, N, Briskin, L., & McPhail, M. (1988). *Feminists organizing for change.* Toronto: Oxford University Press.

Addams, J. (1935). *Twenty years at Hull-House.* New York: MacMillan.

Arnold, E. (1982). *Community as social ideal.* New York: St. Martin's Press.

Cruikshank, B. (1999). *The will to empower: Democratic citizens and other subjects.* Ithaca, NY: Cornell University Press.

Gordon, A. (1997). *Ghostly matters: Haunting and the sociological imagination.* Minneapolis: University of Minnesota Press.

Grant, J. (1990). Civil rights women: A source for doing womanist theology. In V. Crawford, J.A. Rouse, & B. Woods (Eds.), *Women in the civil rights movement: Trailblazers and torchbearers, 1941–1965* (pp. 39-50). Bloomington and Indianapolis, IN: Indiana University Press.

Heron, B. (1999). *Desire for development: The education of white women as development workers.* Unpublished doctoral dissertation, OISE/University of Toronto.

Lelwica, M. (1998). From superstition to enlightenment to race for pure consciousness. *Journal of Feminist Studies in Religion, 14*(2), 108–122.

Lernoux, P. (1982*). Cry of the people: The struggle for human rights in Latin America — The Catholic Church in conflict with U.S. policy.* New York: Penguin.

McRoberts, O. (1999). Understanding the "new" black Pentecostal activism: Lessons from ecumenical urban ministries in Boston. *Sociology of Religion, 60*(1), 47–70.

Mitchinson, W. (1987). Early women's organizations and social reform. In A. Moscovitch and J. Albert (Eds.), *The benevolent state* (pp. 79-92). Toronto: Garamond.

Moffatt, K. (2001). *A poetics of social work: Personal agency and social transformation in Canada, 1920–1939.* Toronto: University of Toronto Press.

Naples, N. (1998). Women's community activism and feminist activist research. In N. Naples (Ed.), *Community activism and feminist politics: Organizing across race, class, gender* (pp. 1-27). New York: Routledge.

Razack, S., & Fellows, M.L. (1998). The race to innocence: Confronting hierarchical relations among women. *Journal of Gender, Race, and Justice, 2*, 335–352.

Roger, K. (1998). *"Fairy fictions": White women as helping professionals.* Unpublished doctoral dissertation, OISE/University of Toronto.

Sands, K. (1992). Uses of the thea(o)logian: Sex and theodicy in religious feminism. *Journal of Feminism Studies in Religion, 8*(1), 7–33.

Shortell, T. (2001). Radicalization of religious discourse in El Salvador: The case of Oscar A. Romero. *Sociology of Religion, 62*: 87–103.

Stebner, E. (1997). *The women of Hull House: A study in spirituality, vocation, and friendship.* Albany, NY: State University of New York Press.

Valverde, M. (1991). *In the age of light, soap, and water: Moral reform in English Canada 1885–1925.* Toronto: McClelland and Stewart.

Wang, F. (1999). Resistance and old age: The subject behind the American seniors' movement. In A. Chambon, A. Irving, & L. Epstein (Eds.), *Reading Foucault for social work* (pp. 189–218). New York: Columbia University Press.

Wills, G. (1992). Values of community practice: Legacy of the radical Social Gospel. *Canadian Social Work Review, 9*(1), 28–39.

Wine, J.D., & Ristock, J.L. (1991). *Women and social change.* Toronto: James Lorimer.

Wood, R. (1999). Religious culture and political activism. *Sociological Theory, 17*(3), 307–331.

CHAPTER 11

ENGAGING WITH SPIRITUALITY:

A QUALITATIVE STUDY OF GRIEF AND HIV/AIDS

SUSAN CADELL, LINDA JANZEN, AND DENNIS J. HAUBRICH

As the AIDS epidemic continues, there are increased numbers of people
who have cared about someone who has died. This research was designed
to explore spiritual experiences in the context of AIDS grief. Fifteen
bereaved individuals were interviewed in 5 Canadian cities. The theme
that emerged overall was one of engagement. The bereaved individuals
engaged with HIV disease, with their own mortality, with their sense of
self, with the world, and with the deceased person or people as well as
with spirituality itself. The participants reconstructed meaning in their
lives after their losses.

❖ INTRODUCTION

As the AIDS epidemic continues, there are increased numbers of people
who have cared about someone who has died. Grief in the context of HIV
is associated with many stresses. These stresses include the stigma that
is still attached to HIV illness and the fact that many of the bereaved are
themselves HIV-positive. The number of losses that continue to accumulate
after someone has died is staggering, because those who are bereaved by
AIDS have often experienced multiple deaths. Further, many relationships
in the context of HIV are not recognized and valued by society, thus
disenfranchising the mourner. For those who continue to live with HIV/
AIDS, complex issues in grief arise as a result of these multiple and often
unrecognized losses.

The research concerning AIDS has concentrated on negative aspects,
and the resultant stresses have been well documented. In North America

the losses due to HIV/AIDS within the lesbian, gay, bisexual, and transgendered community have been enormous. It is not unusual for gay men to have lost dozens of friends and acquaintances (Shernoff, 1995, 1997b); numbers of deaths in studies have ranged from an average of 8 up to 67.7 (Nord, 1996a). The magnitude of AIDS-related losses has led to the suggestion that death has become normative in the lesbian and gay community (Goodkin, Blaney, Tuttle, et al., 1996; Neugebauer, Rabkin, Williams, Remien, Goetz, & Gorman, 1992). Grief is an inseparable part of HIV disease; it has been referred to as the secondary epidemic of AIDS (Wardlaw, 1994). The unrelenting losses associated with HIV disease are often potentially traumatizing (Nord, 1996a, 1996b, 1997, 1998; Shernoff, 1997a). Individuals who experience multiple losses show evidence of traumatic stress (Bigelow & Hollinger, 1996; Gluhoski, Fishman, & Perry, 1997a, 1997b; Goodkin, et al., 1996; Houseman & Pheifer, 1988; Martin & Dean, 1993; Sikkema, Kalichman, Kelly, & Koob, 1995). For both those who are HIV-positive and those who care about them, heterosexism and homophobia may create additional layers of stigma, as well as the potential for adding much stress to their lives.

Religion offers an additional layer of stressors in the context of HIV/AIDS. Many lesbian, gay, bisexual, and transgendered individuals have become estranged from religion (Hardy, 1998). Religion offers "an ultimate vision of what people should be striving for in their lives individually and collectively ... [and] provides its adherents with a set of practical methods, a 'map' to keep them on the proper path toward the ultimate designation" (Pargament & Park, 1995, p. 15). The "map" of religion often does not include acceptance of oneself as a whole and worthy person who is gay, lesbian, bisexual, and/or transgendered, leaving them estranged from their religious institutions. Helminiak (1995, p. 308) describes this process of estrangement:

> The choice, as it often still remains, was pretty much between self and respectability, pure and simple. And the gay men and lesbians chose self. They chose to act honestly. They chose to trust things as they really are. They chose to live life without illusion. If in the process, for whatever complex reasons, that choice meant even rejection of God, they had the courage and the wisdom to opt for what is the more basic.

Those in the lesbian, gay, bisexual, and transgendered communities, and their allies sometimes cannot reconcile their own values and beliefs about humanity and their experiences with religion and the various conceptions of homosexuality that are involved. Helminiak considers that choosing self, even if it means rejecting God, is the choice that is "more basic" (1995, p. 308). While the lesbian, gay, bisexual, and transgendered communities may struggle with religion and its rigid framework, spirituality is often viewed differently. Hardy (1982, p. 154) defines spirituality as a "frame of mind which breaks the human person out of the isolating self." Humans seek connections to one another in order to grow. Spirituality, when defined as such, can be religious or non-religious, depending on the individual.

Little research has explored the role of spirituality in the lives of those bereaved by HIV. One such study took data gathered from the University of California, San Francisco's (UCSF) Coping Project, wherein gay or bisexual men in long-term relationships were interviewed. Participants were caregivers to their partner with AIDS. The qualitative and quantitative data gathered over 7 years was used to examine various aspects of the coping responses of the caregivers (Folkman, Chesney, Collette, Boccellari, & Cooke, 1996; Folkman & Moskowitz, 2000; Folkman, Moskowitz, Ozer, & Park, 1997; Moskowitz, Folkman, Collette, & Vittinghoff, 1996; Wrubel & Folkman, 1997). A number of the participants were bereaved while participating in the project. In interviews after the death of the care recipients, spirituality emerged as one of the coping mechanisms (Richards & Folkman, 1997). Three to 4 years after bereavement, spirituality remained important to the majority of caregivers, but its role in their lives had changed (Richards, Acree, & Folkman, 1999). The self-identified limitation of these 2 studies was that the data about spirituality was not solicited explicitly. No question specifically addressed spirituality. In those interviews where it did not emerge spontaneously, there was no way of knowing whether this indicated a participant's lack of spirituality or was testament to some barrier to disclosing.

Meaning-making is a central tenet of coping with stress (Gottlieb, 1997; Moos & Schaefer, 1986; Park, Cohen, & Murch, 1996). Meaning-making involves the creation or re-creation of significance attached to an event or a life experience. The construction of meaning is essential to human beings, who rely, not on instinct as animals do, but rather on the significance attributed to any event (Saleebey, 2001). Meaning-making coping refers to the significance that the individual ascribes to the stress or trauma (Park & Folkman, 1997). Adverse events challenge how individuals view themselves, the world, and themselves in relation to the world (Janoff-Bulman, 1992). In order to cope with and recover from trauma, individuals must reconcile the event with their beliefs, by altering how they view the event, themselves, and/or the world (Horowitz, 1991, 1998; Janoff-Bulman,

1992). The search for meaning provides the basis of spirituality. In the sense that all humans are searching for significance in their lives (Frankl, 1962, 1997), all human creatures are then spiritual in its broadest sense.

Schwartzberg (1993) examined how gay men made sense of their HIV seropositivity. He found that many of the 19 participants viewed their diagnosis as an opportunity for spiritual or personal growth and it increased their sense of belonging to their community. Among other themes found, HIV was also seen as an irreparable loss, an isolating factor and even as punishment in some cases. Many of these constructions existed simultaneously for HIV-positive individuals. Regardless of the particular interpretations each made, all the gay men Schwartzberg interviewed struggled to find meaning in being HIV-positive. Similar searches for personal meaning were found in the 15 seropositive men interviewed by Borden (1991).

Given this context of complex bereavement and the dynamic tension between religion and spirituality in the lesbian, gay, bisexual, and transgendered communities, this research was designed to explore spiritual experiences in the context of AIDS grief. The theoretical framework of this research is the transactional approach to stress and coping (Folkman, 1997; Lazarus & Folkman, 1984). The results of the UCSF Coping Project caused Susan Folkman to rework the original transactional model of stress and coping (Lazarus & Folkman, 1984) to include positive psychological states and meaning-making coping (Folkman, 1997). Positive states only occurred in the original model when there was satisfactory resolution to the stressor. In the revised model, meaning-based coping can occur after unfavourable or no resolution in a feedback loop that has the potential to influence the re-appraisal of the stressor or to sustain the person in the coping process. In the theoretical context of the transactional model, the aim of this research was to explore spirituality within the negative and the positive changes in people's lives after HIV bereavement.

❖ METHOD

The sample was drawn from a larger study reported elsewhere (Cadell, 2001, 2003; Cadell, Regehr, & Hemsworth, 2003). Participants for that study were recruited because they had cared for someone who had died of HIV-related causes. Recruitment was done by the distribution of posters in AIDS service organizations, gay pride events, and AIDS-related conferences. Those who volunteered did so by leaving a message at a toll free number.

When contacted, the study was explained to potential participants. If they agreed to participate, a survey was mailed; surveys included a question about each person's willingness to be contacted for a follow-up interview. Of those who identified themselves as willing, the participants who were chosen for interviews lived in or near major Canadian cities: Toronto, Vancouver, Montréal, and Québec. This enabled face-to-face interviews, as telephone interviewing was unsuitable for such a sensitive topic.

Interview Protocol

The interviews were designed to be semi-structured and followed an interview schedule. The schedule was based on extant literature concerning caregiving and HIV/AIDS (Folkman, Chesney, Collette, Boccellari, & Cooke, 1996; Folkman, Chesney, Cooke, Boccellari, & Collette, 1994; Folkman, Moskowitz, Ozer, & Park, 1997; Richards, Acree, & Folkman, 1999). Each interview began by asking the person to talk about the person who had died and continued with open-ended questions about changes in their lives since then. Spirituality was one of the lines of inquiry with probes such as "Could you talk about how spirituality has had any influence in your life?"

Sample

Demographic information was collected through both the survey and the interviews. All 15 individuals were self-identified gay, lesbian, bisexual, and/or transgendered, or were allied with the community and had experienced at least one AIDS-related bereavement.

Table 11.1 Sample

	Male	Female	Transgendered
Number	8	4	3
Interview language	2 English	3 English	3 English
	6 French	1 French	
HIV status	6 positive	0 positive	3 positive
	2 negative	4 negative	0 negative
Self-identified sexuality	8 gay	1 lesbian	2 gay
	1 bisexual	1 heterosexual	
	2 heterosexual		

Procedures
The interviews were conducted by the first author in either French or English according to the choice of participant. The location of interview was also their choice. Eight were interviewed in their own homes and 7 in private locations in a public place. Interviews were audiotaped and then transcribed verbatim. All interviewees signed consent forms that had been approved by an ethics board; all were informed that they could terminate the interview at any time they wished without personal consequences. Twenty dollars remuneration was provided to each person.

Analysis
The analysis in this study concentrates on the explication of categories pertinent to spirituality. The analysis was conducted using grounded theory with open, axial, and selective coding (Lincoln & Guba, 1985; Strauss & Corbin, 1990). The first and third authors conducted all stages of the analysis. Open coding constituted the first stage of the analysis in order to articulate themes. Meetings were held to establish perspectives and to reconcile any differences in coding. The second phase of analysis, axial coding, involved evaluating the connection among the themes. The overarching theme of engagement was identified in the final stage of selective coding.

❖ RESULTS

The overarching theme of the data was one of engagement as a broad expression of spirituality. The participants engaged in the various subthemes of HIV/AIDS, mortality, self, the world, the deceased, and spirituality. Quotations will be used to illustrate exemplars of each theme; they have been translated from French where applicable. Pseudonyms have been used to protect confidentiality.

Engagement with HIV/AIDS
The people who were interviewed had fully engaged with the disease and its impact on their lives. Through meaning-making engagements with HIV/AIDS in their day-to-day lives, Joseph, Chantal, and Rosemary contest prevailing dismal constructions of what it is like to be living with or affected by HIV/AIDS. They construct their engagements with HIV/AIDS in ways that are representative of personal empowerment—as challenge, opportunity, and fulfillment.

Joseph was 50 years old at the time of his interview. He had been HIV-positive for more than 10 years. Joseph had transformed the French

equivalent of HIV (VIH) to represent *Vivre Intensément l'Humain*: Live
Humanity Intensely. Joseph considered that instead of being a death
sentence, HIV was an opportunity for him to live his life to the fullest.
Joseph credited this interpretation with allowing him to survive for so
long.

Chantal, a 46-year-old male-to-female transsexual who had been HIV-
positive for 15 years, worked as a full-time volunteer in an AIDS service
organization. She had devoted most of her life to HIV issues. Chantal
considered that HIV had "enriched my life. I think I've lived with the
disease for so long now that if they came tomorrow and said I didn't have
this disease, I was cured that you know, I think I'd be more devastated
than when I got it." Chantal had so strongly engaged with HIV that it had
become, to a great extent, her whole identity.

Rosemary was 52 at the time of the interview. She was HIV-negative
and had worked in an AIDS service organization for many years. Rosemary
had fully engaged with HIV disease, both personally and professionally.
She stated: "I owe AIDS nothing, but I sure owe a lot to the people who
have contributed in very remarkable ways to my happiness. Not my
sadness, my happiness."

Engagement with Mortality
Participants often expressed changed feelings in relation to death. Many
feared death less since they had experienced the loss of the person with
HIV. The following examples demonstrate the various ways in which
individuals were able to engage with mortality. Paul, a 39–year-old HIV-
positive gay man who was interviewed in French, considered that it would
not bother him to be told that he would die in three days: "Because I've
been going through that all since 1997. I've been through it. I've seen other
people die." Paul's engagement with his own mortality was significantly
affected by his prior losses. In processing these, he learned to face his own
death.

Michael, a 50-year-old HIV-negative gay man whose partner died ten
years before the interview, commented: "that's why I am not afraid [of
death], because it's like going somewhere and there's already someone
there. We're not arriving at an empty house. There is already someone
there to welcome us." Michael's spiritual beliefs supported him in engaging
with mortality.

Rosemary came to realize in her work with people with AIDS that she
could not "stop people from dying. That was a hard realization to come to,
but I can walk the journey." This is a common struggle for caregivers who

must come to terms with the mortality of their loved one. Amy, a bisexual woman who had worked in an AIDS organization commented: "I truly believe you cannot really live if you don't know you're going to die." For Amy, facing her own mortality through experiencing the loss of others heightened her ability to live to the fullest.

The death of the care recipient personifies the mortality of the caregiver. The integration of a personal mortality informs the significance of present life, as well as in the case of Michael to signify a continued relationship with the person he has lost.

Engagement with Self

This theme involved the finding of purpose in one's life and the process of reconstructing one's self after losing a friend or a partner. Finding purpose, or making meaning, was experienced in many ways. Julien, a 46-year-old HIV-positive gay man, lost his partner 7 years before the interview. Julien derived great satisfaction in himself from the feeling that he had done everything that he could to care for his partner. Rosemary commented that she had "learned a huge amount about how I should live life, about my capacity for pain, joy, sadness, grief, tenderness, and love."

Gary was a 39-year-old HIV-positive gay man whose partner had died 1 1/2 years before the interview. Both Joseph and Gary had become highly involved in public speaking engagements to raise awareness about HIV prevention programs in schools. Both of them derived enormous satisfaction with these activities and expressed those feelings. Joseph used the transformation of HIV (*Vivre Intensément l'Humain*) described above in his talks. Gary said: "we all have a mission in life. I understood that I had work to do and ... I decided to do prevention in schools."

Ted, a 64-year-old HIV-negative gay man, had participated in more than 50 care teams caring for individuals with AIDS. Ted considered that these experiences had made him "a better person, a brighter person." Sarah, a 44-year-old heterosexual transsexual whose partner had died said:

> what I got from [her partner] is I really like who I am ... [he] accepted me wholeheartedly, he loved me, and even he was sick, and he came home. And you know it was funny how he did it. But he really loved me. You know he would worry about me eh? And you can't get that kind of love. And what it's given me an even stronger acceptance for who I am.

"Engagement with self" addresses the relationship of the self to the self in an evolving identity. Our identities and life purposes are constructed in accordance to relational others. Among the participants, the death of the care recipient necessitated the relinquishment of cherished roles and identities, and precipitated the search for meaning and purpose.

For one participant the struggle to make meaning was overwhelming. Andy remained trapped in his grief and he had not been able to move forward in a positive manner. HIV-positive himself, Andy, at 31 years of age, had considered that his partner had been his reason for living. He had been unable to find a new purpose in life after the death of his partner. In the 4 years since he assisted in his partner's death, Andy had attempted suicide and referred to himself as a "rudderless" ship.

Engagement with World

Themes of nature and of how human beings should interact with one another occur in this category. The participants' reflective engagements with the outside world exude a "kind and gentle" stance, a wonderment that is mindful of our connectedness to others and the natural world. Ted explained his philosophy about life: "to be loving and caring because if you're loving and caring, you're going to get loving and caring back."

Andy, who could find no meaning in his life, did derive some satisfaction and pride from his relationship with his dog. Michael talked about his experience of looking out the hospital window when his partner had died and seeing people as ants who are scurrying along with no idea of what he was going through. Through his traumatic experience, he grew in his capacity to be compassionate to others. He comments: "So we want to go looking for a little compassion, we want the world to be a little more compatible with our pain."

Julien tells the story of passing by a fallen baby bird because he was in a hurry to run errands before going to the hospice where his lover was dying. Julien picked up the baby bird when he found it was still there on his way back. Later that day another bird, Julien believed it was the mother, entered the room repeatedly until the adult and the baby bird flew away together. Julien considered this a fairy tale ending. He likened his partner's death a few weeks later to the flight of the baby bird.

Engagement with Deceased

Many of the bereaved participants had continuing connections to their friends or partner who had died. They had developed ways of maintaining healthy relationships with the deceased, and of bringing those relationships forward into their lives. Sarah said, "I went over and I held his picture … what it is doing is having a conversation with him."

Henry, a 33-year-old HIV-positive transgendered individual, had experienced the death of a foster child, of his best friend, and of numerous other friends. Henry commented:

> I travel all around the world to places that my friends would want to go. The ones that I've cared for. And I bring a picture of them and I let it float in the water: I let it go, you're here now.

Rosemary kept pictures on the wall of her office of people she cared about who had died. She referred to these people as her angels:

> My angels are different than other people's angels. My angels are all the people that have died of AIDS that I've loved.... But they're not perfect by any stretch of the imagination.

Spiritual engagement with the deceased demonstrates mindfulness of the continuing presence of those who have died through memories and concrete representations. To grieve is to cherish and to mindfully make present the ones we have lost.

Engagement with Spirituality

Participants often defined their own spirituality; and in their definitions, many were adamant that their spirituality did not constitute religion. The participants constructed the spirituality of their grief outside of the ascribed constraints of religiosity. Their spirituality may have been drawn in part from aspects of religiosity, but what was most characteristic of participants' spiritualities was their autonomy.

Amy, a 27-year-old HIV-negative bisexual woman specified that she did not believe in God. She had rejected her Christian upbringing after her father died when she was 12 and relatives told her that God needed her father more than her. Amy wore a rune, had a Wiccan spell bottle, and, in spite of her rejection of Christianity, kept a bible in her apartment. Amy stated:

> You should give back things that you take and I believe that you should take care of the people around you. I mean I'm sure that a lot of what I believe comes from this religion and that religion.

Henry, who was Métis, had "become more spiritual, connecting myself with my native culture" since experiencing loss. Daniel had studied theology and had reflected a great deal on his spirituality but had never talked to anyone about it before the interview. Daniel was 36 at the time of the interview, was HIV-positive, and had experienced the death of a partner and two friends. Daniel says:

> The bible was written by man more than 2000 years ago. You take some, you leave some, that's my spirituality … it is said that two men together is sinful. Well, that's strange because a few pages before God says "love one another" … my spirituality is that God accepts me.

Joseph had also reflected on his Christian upbringing:

> The Christian cross has two directions: there is the obvious vertical direction which is for me at least, the symbol of the relationship between people and God and it is true that there is the traverse, the horizontal direction, which is the relationship between people, between equals…. Spirituality and sexuality are for me the poles that absolutely join one another…. My own sexuality would like to be more spiritual.

❖ DISCUSSION

This study examined the spirituality and/or religiosity of individuals who had cared about someone who had died of AIDS related complications. Many, but not all, of the participants were themselves HIV positive. The participants' spirituality grew to include engagement at many levels: with HIV disease, with their own mortality, with their sense of self, with their assumptive worlds, and with the deceased person or people in their lives. They also engaged with spirituality and/or religion. The engagement of these bereaved individuals involves mindful process (Langer, 1997). Mindfulness is seen in the choices they have made in their lives: how they have chosen to live, how they approach death, how they relate to spirituality, and how they interact with others.

The participants have created meaning and purpose in their lives, not only from the death of the person or people they cared about, but for many of them from facing their own mortality in living with this disease. Many of them shifted the focus in their lives, reconstructing their beliefs about what is important to them, and how they function in the world, a process of grieving that has been gaining attention (Neimeyer, 2001). The (re)construction of meaning and purpose in life for these bereaved individuals has led to a stronger sense of self, and to the embracing of a greater participation in and appreciation for life. Where this adaptive meaning was not established, the participant struggled significantly with engagement with self, life, and the world.

Through their individual grieving processes, most of the participants have developed a spiritual connection to the person or people for whom they cared. They have found ways to incorporate the deceased into their daily lives and have continued their bonds adaptively with the deceased (Janzen, Cadell, & Westhues, 2004; Klass, 2001; Klass, Silverman, & Nickman, 1996). Many were able to identify what they have learned from the deceased in their living and dying and have incorporated those facets of the deceased into their own lives. In doing so, they have strengthened the spiritual connection between self and deceased. This has contributed to their well-being at a deep level. Their spiritual connection to the deceased helps them live each day to the fullest, and for most has removed the fear of death. The spiritual connection to the deceased has strengthened their spiritual beliefs and sense of self as a spiritual being.

Spirituality for most participants was viewed as distinct from religion. The emphasis on spirituality was strong. The perceived inconsistency of biblical texts that extol followers to accept and love all humanity, and then decry homosexuality as a sin, has led many participants to embrace their own spirituality, rather than any particular religious movement. Spirituality for many participants allowed them to feel whole in their sexuality and lifestyle choices. It has strengthened their ability to create meaning and purpose in their lives, and to go forward embracing life, even in the face of their own disease and death.

The results of this study parallel closely the experience of HIV/AIDS caregivers in the UCSF Coping Project and their spiritual resources (Richards, 2001; Richards, Acree, & Folkman, 1999; Richards & Folkman, 1997). This research, however, in contrast to the Coping Project, sought information about spirituality.

The themes of engagement with HIV, mortality, self, world, the deceased person, and spirituality echo the domains of posttraumatic growth (Cadell, 2001, 2003; Cadell, Regehr, & Hemsworth, 2003; Calhoun & Tedeschi, 2001; Tedeschi & Calhoun, 1995, 2004; Tedeschi, Park, & Calhoun, 1998). Posttraumatic growth is conceptualized as the outcome of the process of dealing with the aftermath of trauma; it is not considered that growth is a result of the trauma itself. Growth and wisdom and enduring distress are the simultaneous three outcomes that can occur (Tedeschi & Calhoun, 2004). New possibilities, relating to others, personal strength, appreciation of life, and spiritual change are considered to be the domains of posttraumatic growth (Tedeschi & Calhoun, 1996, 2004).

The grief of the individuals in this study has aspects that are potentially traumatic: from the multitude of losses associated with HIV to the loss of someone to a disease that can disfigure someone and/or cause a long dying process. An additional trauma lies in the possibility of observing one's own demise in a similar manner, as so many of the people were HIV-positive themselves. These individuals demonstrated growth similar to the domains of posttraumatic growth. The engagement with HIV disease demonstrated by these individuals relates to the category of new possibilities. By reconstructing the meaning of the disease, they created new possibilities for themselves. Engagement with the world and the deceased person both reflect aspects of relating of others. Personal strength is demonstrated in these people's engagement with their self, while the changing views of death are an example of their greater appreciation of life. Finally, the domain of spiritual change is exemplified by the engagement with spirituality. The entire framework of engagement can be considered spiritual change. Future research is needed to further explore spirituality in the phenomenon of posttraumatic growth, as this study suggests that it may have a larger role than has been previously conceptualized.

❖ CONCLUSION

Throughout this study spirituality was clearly expressed through the various forms of engagement experienced by the participants. Spirituality was identified as a key factor in moving forward in an adaptive fashion to face their lives and in some cases their own HIV disease. The strengthening of spirituality has greatly assisted these bereaved individuals in meaning-making and the development of purpose in life in the face of this disease and its sequelae.

REFERENCES

Bigelow, G., & Hollinger, J. (1996). Grief and AIDS: Surviving catastrophic multiple loss. *The Hospice Journal, 11*(4), 83–96.

Borden, W. (1991). Beneficial outcomes in adjustment to HIV seropositivity. *Social Service Review, 65*(3), 434–449.

Cadell, S. (2001). Post-traumatic growth in HIV/AIDS caregivers in Quebec. *Canadian Social Work, 3*(1), 86–94.

Cadell, S. (2003). Trauma and growth in Canadian carers. *AIDS Care, 15*(5), 639–648.

Cadell, S., Regehr, C., & Hemsworth, D. (2003). Factors contributing to post-traumatic growth: A proposed structural equation model. *American Journal of Orthopsychiatry, 73*(3), 279–287.

Calhoun, L.G., & Tedeschi, R.G. (2001). Posttraumatic growth: The positive lessons of loss. In R.A. Neimeyer (Ed.), *Meaning reconstruction and the experience of loss* (pp. 157–172). Washington, DC: American Psychological Association.

Folkman, S. (1997). Positive psychological states and coping with severe stress. *Social Science and Medicine, 45*(8), 1207–1221.

Folkman, S., Chesney, M., Collette, L., Boccellari, A., & Cooke, M. (1996). Postbereavement depressive mood and its prebereavement predictors in HIV+ and HIV- gay men. *Journal of Personality and Social Psychology, 70*(2), 336–348.

Folkman, S., Chesney, M.A., Cooke, M., & Boccellari, A. (1994). Caregiver burden in HIV-positive and HIV-negative partners of men with AIDS. *Jounral of Consulting and Clinical Psychology 62*(4), 746-756.

Folkman, S. & Moskowitz, J.T. (2000). Stress, positive emotion, and coping. *Current Directions in Psycological Science, 9*(4), 115–118.

Folkman, S., Moskowitz, J.T., Ozer, E.M., & Park, C.L. (1997). Positive meaningful events and coping in the context of HIV/AIDS. In B.H. Gottlieb (Ed.), *Coping with chronic stress* (pp. 293-314). New York: Plenum Press.

Frankl, V.E. (1962). *Man's search for meaning.* Boston: Beacon Press.

Frankl, V.E. (1997). *Man's search for ultimate meaning.* New York: Plenum Press.

Gluhoski, V.L., Fishman, B., & Perry S.W. (1997a). The impact of multiple bereavement in a gay male sample. *AIDS Education and Prevention 9*(6), 521-531.

Gluhoski, V.L., Fishman, B., & Perry, S.W. (1997b). Moderators of bereavement distress in a gay male sample. *Personality and Individual Differences, 23*(5), 761–767.

Gluhoski, V.L. & Wortman, C.B. (1996). The impact of trauma on world views. *Journal of Social and Clinical Psychology, 15*(4), 417–429.

Goodkin, K., Blaney, N.T., Tuttle, R.S., Nelson, R.H., Baldewicz, T., Kumar, M., Fletcher, M.A., Leeds, B., & Feaster, D.J. (1996). Bereavement and HIV Infection. *International Review of Psychiatry, 8*, 201–216.

Gottlieb, B.H. (1997). Conceptual and measurement issues in the study of coping with chronic stress. In B.H. Gottlieb (Ed.), *Coping with chronic stress* (pp. 3–40). New York: Plenum Press.

Hardy, R.P. (1982). Christian spirituality today: Notes on its meaning. *Spiritual Life, 28*, 151–159.

Hardy, R.P. (1998). *Loving men: Gay partners, spirituality, and AIDS.* New York: Continuum.

Helminiak, D.A. (1995). Non-religious lesbians and gays facing AIDS: A fully psychological approach to spirituality. *Pastoral Psychology, 43*(5), 301–318.

Horowitz, M.J. (1991). Person schemas. In M.J. Horowitz (Ed.), *Person schemas and maladaptive interpersonal patterns.* Chicago: University of Chicago Press.

Horowitz, M.J. (1998). Organizational levels of self and other schematization. In P.M. Westenberg, A. Blasi, & L.D. Cohn (Eds.), *Personality development: Theoretical, empirical, and clinical investigations of Loevinger's conception of ego development.* Mahwah, NJ: Lawrence Erlbaum.

Houseman, C., & Pheifer, W.G. (1988). Potential for unresolved grief in survivors of persons with AIDS. *Archives of Psychiatric Nursing, 2*(5), 296–301.

Janoff-Bulman, R. (1992*). Shattered assumptions: Towards a new psychology of trauma.* New York: The Free Press.

Janzen, L.M., Cadell, S., & Westhues, A. (2004). Dealing with the sudden death of a child: Advice to professionals from parents. *Omega: Journal of Death and Dying, 48*(2), 175–190.

Klass, D. (2001). The inner representation of the dead child in the psychic and social narratives of bereaved parents. In R.A. Neimeyer (Ed.), *Meaning reconstruction and the experience of loss* (pp. 77–94). Washington, DC: American Psychological Association.

Klass, D., Silverman, P.R., & Nickman, S.L. (1996). *Continuing bonds: New understandings of grief.* Washington, DC: Taylor & Francis.

Langer, E.J. (1997). *The power of mindful learning.* Reading, MA: Addison-Wesley Publishing.

Lazarus, R.S., & Folkman, S. (1984). *Stress, appraisal, and coping.* New York: Springer Publishing Company.

Lincoln, Y.S., & Guba, E.G. (1985). *Naturalistic inquiry.* Beverly Hills, CA: Sage Publications.

Martin, J.L., & Dean, L. (1993). Effects of AIDS-related bereavement and HIV-related illness on psychological distress among gay men: A 7-year longitudinal study, 1985-1991. *Journal of Consulting and Clinical Psychology, 61*(1), 94–103.

Moos, R.H., & Schaefer, J.A. (1986). Life transitions and crises: A conceptual overview. In R.H. Moos (Ed.), *Coping with life crises: An integrated approach* (pp. 1-28). New York: Plenum Press.

Moskowitz, J.T., Folkman, S., Collette, L., & Vittinghoff, E. (1996). Coping and mood during AIDS-related caregiving and bereavement. *Annals of Behavioral Medicine, 18*(1), 49–57.

Neimeyer, R.A. (2001). Meaning reconstruction and loss. In R.A. Neimeyer (Ed.), *Meaning reconstruction and the experience of loss* (pp. 1–9). Washington, DC: American Psychological Association.

Neugebauer, R., Rabkin, J.G., Williams, J.B.W., Remien, R.H., Goetz, R., & Gorman, J.M. (1992). Bereavement reactions among homosexual men experiencing multiple losses in the AIDS epidemic. *American Journal of Psychiatry, 149*(10), 1374–1379.

Nord, D. (1996a). Assessing the negative effects of multiple AIDS-related loss on the gay individual and community. *Journal of Gay and Lesbian Social Services, 4*(3), 1–34.

Nord, D. (1996b). Issues and implications in the counseling of survivors of multiple AIDS-related loss. *Death Studies, 20*(4), 389–413.

Nord, D. (1997). *Multiple AIDS-related loss: A handbook for understanding and surviving a perpetual fall.* Washington, DC: Taylor & Francis.

Nord, D. (1998). Traumatization in survivors of multiple AIDS-related loss. *Omega: Journal of Death and Dying, 37*(3), 215–240.

Pargament, K.I., & Park, C.L. (1995). Merely a defense? The variety of religious means and ends. *Journal of Social Issues, 51*(2), 13–32.

Park, C.L., Cohen, L.H., & Murch, R.L. (1996). Assessment and prediction of stress-related growth. *Journal of Personality, 64*(1), 71–105.

Park, C.L., & Folkman, S. (1997). Meaning in the context of stress and coping. *Review of General Psychology, 1*(2), 115–144.

Richards, T.A. (2001). Spiritual resources following a partner's death from AIDS. In R.A. Neimeyer (Ed.), *Meaning reconstruction and the experience of loss* (pp. 173–190). Washington, DC: American Psychological Association.

Richards, T.A., Acree, M., & Folkman, S. (1999). Spiritual aspects of loss among partners of men with AIDS: Postbereavement follow-up. *Death Studies, 23*(2), 105–127.

Richards, T.A., & Folkman, S. (1997). Spiritual aspects of loss at the time of a partner's death from AIDS. *Death Studies, 21*(6), 527–552.

Saleebey, D. (2001). *Human behavior and social environments: A biopsychosocial approach.* New York: Columbia University Press.

Schwartzberg, S.S. (1993). Struggling for meaning: How HIV-Positive Gay men make sense of AIDS. *Professional Psychology: Research and Practice, 24*(4), 483–490.

Shernoff, M. (1995). Reflections on living with AIDS. *Journal of Gay and Lesbian Social Services, 3*(4), 83–89.

Shernoff, M. (1997a). Conclusion: Mental health considerations of gay widowers. *Journal of Gay and Lesbian Social Services, 7*(2), 137–155.

Shernoff, M. (1997b). Do you have a partner? *Journal of Gay and Lesbian Social Services, 7*(2), 15–28.

Sikkema, K.J., Kalichman, S.C., Kelly, J.A., & Koob, J.J. (1995). Group intervention to improve coping with AIDS-related bereavement: Model development and an illustrative clinical example. *AIDS Care, 7*(4), 463–475.

Strauss, A., & Corbin, J. (1990). *Basics of qualitative research: Grounded theory procedures and techniques.* Newbury Park, CA: Sage Publications.

Tedeschi, R.G., & Calhoun, L.G. (1995). *Trauma and transformation: Growing in the aftermath of suffering.* Thousand Oaks, CA: Sage Publications.

Tedeschi, R.G., & Calhoun, L.G. (1996). The post traumatic growth inventory: Measuring the positive legacy of trauma. *Journal of Traumatic Stress, 9*(3), 455–471.

Tedeschi, R.G. & Calhoun, L.G. (2004). Posttraumatic growth: Conceptual foundations and empirical evidence. *Psychological Inquiry, 15*(1), 1–18.

Tedeschi, R.G., Park, C.L., & Calhoun, L.G. (1998). *Posttraumatic growth: Positive changes in the aftermath of crisis.* Mahwah, NJ: Lawrence Erlbaum Associates.

Wardlaw, L.A. (1994). Sustaining informal caregivers for persons with AIDS. *Families in Society, 75*(6), 373–384.

Wrubel, J. & Folkman, S. (1997). What informal caregivers actually do: The caregiving skills of partners of men with AIDS. *AIDS Care, 9*(6), 691–706.

CHAPTER 12

CIRCLES OF RESISTANCE:

SPIRITUALITY AND TRANSFORMATIVE CHANGE

IN SOCIAL WORK EDUCATION AND PRACTICE

CYNDY BASKIN

Spirituality comes from within and outside the self. It is meant to assist us as individuals, families, and communities. It is also about resistance and it connects us to the work of social change.

The topic of spirituality is an important dialogue that educators must have with their students. In my four years of teaching, I have brought spirituality into the classroom not only by speaking about it, but by doing it. What I have learned so far, is that if I open those doors by taking the lead, it creates a safe place where students can share their spirituality.

As important as spirituality is to each individual's well-being and strength, each of us has a responsibility to use it in creating a better world. It is the role of the social worker to resist oppression and become involved in political activism. The structural social work approach guides us in this role, but it lacks any spiritual dimension. What social workers need is direction based on action-oriented spirituality.

❖ INTRODUCTION

In my experiences outside Indigenous communities, the topic of spirituality is usually met with silence and a lowering of the eyes. It appears to make people uncomfortable, which is difficult for me to understand, as I see it simply as existence. In order to write about spirituality, I am faced with the dilemma of having to separate it from the whole, which, of course, is problematic in itself. However, because I have had so many uplifting experiences as a social work practitioner, hopeful ones as a recent educator and student, and am committed to inclusive schooling, I have an unavoidable calling to incorporate spirituality into my research in the academy.

I believe spirituality is the connection to all that is in existence. It comes from within and outside the self. It is meant to assist us as individuals, families, and communities. Spirituality is also about resistance and it connects us to the work of social change.

Thus, this chapter will focus on the use of spirituality in social work practice, the teaching of it in social work programs and its importance to social change.

❖ DEFINITION

The social work literature is consistent in its definition of spirituality as encompassing an individual's ultimate values, her/his relationship with others, and one's perception of the sacred (Canda, 1988; Titone, 1991; Ingersoll, 1994; O'Rouke, 1997; Pellebon, Anderson, & Angell, 1999; Gilbert, 2000). Carolyn Jacobs (1997) defines spirituality as "heart knowledge where wholeness, meaning, and inner peace occur. Spirituality is a sense of being at one with the inner and outer worlds" (p. 172).

The literature also emphasizes that although religion can be a part of spirituality, they are not interchangeable. Religion is seen as a formalized practice that includes "an integrated belief system that provides principles of behaviour, purposes of existence, meaning of death, and an expression of reverence for a supernatural being (or beings)" (Canda, 1989, p. 37). Spirituality, on the other hand, is distinguished as "a set of personal beliefs derived from the individual's perception of self and his or her relationship to both the natural world and some metaphysical realm" (*ibid.*). The significant difference between the two is that religion is a structured form of spirituality that usually has a group following, whereas spirituality can include individual experiences with or without a structured belief system.

In researching the historical origins of social work, it is evident that its practice is grounded in religious-sponsored agencies. Kilpatrick and Holland (1990) state that

> Our professional grandparents viewed their efforts as a way of evidencing two religious values that were immediately present in their understanding of the meaning of life—love and justice for their fellow human beings. The origins of this profession, the values which gave it birth, are to be found in the concerns of people who not only believed in individual charity but

also understood that their faith called for community responses of mutual responsibility (p. 127).

I am honoured to be a part of a profession that grew out of the values of love, justice, community, and mutual responsibility. Each of these values encompasses my own spirituality. They also speak clearly to the role of social work in the arena of social change as linked to spirituality.

My understanding of Aboriginal spirituality, according to the teachings that have been passed on to me, is that it is an interconnectedness and interrelationship with all life. All (both "animate" and "inanimate") are seen as being equal and interdependent, part of the great whole and as having a spirit. This view permeates the entire Aboriginal vision of life and the universe. Comparatively, there is little published writing on Aboriginal spirituality that is, in fact, conducive to our way of responsibly imparting knowledge through oral tradition. However, Sioui (1992) explains as follows:

> Where their human kin are concerned, the Amerindians' attitude is the same: all human beings are sacred because they are an expression of the will of the Great Mystery. Thus, we all possess within ourselves a sacred vision, that is, a unique power that we must discover in the course of our lives in order to actualize the Great Spirit's vision, of which we are an expression. Each man and woman, therefore, finds his or her personal meaning through that unique relationship with the Great Power of the universe. (p. 9)

❖ USE OF SPIRITUALITY IN PRACTICE AND EDUCATION

For me not to implement spirituality into my social work roles as educator and practitioner is unnatural. To not be able to do so makes me feel both empty and insincere. It is a form of spiritual abuse that I experience as deeply wounding. With regards to my social work practice, I have had the good fortune to incorporate spirituality into almost all settings and situations mainly due to the fact that my work has always been within Aboriginal communities. As a social work student, I had no "education" regarding spirituality in my programs. As an educator, I am finding it infinitely challenging but increasingly rewarding to invite spirituality into the classroom.

Once again, the literature is consistent regarding the role of spirituality in social work education. Three major research studies indicate that 88.5%,

65.7%, and 79% of social work students received little or no "training" on spirituality in their programs (Sheridan, Wilmer, & Atcheson, 1994; Sheridan & Hemert, 1999; Miller, 2001).

With regards to the use of spirituality in social work practice, a literature review indicates that the topic has been largely neglected by the profession (Sermabeikian, 1994; Pellebon, et al., 1999; Gilbert, 2000; Damianakis, 2001; Gotterer, 2001).

An obvious question emerges at this point. Why is it that the profession of social work has strayed so far from its roots, which lie largely within the realm of spirituality? I assert that as social work moved into the period of modernity it allied itself with science, thereby embracing a rational, linear, reductionist view of the world. This move towards gaining credibility by the social sciences and medical professions meant that spirituality would have to be severed from social work because it does not conform to this view of the world.

Practice
The small body of literature on spirituality in social work practice focuses on grief counselling and hospice work. To be sure, these are significant areas in which spirituality is needed. However, I advocate that it be implemented within all aspects of social work. Spirituality is not only about death and dying—it is about life and living!

Social work practice cannot be whole without including the spiritual dimension. If practitioners ignore it, then they are not fully responding to their "clients." Ideally, social work practice focuses on client strengths. Spirituality is the most powerful source of strength because everyone who chooses to go on in this world operates on some form of faith. A spiritual value or belief can be a powerful resource in a client's life that can be used in problem solving, coping, and recovering from trauma.

Many Aboriginal helpers and writers identify a revitalization of spirituality in the lives of Aboriginal peoples. In a 1995 study by McCormick, which looked at the facilitation of healing for Aboriginal peoples in British Columbia, "establishing a spiritual connection" and "participation in spiritual ceremonies" were ranked amongst the most important components by participants (pp. 280–282). Fyre Jean Graveline (1998) refers to this revival as "spiritual resistance [that] flourishes through treasuring our children and honouring the visions and words of our Ancestors" (p. 45). In her research regarding Aboriginal women, writer Kim Anderson (2000) shares that "many Native women told me it felt like they had finally found something that was 'ours' when they began to practice Native spirituality" (p. 133).

Often, this reclaiming of spirituality begins in healing processes with Aboriginal social workers and other helpers. It is important that the profession of social work pick up this work since "spiritual healing requires special attention because it is the spiritual aspect of Aboriginal identity that has suffered most from the effects of cultural colonialism" (Morrissette, McKenzie, & Morrissette, 1993, p. 99). Thus, some healing programs ensure that they place emphasis on activism, resistance, and social change as well as community recovery (Avalos, Arger, Levesque, & Pike, 1997; Baskin, 1997).

Most importantly, perhaps, is the concept of incorporating spirituality as power and knowledge throughout everyday life. In social work discourse, this is called "prevention." It involves reflexive knowledge that is less preoccupied with the outcome and more concerned with the process. It encourages social workers not to construct an understanding of the client's reality through knowledge derived only empirically, as this may block other ways of knowing. Such a position begins to move the profession of social work from modernity into postmodern thought. According to this discourse, alternative means to knowledge acquisition and power are emphasized, such as those that arise from emotion and intuition. Intuition, in particular, allows the social worker to have "direct, immediate knowledge of something without relying on the conscious use of reason or sense perception" (Percesepe, 1991, as cited in Damianakis, 2001). With respect to spirituality, intuition is usually rooted in a collective unconscious. In its most valuable application, social workers' offerings of intuitive insights or hunches with their clients can affect those who experience them in integrative, powerful, and meaningful ways (Richards and Bergin, 1997). To make this even more powerful, however, practitioners can assist their clients in learning how to access and implement their own intuitions and other spiritual gifts. In addition, they can also help with clients' positive identity formation through a relationship with the collective unconscious that they share with other people.

It may be that postmodern discourse makes it much easier to begin to talk about Indigenous ways of knowing and helping. There are, of course, no Aboriginal terms for social work, but there are certainly words for helping and healing, which I have always seen as my role in this area.

Aboriginal cultures make use of many spiritual techniques in healing. In fact, I do not believe that healing can occur outside of spirituality. As Aboriginal social worker Michael Hart (2002) states, "Aboriginal philosophy and ways of knowing encompass spirituality to such a degree that it almost dictates the necessity of including spirituality in this approach" (p. 46).

Traditional teachings, ceremonies, rituals, stones, water, the pipe, herbs, sitting on the earth, fasting, prayer, dreams, visions, channelling, out of body experiences, touch, and food are all part of the journey to spiritual balance and well-being. In addition, those who are the helpers are said to be containers or channels for healing. Their abilities come from the spirits and live inside them through blood memory. The assistance that helpers or healers pass on to others is more spiritual than any other dimension. According to Ojibway helper Calvin Morrisseau (1998), "without the recognition of spirituality, our relationships are superficial at best" (p. 103). Thus, social work practice from an Aboriginal world view deeply involves spirituality and cannot be truly effective without it.

A significant area that I believe must be of great concern to social work is the connection, and confusion, between mental health and spirituality. I view the line between a spiritual and a psychotic experience as blurred. However, practitioners tend to diagnose some spiritual experiences and practices as "pathological symptoms of delusions, immaturity, regression, escapism, or neurosis" (Gilbert, 2000, p. 79).

In fact, what some clients see as spiritual strength is often pathologized by practitioners. Clients learn that they cannot discuss their spiritual beliefs and experiences with social workers for fear of being judged as "crazy." This has become a problematic situation for many Indigenous peoples. In Aboriginal cultures, a major focus of spirituality is the ability to communicate with the spirit world. There are many practices, such as fasting and ceremony, that are designed to help us enhance this ability. To hear the voices of spirits, then, is considered to be a strength. Yet in my social work practice, many Aboriginal clients came to me with the misdiagnosis of schizophrenia.

Another issue that concerns the connection between spirituality and mental health is depression. According to many Aboriginal elders and medicine people, the roots of depression are due to an "abandonment of respect for a spiritual way of life in exchange for materialistic things which overwhelm people, preventing them from looking at themselves as they really are" (Timpson, et. al., 1988, p. 6). This process involves losing conscious contact with the Creator and the spiritual parts of all life. The more this conscious contact is lost, the more our consciousness becomes numb. We lose our sense of where we are from and the direction in which we are going. Hence, depression is considered to be a spiritual illness and spiritual practices must be a part of the healing process.

Indigenous peoples have been practising holism, which includes spirituality, since the beginning of creation. It is only recently that some

Western methods are making space for incorporating these practices as it has been "proven" that they are helpful in maintaining good holistic health. In addition, it is clear that the problems of the world are not being solved by professional expertise. There is an obvious interest in self and spiritual development since books on this topic are the fastest growing reading materials in terms of non-fiction in both North America and Europe (Jayanti, 1999). Aboriginal peoples are leaders in including spirituality in the helping process. We have so much to offer in assisting in the healing of all humankind.

Around the globe, Aboriginal peoples are incorporating spirituality into research methodologies, healing, and activism. Aboriginal scholars such as Linda Tuhiwai Smith, Graham Smith, and Russell Bishop of New Zealand, for instance, are now publishing leading works in this area. According to Tuhiwai Smith (2001), decolonization for Aboriginal peoples worldwide must contain a spiritual element. She adds words of caution, however, about Westerners appropriating Aboriginal spiritual beliefs: "the spirituality industry will continue to expand as people, particularly those in First World nations, become more uncertain about their identities, rights, privileges, and very existence" (p. 102). The message is clear: spirituality is essential for all peoples, but we all must go to our own.

Do social workers want to include spirituality in their practice? According to a 1994 study on the topic, they do (Sheridan, et al., 1994). However, the vast majority of respondents (90.1%) supported this inclusion based on its relevance to multicultural diversity rather than on the belief that there is a spiritual dimension to human existence that needs to be addressed by social workers. This information is presented in this chapter in a positive light without any critique. Clearly, it suggests that many social workers are not comfortable with spirituality being on an equal footing with the biopsychosocial components of social work's current human behaviour framework. Even more troubling, however, is the implied notion that spirituality only applies to "multicultural others." When an area is assigned to multiculturalism, it means tolerance rather than equality. Thus, it lacks importance or seriousness. Furthermore, it excludes Aboriginal peoples who are not a part of multiculturalism. Certainly this area of social work needs further research from a decolonizing framework.

Education
As a "spirituality in education advocate," I would like to see social work programs including this topic throughout core courses on practice, policy, and research. Currently, no such program exists. Certainly, however, there

are social work educators like myself who bring the topic of spirituality
to the faculty table and into the classroom. I believe this is pertinent for
the benefit of both the clients and the students. The topic of spirituality
is an important dialogue that educators must have with their students.
We need to inquire about their perspectives. As consumers of our
educational programs and as future professionals, their voices are valuable
contributions. I also feel strongly that we have a responsibility to teach our
students about self-care in doing this draining work. In my community, we
refer to this as "help for the helpers." What greater help is there than the
spiritual kind?

In bringing spirituality into the social work classroom, all students
must be accommodated and included, which means that more than Judeo-
Christian beliefs be expressed. This can be addressed by looking to the
students themselves, as a dialogue on spirituality "must take into account
the bodies, minds, and souls present in the classroom" (Dei, James,
Karumanchery, James-Wilson, & Zine, 2000, p. 88).

The saying "build it and they will come" seems to fit my social work
teaching experiences over the past four years. In teaching a course on
becoming an ally to First Nations people, I bring our spirituality into
the classroom not only by speaking about it, but by doing it. This is
accomplished through the use of space, guest speakers, sacred objects,
offsite visits, and experiential learning. I have found most students to be
open, respectful, and enlightened by these other ways of learning and
knowing. It appears that students agree, as the class has grown from 10
in the first year to 44 this year. Of course, one could argue that students
would be receptive to spirituality in a course on First Nations issues
because, after all, we are "such spiritual people." So I decided two years
ago to take a risk and invite the spiritual dimension into the other courses
I teach—anti-oppression and human diversity, and advanced social work
theory and practice. To my joyful surprise, this has been met with interest
and tentative participation by many students. What I have learned so far is
that if I open those doorways by taking the lead in progressively speaking
about spirituality, it creates a safe place where it becomes "normal" to
have a spiritual dialogue. Some students then join me as leaders in these
discussions where they share what spirituality means to them. This is a
living example of how "the strength of our diversity is that each of us
brings some contribution to the table. When we begin to think in circles
rather than in hierarchies … we all gain from the knowledge sharing" (Dei,
2002, p. 6). It is during these moments when I know I am living my spiritual
name, which translates as something like "The Woman Who Passes On
The Teachings."

I am convinced that the teaching and learning about spirituality has a definite place in the classroom. It is very conducive to my understandings of how spirituality and traditional teachings are to be passed on. I have been taught that these teachings are passed on in a context of relationship and, therefore, trust and readiness to learn on the part of the listener. This face-to-face interaction is necessary because the teacher has a responsibility to both the teachings and the listener. Hence, because she knows the listener, she can decide what can be passed on, she can answer questions and ensure that the listener understands and knows what to do with the teachings. She can even ask that listener to mirror back to her what has been said. This is often the root of many Aboriginal people's reluctance to pass on spiritual teachings through writing—there is no relationship with or responsibility to the listener and what that person will do with the knowledge.

❖ SOCIAL CHANGE

Since spirituality encompasses everything in our lives, it cannot be seen only as an inward journey. As important as this is to an individual's source of peace, well-being, and strength, each of us has a responsibility to use our spirituality in creating a better world. How I value my life, value others and through this create a life in which I can be valuable to my community and the world is the connection that explains my existence.

This connection and its emphasis on spirituality is succinctly explained by Kurt Alan ver Beek (2000) who writes, "a sick child, dying livestock, or the question of whether to participate in risky social action are spiritual as well as physical problems, requiring both prayer and action" (p. 33). His description of Lenca "pilgrims" marching, "singing religious songs ... and blowing on their conch shells—all traditional means of calling villagers to worship" reminds me of my own community's spiritual and holistic approach to social action (p. 34). When Aboriginal peoples engage in social justice activities, our Elders, prayer, medicines, song, sacred fire, and the drum are always present as sanctions of the spiritual importance of the activities.

On a deeper spiritual level is the involvement of our Elders in their communicating to us blood memories that guide us in our current efforts for social justice. In discussing research with her Hawaiian Elders, Leilani Holmes states, "the stories of kupuna contain historic discourses about knowledge, memory, land, and social change. It would be useful to ask how living memory and the stories of Indigenous elders may eclipse histories taught through schooling and offer indigenous peoples a way to envision and enact social change" (Holmes, 2000, p. 49).

Indigenous peoples also have allies within the social change movement. Ver Beek writes about a large group of priests supporting the Lenca through their use of "scripture, tradition, and their 'pulpits' to frame the pilgrimage as a spiritual responsibility"(2000, p. 34). This action is, of course, embedded in Catholicism's liberation theology, which emphasizes changing larger economic and political structures rather than merely changing individuals (Dudley and Helfgott, 1990).

I like the term "a spirituality of resistance" because, for me, it links my individual and community spirituality to social change. This helps me understand that my spirituality is not meant to simply make me feel better in times of distress.

Spirituality as responsibility, then, involves resisting the evil in this world. The evil is oppression and all it entails in its harm to all creatures of the earth and the earth herself. This resistance has always been present in the lives of spiritual people. Historically, for prophets "a spiritual form of life had to include responsiveness to the hunger or anguish of those around us, as well as seeing and resisting the authority of the arrogant and privileged who controlled the kingdom" (Gottlieb, 1999, p. 26). There have been more recent resistors such as Martin Luther King, Jr. and Gandhi. There have also been Aboriginal leaders who have resisted colonization such as Crazy Horse, Louis Riel, and Leonard Peltier.

In today's world, it is the role of social workers to respond to the hunger and anguish of those around them. I argue that it is also the role of the social worker to resist oppression and become involved in political activism. As has been seen, this will best be accomplished within the context of action-oriented spirituality.

Within the profession of social work is a model that focuses on transformative change. It is structural social work, which is defined as viewing

> social problems as arising from a specific societal context—liberal neo-conservative capitalism—rather than from the failings of individuals. The essence of socialist ideology, radical social work, critical theory, and the conflict perspective is that inequality: (1) is a natural, inherent (i.e., structural) part of capitalism; (2) falls along the lines of class, gender, race, sexual orientation, age, ability, and geographical region; (3) excludes these groups from opportunities, meaningful participation in society, and a satisfactory quality of life; and (4) is self-perpetuating. (Mullaly, 1997, p. 133)

Thus, structural social work's primary focus is the recognition that oppression is at the core of social problems. It emphasizes that social work is to be carried out with, or on the behalf of, oppressed people. This perspective peels away the mythical belief system that if a person works hard enough and is good enough, then he/she can overcome any obstacle that life throws at him/her. In other words, the myth that all social problems can be overcome and all successes in life are achieved through individual merit alone. This is, of course, the myth of equality.

Structural social work is different from other social work models because it focuses on the structures in society (i.e., patriarchy, capitalism, racism) that oppress certain groups of people. Rather than blaming the victim for her/his situation, this approach examines the structures that create barriers to accessing resources, services, and social goods. Another way in which structural social work is different from other social work models is through consciousness-raising. Mullaly (1997) emphasizes that "much of consciousness-raising occurs in the form of political education whereby structural social workers, in the course of their daily work attempt to educate service users about their own oppression and how to combat it" (p. 171). Structural social workers advocate that educating oppressed people about their oppression helps with the empowerment process. Most importantly, it stresses that social workers cannot empower people. Rather, they can only assist with the empowerment process. Structural social workers work collaboratively with those who are oppressed to help them have their own voices heard.

Structural social work also includes a historical analysis of society. This understanding is critical when viewing the impact of the harmful experiences that oppressed groups have been forced to endure and how this applies to the present day.

This analysis is particularly applicable to the destruction caused by the colonization of Aboriginal peoples in Canada. Thus, a structural approach acknowledges that history has an impact on groups of people and that a people's past is linked to their present conditions of oppression.

Although structural social work includes this historical perspective in its analysis of oppression, it lacks any discussion of culture, values, and spirituality. This is problematic from an Aboriginal perspective, as it omits the significance of a spiritual foundation. Hence, with regards to spirituality, structural social work is no different from conventional social work. This is where I challenge it because it does not allow for this important aspect that is so significant to Aboriginal communities and other Indigenous peoples worldwide. While structural social work is anti-oppressive and focuses on social change, which is vital for working with Aboriginal communities, it does not incorporate spirituality in any way and, therefore, is not a holistic approach.

Despite acknowledging structural social work as beneficial to a critical analysis of oppression, I would not fall into the typical response, which is to adapt or amend the theory to fit social work with Aboriginal communities. Rather, we as Aboriginal social workers need to go beyond structural social work perspectives to those that focus on our own knowledges and world views. This would, of course, be firmly embedded in a spiritual base which is action-oriented.

❖ CONCLUSION

Social work practitioners and educators need to be willing to let go of and challenge the conventional assumptions rooted in modernity and risk engaging in more holistic ways of experiencing our world. At the same time, we must be prepared to deal with the consequences that go with doing anti-oppression social work and social change. It is spirituality that will assist us in experiencing our world and our work in a fuller way. It is also spirituality that will help us face and overcome the consequences that will be placed in front of us.

REFERENCES

Anderson, K. (2000). A recognition of being: Reconstructing Native womanhood. Toronto: Second Story.

Avalos, C., Arger, L., Levesque, E., & Pike, R. (1997). Mooka'am (a new dawn). Native Social Work Journal, 1(1), 11–24.

Baskin, C. (1997). Mino-yaa-daa: An urban community based approach. Native Social Work Journal, 1(1), 55–67.

Canda, E. (1988, Winter). Conceptualizing spirituality for social work: Insights from diverse perspectives. Social Thought, 30–46.

Canda, E. (1989). Religious content in social work education: A comparative approach. Journal of Social Work Education, 25(1), 36–45.

Damianakis, T. (2001). Postmodernism, spirituality, and the creative writing process: Implications for social work practice. Families in Society, 82(1), 23–34.

Dei, G. (2002). The resistance to amputation: Spiritual knowing, transformative learning, and anti-racism. Toronto: OISE/University of Toronto.

Dei, G., Hall, B., & Rosenberg, D. (2000). *Indigenous knowledges in global contexts*. Toronto: University of Toronto Press.

Dei, G., James, I., Karumanchery, L., James-Wilson, S., & Zine, J. (2000). *Removing the margins*. Toronto: Canadian Scholars' Press.

Dudley, J., & Helfgott, C. (1990). Exploring a place for spirituality in the social work curriculum. *Journal of Social Work Education, 26*(3), 287–293.

Gilbert, M. (2000). Spirituality in social work groups: Practitioners speak out. *Social Work with Groups, 22*(4), 67–83.

Gotterer, R. (2001). The spiritual dimension in clinical social work practice: A client perspective. *Families in Society, 82*(2), 187–193.

Gottlieb, R.S. (1999). *A spirituality of resistance*. New York: Crossroads.

Graveline, F.J. (1998). *Circle works: Transforming Eurocentric consciousness*. Halifax, NS: Fernwood.

Hanohano, P. (1999). The spiritual imperative of Native epistemology: Restoring harmony and balance to education. *Canadian Journal of Native Education, 23*(2), 206–219.

Hart, M.A. (2002). *Seeking mino-pimatisiwin: An Aboriginal approach to helping*. Halifax, NS: Fernwood.

Hill, D. (1995). *Aboriginal access to post-secondary education: Prior learning assessment and its use within Aboriginal programs of learning*. Deseronto, ON: First Nations Technical Institute.

Holmes, L. (2000). Heart knowledge, blood memory, and the voice of the land: Implications of research among Hawaiian Elders. In G. Dei, B.L. Hall, & D.G. Rosenberg (Eds.) *Indigenous Knowledges in Global Contexts*, 37-53. Toronto: University of Toronto Press.

Ingersoll, R.E. (1994). Spirituality, religion, and counselling: Dimensions and relationships. *Counselling and Values, 38*(2), 98–111.

Jacobs, C. (1997). On spirituality and social work practice. *Smith College Studies in Social Work, 67*(2), 171–175.

Jayanti, Sister. (1999). Valuing the future: Education for spiritual development. In *Experiencing the difference: The role of experiential learning in youth development*. Brathlay Youth Conference Report, Ambleside, UK, 42–50.

Kilpatrick, A., & Holland, T. (1990). Spiritual dimensions of practice. *The clinical supervisor, 8*(2), 125–140.

McCormick, R. (1995). The facilitation of healing for the First Nations people of British Columbia. *Canadian Journal of Native Education, 21*(2), 249–322.

Miller, D. (2001). Programs in social work embrace the teaching of spirituality. *The Chronicle of Higher Education, 47*(36), 12–16.

Morrisseau, C. (1998). *Into the daylight: A wholistic approach to healing*. Toronto: University of Toronto Press.

Morrissette, V., McKenzie, B., & Morrissette, L. (1993). Towards an Aboriginal model of social work practice: Cultural knowledge and traditional practices. *Canadian Social Work Review, 10*(1), 91–108.

Mullaly, R.P. (1997). *Structural social work*. Toronto: Oxford University Press.

O'Rourke, C. (1997). Listening for the sacred: Addressing spiritual issues in the group treatment of adults with mental illness. *Smith College Studies in Social Work, 67*(2), 177–195.

Pellebon, D., Anderson, S., & Angell, G. (1999). Understanding the life issues of spiritually-based clients: Another view. *Families in Society, 80*(3), 229–239.

Percesepe, G. (1991). *Philosophy: An introduction to the labour of reason.* New York: Macmillan.

Richards, P., & Bergin, A. (1997). *A spiritual strategy for counselling and psychotherapy.* Washington: American Psychological Association.

Sermabeikian, P. (1994). Our clients, ourselves: The spiritual perspective and social work practice. *Journal of the National Association of Social Workers, 39*(2), 178–183.

Sheridan, M., & Hemert, K. (1999). The role of religion and spirituality in social work education and practice: A survey of student views and experiences. *Journal of Social Work Education, 35*(1), 51–69.

Sheridan, M., Wilmer, C., & Atcheson, L. (1994). Inclusion of content on religion and spirituality in the social work curriculum: A study of faculty views. *Journal of Social Work Education, 30*(3), 363–375.

Sioui, G. (1992). *For an Amerindian autohistory: An essay on the foundations of a social ethic.* Montreal: McGill University Press.

Timpson, J., McKay, S., Kakegamic, S., Roundhead, D., Cohen, C., & Matewapit, G. (1988, June/September). Depression in a Native Canadian in northwestern Ontario: Sadness, grief or spiritual illness? *Canada's Mental Health*, 5–8.

Titone, A.M. (1991). Spirituality and psychology in social work practice. *Spirituality and Social Work Communicator, 2*(1), 7–9.

Tuhiwai Smith, L. (2001). *Decolonizing methodologies: Research and Indigenous peoples.* Dunedin, New Zealand: University of Otago Press.

Ver Beek, K. (2000). Spirituality: A developmental taboo. *Development in Practice, 10*(1), 31–43.

SECTION 3

SPIRITUALITY AND EMERGING AREAS OF PRACTICE

INTRODUCTION

JOHN COATES

In social work the re-emergence of spirituality has coincided with the rise in prominence of environmentalism and indigenization. As well, with the importance of spirituality becoming more widespread, its relevance is being considered in a variety of other helping contexts and situations (see section 2) and as a resource for the workplace. For example, the School of Business Administration at UPEI offered, in 2003, the first course in Canada in Spirituality in Business. In recent years, conferences, websites, and centres focusing on spirituality have been sponsored in Canada, not only by helping professions such as medicine, social work, and counselling, but also by schools of business. These developments, while presently on the fringe of mainstream social work, have found in spirituality a welcoming and mutually reinforcing discourse, which, if taken seriously, has the potential to significantly shift how we have come to both understand and practice social work.

The modern environmental movement is credited to have begun with Rachel Carson's *Silent Spring* (1962), and has been advanced by scientists (Capra, 1982); sociologists (Clark, 1989), cultural historians (Berry, 1988, 1999), theologians (O'Murchu, 1997), and philosophers (Naess, 1989), among others. The first major environmentalist publication in social work, by Marie Hoff and John McNutt, was published in 1994, but mainstream social work has remained resistant to widespread engagement. Many of the above writers critiqued modern society's assumptions that nature has no spirit or intrinsic value and is to be regarded primarily as a resource for human needs and wants. People are being challenged, as the modern story of progress, technology, and exploitation is being confronted, and people are questioning their relationship with nature and the role of the human on the planet (see Coates, 2003).

For many, the human search for meaning has begun to shift away from an orientation that is individualistic, materialist, and focused on personal salvation toward a holistic conception of nature, and of seeing humanity and human identity as embedded in nature. This search for meaning creates a strong link between spirituality and ecology/environmentalism. Dualism, exploitation, and attitudes of human superiority are replaced by interdependence, sustainability, diversity, and emergence as people seek what Berry referred to as a mutually enhancing human/earth relationship (1988, p. xiii). The search for meaning and direction has led many humans to reconsider the big story that governs their lives.

One of the hopeful steps that is occurring has been referred to by Besthorn as the "greening of spirituality" (2002, p. 6). He goes on to say that

> Ecological spirituality recognizes that humans share a common destiny with the earth. It celebrates an ongoing cultivation of a deeper identification of self with the whole of the earth. Humanity and nature cannot be separated, the sacred is in and of both. A deeply infused ecological spirituality acknowledges that we belong, from the very core of our physical bodies to the highest aspirations of our cognitive minds, to a constantly emerging cosmic/spiritual process. Humans emerge from, are dependent upon and shall return to an underlying energy or Divine presence pervading all reality. Nothing exists outside of this relationship cycle. (Besthorn, 2002, p. 15)

Not only are religions and their various traditions concentrating more attention on environmental and social justice issues (see, for example, the Forum on Religion and Ecology (Tucker and Grimm, 2005)), but so are professions such as social work. This is reflected in Ed Canda's comment, "When social work is infused with spirituality, promoting human fulfillment can become a process that creatively connects personal growth, social justice, and ecojustice" (1998, p. 104).

Spirituality's emphasis on inclusion and intimate connection with nature and ecology's emphasis on interdependence and diversity have created fertile ground in support of localization and indigenization—that is, the acceptance and valuing of traditions and practices that are rooted locally, and the adapting of mainstream practices to fit the local context (Barise, 2005). Indigenization as professional social work has become more international; the longstanding importance of cultural sensitivity has led to many efforts to encourage cross-cultural competence (see Hokenstad

& Midgley, 1997). It is here that mainstream social work's first tenuous steps into exploring the benefits of traditional knowledge and alternative healing practices have much to gain from local and indigenous knowledge and practices. Up to the present time, mainstream social work's attempts to deal with diversity have spawned several bodies of knowledge relating to, among other things, cross-cultural and anti-oppressive social work practice (Gray, Coates, & Hetherington, 2007). However, Gray, et al. argue that these models have frequently supplanted local, indigenous approaches and practices, resulting in many scholars critiquing social work's track record when working cross-culturally (see for example, Ling, 2003; Nagpaul, 1993; Nimmagadda & Cowger, 1999; Tsang & Yan, 2001; Tsang, Yan, & Shera, 2000; Yip, 2004).

In response to this colonization and globalization of knowledge, which reaffirms the West's view of itself as the source and centre of legitimate knowledge, (Smith in Hart, 2002, p. 29), Indigenous movements have arisen to promote the acceptance of local traditions and practices. This is reflected not only in efforts to pursue treaty rights, self-government, and self-determination, but also in efforts to utilize local healing traditions and practices. In many ways, the growth in interest in spirituality can be seen to reflect social work's growing cross-cultural practice (in Canada and elsewhere) and the increasing emphasis on understanding the client's world view and starting where the client is. The ability to integrate spirituality and religion into social work will increase in importance and relevance as the profession adopts holistic, empowerment-focused, and culturally appropriate approaches (Van Hook, Hugen, & Aguira, 2001, p. 3).

Spirituality and ecology, with their emphasis on greater acceptance of alternative world views, interdependence, holism, and the centrality of human/Earth relationships, have created an inviting space, as these views reflect a value base that is more consistent with traditional Indigenous forms of healing and helping. Diversity is celebrated, Earth is honoured, and inclusion promoted. It is quite understandable, then, that the social work literature on spirituality incorporates attention to sustaining the natural environment as well as celebrating Indigenous knowledge and local traditions and practices.

The chapters in this section by Coates and Zapf reflect how the literature on spirituality and social work attempts to bridge environmental concerns and spiritual realities, thereby enabling a reconceptualization of foundational knowledge and practices. Coates draws attention to the overlapping nature of deep ecological commitments, spirituality, social justice, and to the value of a new foundational assumption—one based on the interdependence of all things.

Zapf draws attention to urban/rural differences, and his arguments, which he acknowledges are informed by Aboriginal perspectives, challenge the disconnect between people and place. Our physical environment shapes and nurtures us, and these chapters challenge us to reconceptualize how we understand and live with place.

Continuing with the importance of place, but from a different knowledge base, Csiernik and Adams present evidence from people in a variety of professions and settings that indicates that work can be dangerous to one's soul. While the impact of pressures at work is quite familiar to almost of all readers, this study points to the importance that attention to spirituality can have in decreasing stress at work and enhancing personal health. The three chapters approach spirituality from different perspectives, but each emphasizes the importance that spirituality can play as a central aspect of people's lives and as a force enabling people to feel connected and whole.

REFERENCES

Barise, A. (2005). Social work with Muslims: Insights from the teachings of Islam. *Critical Social Work, 6*(2). Retrieved 24 January 2006 from http://www.criticalsocialwork.com/units/socialwork/critical.nsf/EditDoNotShowInTOC/554026006519AFC38525700F004B57B6.

Berry, T. (1988). *The dream of the Earth*. San Francisco: Sierra Club.

Berry, T. (1999). *The great work: Our way into the future*. New York: Bell Tower.

Besthorn, F. (2002). Expanding spiritual diversity in social work: Perspectives on the greening of spirituality. *Currents: New Scholarship in the Human Services, 1*(1), p. 339.

Canda, E.R. (Ed.). (1998). *Spirituality and social work: New directions*. Binghamton, NY: Haworth Pastoral Press.

Capra, F. (1982). *The turning point*. New York: Simon and Schuster.

Carson, R. (1962). *Silent spring*. Boston: Houghton Mifflin.

Clark, M. (1989). *Ariadne's thread: The search for new modes of thinking*. New York: St. Martin's Press.

Coates, J. (2003) *Ecology and social work: Toward a new paradigm*. Halifax, NS: Fernwood Publishing.

Gray, M., Coates, J., & Hetherington, T. (2007). Hearing Indigenous voices in mainstream social work, *Families in Society, 88*(1), 55–66.

Hart, M.A. (2002). *Seeking mino-pimatisiwin: An aboriginal approach to helping*. Halifax, NS: Fernwood Publishing.

Hoff, M., & McNutt, J. (Eds.). (1994). *The global environmental crisis: Implications for social welfare and social work*. Brookefield, VT: Avebury.

Hokenstad, M.C., & Midgley, J. (Eds). (1997). *Lessons from abroad: Adapting international social welfare innovations*. Washington, DC: NASW Press.

Ling, H.K. (2003). Drawing lessons from locally designated helpers to develop culturally appropriate social work practice. *Asia Pacific Journal of Social Work, 13*(2), 26–44.

Naess, A. (1989). *Ecology, community, and lifestyle* (D. Rothenberg, Trans. & Ed.). Cambridge: Cambridge University Press.

Nagpaul, H. (1993). Analysis of social work teaching material in India: The need for indigenous foundations. *International Social Work, 36*, 207–220.

Nimmagadda, J., & Cowger, C. (1999). Cross-cultural practice: Social worker ingenuity in the indigenisation of practice knowledge. *International Social Work, 42*(3), 261–276.

O'Murchu, D. (1997). *Quantum theology: Spiritual implications of the new physics*. New York: Crossroad Publishing.

Tsang, A.K.T., & Yan, M.-C. (2001). Chinese corpus, western application: The Chinese strategy of engagement with western social work discourse. *International Social Work, 44*(4), 433–454.

Tsang, A., Yan, M., & Shera, W. (2000). Negotiating multiple agendas in international social work: The case of the China-Canada collaborative project. *Canadian Social Work, 2*(1), 147–161.

Tucker, M.E., and Grimm, J. (2005). Religions of the world and ecology: Discovering the common ground. *The Forum on Religion and Ecology*. Lewisburg, PA: The Forum on Religion and Ecology. Retrieved on 20 January 2007 from http://environment.harvard.edu/religion/information/index.html.

Van Hook, M., Hugen, B., & Aguira, M. (Eds.). (2001). *Spirituality within religious traditions in social work*. Belmont, CA: Wadsworth Publishing.

Yip, K. (2004). A Chinese cultural critique of the global qualifying standards for social work education. *Social Work Education, 23*(5), 597–612.

CHAPTER 13

FROM ECOLOGY

TO SPIRITUALITY AND SOCIAL JUSTICE[1]

JOHN COATES

Many social workers, and individuals from all walks of life, are deeply concerned about the environment and the problems created by pollution, habitat destruction, and the exploitation of renewable and non-renewable resources, to name a few. The motivation to take part in action to protect the environment rests on many and varied factors including opposition to local destruction and concern for our species' survival. For many people environmental action has contributed to a deepening of their appreciation of the interdependence of all things; this experience can expand toward a deeper sense of one's connectedness to Earth, and to everyone and everything on it. This sense of connectedness provides a spiritual foundation for strong convictions in support of ecological and social justice. Concern for the environment expands toward a holistic conception of the relationship of people and nature, and can be a foundation for action against all forms of exploitation.

❖ INTRODUCTION

> The more deeply I search for the roots of the global environmental crisis,
> the more I'm convinced that it is the outer manifestation of an inner crisis
> that is, for the lack of a better word, spiritual.
>
> Al Gore (1992, p. 98)

In recent years efforts have been made to encourage social workers and social work students to become more sensitive to the relationship between people and the natural environment (for example, Besthorn,

2000; Coates, 2003; Hoff & McNutt, 1994). The goals of these efforts are to have social workers who are both environmentally aware and able to link environmental problems to the kinds of issues with which social workers deal. Considerable evidence points out that, if current patterns of environmental destruction continue, the quality of life as we have come to know it and our day-to-day social interactions will change (see Berry, 1988; Daly & Cobb, 1989; Meadows, Meadows, Randers, & Behrens, 1972).

This chapter argues that involvement in, and reflection on, activities to protect the environment can lead to a shift in world view. In the author's experience, the more deeply he has explored environmental issues, the more he has brought into question the foundational beliefs of our profession and society. Such a shift can be fundamentally spiritual,[2] as it draws into question our relationship with nature, the role of humans on the planet, and what is of ultimate value. The transition from a modern to a holistic and inclusive world view, can be a spiritual transformation[3] that opens social workers to a deeper understanding not only of environmental justice, but also of social justice. For social workers this awareness of interdependence can expand the scope of social work practice.

❖ ENVIRONMENTAL DESTRUCTION IS A SOCIETAL CRISIS

Few people in our society today are unfamiliar with concerns regarding what generally is known as the environmental crisis.[4] Individuals from all walks of life, including social workers, have heard about, for example, the decimation of Canada's East Coast cod fishery, the decline of Pacific and Atlantic wild salmon, climate change, air pollution, contaminated drinking water, habitat destruction, and the exploitation of renewable and non-renewable resources, to name a few. This awareness has led to global efforts such as the Kyoto Protocol, and local community action to address the consequences or the causes of ecological destruction. For example, St. Thomas University (2003) recently established, as have several other North American universities, an advisory committee on "matters relating to the implementation and maintenance of environmentally-sensitive choices in the management of the University's resources." However, in Canada and I suspect in the USA, initiatives to preserve the environment or to combat environmental decline, have not garnered widespread support. The reason for this rests, I think, on the reality that environmental destruction, just like social injustice, is a societal problem stemming directly from the values and beliefs (modernism) that are inherent in the structure of modern society.

The world view of modernism facilitates consumerism, materialism, anthropocentrism, and the exploitation of people and nature (see Berry, 1988; Spretnak, 1997). While modernist values have enabled humans to gain considerable autonomy as individuals and as a species, this has taken place at the expense of both human integration with the rest of nature and the viability of Earth's creative processes. "This detachment is like a 'virtual reality' where people have the impression they are living in a 'real' world when in fact it is totally synthetic and isolated" (Coates, 2003, p. 93).

Edward Goldsmith (1998) supports this conclusion when he argues that in modern society, all the benefits—what is considered real wealth—are human made. He states that "to maximize all benefits and hence our welfare and our wealth, we must maximize development or progress" (pp. xi–xii). Within such a belief system nature is but a context for the human, a background for the more important human events, a provider of resources, and is without innate value. Nature can be used and destroyed as humans devour or pollute increasing amounts of natural resources as we turn them into products for trade (benefits). Within modernism it makes sense to clear-cut a forest if one can earn more interest from the money invested from the sale of the timber than from sustainable logging practices (Rees in Suzuki, 1999); it is normal to dump toxic effluent into a river or the atmosphere if it increases a product's marketability; it is normal to pay poverty level wages and for people to work in sweat-shops if such practices enhance profits.

This reduction of almost everything to commodity relations (Polanyi, 1957) includes human relationships. For example, almost every government and large business has established departments of human resources. Goldsmith argues that what we see as normal is a system that is "totally aberrant and destructive" (1998, p. xv). He argues that just as an abandoned child who is forced to survive on the streets of a large city accepts that living in alleys and sewers and surviving by prostitution and theft is normal, so also do modern humans see as normal polluted rivers, air pollution, poverty, and watching violence in films and games (1998, p. xii). So pervasive is this system that most of us "moderns" see the emphasis on progress and growth and the related ecological and social exploitation as normal, as expected and beyond question (such is the nature of paradigms—see Barker, 1990; Kuhn, 1970). Modern society places almost divine value on economic growth, progress, and the need for an ever-expanding gross domestic product (GDP). Both nature and people are seen primarily as commodities—as resources with monetary value.

As a result, the world order is governed by the primacy of accumulation, and supports the removal of barriers to trade and the political monoculture of capitalistic democracy (Korten, 1995, 1999). The offspring of this ideology includes the exploitation of people and the environment, an increased gap between the rich and the poor, an increase in low-income employment opportunities, and a decline in the state's compassion for those who are disadvantaged (see Chossudovsky, 1998; Latouche, 1991, 1993).

In the absence of a holistic and inclusive framework, modern society and the social work profession have not been able to see that the root of exploitation is modernism and the industrial process that adheres to the mistaken belief that abundance will solve the problem of want (and of all other problems as well).

❖ THE POLITICAL IS PERSONAL

The motivation to take part in action to protect the environment rests on many and varied factors.[5] However, a major reason for a lack of widespread commitment toward environmental action stems from the modernist understanding of nature. Nature is regarded primarily "as the embodiment of resources for exploitation, management, restoration, and visitation" (Keefe, 2003, p. 2). Nature is seen as a location for human activity, an element to be brought under human control, and as a resource for human production. In modern society, nature is seen as "other." Dualistic thinking (see Coates, 2003; Spretnak, 1997), which leads to a disregard for the impact of human activity on nature and the tendency to treat all things, both human and non-human, as commodities, is one of the primary forces that contribute to ecological and human exploitation.

Technology, consumerism, and materialism have certainly led to many benefits, especially for people in economically privileged countries (see Chossudovsky, 1998). However, they appear to have become ends in themselves, as society has become so embedded in modernity that we have been unable to step back from it, evaluate it, and critique it. "Modernity acts as an 'ideological prosthesis' (Livingston, 1994) standing in the way of our unity with nature and supporting a belief in our superiority over it" (Coates, 2003, p. 58). For many people individual identity becomes a "commodity identity" (Keefe, 2003) void of concern for the larger environment and the impact of one's lifestyle on others. As a result, many people have limited perspectives on life's purpose and what is of ultimate value. For example, many young people see their life path as simply getting an education to secure a good job, so they can make lots of money, so they can buy more things (see Swimme, 1997).

While the society at large and the majority of its citizens have not yet fully recognized the significance and pervasiveness of dualistic thinking, many people are coming to the realization that what happens outside mirrors the thinking on the inside. The political is certainly personal (see Bricker-Jenkins & Hooyman, 1986). If we look carefully and critically at the environmental crisis and seek out its causes, we can see that the root of the crisis is situated in the values and beliefs of modern society, which have made everything a commodity and rendered economic worth to be the primary, and often sole, source of value (Clark, 1989). The patterns of exploitation that impoverish the Earth and create the environmental crisis can be seen as the same patterns, values, and beliefs that contribute to the exploitation of people. If ecological and social justice are to be attained, humanity requires what Berry (1988) refers to as a "new story," perhaps even a "radical re-storying" (Kenyon & Randall, 1997), that can eliminate the dualism and exploitation inherent in modern society.

❖ TRANSITION: TOWARD A HOLISTIC WORLD VIEW

When people become involved in action to protect the environment, and begin to reflect on this activity, they begin to challenge the values and beliefs of modernism. This challenge is the beginning of a transition of world views (see Harris & Morrison, 2003), from the dualistic, anthropocentric, and materialist world view of modernism to a world view in which "all in nature" is seen to have value, each in its own right. Within this holistic world view, humans act on their awareness and concerns about the impact of their behaviour. The separation of people from nature, people from each other, and people from the transcendent (however understood), are seen to be false dichotomies. In a similar way we begin to see the inappropriateness of the right of certain humans to dominate and make subservient both nature and other people. This transition toward a holistic conception of the relationship of people and nature, toward a world view in which humans and the rest of nature are seen as interdependent and intimately connected, is of such significance that it can be, at its roots, a spiritual transformation. To seriously confront environmental problems is to challenge deeply held societal and personal beliefs—our world view. The modern person is challenged to shake off our what Macy (1989) refers to as the "false self-concept" and "mistaken identity," which have us seeing ourselves as possessive, competitive individualists, quite separate from each other and the Earth. When people confront their sense of identity and sources of meaning, deeply spiritual questioning frequently follows. This perspective transformation (Mezirow, 1978) is a transition through which humans break free of a sense of superiority and separateness.

This consciousness reflects a deeper sense of our connectedness to Earth, and to everyone and everything on it. This growing awareness of the interdependence of all things challenges individualism and anthropocentrism, and can lead to a new understanding of human/Earth relationships and of the role of the human on the planet. The awareness of everything being connected and of everything being part of the creativity[6] of Earth's evolution can be a spiritual awakening that can provide a foundation for action against all forms of exploitation.

This "experience of profound interconnectedness with all life" (Macy, 1990) occurs when a personal sense of identity transcends separateness and self-interest, and becomes synonymous with the well-being of all life. People become empowered "to be partners in the unfolding prosperity and generosity of Earth's creative process" (Coates, 2003, p. 63). This cosmology calls humans to a new role that is in "solidarity with all other creatures of the earth" (McFague, 1993) and to seek what Berry identifies as "mutually enhancing human-Earth relationships" (1988, p. xiii). The transition can be understood as an awakening to our interconnectedness with all things, to what Naess (1989) refers to as "ever-widening identification," and what Homer-Dixon (2001) expresses as a "species-wide sense of humanity." It is an identity in which humans see themselves, along with all other life forms, as integral to Earth and as part of the Earth's unfolding.

However, consumerism, materialism, domination, and economism, for example, are so embedded in our culture that they are adhered to with "religious fervour" (Swimme, 1997, p. 12). Swimme argues that to move forward humans will require a "larger, vaster, and deeper context—a deeper cosmology" (1997, p. 12). An intense sense of personal connectedness can motivate people to seek an escape from consumerism's powerful hold. If large numbers of people come to the conclusion that we, along with all plants and animals, all mountains and rivers, are on a one-of-a-kind, terminal, creative journey—if we regard the Earth as a sacred[7] place—then we might have the insight and passion required to treat the Earth and all of its inhabitants as fellow participants in the journey of life.

❖ STEPS TOWARD TRANSFORMATION

The transformation, however, from a dualistic to a holistic world view involves "a profound change of mind and heart" (O'Murchu, 1997, p. 26): a shift from human-centred to Earth-centred, from individualism to individuality-in-community. The transition involves a shift in our thinking and in the internalized collection of stories/memories/symbols and their meanings. If we take this change seriously it is important, first of all, to challenge our sense of superiority and arrogance that sees humankind in control of and superior to other species. The modernist story of progress, technology, and economic growth (along with exploitation, centralization, and imperialism) supports ecological destruction and social injustice. No alternative is possible within its economic and materialist limitations. The drive toward development, along with attitudes of superiority, forestalls the realization of a long-term solution.

Secondly, we are challenged to discover how people can achieve fulfillment in the context of a healthy and thriving Earth. The understanding required to support Earth on its creative journey can stem from our ability to reject the self-centred competitiveness of modernity, and to identify one's own well-being with the well-being, growth, and fulfillment of all other people and all of creation. Such an understanding led Livingston (1994) to conclude that ecological destruction is a failure in self-development.

When a person develops holistic thinking and explores relationships and interdependencies, he/she quickly realizes the interconnectedness of all things; this leads to a questioning of the interconnections in one's own life. A sense of personal responsibility emerges when we begin to question not only the role of humans and our society but also the personal role that each of us plays. The consciousness of unity and interdependence can manifest itself in our reasoning, but, as Naess (1989) points out, it shows itself primarily in our ethics—our responsibility for our conduct toward others. Clark (1989), Earley (1997), Griffin (1990), O'Murchu (1997), and Spretnak (1997) point out that many of the personal attributes required in the transition can be understood as the consequence of spiritual development. These attributes include compassion and empathy for people who are different from ourselves, the loss of a self-serving and self-interested individualism, a willingness to act for the common good, and identification with all of nature, all of humankind, and Earth itself. As a result, superficial human wants would not necessarily be seen as superior to, and may be seen as subservient to, the needs of other species.

The transition is advanced through learning about exploitation, and acting against ecological and social injustices. At a societal level we begin to understand that injustice involves not only such things as large industrial pollution and disasters, but it is also connected to inequality arising from international trade agreements, international finance, agricultural practices, and lifestyle. At yet another level, we begin to understand how very small yet complex interactions have impacts of enormous proportions. For example, research reveals that a deficiency of folic acid (Picard, 2003) or the presence of trace elements of toxins (Colborn, Dumanoski, & Myers 1997) at certain moments in fetal development can cause severe and life-long defects in people and other animals.

The transformation or shift is realized when we feel discomfort in response to the abuse of the Earth and of people—e.g., loss of a fishery, extinction, homelessness, and famine. What was a commodity identity has shifted toward what Earley (1997), Elgin (2000), and Hubbard (1998) called "global consciousness," an awareness in which our well-being is tied to the well-being of all. We no longer view ourselves as separated, isolated beings. Human fulfillment is not limited to our own self-actualization (though this is indeed part of the process); it expands beyond self to incorporate a compassion for the needs of all people and species on Earth. It can lead to a conscious participation in the personal and communal struggle to live in the knowledge of our "common connection with the community of life" (Elgin, 2000, p. 114). As David Korten (1999) argues,

> Wholeness and coherence in one's own life and relationships are essential foundations of both individual freedom and coherence of society.... When we are spiritually whole and experience the caring support of community, thrift and concern for the well-being of the whole become natural parts of a full and disciplined life. One of the greatest challenges is to re-create caring communities that nurture our wholeness. (p. 146)

Such a deeply ecological spirituality can be understood to be the realization or experience of a connectedness to all things; and a sense of awe and wonder at the spectacular diversity, complexity, and creativity that exist in the life-forms and geology of the planet. It involves a world view that not only values all life forms and all of Earth, but sees humans as but one of the many species that have equal claims to existence and to fulfillment. A spirituality rooted in ecology incorporates an inclusiveness and interdependence that leads humans to challenge both the commodification of everything, and the foundational assumptions of modernism. It leads us to re-examine human identity, the relationship of humans to the rest of nature, and, most fundamentally, the role of the human in Earth's evolution.

An "authentic global spirituality will also have a profound sense of the divine consciousness that informs every species and every atom of the earth and universe" (Mische, 1982/1998, p. 8). Elgin captures this reality as he states, "When humanity consciously recognizes itself as a single community with responsibilities to the rest of life, both present and future, we will cross the threshold to a new level of maturity and a new culture and consciousness will begin to grow in the world" (2000, p. 131). This consciousness can lead to a search for sustainable economic and social practices and, in developed countries in particular, to an awareness of the need for voluntary limits on consumption and personal wants due to the needs of others and the Earth (Earley, 1997; Macy, 1990; Naess, 1989). Humans can find meaning as we transcend ourselves in response to the larger issues that history places before us.

A global consciousness that incorporates the well-being of Earth and of present and future generations is inherent in traditional indigenous world views: for example, the emphasis on harmony, wholeness, connectedness, and balance, to name a few (see Four Worlds Development Project, 1982; Hart, 2002). Such perspectives offer a wealth of understanding and practices that can become part of what Hubbard (1998) refers to as a "life enhancing global society" and what Macy and Brown (1998) refer to as a "life-sustaining society."[8]

❖ SOCIAL WORK

While there are notable exceptions (for example, Berger & Kelly, 1993; Besthorn, 1997, 2000; Coates, 2003; Hoff & McNutt, 1994), the social work profession overall has been absent from environmental discourse. Social workers commonly view social problems as quite distinct from environmental ones, and few social workers are in the front lines of environmental education, protest, or research. Large numbers of social workers, like most people in our culture, focus on human nature and social interaction, which are seen to be quite separate from nature, which is benign background for human concern and activity. As a result, the profession has generally ignored the physical environment. Many professions and industries share this lack of consideration, as "Western Eurasian" societies (Diamond, 1997) are embedded in the modern story, complete with its beliefs of progress, individualism, dualism, domination, technology, and materialism.

Social work developed within and functions within modernity, and has been constrained by its assumptions and boundaries. Professional ethics and conceptions of humanitarianism and human fulfillment for example, are defined within modernity. "Humanitarianism is operationalized as compassion for those who fall by the wayside of industrial progress, equality is viewed as an equal distribution of wealth, and personal fulfillment is seen to equal success with regards to ones' acquisitions and status in industrial society" (Coates, 2003, p. 58). While structural, feminist, and anti-oppressive approaches have attempted to deal with some of the problems that are endemic to modern society, they have largely focused on the unequal distribution of money, status, and power. For the most part, however, these positive developments have taken place without serious critique of the parameters of the world view within which social work functions.

Social work's narrow, human-centred understanding of environment (see Besthorn, 1997; Coates, 2003) has led the profession to use ecological metaphors while seeing the environment as almost exclusively social. Social work has lacked a deeper, more inclusive framework with which one can step back and critically analyze what is taking place in society and our professional lives. As a result, social work might be called a "domesticated profession" (Coates, 2003) that has been dependent on modern society for its existence and, in turn, has been limited by the roles and definitions it has been assigned.

Lacking a holistic and inclusive framework, the profession has not been able to see that it is the characteristics of modernism—consumerism, materialism, anthropocentrism, along with the industrial process itself— that reinforce misplaced confidence that abundance will benefit everyone. The search for long-term resolution of ecological and social injustice points to the need to move to a broader and more encompassing level of analysis. Such a level can be found in a global consciousness nurtured by a holistic and inclusive spirituality.

A more holistic conception of human/Earth relationships provides an alternative path for social work and all of humanity. Several writers who have explored alternatives to modernism from a variety of perspectives, such as evolution (Sahtouris, 1989, 1995; Swimme & Berry, 1992), anthropology (Eisler, 1987), philosophy (Naess, 1989), sociology (Clark, 1989), theology (McFague, 1993), spirituality (O'Murchu, 1998; Spretnak, 1997), eco-feminism (Mies & Shiva, 1993; Plant, 1989), and futurists (Hubbard, 1998; Milbrath, 1989), have arrived at a fundamental shift in values and beliefs. These alternative perspectives may provide social work with critical insight into its values and beliefs, as well as potential areas and directions for practice.

Within a foundation that stresses the unity and connectedness of all things, social work practice can begin to operate from an underpinning quite different from modernity, which "has been incapable of establishing human-environment relations that would guarantee our future on the planet" (Tester, 1994, p. 80). When we see ourselves as living in a sacred place, respect for our community and ecosystems become central features in all aspects of social work.

Within this global consciousness many social work interventions can be expanded and utilized (see for example, Global Alliance for Deep Ecological Social Work, www.ecosocialwork.org). The direction of social work shifts from that of fitting in with modernity to one of sustainability, and participation in the creativity of Earth. Inclusion, interdependence, and cooperation in community-enriching activities (see Naess, 1989) become central, as living becomes more celebratory, less isolating, and material. The manner in which individuals carry out their lives and interact with others, as well as how social workers carry out their professional work, become essential aspects of individual and social transformation. Issues of well-being, participation, and equality—long-standing concerns of radical and structural social work—rise in importance as social justice incorporates environmental justice. The well-being of each person is dependent on the well-being of others.

Such a foundation places importance on three general professional social work activities. The first of these is helping people to see all life as sacred and to see the importance of personal choices and actions. Empowerment, education, and consciousness raising are essential interventions to overcome powerlessness. People can be helped to recognize their skills and talents, along with their contributions and responsibilities to community (both social and ecological). More specific activities include the following:

1. Supporting personal and communal empowerment through which people see themselves as competent and capable of having an impact on their environment (see Saleeby, 1997; Dominelli, 1997).
2. Learning about the impact of personal behaviours and choices (lifestyle) on our health and the health of the ecosystems in which we live.
3. Modelling in our families, work and community, a culture of sustainability (for example, by walking rather than driving, buying local and fair-trade products, and taking David Suzuki's "Nature Challenge" [Suzuki, 2003]).
4. Choosing behaviours that reduce the tendency toward violence.

A second general activity that should be emphasized is taking a significant role in developing social structures that support the well-being of all life. This includes, for example:

1. Working to ensure that people have sufficient resources to meet their basic needs.
2. Supporting local organizations that work toward local control of local organizations for local benefit (such as community supported agriculture, community gardens, credit unions, and co-ops).
3. Establishing and preserving "green space," parks, and wildlife reserves that give priority to sustainability over profit.
4. Supporting community initiatives that promote inclusion and celebrate diversity.

A third general activity to note is challenging those structures that block individual and communal well-being. This includes:

1. Resistance and "holding actions" (Macy & Brown, 1998) through which people boycott businesses that, for example, produce weapons or fail to support fair trade, or whose practices exploit workers or endanger the environment.
2. Conducting research, writing reports, and supporting protests and letter writing to government officials in efforts to bring about policies and legislation promoting social and environmental justice.
3. Protesting international trade agreements that jeopardize the ability of governments to implement social and environmental legislation; and lobbying all levels of governments to insist that all household, municipal, and industrial sewage be effectively treated.

Social work is in a solid position for it to assume a substantial role in the movement to bring about not only social justice but Berry's "mutually enhancing human-Earth relationships" (1988, p. xiii). The profession has an understanding of human suffering and community breakdown, a history of individual and community interventions, and progressive critiques of social policy (for example, Mullaly, 1997; Pulkingham & Ternowetsky, 1996). However, to proceed toward a more active role in the movement toward sustainability, social work must progress beyond both focusing its critique primarily on the social and advocating only for adjustments and improvements to industrial-growth and market-dominated social structures. For example, in its educational and scholarly activity, social work can expose and challenge the foundational values and beliefs of modernity's industrial growth imperative and present an alternative. Such an alternative perspective values the interdependence of all things and the need for human actions to enrich and sustain, rather than be destructive toward, life on Earth.

The opportunity exists for humanity to assume a positive role in Earth's creative evolution. However, the potential to create a more hopeful future requires a willingness on our part to see and act as persons intimately connected with all life. A major challenge is to shift our source of meaning and ultimate value away from the individualism of consumerism and materialism, toward the community of life. This transition is one of such magnitude that, to be sustained, it requires a deep spiritual foundation through which we not only identify the roots of so much suffering and destruction, but also the alternatives that can lead people to act in support of the "not yet but possible future" (Mische, 1982/1998, p. 13). When humans see themselves, all creatures, and Earth in its entirety as sacred, we can become conscious participants in the transformation toward ecological and social justice. Social work can play a visionary role as it brings this potential to the attention of society.

NOTES

1. This manuscript is based on a presentation made at the Second Annual Canadian Conference on Spirituality and Social Work, Dalhousie University, Halifax, NS, June 4–5, 2003. Parts of this chapter are adapted from Coates, 2003. The author wishes to thank Brian Ouellette, and the reviewers at *Currents: New Scholarship in the Human Services*, for their helpful comments on earlier drafts of this chapter.
2. Spirituality is seen as integral to being human; it is the quest for meaning and purpose, to understand what is of ultimate value. It is different from religion, which is seen as the structures built around certain beliefs and values. Religion can be a means of spiritual expression and experience.
3. This chapter focuses on a spirituality that is inclusive rather than exclusive (Baum, 2003). This author writes from a deeply ecological spirituality, but other writers have come to similar conclusions from Aboriginal spirituality (Hart, 2002), feminism (Macy & Brown, 1998; Plant, 1989) and economics (Hawken, 1993).
4. The environmental crisis occurs as levels of consumption and pollution exceed the Earth's capacity to replenish and renew.
5. Motivations include survivalist fear arising from concern regarding the impact that habitat destruction and pollution have on people, and a desire to preserve the beauty of nature or to conserve resources for human use (see Eckersley, 1992).

6. This view sees the creative energy that informs the Universe as present in all things. It is panentheistic as opposed to a concept of the divine as totally separate from nature, or of the divine as existing only in nature (pantheism).

7. Sacred as used here can be understood as related to your spiritual nature. It may also be seen as an expression of the will of the divine, however this is understood. This evolutionary journey has been considered a sacred process: as "cosmic revelation" (Teasdale, 1991), the "primary scripture" (Berry 1988), and the "revelation of the Ultimate Truth" (Griffiths, 1982).

8. In contrast to the "Industrial Growth Society," Macy and Brown (1998, p. 16) see a "life-sustaining society" as one that "operates within the 'carrying capacity' of its life-support system, regional and planetary, both in the resources it consumes and the waste it produces."

REFERENCES

Barker, J. (1990). *The business of paradigms* [Film]. Available from Charthouse International Learning Corporation, 221 River Ridge Circle, Burnsville, MN 55337.

Baum, G. (2003). *Spirituality and social justice.* Keynote Presentation, Second Annual Canadian Conference on Spirituality and Social Work, Dalhousie University, Halifax, NS, June 4, 2003.

Berger, R., & Kelly, J. (1993). Social work in the ecological crisis. *Social Work, 38*(5), 521–526.

Berry, T. (1988). *The dream of the Earth.* San Francisco, CA: Sierra Club.

Besthorn, F. (1997). *Reconceptualizing social work's person-in-environment perspective: Explorations in radical environmental thought.* Unpublished doctoral dissertation, University of Kansas. (Ann Arbor, MI: UMI Microform 981157.)

Besthorn, F. (2000). Toward a deep-ecological social work: Its environmental, spiritual, and political dimensions. *The Spirituality and Social Work Forum, 7*(2), 1, 6–7.

Bricker-Jenkins, M. & Hooyman, N. (1986). A feminist world view: Ideological themes from the feminist movement. In M. Bricker-Jenkins & N. Hooyman (Eds.), *Not for women only: Social work practice with a feminist future* (pp. 7–22). Silver Spring, MD: National Association of Social Workers.

Chossudovsky, M. (1998). *The globalization of poverty.* Halifax, NS: Fernwood.

Clark, M. (1989). *Ariadne's thread: The search for new modes of thinking.* New York: St. Martin's Press.

Coates, J. (2003). *Ecology and social work: Toward a new paradigm.* Halifax, NS: Fernwood Publishing.

Colborn, T., Dumanoski, D., & Myers, J. (1997). *Our stolen future.* New York: Penguin.

Daly, H., & Cobb, J. (1989). *For the common good: Redirecting the economy toward community, the environment, and a sustainable future.* Boston, MA: Beacon Press.

Diamond, J. (1997). *Guns, germs, and steel: The fate of human societies.* New York: Norton.

Dominelli, L. (1997). *Anti-racist social work* (2nd ed.). Basingstoke, UK: Macmillan.

Earley, J. (1997). *Transforming human culture.* Albany, NY: SUNY Press.

Eckersley, R. (1992). *Environmentalism and political theory: Toward an ecocentric approach.* Albany, NY: SUNY Press.

Eisler, R. (1987). *The chalice and the blade*. San Francisco, CA: Harper.

Elgin, D. (2000). *Promise ahead: A vision of hope and action for humanity's future*. New York: William Morrow.

Four Worlds Development Project. (1982). *Twelve principles of Indian philosophy*. Lethbridge, AB: University of Lethbridge.

Goldsmith, E. (1998). *The way*. London: Rider.

Gore, A. (1992). *Earth in the balance: Ecology and the human spirit*. New York: Houghton Mifflin.

Griffin, D. (Ed.). (1990). *Sacred interconnections*. Albany, NY: SUNY Press.

Griffiths, B. (1982). *The marriage of east and west*. Springfield, IL: Templegate.

Harris, I., & Morrison, M. (2003). *Peace education* (2nd ed.). Jefferson, NC: McFarland and Co.

Hart, M.A. (2002). *Seeking mino-pimatisiwin: An Aboriginal approach to helping*. Halifax, NS: Fernwood Publishing.

Hawken, P. (1993). *The ecology of commerce*. New York: Harper Business.

Hoff, M., & McNutt, J. (Eds.). (1994). *The global environmental crisis: Implications for social welfare and social work*. Brookefield, VT: Avebury.

Homer-Dixon, T. (2001, September 20). *Can we solve the problems of the future?* Presentation sponsored by the Environment and Sustainable Development Research Centre, University of New Brunswick, Fredericton, NB.

Hubbard, B. (1998). *Conscious evolution: Awakening our social potential*. Novato, CA: New World Library.

Keefe, T. (2003). The bio-psycho-social-spiritual origins of environmental justice. *Critical Social Work, 3*(1), 1–17. Retrieved 10 October 2003 from www.criticalsocialwork. com/units/socialwork/critical.nsf/982f0e5f06b5c9a285256d6e006cff78/ 2a71f4a30d70ba5485256f0200425a7b?OpenDocument.

Kenyon, G., & Randall, W. (1997). *Restorying our lives: Personal growth through autobiographical reflection*. Westport, CT: Praeger.

Korten, D. (1995). *When corporations rule the world*. San Francisco: Kumarian and Berrett-Koehler.

Korten, D. (1999). *The post-corporate world: Life after capitalism*. San Francisco: Kumarian and Berrett-Koehler.

Kuhn, T. (1970). *The structure of scientific revolutions*. Chicago: University of Chicago Press.

Latouche, S. (1991/1993). *In the wake of the affluent society: An exploration of post-development* (M. O'Connor & R. Arnoux, Trans.). London: Zed Books.

Livingston, J. (1994). *Rogue primate: An exploration of human domestication*. Toronto: Key Porter.

Macy, J. (1989). Awakening to the ecological self. In J. Plant (Ed.), *Healing the wounds: The promise of ecofeminism* (pp. 210–211). Santa Cruz, CA: New Society.

Macy, J. (1990). The ecological self: Postmodern ground for right action. In D.R. Griffin (Ed.), *Sacred Interconnections* (pp. 35–48). Albany: State University of New York Press.

Macy, J., & Brown, M. (1998). *Coming back to life: Practices to reconnect our lives, our world*. Gabriola Island, BC: New Society.

McFague, S. (1993). *The body of God: An ecological theology*. Minneapolis: Fortress.

Meadows, D., Meadows, D., Randers, J., & Behrens, W., III. (1972). *The limits to growth: A report for the Club of Rome's project on the predicament of mankind*. New York: Universe Books.

Mezirow, J. (1978). Perspective transformation. *Adult Education, 28*(2), 100–110.

Mies, M., & Shiva, V. (1993). *Ecofeminism*. Halifax, NS: Fernwood Publishing.

Milbrath, L. (1989). *Envisioning a sustainable society: Learning our way out*. Albany, NY: SUNY Press.

Mische, P. (1982/1998). *Toward a global spirituality* (Rev. ed.). New York: Global Education Associates.

Mullaly, R. (1997). *Structural social work: Ideology, theory, and practice* (2nd Ed.). Toronto: Oxford University Press.

Naess, A. (1989). *Ecology, community, and lifestyle* (D. Rothenberg, Trans. & Ed.). Cambridge: Cambridge University Press.

O'Murchu, D. (1997). *Quantum theology: Spiritual implications of the new physics*. New York: Crossroad.

O'Murchu, D. (1998). *Reclaiming spirituality*. New York: Crossroad.

Picard, A. (2003, December 9). Folic acid crucial for mothers, research suggests. *The Globe and Mail*, p. A3.

Plant, J. (Ed.). (1989). *Healing the wounds: The promise of ecofeminism*. Philadelphia: New Society.

Polanyi, K. (1957). *The great transformation*. Boston: Beacon.

Pulkingham, J., & Ternowetsky, G. (Eds.). (1996). *Remaking Canadian social policy: Social security in the later 1990s*. Halifax, NS: Fernwood.

Sahtouris, E. (1989). *Gaia: The human journey from chaos to cosmos*. Toronto: Simon and Schuster.

Sahtouris, E. (1995). *Earthdance: Living systems in evolution*. Retrieved 15 April 2003 from www.ratical.org/LifeWeb/Erthdnce/erthdnce.txt.gz.

Saleebey, D. (1997). *The strengths perspective in social work practice*. New York: Longman.

Spretnak, C. (1997). *The resurgence of the real*. Don Mills, ON: Addison-Wesley.

St. Thomas University. (2003). *Draft terms of reference: President's advisory committee on campus environmental issues*. Fredericton, NB: Author.

Suzuki, D. (1999). *From naked ape to superspecies* [Radio program]. Toronto: CBC Radio.

Suzuki, D. (2003). *Nature Challenge*. Retrieved 15 April 2003 from www.davidsuzuki.org/WOL/Challenge/.

Swimme, B. (1997, June). Where does your faith fit in the cosmos? *U.S. Catholic*, 8-16.

Swimme, B., & Berry, T. (1992). *The universe story*. San Francisco, CA: Harper.

Teasdale, W. (1991). Nature-mysticism as the basis for eco-spirituality. *Studies in Formative Spirituality, 12*, 215–231.

Tester, F. (1994). In an age of ecology: Limits to voluntarism and traditional theory in social practice. In M. Hoff & J. McNutt (Eds.), *Global environmental crisis: Implications for social welfare and social work*, (pp. 75-99). Brookfield, VT: Avebury.

CHAPTER 14

PROFOUND CONNECTIONS BETWEEN PERSON AND PLACE: EXPLORING LOCATION, SPIRITUALITY, AND SOCIAL WORK

MICHAEL KIM ZAPF

Recent efforts to incorporate spirituality into the knowledge foundation of the urban-based social work profession have often presented spirituality as either an additional aspect of the individual client to be assessed or as just another resource for use in clinical practice. A rural perspective, with particular attention to the world view offered by traditional knowledge systems, suggests a very different understanding of spirituality that does not separate person from place. When the environment is understood as a conscious entity, a partner, then spiritual transformation must occur *with* the environment or *as* the environment, not *in* it.

❖ INTRODUCTION

Canda's (1988) influential definition of spirituality as "the human quest for personal meaning and mutually fulfilling relationships among people, the non-human environment, and, for some, God" (p. 243) has been the starting point for many discussions of spirituality in the social work literature. An integral component of this definition is the meaningful connection between people and the physical environment, yet this fundamental relationship quickly disappears, without explanation, from most accounts of spirituality in the social work literature. The following discussion examines recent efforts in the mainstream social work literature to incorporate spirituality into the foundation of the urban-based profession. I argue that most authors have presented spirituality as either one more aspect of the individual client to be assessed or as simply another resource for possible use in clinical practice. From rural social work (with particular emphasis on the world view from Aboriginal social work), a much broader perspective emerges that demands a very different understanding of spirituality that does not separate person from place.

I must acknowledge at the outset of this discussion that I have deliberately used grand generalizations to make a point and highlight the differences between two approaches to spirituality and social work. Of course, urban peoples are not homogeneous in their understanding and expression of spirituality. Similar diversity is apparent among rural groups as well. But I would argue that the perspectives on spirituality evident in the mainstream urban social work literature differ from the perspectives commonly found in the rural social work material. Some might contend that the differences explored here might be more appropriately contrasted as Western European/Aboriginal rather than urban/rural. Debatable labels or categories, however, are not as important to my argument as recognition of some of the dangerous and constraining assumptions underlying the treatment of spirituality in much of the Western urban mainstream social work literature.

❖ SOCIAL WORK AND *PERSON-IN-ENVIRONMENT*

A perspective of *person-in-environment* has been a popular starting point in the social work literature for some time, but urban practice and education have tended to focus more on the personal side of this declared duality at the expense of environmental considerations. The individual person or group has usually been the subject, the main concern, while the environment has been presented as a modifier or context. In the social work literature, one finds many more categories for understanding people than environments. We have tended to view the environment merely as a setting, a lifeless backdrop for the more important activities of human communication, growth, and interaction.

Furthermore, it is common in the mainstream Canadian and American social work literature for the broad notion of *environment* to be reduced quickly to the much narrower *social environment* with no rationale or justification offered (Zapf, 2001). Such narrowing of focus to only the social environment is not surprising given that many of the disciplines contributing to the knowledge base for social work (psychology, sociology, anthropology, economics, history, political science, psychiatry, physiology, and biology) tend to emphasize the individual and/or society over the natural world. I am reminded of comedian George Carlin (1990) who lamented that, sometime in his lifetime without notification or permission, several major changes had taken place: "toilet paper" had become "bathroom tissue," "dumps" had become "landfills," and "the poor" had become "economically disadvantaged." Sometime during my social work career, it seems "the environment" became "the social environment" without formal notification, permission, or even rationale.

Now there are calls in the social work literature for the profession to incorporate spirituality as part of the knowledge base and practice foundation. Just as we limited our understanding of environment to only the social environment, I am concerned that we may also inadvertently be limiting our understanding of the broad concept of spirituality to simply a component of the individual person. We could be missing a broad and exciting concept that holds the potential to expand our understanding of the profession's foundational *person/environment* relationship.

❖ URBAN SOCIAL WORK AND SPIRITUALITY

Given that most social workers are employed by government agencies, the historical separation of church and state in Western countries may help explain why issues of spirituality have long been ignored, neglected, or even actively discouraged by the profession. Seeking to improve its status as an evidence-based, scientific discipline, social work may have avoided spiritual issues that could be perceived as unscientific or difficult to categorize and use in practice. In the Western helping professions, religious and spiritual factors have often been linked more to pathology and impediments rather than seen as strengths or resources in a client's situation. For practitioners seeking to demonstrate professional competence with intervention techniques that are under their own control, the very scope of spiritual practice and understandings can be threatening. In spite of these trends, however, there is recent evidence in the social work literature of a renewed interest in spirituality. Drouin (2002) attributes this renewal to "a longing for profound and meaningful connections to each other, to ourselves, and to something greater than ourselves" (p. 34) that has arisen because the Western mindset of individualism and materialism has ruined the environment and destroyed community. He sees evidence of "growing spiritual longing" in social work practitioners, in clients, and in Western society as a whole (p. 36).

Almost all of the recent authors addressing spirituality and social work begin with making a distinction between spirituality and religion. The defining characteristic of religion appears to be some observable expression of a belief system through prescribed activity or ceremony (Cascio, 1999; Gilbert, 2000). Spirituality, on the other hand, is presented as a much broader concept as evident from Canda's (1988) previously quoted definition of spirituality as "the human quest for personal meaning and mutually fulfilling relationships among people, the non-human environment, and, for some, God" (p. 243).

Just as the concept of *environment* quickly became limited to the *social environment* in the social work literature, I see evidence that Canda's broad notion of *spirituality* as meaningful connection has been narrowed to simply an *internal quality of the individual*. Spirituality has been described as "the divine essence of the individual" (Carroll, 1997, p. 29) and "an innate human quality" (Faiver, Ingersoll, O'Brien, & McNally, 2001, p. 2). Tolliver (1997) concentrates on "the spiritual dimension of the self" (p. 483), supported by Drouin's (2002) assertion that "spirituality always begins by exploring one's interior life" (p. 38). Csiernik and Adams (2003) present spirituality as "an essential component of comprehensive social work assessment" and a "foundation of client and personal wellness" (p. 65). Sermabeikian (1994) offers a "theoretical framework for understanding spirituality within the individual" (p. 178). Cornett (1992) sees spirituality as "a legitimate clinical focus" arguing that the "psychosocial perspective" that became the "biopsychosocial perspective" must now become a "biopsychosocial-spiritual model" (p. 102). Ortiz and Smith (1999) similarly advocate a "social-cultural-spiritual context" (p. 318) for social work interventions. Recent inclusion of spiritual problems in the DSM-IV (Foley, 2001; Jacobs, 1997) is viewed as a new push for social workers to consider a client's spiritual values as a legitimate focus for clinical intervention, a potentially important aspect of the individual's development and behaviour.

Carroll (2001) describes two dimensions of spirituality: a vertical dimension or "relationship with the transcendent," and a horizontal dimension or "all other relationships—with self, others, and the environment" (p. 7). Later in the very same paragraph, however, she refers to the horizontal dimension as "the kind and quality of one's relationships with self and others, to well-being in relation to self and others, and to a sense of life purpose and satisfaction." What happened to relationships with the environment? It has been lost as spirituality focuses on the individual and social relations.

On the practice side, Bullis (1996) offers a list of spiritual interventions, 25 of them ranging from the sharing of religious books to the practice of exorcism. Faiver, Ingersoll, O'Brien, and McNally (2001) discuss spiritual problems experienced by clients and put forward their own list of 13 spiritual interventions. Frame (2003) also presents a series of "explicit religious and spiritual strategies for counselling" (p. 183) ranging from prayer and meditation through spiritual journaling, forgiveness, repentance, and surrender. Russell (1998) calls for research on the "efficacy of spiritually derived interventions" (p. 27), while Hodge (2001) finds evidence in reported findings documenting "spirituality's salience in a wide variety of areas" and concludes that spirituality can be a "significant variable in recovery" (p. 203). Cascio (1998) argues that the addition of spiritual content in social work education "need not force significant restructuring of existing classes ... the spiritual dimension can thus be presented as an additional aspect to be considered" (p. 530). It would appear from this overall perspective that spirituality is something to be used in clinical practice, another intervention technique added to the worker's repertoire, another variable to be considered for outcome research. Kasiram (1998) actually refers to "the use of God" as a resource in therapy (p. 172)!

Although the initial broad definition of spirituality included connections with the physical environment, specific treatment of the concept within the social work literature has ignored this aspect. Cowley and Derezotes (1994) specifically described spirituality as "non-local" (p. 478). Ortiz and Smith (1999) conducted a content analysis of the term "spirituality" in the social work literature and found "the common themes of interconnectedness between self, others, and sense of ultimacy as well as the individual's need for generativity and inner meaning" (p. 309); none of these themes mentioned connection with place or the physical environment. Canda and Furman (1999) also identified common attributes of spirituality (pp. 44–45), but, again, none of these made reference to place. They later acknowledge that rapport with the natural environment can be helpful for clients, but the "beauty and inspiring qualities of nature" are relegated to the margins as attending to "the aesthetics of helping" (pp. 192–193).

According to Deloria (1999), Western society can "attribute to the landscape only the aesthetic and not the sacred perspective" (p. 257) because we relate to the physical environment through technology. Cajete (1994) also lamented modern society's "cosmological disconnection from the natural world" (p. 25). In urban society, we view the physical environment as separate from ourselves, as an objective thing, as a commodity to be developed or traded or wasted or exploited, as an economic unit, as property. The dominant Western urban culture has been described as "hostile to nature" (Spretnak, 1991, p. 102) and antagonistic to any concept of personhood beyond individualism. Even if hostility is too strong a word, most of us now live, as Suzuki (1999) observed, in "the human-created environment of big cities where it's easy to believe the illusion that we have escaped our biological dependence on the natural world" (p. 45).

This urban neglect or hostility toward nature may help explain why our treatment of spirituality in the social work literature has been so limited to a narrow person-centred perspective. A rural perspective (especially from the developing literature on Aboriginal social work) offers alternative understandings of the connection between person and environment.

❖ RURAL SOCIAL WORK AND SPIRITUALITY

Rural social work has a long tradition of exploring spiritual connections between persons and the places they inhabit. Rural values such as sharing, harmony with nature, cooperation, stewardship, and coexistence have been contrasted with values of the dominant urban society, such as individual autonomy, private property, and manipulation of the environment for profit. In rural settings, a shared history and lifestyle lead to a rural identity rooted in a sense of belonging and a profound attachment to place (Cheers, 1998; Collier, 1993; Ginsberg, 1998; Johnson, 1997; McKenzie, 2001; Stuart, 2004; Watkins, 2004; Zapf, 2002). This profound connection between identity and place is perhaps expressed most clearly in the developing literature on Aboriginal social work grounded in traditional knowledge.

Traditional knowledge has been described as "knowledge and values which have been acquired through experience, observation, and from the land or from spiritual teachings, and handed down from one generation to another" (Wenzel, 1999, p. 113). Prominent in this definition is an element of the land, of the physical environment, of place. Sahtouris (1992) explained further how the traditional way of knowing "is not a science that stands apart from nature to look at it objectively; it does not eliminate the sacred, but integrates it. It fosters dialogue between humans and the rest of nature" (p. 4).

Some authors have attempted to include traditional knowledge or Aboriginal theory as part of the knowledge base for mainstream social work practice, but any assumption of traditional knowledge as just another theory base disguises a fundamental difference in world view (Zapf, 1999). The essence of this difference was expressed effectively by Morrissette, McKenzie, & Morrissette (1993):

> While Aboriginal people do not embrace a single philosophy, there are fundamental differences between the dominant Euro-Canadian and traditional Aboriginal societies, and these have their roots in differing perceptions of one's relationship with the universe and the Creator. (p. 93)

As a Western discipline with a focus on person-environment interaction, social work can be seen as problematic from the perspective of traditional knowledge because the person and the environment are still understood as two separate (although interacting) entities, with one (the person) commanding all the attention. In contrast to this Western notion, the foundation metaphor of traditional knowledge has been characterized as a perspective of "I am I and the Environment," (Ortega y Gasset, 1985), "I'm not in the place but the place is in me" (Suopajarvi, 1998, p. 3), or "the earth knows us" (Spretnak, 1991, p. 91). These Aboriginal expressions of "world-image identity" contrast sharply with Western culture's "self-image concepts" (Stairs & Wenzel, 1992).

Aboriginal cultural identities are directly connected to the physical environment, to the land and concepts of place (Cheers, 1998; McCormack, 1998). When inhabitants of a region have been there for many generations, their identity incorporates the place and their relationship to it. Graveline (1998) referred to this as a link between "geographical space and world view" (p. 19). As explained by Spretnak (1991), "a people rooted in the land over time have exchanged their tears, their breath, their bones, all of their elements—oxygen, carbon, nitrogen, hydrogen, phosphorus, sulfur, all the rest—with their habitat many times over. Here nature knows us" (p. 91). With specific reference to the Western Apache, Basso (1996) elaborated on the interconnectedness of place, spirit, and self:

> As Apache men and women set about drinking from places—as they acquire knowledge of their natural surroundings, commit it to permanent memory, and apply it productively to the workings of their minds—they show by their actions that their surroundings live in them. Like their ancestors before them, they display by word and deed that beyond the visible reality of place lies a moral reality which they themselves have come to embody. And whether or not they finally succeed in becoming fully wise, it is this interior landscape—this landscape of the moral imagination—that most deeply influences their vital sense of place, and also, I believe, their unshakable sense of self ... selfhood and placehood are completely intertwined. (p. 146)

Aboriginal spirituality is deeply connected with land and place. Holst (1997) observed that "a spiritual landscape exists within the physical landscape" (p. 150). It seems that some places within this living landscape hold more power or spiritual energy than others do, and these are often called sacred sites. Cummins and Whiteduck (1998) argue that Western society is not able to recognize such sacred sites or appreciate their power due to a number of cultural traits. These include "an emphasis upon the rights of the individual to pursue economic gain as opposed to the communal good, and a belief that humankind is separate from, as opposed to a part of, the natural world" (p. 12). In Walker's (1998) terms, such "portals to the sacred" are "geographic points that permit direct access to the embedded sacredness in nature" (p. 6). Peat (1994) also explored this notion of natural energy connected closely with a geographic sense of place:

> Unlike Western science, the importance of the landscape, and specific places in it, is a characteristic of all Indigenous science…. Within Indigenous science there is an association of spirit or energy with particular places, and it is important to visit these places and carry out ceremonies there…. This idea of the significance of place and the energies associated with it is common to Indigenous sciences all over the world…. Western science does not appear to have a corresponding concept. (pp. 265–267)

Aboriginal healing practices derive from this profound connection with the land, a living physical environment that is a source of energy and knowledge (Colorado, 1991; Ellerby, 2000; Hart, 2002; Neil & Smith, 1998; Proulx & Perrault, 2000; Rajotte, 1998). Rather than a passive background, the environment is a "sensate conscious entity suffused with spiritual powers" (Spretnak, 1991, p. 90). With specific reference to social work, Hart (1996) explained the Western and Aboriginal approaches in this way:

> Western models of healing separate and detach individuals from their social, physical, and spiritual environments, isolating "patients" for treatment purposes and then re-introducing them into the world. Traditional healers are concerned with balancing emotional, physical, mental, spiritual aspects of people, the environment, and the spirit world. (p. 63)

❖ PROPOSITIONS AND PREPOSITIONS

How far has the mainstream urban profession gone down the road of defining spirituality within the person and paying lip service to the natural environment? Can the urban-based profession consider a broader alternative, a spiritual connection between person and place?

There have been some encouraging signs in the literature, but they are rare and typically introduced, then quickly dropped as undeveloped hints of what might be possible. Foley (2001) presented the new spirituality as holistic, a "new awareness of the human within the intrinsic dynamics of the earth itself" (p. 356). The recent Spiritual Wellness Inventory (Ingersoll, 2001) included a component of connections with the natural environment. Canda (1998) called for social work to revisit the *person-in-environment* concept "in a dramatic way" because the person is "not separable" (p. 103) from the environment. Canda and Furman (1999) further challenged the profession to reconsider "what is the whole person and what is the whole environment" (p. 194), but the holistic models they offered still did not focus on place. In the set of definitions at the outset of their generalist practice text, Hull Jr. and Kirst-Ashman (2004) defined "energy" as "the natural power of active involvement among people and their environments" (p. 10), yet they did not return to this concept in the rest of the book.

The developing approach of deep ecology holds great promise in this regard. Consistent with Canda's (1988) broad definition of spirituality, deep ecology clearly rejects divisions "between the human and non-human realm" and suggests instead that self-identity derives from an ecological consciousness, a

> moving away from a view of person-in-environment to one of self as part of a "relational total-field."... Rather than experiencing ourselves as separate from our environment and existing in it, we begin to cultivate the insight that we are with our environment. (Besthorn, 2001, p. 31)

At first glance, this might be dismissed as a minor issue of semantics — substituting one preposition for another. Yet living *with* our environment is a profoundly different perspective and value position than living *in* our environment.

Ungar (2003) offers a fascinating discussion of deep ecology as a "more politicized environmentalism" (p. 14) that demands we understand "our place in nature" and come to value the natural environment for itself rather than simply for the resources we can extract and exploit. Observing that deep ecology has been "accused of being overly spiritual" (p. 14), Ungar proceeds to extract a set of anti-oppressive intervention principles, "axioms for theoretically sound ecological human services" (p. 15), with the natural environment serving as a model for a new egalitarian social order. This is creative and challenging work, but the natural environment appears once again to take a back seat to "individuals and their communities" as a focus for the new "social ecologists" (p. 20).

In the near future, I think it unlikely that the urban-based profession of social work, or the dominant society for that matter, will easily embrace a rural perspective, an Aboriginal world view, or a deeper ecological understanding of the profound connections between person and place. Does that mean that social workers are doomed to accept a limited notion of spirituality as a disconnected client characteristic, while the land remains a passive and lifeless background for human activity? Is it possible for social work to help Western society "learn to live attentively in place" or "to reinhabit" our world? (Spretnak, 1991, p. 82). Can we come to better understand our environment in spiritual terms, to appreciate and express and celebrate our connectedness?

In a simple yet profound question put forward by Haas and Nachtigal (1998), I found a possible starting point for rethinking social work's commitment to *person-in-environment*. Their question was "what does it mean to live well in this place?" I concur that wellness cannot be separated from place as easily as our limited notion of *person-in-environment* has pretended. But I am troubled by that preposition "in" because it maintains the dominance of human activity with the environment as secondary, a passive backdrop. As we saw earlier, deep ecology suggests substituting the preposition "with" for "in," thereby changing the fundamental question to "what does it mean to live well *with* this place?" This is certainly a step in the right direction, a notion of living in full partnership with a living conscious environment that sustains us and toward which we have powerful and respectful obligations for mutual survival.

Still, I wonder if we could even move beyond "with" to understand the question as "what does it mean to live well *as* this place?" — thereby rejecting the fundamental distinction between person and place in favour of a unifying spiritual connection.

REFERENCES

Basso, K.H. (1996). *Wisdom sits in places: Landscape and language among the Western Apache*. Albuquerque: University of New Mexico Press.

Besthorn, F.H. (2001). Transpersonal psychology and deep ecological philosophy: Exploring linkages and applications for social work. In E.R. Canda & E.D. Smith (Eds.), *Transpersonal perspectives on spirituality in social work* (pp. 23–44). New York: Haworth Press.

Bullis, R.K. (1996). *Spirituality in social work practice*. Washington, DC: Taylor & Francis.

Cajete, G. (1994). *Look to the mountain: An ecology of indigenous education*. Durango, CO: Kivaki Press.

Canda, E.R. (1988). Spirituality, diversity, and social work practice. *Social Casework, 69*(4), 238–247.

Canda, E.R. (1998). Afterword: Linking spirituality and social work: Five themes for innovation. In E.R. Canda (Ed.), *Spirituality in social work: New directions* (pp. 97–106). New York: Haworth Press.

Canda, E.R., & Furman, L.D. (1999). *Spiritual diversity in social work practice: The heart of helping.* New York: Free Press.

Carlin, G. (1990). *Euphemisms* (Cassette Recording No. 79 15934). Scarborough, ON: Atlantic Recording Corporation and WEA Music of Canada.

Carroll, M.M. (1997). Spirituality and clinical social work: Implications of past and current perspectives. *Arete, 22*(1), 25–34.

Carroll, M.M. (2001). Conceptual models of spirituality. In E.R. Canda & E.D. Smith (Eds.), *Transpersonal perspectives on spirituality in social work* (pp. 5–21). New York: Haworth Press.

Cascio, T. (1998). Incorporating spirituality into social work practice: A review of what to do. *Families in Society: The Journal of Contemporary Human Services, 79*(5), 523–531.

Cascio, T. (1999). Religion and spirituality: Diversity issues for the future. *Journal of Multicultural Social Work, 7*(3/4), 129–145.

Cheers, B. (1998). *Welfare bushed: Social care in rural Australia.* Hants, UK: Ashgate Publishing.

Collier, K. (1993). *Social work with rural peoples: Theory and practice* (2nd ed.). Vancouver: New Star Books.

Colorado, P. (1991). A meeting between brothers: Indigenous Science (interview with J. Carroll). *Beshara, 13,* 20–27.

Cornett, C. (1992). Toward a more comprehensive personology: Integrating a spiritual perspective into social work practice. *Social Work, 37*(2), 101–102.

Cowley, A.S., & Derezotes, D. (1994). Transpersonal psychology and social work education. *Journal of Social Work Education, 30*(1), 32–41.

Csiernik, R., & Adams, D.W. (2003). Social work students and spirituality: An initial exploration. *Canadian Social Work, 5*(1), 65–79.

Cummins, B., & Whiteduck, K. (1998). Towards a model for identification and recognition of sacred sites. In J. Oakes, R. Riewe, K. Kinew, & E. Maloney (Eds.), *Sacred lands: Aboriginal world views, claims, and conflicts* (pp. 3–14). Edmonton: Canadian Circumpolar Institute (University of Alberta).

Deloria, V., Jr. (1999). *For this land: Writings on religion in North America.* New York: Routledge.

Diaz, P., & Gingrich, P. (1992). Crisis and community in rural Saskatchewan. In D. Hay & G. Basran (Eds.), *Rural sociology in Canada.* Toronto: Oxford University Press.

Drouin, H.A. (2002). Spirituality in social work practice. In F.J. Turner (Ed.), *Social work practice: A Canadian perspective* (2nd ed., pp. 33–45). Toronto: Prentice Hall.

Ellerby, L. (2000). Striving towards balance: A blended treatment/healing approach with Aboriginal sexual offenders. In J. Proulx & S. Perrault (Eds.), *No place for violence: Canadian Aboriginal alternatives* (pp. 78–98). Halifax, NS: Fernwood Publishing and RESOLVE (Research and Education for Solutions to Violence and Abuse).

Faiver, C., Ingersoll, R.E., O'Brien, E., & McNally, C. (2001). *Explorations in counselling and spirituality: Philosophical, practical, and personal reflections.* Belmont, CA: Wadsworth/Thomson Learning.

Foley, M.S. (2001). Spirituality as empowerment in social work practice. In R. Perez-Koenig & B. Rock (Eds.), *Social work in the era of devolution: Toward a just practice* (pp. 351–369). New York: Fordham University Press.

Frame, M.W. (2003). *Integrating religion and spirituality into counselling: A comprehensive approach.* Pacific Grove, CA: Brooks/Cole/Thomson Learning.

Gilbert, M.C. (2000). Spirituality in social work groups: practitioners speak out. *Social Work with Groups, 22*(4), 67–84.

Ginsberg, L.H. (1998). Introduction: An overview of rural social work. In L.H. Ginsberg (Ed.), *Social work in rural communities* (3rd ed., pp. 3–22). Alexandria, VA: Council on Social Work Education.

Graveline, F.J. (1998). *Circle works: Transforming Eurocentric consciousness.* Halifax, NS: Fernwood Publishing.

Haas, T., & Nachtigal, P. (1998). *Place value: An educator's guide to good literature on rural lifeways, environments, and purposes of education.* Charleston, WV: Appalachia Educational Laboratory.

Hart, M.A. (1996). Sharing circles: Utilizing traditional practice methods for teaching, helping, and supporting. In S. O'Meara & D.A. West (Eds.), *From our eyes: Learning from Indigenous peoples* (pp. 59–72). Toronto: Garamond Press.

Hart, M.A. (2002). *Seeking Mino-pimatisiwin: An Aboriginal approach to healing.* Halifax, NS: Fernwood Publishing.

Hodge, D.R. (2001). Spiritual assessment: A review of major qualitative methods and a new framework for assessing spirituality. *Social Work, 46*(3), 203–214.

Holst, W. (1997). Aboriginal spirituality and environmental respect. *Social Compass, 44*(1), 145–156.

Hull, G.H., Jr., & Kirst-Ashman, K.K. (2004). *The generalist model of human services practice.* Pacific Grove, CA: Brooks/Cole.

Ingersoll, E. (2001). The spiritual wellness inventory. In C. Faiver, R.E. Ingersoll, E. O'Brien, & C. McNally (Eds.), *Explorations in counselling and spirituality: Philosophical, practical, and personal reflections* (pp. 185–194). Belmont, CA: Wadsworth/Thomson Learning.

Jacobs, C. (1997). On spirituality and social work practice. *Smith College Studies in Social Work, 67*(2), 171–175.

Johnson, S.K. (1997). Does spirituality have a place in rural social work? *Social work and Christianity, 24*(1), 58–66.

Kasiram, M.I. (1998). Achieving balance and wellness through spirituality: A family therapy perspective. *Social Work/Maatskaplike (South Africa), 34*(2), 171–175.

McCormack, P. (1998). Native homelands as cultural landscape: Decentring the wilderness paradigm. In J. Oakes, R. Riewe, K. Kinew, & E. Maloney (Eds.), *Sacred lands: Aboriginal world views, claims, and conflicts* (pp. 25–32). Edmonton: Canadian Circumpolar Institute (University of Alberta).

McKenzie, P. (2001). Aging people in aging places: Addressing the needs of older adults in rural Saskatchewan. *Rural Social Work, 6*(3), 74–83.

Morrissette, V., McKenzie, B., & Morrissette, L. (1993). Towards an Aboriginal model of social work practice: Cultural knowledge and traditional practices. *Canadian Social Work Review, 10*(1), 91–108.

Neil, R., & Smith, M. (1998). Education and sacred land: First Nations, Metis, and Taoist views. In J. Oakes, R. Riewe, K. Kinew, & E. Maloney (Eds.), *Sacred lands: Aboriginal world views, claims, and conflicts* (pp. 87–100). Edmonton: Canadian Circumpolar Institute (University of Alberta).

Ortega y Gasset, J. (1985). *Meditations on hunting.* New York: Scribners.

Ortiz, L., & Smith, G. (1999). The role of spirituality in empowerment practice. In W. Shera & L.M. Wells (Eds.), *Empowerment practice in social work: Developing richer conceptual foundations* (pp. 307–319). Toronto: Canadian Scholars' Press.

Peat, F.D. (1994). *Lighting the seventh fire: The spiritual ways, healing, and science of the Native American.* New York: Birch Lane Press.

Proulx, J., & Perrault, S. (2000). Introduction. In J. Proulx & S. Perrault (Eds.), *No place for violence: Canadian Aboriginal alternatives* (pp. 13–21). Halifax, NS: Fernwood Publishing and RESOLVE (Research and Education for Solutions to Violence and Abuse).

Rajotte, F. (1998). *First Nations faith and ecology.* Toronto: Anglican Book Centre & United Church Publishing House.

Russel, R. (1998). Spirituality and religion in graduate social work education. In E.R. Canda (Ed.), *Spirituality in social work: New directions* (pp. 15–30). New York: Haworth Press.

Sahtouris, E. (1992). *The survival path: Cooperation between indigenous and industrial humanity.* Proceedings of the United Nations Policy Meeting on Indigenous Peoples, Santiago, Chile. Retrieved from www.ratical.com/LifeWeb/Articles/survival.html.

Sermabeikian, P. (1994). Our clients, ourselves: The spiritual perspective and social work practice. *Social Work, 39*(2), 178–183.

Spretnak, C. (1991). States *of grace: The recovery of meaning in the postmodern age.* New York: Harper Collins.

Stairs, A., & Wenzel, G. (1992). "I am I and the environment": Inuit hunting, community, and identity. *Journal of Indigenous Studies, 3*(1), 1–12.

Stuart, P.H. (2004). Social welfare and rural people: From the colonial era to the present. In T.L. Scales & C.L. Streeter (Eds.), *Rural social work: Building and sustaining community assets* (pp. 21–33). Belmont, CA: Brooks/Cole/Thomson Learning.

Suopajarvi, L. (1998). *Regional identity in Finnish Lapland.* Paper presented at the Third International Congress of Arctic Social Sciences, Copenhagen, Denmark.

Suzuki, D.T. (1999, June 14). Saving the Earth (Essays on the Millenium series). *Maclean's, 112*(24), 42–45.

Tolliver, W.F. (1997). Invoking the spirit: A model for incorporating the spiritual dimension of human functioning into social work practice. *Smith College Studies in Social Work, 67*(3), 477–486.

Ungar, M. (2003). The professional social ecologist: Social work redefined. *Canadian Social Work Review, 20*(1), 5–23.

Walker, D.E. (1998). Sacred geography in northwestern North America. Retrieved 11 April 2002 from www.indigenouspeople.org/natlit/sacred.htm.

Watkins, T.R. (2004). Natural helping networks: Assets for rural communities. In T.L. Scales & C.L. Streeter (Eds.), *Rural social work: Building and sustaining community assets* (pp. 65–76). Belmont, CA: Brooks/Cole/Thomson Learning.

Wenzel, G.W. (1999).Traditional ecological knowledge and Inuit: Reflections on TEK research and ethics. *Arctic, 52*(2), 113–124.

Zapf, M.K. (1999). Location and knowledge-building: Exploring the fit of western social work with traditional knowledge. *Native Social Work Journal, 2*(1), 139–153.

Zapf, M.K. (2001). The geographic base of Canadian social welfare. In J.C. Turner & F.J. Turner (Eds.), *Canadian social welfare* (4th ed., pp. 67–79). Toronto: Pearson Education Canada.

Zapf, M.K. (2002). Geography and Canadian social work practice. In F.J. Turner (Ed.). *Social work practice: A Canadian perspective* (2nd ed., pp. 69–83). Toronto: Pearson Education Canada.

CHAPTER 15

SPIRITUALITY, STRESS, AND WORK

RICK CSIERNIK AND DAVID W. ADAMS

Work is love made visible. And if you cannot work with love but only with distaste, it is better that you should leave your work and sit at the gate of the temple and take alms of those who work with joy. (Gibran, 1965, p. 28)

The role of stressful life and workplace events in creating illness has been well documented (Eakin, 1992; Hamilton-Smith, 1992; Hyatt, 2002; Karasek & Theorell, 1990; Noer, 1993; Shehadeh & Shain, 1990). Historically, Employee Assistance Programs have focused upon psychosocial issues, while physical health maintenance has been the primary focus of wellness initiatives. However, the idea of wellness is more than that, it is a synthesis of five areas of health: physical, psychological, social, intellectual, and spiritual (Csiernik, 1995a; Sefton, et al., 1992). Not surprisingly, spirituality has been the dimension that has been studied the least empirically and that has been the most difficult to openly discuss in the context of work. However, there has been a growing interest in what had traditionally been the most neglected aspect of wellness, and in its relationship to both work and the workplace (Adams & Csiernik, 2001, 2002; Ambrose, 1997; Conger, 1994; Hawley, 1993; Lee & Zemke, 1993; Neal, 2000). Fox (1994) has even gone as far as to claim that work is an expression of our soul and our inner being and that our work is an expression of our spirituality. Percy (1997) has gone a step further and compared his six stations of the inner journey that explore personal spiritual development with the spiritual journey of corporations.

Morgan (1993) states that spirituality entails the ability to transcend the physical limits of time and space, the ability to reason, to will, be creative, and to seek meaning. Spirituality also includes our perception of ourselves, an adherence to values, of being ethical, and being connected with others, while maintaining a belief system that typically includes some religious dimension. It is an evolutionary process that necessitates a striving for transcendental values and meanings, and discovering knowledge of an ultimate reality. Anderson and Worthen (1997) suggest that spirituality is premised upon three critical factors:

1. an awareness of the existence of a supreme power or force;
2. the innate yearning of people for connection with this divine entity; and,
3. the belief that this power is interested in humans and acts upon this relationship in order to promote changes that benefit humans.

However, downsizing, reorganizations and restructuring have left many employees devoid of energy and no longer feeling connected (Laabs, 1995). During this time many organizations attempted to respond by enhancing employee participation and fostering employee empowerment. Initiatives included TQM—total quality management—quality control circles, and introducing quality of life working programs (Csiernik, 1995b). Elmes and Smith (2001) claim that empowering employees to participate in fulfilling the mission and vision of the organization has distinct spiritual overtones and that empowerment has a spiritual idealism that can be also seen in Christian and utopian thinking. It is an attempt to help reconnect.

However, there has been little empirical study of the relationship of spirituality to the workplace or to workplace stress. Holder and Vaux (1998) reported that spirituality had no relationship to job satisfaction in their study of African Americans working in predominantly White work settings. However, we believe from the anecdotal discussions of our clients and based upon recent qualitative work (Neal, 2000) that spirituality is an important factor is dealing with workplace stress and is a prominent component of wellness. Thus, we undertook this exploratory study to examine if spirituality did contribute to creating wellness through mitigating stress.

❖ METHODOLOGY

The study's sample was drawn from participants attending a Death and Dying conference held in June 2000, in London, Ontario, Canada.

A questionnaire was included in each delegate's package. Of the 449 attendees, 154 (34.3%) returned questionnaires prior to the end of the conference. The 154 respondents completed a six-page instrument consisting of four sections. The initial section asked individuals their occupation and their workplace along with inquiring about the extent to which workplace stress had an impact on their spirituality and the degree to which their spirituality helped to minimize the stress that they felt at work. The latter two items used a five-point Likert scale. Section two was Peele's (1988) *Organization Health Climate Chart*. This is a ten-item true/false instrument used to assess a workplace's health. The scale runs from "this is a good model of a healthy organization" (1) to "this organization is risking significant health consequences" (5). Section three was Forbes' (1979) 20-item yes/no instrument examining *Signs of an Over-Stressed Organization*. Total scores are ranked from one to four with one (a score from one to five of the 20 items) indicating that a healthy organizational climate exists to four (a score of 16 to 20) indicating that the organization is in danger of not functioning. The final component of the survey distributed to conference participants was the 21-item *JAREL Spiritual Well-Being Scale* developed by Hunglemann, Kenkel-Rossi, Klassen, and Stollenwerk (1987). The *JAREL* scale consists of 21 items each on a six-point Likert scale with a maximum possible score of 126.

❖ RESULTS

Of the 154 respondents 57 (37.0%) were clergy, 17 (11.0%) were nurses, 13 (8.4%) educators, 11 (7.1%) social workers or related counselling professionals; another 11 (7.1%) were students while 10 (6.5%) were bereavement counsellors, 9 (5.8%) were volunteers and 8 worked in pastoral care (5.2%). The remaining 18 persons identified themselves as administrators (6), hospice workers (5), physicians (4) and funeral directors (3) (Table 15.1). The workplaces of the survey respondents were nearly as varied as were their occupation categories. The largest number of survey respondents, 44 (28.6%), worked in a hospital setting, followed by 36 (23.4%) persons who worked in a community-based health or social service organization. Twenty-three (14.9%) worked in a church while 18 (11.7%) were based in a hospice, 11 (7.1%) in a post-secondary institution, 6 (3.9%) in a funeral home, and 4 (2.6%) in private practice (Table 15.2).

The eight pastoral care workers had the highest average score (112.5) on the *JAREL Spiritual Well-Being Scale* followed by clergy (109.5), educators (108.8), several of whom were clergy as well, physicians (108.0), and social

Table 15.1 Responses by occupation

Occupation	n	JAREL spirituality well-being scale	Work stress impact on spirituality	Spirituality's role in decreasing work stress	Organization health climate	Level of workplace stress
Clergy	57	109.5	3.6	4.1	2.6	1.7
Nurse	17	98.5	3.4	3.7	3.1	2.2
Educator	13	108.8	2.9	3.9	2.6	2.0
Social worker/counsellor	11	106.6	3.5	4.3	3.3	2.0
Student	11	102.4	3.6	3.6	2.4	2.2
Bereavement counsellor	10	104.2	3.4	4.1	2.4	2.1
Volunteer	9	105.5	3.2	3.8	3.1	2.0
Pastoral care worker	8	112.5	2.6	4.3	2.6	1.4
Administrator	6	102.3	3.7	4.5	1.8	2.0
Hospice worker	5	93.8	3.2	3.8	2.0	1.0
Physician	4	108.0	4.0	4.5	2.8	1.3
Funeral director	3	96.0	3.7	3.0	3.7	1.3
Total	154					
Mean		106.3	3.5	4.0	2.7	1.8
Maximum score		126	5	5	5	4

Table 15.2 Responses by workplace

Workplace	n	JAREL spirituality well-being scale	Work stress impact on spirituality	Spirituality's role in decreasing work stress	Organization health climate	Level of workplace stress
Hospital	44	107.4	3.4	4.2	2.8	1.7
Community-based agency	36	103.9	3.4	4.1	2.7	2.1
Church	23	109.3	3.7	3.6	2.6	1.9
Hospice	18	104.9	3.3	3.9	2.4	1.4
College/university	11	106.3	3.0	3.9	2.6	1.8
Funeral home	6	105.8	3.8	3.8	3.0	1.7
Private practice	4	108.3	3.3	4.3	2.5	2.5
Other	12	105.2	3.7	3.0	2.6	2.1
Total	154					
Mean		106.3	3.5	4.0	2.7	1.8
Maximum score		126	5	5	5	4

workers (106.6). The groups that had the lowest mean scores were hospice workers (93.8), funeral directors (96.0), and nurses (98.5), though funeral directors (n = 3) and hospice workers (n = 5) were among the occupational groups with the fewest respondents. Groups scoring above the mean when asked if workplace stress had an impact on their spirituality were physicians (4.0), funeral directors (3.7), administrators (3.7), clergy (3.6) and students (3.6). The lowest averages were those of pastoral care workers (2.6) and educators (2.9) (Table 15.1).

When asked is their spirituality helped to minimize stress felt at work, the groups that ranked highest were physicians (4.5), administrators (4.5), social workers (4.3), pastoral care workers (4.3), clergy (4.1), and bereavement counsellors (4.1). The remaining groups were also just slightly below the mean of 4.0, except for the three funeral directors whose average score for the question was 3.0 (Table 15.1).

Those who rated their organization least healthy on the *Organizational Health Climate Chart* were funeral directors (3.7), social workers (3.3), and nurses (3.1). Interestingly it was hospice workers (2.0) along with administrators (1.8) who rated their organizations as being unusually healthy. There was not a great deal of variance between occupational groups on the *Signs of an Over-Stressed Organization* scale with hospice workers (1.0), funeral directors (1.3), physicians (1.3), and pastoral care workers (1.4) being at the low end, while nurses had the highest mean score of 2.2. Based on the summaries presented in Table 15.1, hospice workers, clergy, and those working in pastoral care perceived their organizations as producing the least amount of stress while social workers and nurses found their organizations the most stressful.

Not surprisingly, those whose primary place of work was a church had the highest score (109.3) on the *JAREL Spiritual Well-Being Scale* followed by those in private practice (108.3) and those employed by a hospital (107.4). The workplaces that had the lowest mean scores were community-based health and social service agencies (103.9) and hospices (104.9). Workplace sectors that had their spirituality most negatively affected by workplace stress were funeral homes (3.8) and churches (3.7), while the least impact was reported by those working at post-secondary institutions (3.0), in private practice (3.3), and at hospices (3.3) (Table 15.2).

When asked is their spirituality helped to minimize stress felt at work, the workplaces with the greatest scores were private practice settings (4.3), hospitals (4.2), and community-based health and social service agencies (4.1). Those employed by churches had the lowest score (3.6) on this question, followed by employees of hospices (3.9), colleges and universities

(3.9), and funeral homes (3.8), the latter three all just barely falling below the mean of 4.0 (Table 15.2).

Those who rated their organization least healthy on the *Organizational Health Climate Chart* worked in funeral homes (3.0), hospitals (2.8), or community-based agencies (2.7). The remaining scores all fell under the mean of 2.7 and were also all clustered closely together with the group reporting the lowest score being those employed by hospices (2.4). Similarly, those working at a hospice rated their organization as having the least stress based on the *Signs of an Over-Stressed Organization* scale (1.4). What was more interesting was that the workplaces also indicating a positive emotional climate were funeral homes (1.7), hospitals (1.7), and colleges and universities (1.8). Churches (1.9), community health and social service agencies (2.1), and private practice (2.5) all scored above the mean of 1.8. There was no consistent pattern that emerged in Table 15.2 between place of work and the questions asked and scales completed other than the fact hospices again emerged as the organizations that created the least amount of stress for their employees followed by post-secondary institutions.

However, some interesting correlations were discovered. There was a positive correlation (r = .523, 0.01 significance level) between the *JAREL Spiritual Well-Being Scale* and the perceived role of spirituality on minimizing work stress. Individuals who believed that their spirituality was a mitigating factor on the stress they felt at work tended to have higher spiritual well-being scores than those who did not perceive their spirituality as an ameliorating factor. There was also a weak negative correlation (r = –.164, 0.05 significance level) between the *JAREL* score and *Signs of an Over-Stressed Organization* score. Thus, those who scored higher on the *JAREL* scale also tended to perceive their organizations as having a more positive emotional climate. The degree to which spirituality mitigated the stress felt at work was also negatively correlated weakly with the *Signs of an Over-Stressed Organization* scale (r = –.185, 0.05 significance) and with the *Organizational Health Climate Chart* (r = –1.86, 0.05 significance).

❖ DISCUSSION

> In fact, some feel that work is destructive to their souls. (Neal, 2000, p. 1318)

Spirituality has historically been seen as an inner source of strength especially when dealing with uncertainty and chaos in one's personal life. That it should also help in ameliorating workplace stress and be important in one's working life should then be no surprise. However, it remains that organizations still have difficulty incorporating the idea of spirituality into their workplace wellness and Employee Assistance Programs. This is despite the supposition that "spirituality-in-business suggests that a spiritual basis for working enables workers to feel whole and complete and their organizations to prosper" (Elmes & Smith, 2001, p. 35).

This study's results indicate that one's spirituality does help decrease the perception of workplace stressors and thus contributes to a sense of wellness. Study participants who indicated a greater sense of spirituality perceived lower levels of workplace stress than less spiritually inclined colleagues. It was also interesting to note that those with a greater sense of spirituality also perceived their organizations as being healthier. Not surprisingly, the majority of respondents also indicated that workplace stress had a negative impact on their spiritual health. The two correlations between spirituality and the *Signs of an Overstress Organization* scale and *Organizational Health Climate Chart* further add to the belief that a strong sense of spirituality contributes to health and is valuable in counteracting workplace stressors. The challenge then becomes how to introduce, channel, and better use spirituality in the workplace to enhance our Employee Assistance Programs and to increase worker and workplace wellness.

REFERENCES

Adams, D.W., & Csiernik, R. (2001). A beginning examination of the spirituality of health care practitioners. In R. Gilbert (Ed.), *Health Care and Spirituality: Listening, Assessing, Caring*. Amityville, NY: Baywood Books.

Adams, D.W., & Csiernik, R. (2002). Seeking the lost spirit: Understanding spirituality and restoring it to the workplace. *Employee Assistance Quarterly, 17*(4), 31–44.

Ambrose, D. (1997). *Healing the downsized organization*. New York: Harmony Books.

Anderson, D.A., & Worthen, D. (1997). Exploring a fourth dimension: Spirituality as a resource for the couple therapist. *Journal of Marital and Family Therapy, 23*(1), 2–12.

Conger, J. (Ed.). (1994). *Spirit at work: Discovering the spirituality in leadership*. San Francisco: Jossey-Bass.

Csiernik, R. (1995a). Wellness, work, and employee assistance programming. *Employee Assistance Quarterly, 11*(2), 1-12.

Csiernik, R. (1995b). *The development of an integrated model of occupational assistance*. Toronto: University of Toronto.

Eakin, J. (1992). Psychosocial aspects of workplace health. Canadian Centre For Occupational Health and Safety, April 8-10, Hamilton, ON.

Elmes, M. & Smith, C. (2001). Moved by the spirit: Contextualizing workplace empowerment in American spiritual ideals. *Journal of Applied Behavioral Science, 37*(1), 33–50.

Forbes, R. (1979). *Corporate Stress.* Garden City, NY: Doubleday.

Fox, M. (1994). *The reinvention of work: A new vision of livelihood for our time.* San Francisco: Harper Collins.

Gibran, K. (1965). *The Prophet.* New York: Alfred A. Knopf.

Hamilton-Smith, E. (1992, March 12–13). *Why the word wellness?* Paper presented at the National Recreation and Wellness Conference, Coburg, Australia.

Hawley, J. (1993). *Reawakening the spirit in work: The power of Dharmic management.* San Francisco: Berrett-Koehler.

Holder, J., & Vaux, A. (1998). African American professionals: Coping with occupational stress in predominantly White work environments. *Journal of Vocational Behavior, 53*(3), 315–333.

Hungelmann, J., Kenkel-Rossi, E., Klassen, L., & Stollenwerk, R. (1987). *JAREL Spiritual Well-Being Scale.* Milwaukee: Marquette University College of Nursing.

Hyatt, L. (2002, January). Job stress: Have we reached the breaking point? *Workplace Today, 14–16,* 37.

Karasek, R., and Theorell, T. (1990). *Healthy work: Stress, productivity, and reconstruction of working life.* New York: Basic Books.

Laabs, J. (1995, January). Balancing spirituality and work. *Personnel Journal,* 60–76.

Lee, C., & Zemke, R. (1993, June). The search for spirit in the workplace. *Training,* 21–28.

Morgan, J.D. (1993). The existential quest for meaning. In K. Doka & J.D. Morgan (Eds.), *Death and Spirituality.* Amityville, NY: Baywood Books.

Neal, J. (2000). Work as service to the Divine. *American Behavioral Scientist, 43*(8), 1316–1333.

Noer, D. (1993). *Healing the wounds: Overcoming the trauma of layoffs and revitalizing downsized organizations.* San Francisco: Jossey-Bass.

Peele, S. (1988). *How Healthy is Your Workplace?* Morristown, NJ: Organizational Health Systems.

Percy, I. (1997). *Going Deep in Life and Leadership.* Toronto: MacMillan.

Sefton, J., Wankel, L., Quinney, H., Webber, J., Marshall, J., & Horne, T. (1992). Working towards well-being in Alberta. In National Recreation and Wellness Conference, Coburg, Australia, March 12-13, 1992.

Shehadeh, V., & Shain, M. (1990). *Influences on wellness in the workplace: A multivariate approach.* Ottawa: Health and Welfare Canada.

SECTION 4

DIVERSITY AND
FAITH TRADITIONS

INTRODUCTION

BARBARA SWARTZENTRUBER

The chapters in this section provide a variety of perspectives for social work in relation to diversity and faith traditions. They serve to inform social work practice with individuals and faith communities, and they contribute to research and education regarding issues of religious diversity. Spirituality is discussed in relation to the expression of faith traditions within the cultural practices of particular communities and lifeworlds. When religious and spiritual diversity is embraced and welcomed within the helping relationship, it can offer tremendous resources for individual and social change.

In this section's first chapter, Gord Bruyere shares First Nations teachings about the Medicine Wheel and their related expression in the symbol and ceremony of "the Circle." These teachings speak to the connectedness of the First Nations people to Turtle Island, or North America, and are reflected in a variety of cultural practices. This world view and this way of life have been disrupted by the historical colonization, oppression, and exploitation of First Nations people in Canada. However, Bruyere makes note that the current "cultural, social and political resurgence" of the First Nations people and the reclaiming of these teachings and cultural practices that have begun to "mend" this broken circle. He provides an excellent example of this in his description of incorporating the Circle in his approach to education and in the manner in which he draws on the Medicine Wheel teachings to understand "racism as a spiritual force." Here, racism, placed within the context of the "circle of creation," can be seen as a catalyst for the spiritual development of the individual and the community.

In chapter 17, Linda Snyder and Sarah Bowman offer some considerations for developing culturally sensitive practice approaches for human services work with Old Order Mennonites and other conservative religious communities. Based on an exploratory research project, using interviews with members of the Old Order Mennonite community near Waterloo, Ontario, and with human services providers, Snyder and Bowman describe how "professional values such as respect and self-determination" can be used to creatively respond to the needs of this community. The chapter speaks to the importance of "understanding the other's perspective" through gaining further knowledge of a religious tradition and its cultural expression within a particular faith community. The methodology used by Snyder and Bowman is a wonderful example of how research carried out from a position of respect and a genuine desire to understand can both inform and build trust between helping professionals and faith communities.

In chapter 18, David Este outlines the significant role that churches had in the development of a number of black communities in Canada, from the eighteenth century to the twentieth. This historical perspective makes clear the ways in which faith traditions serve as a source for community resilience and capacity in the face of social exclusion and discrimination. As the author points out, "The various ways that African Canadians were excluded by whites served as a catalyst for blacks to develop their own institutions that provided members of the community with feelings of acceptance and belonging, as well as opportunities to develop their leadership and other skills." He describes how the church and related organizations developed by the African-Canadian communities in Nova Scotia, Ontario, and Montreal served as an important vehicle for community development by improving the "quality of life experienced by black Canadians" and through advocacy efforts directed at equitable opportunities.

Finally, Alean Al-Krenawi and John R. Graham provide an overview of Islamic theology and the pillars of Islam, and examine the significance of prayer within this tradition and its implications for social work practice with Muslim clients. In addition, they offer a selected review of the practice literature in relation to social work with Muslim individuals and families. The authors note that "Islam is a total, all-embracing way of life for Muslims" and advise that "social workers should be familiar with the basic beliefs, values, and rituals of Islam as it is practised in the client's milieu." This chapter is an excellent illustration of the importance of bringing together knowledge of theology and religious practices and rituals in order to appropriately adapt social work responses to particular religious traditions. Al-Krenawi and Graham also call for future research that informs "generic cross-cultural principles of working with religious clients, and the lessons that can be mutually applied transculturally, transnationally and across religious traditions."

Collectively, these four chapters deal with the many implications of diversity in relation to particular faith traditions. Faith traditions expressed in cultural practices can be a tremendous resource for community development and cohesion as well as adaptation and growth. Where communities can reclaim and revitalize spiritual traditions that are intimately tied to identity and difference, they can become a source of hope and resilience, particularly in addressing issues of oppression and difference. Through supportive research, social work might assist individuals and communities in this endeavour. Building a mutual understanding between social workers and faith communities requires knowledge of religious and spiritual traditions and their interpretation in the cultural practices of communities and the daily lives of individuals, as well as the relativizing of the helping relationship and practice interventions.

CHAPTER 16

MAKING CIRCLES:

RENEWING FIRST NATIONS WAYS OF HELPING

GORD BRUYERE

Ella Deloria (1944) said that "all peoples who live communally must first find some way to get along together harmoniously and with a measure of decency and order. And that way, by whatever rules and controls it is achieved is, for any people, the scheme of life that works." I would like to share with you my own thoughts and feelings about a particular aspect of the Anishnabe "scheme of life" and explore one application related to social work practice. In sharing my personal understanding, I will attempt to speak predominantly from my own experience and acknowledge that I am engaged in learning, as we all are, and what I know today I will hopefully know better tomorrow. My intention is not only to share my personal understanding but to promote further exploration about how other schemes of life may similarly help human beings address the problems we all face.

This chapter describes a selected set of First Nations teachings known as the Medicine Wheel, which symbolize the relationship between a particular First Nations people, the Anishnabe, and the world around them. These teachings have been used to inform a multiplicity of cultural practices since time immemorial. The "scheme of life that worked," which characterized the diverse nations of peoples of Turtle Island, and the day-to-day practice of the Medicine Wheel teachings were interrupted by the colonization experience in Canada. First Nations peoples are in the process of renewing the cultural practices that make them distinct peoples. One contemporary application of Medicine Wheel teachings, based on an ancient ceremony described as "the Circle," is explained as one example of how that renewal is unfolding. Finally, I will offer an alternative conception of racism as a spiritual force, and explore concomitant ways by which to address it.

❖ THE WINDIGO

In trying to find a way to begin to tell you what I know about racism and how we may move beyond racial divides, I will share this story:

> To begin, I am Anishnabe. It is a name that a people have given themselves, and in accordance with the purpose of naming, "Anishnabe" means more to these people than its literal interpretations, which are "the good people," "the real people," "human beings." Since our creation, Anishnabe people have lived with the land that cradles "gitchi–gaming," those Great Lakes in Ontario, Canada and the mid-western United States.
>
> Anishnabe people still talk about the Windigo. The Windigo has existed in actual physical form as huge misshapen giants with an appearance so horrible that it would take away the breath of human beings and cause plants to wither and die. Mothers would admonish their children to stay close to home and to obey family members or the Windigo would get them.
>
> Besides their ghastly visage, something else caused the people to fear them. You see, the Windigo were once human beings who lived among us as family and who contributed to our society as much as any other person or clan. Yet through the consequence of some agony endured, those human beings were made to eat the flesh of other human beings. Sometimes it was overwhelming hunger brought on by the harshest of winters that caused this to happen. In other instances, people were told through the force of their dreams that they were supposed to commit this act. It was a rare occurrence but it was one that was sure to bring fear to the people. It is said that the cannibalistic act was caused when the Windigo spirit invaded a human being and that you could identify a person inhabited by the Windigo spirit by the vacant, hollow look in their eyes and by the sickly translucence of their flesh. At times people would be so desperate that they would use the most extreme measures to rid the people of the threat of a Windigo. Yet, other than killing a Windigo, there were means by which our medicine people, healers, and most learned elders, could rid a human being of that Windigo spirit. Those means involved the will of the entire community and was a most delicate spiritual, ceremonial matter. (J. Windigo, personal communication, 1993)

❖ A SCHEME OF LIFE THAT WORKS

Anishnabe people and the many diverse Indigenous nations of Turtle Island or North America have always had fecund, complex ways of organizing their societies and continue, to greater and lesser degrees, to practise those ways. In the story of the Windigo, I alluded to ceremonial ways of addressing an extreme social situation. While I am unable to discuss the remedies for that particular situation because of my own limited understanding and the focus of this chapter, I would like to turn our attention to one specific way, one specific scheme if you will.

Since at the present time, I am engaged in my own practice as a teacher, I want to discuss this aspect of our scheme of life in relation to the contemporary context of social work education.

❖ THE CIRCLE AS SYMBOL

Earlier, I rooted the location of Anishnabe people on a particular territory. It is my understanding that our philosophies, values, and beliefs—our scheme of life—are particular to that territory. It is the land herself that teaches us how to live with all of Creation, including other human beings. So it makes sense that the mechanisms that guide our relationships be predicated on what we see around us.

Here I will use the term "Medicine Wheel" to refer to the set of teachings that are encapsulated in this symbol and later I will use the term "Circle" to depict the application of these teachings. I should note that medicine wheels are actual stone formations created by the Plains peoples, and that the term "Medicine Wheel" has come to be used in a contemporary sense as a kind of pan-indigenous rubric to identify sets of similar teachings that have unique histories among a wide variety of First Nations peoples. The historical origins of Medicine Wheel teachings and of the Circle are virtually impossible to pinpoint because their ceremonial and customary usage arose, and predominately continue to arise, out of oral traditions. To be blunt, it is not so important to distinguish their historical origins as it is to understand that they are intrinsic to many First Nations societies (and indeed in many Indigenous societies globally). It is safe to say that these teachings have been discretely elucidated by elders and teachers within our societies and are also simply reinforced through conscious and unconscious personal relationships in the world around us. I should also state that not all First Nations peoples make use of the symbol of the Circle or subscribe to Medicine Wheel teachings. Medicine Wheel teachings also reflect how diverse cultures evolve and grow by adapting and adopting aspects of other cultures.

Many of the peoples indigenous to Turtle Island do make use of the symbol of the circle. It has been described as the Circle of Life (J. Windigo, personal communication, 1993) or the Sacred Hoop (Allen, 1986; Black Elk, 1932) or the Medicine Wheel (Bopp, Bopp, Brown, & Lane, 1984; Buswa & Shawana, 1993). The Circle as symbol is witnessed concretely within the elements of the natural world. Birds' nests, the trunks of trees, the sun and moon, and the unobliterated view of the horizon show the Circle. The representation of life as a cycle is a truth in relation to the passing of seasons, the ebb and flow of tides, the phases of the moon, and a human lifetime. The Circle has no beginning and no end unless one is arbitrarily imposed and so it represents wholeness or completeness and "includes a way of living that emphasizes responsibilities, values, and ethics that ensure achieving balance and harmony" (Longclaws, 1994). Thus we conceive of the Circle as natural law.

Medicine Wheel teachings locate us upon the Earth and place us in relation to all of Creation. Wherever we are is the centre of the Wheel. From where we sit or stand we can look out to four cardinal directions. The East is where the sun rises and symbolizes beginnings, births, or rebirths, the start of a day, the coming of light, warmth, or awareness. The East reminds us of the start of every day that could be our last or our first; so whatever the case, we better be present and make the most of it. The South is the direction where the sun sits highest and strongest in the sky, representing growth and fullness. The West, where the sun sets, helps us to acknowledge the darkness, the unknown. The North, being the fourth direction, brings us to completion or resolution and is the place where wisdom begins. When we place ourselves at the centre of the Four Directions we are reminded that we are but one piece of Creation and, since we are at the centre of Creation at the present time, that we also have a place within all of Creation.

As part of all of Creation, we are taught that human beings and everything else is made up of Four Elements—Earth, Air, Water, and Fire. In acknowledging the universality of these elements, we can understand that we are not any more or less than any other part of Creation and that we are not ever separated from Creation. We are in relationship with Creation.

Those four elements come to us in many guises and part of the shifting face of Creation are the Four Seasons. Where Anishnabe people live there are four distinct faces to Creation. Each season comes with its particular feel and purpose. Of course, Spring is the time where we see many living beings take part in the sacred ritual of change, of birth, rebirth, and renewal. Summer is the season of warmth, rapid growth, and activity. Autumn is the time of harvesting and preparation. Winter is the time of decay, of incubation, and hibernation. The Earth undergoes great change from one season to the next and reminds us that the essence of Creation is change and that life occurs in cycles, that things happen in their own time and in their own way.

In turning our attention to human beings, the Medicine Wheel teaches us that there are four kinds of human beings, Red, Yellow, Black, and White. I was once told a story about how the human beings were lowered to the Earth by the Creator. You see, the Creator had placed all of Creation and had covered the Earth with all kinds of living beings. Yet the Creator thought the Earth needed another kind of being to bring all of Creation together, to serve as custodians for the rest of Creation. The Creator would seek balance, as always, by making those custodians the weakest of all living beings, dependent upon the rest of Creation in order to survive. So the Creator took some Earth, mixed in some Water, blew Air into it and placed it all into a Fire. Four times the Creator did this and each time, the Creator lowered those Four Races to Earth setting them off in different directions.

Often the Medicine Wheel will be drawn divided in four sections. This can be misleading in that the Medicine Wheel and the Circle are not meant to imply division nor are they meant to categorically relegate all human beings to four distinct kinds. The Four Races concept illustrates that difference is part of life and that we all belong to make up the whole.

Each of the Four Races has respective responsibilities for the Four Elements. The Red people are responsible for Earth, the Yellow people are responsible for Air, the Black people are responsible for Water, and the White people are responsible for Fire. While it may connote otherwise, this teaching is designed to show that all human beings have a role to play in custodianship for the Earth.

From the Medicine Wheel we are taught that human beings are comprised of physical, mental, emotional, and spiritual aspects (Bopp, et al., 1988). The development of a human's potential is dependent upon an intentional nurturing of the four aspects. Personal health consists of a conscious balance of these four aspects. The means by which an individual strives for this balance and enactment of potential is the volition or will.

It is not the individual that is the only manner of acknowledging human relationships with the rest of Creation. There are Four Faces of Human Identity—Individual, Family, Community, and Nation. The rights and responsibilities of these Four Faces of Human Identity are interdependent and mutually reinforcing, and reflect the primacy of kinship and relationship for Anishnabe and other First Nations peoples. You can see that when an individual enacts his or her own potential through the volition, he or she contributes to the strengthening of the other Faces of Human Identity and, since there is an interdependence, individual development is not intended to be done in isolation or purely for the benefit of self.

Human beings enacting their potential go through Four Stages of Life—Infancy, Youth, Adulthood, and Elderhood. These stages of life have parallels with the Four Seasons. When we place ourselves at the centre of the Medicine Wheel, these Four Stages of Life indicate that within the life of an individual, family, community, or nations there are opportunities to include all member of that society.

The wisdom-making process itself can also be conceptualized as having four components (Native Child and Family Services of Toronto, 1990). It begins at the Vision stage where we recognize a learning opportunity and make the choice to begin. We may also have some idea what it is we wish to learn. Time is the second component of the learning process, as it takes Time to experience or relate to the people or situations as they exist. It takes Time for the third component of the wisdom-making process to become apparent: the third component of learning is Knowledge. Knowledge is the development of awareness, skills, and understanding within ourselves individually and collectively. The fourth component is Action and it results from behaviour enacted in relation to the other three components of the wisdom-making process. These four components are interdependent and reflect the primacy of relationships within the Medicine Wheel teachings. It also shows that human beings learn in accordance with natural law.

A crucial concept within the Medicine Wheel concerns the Four Sacred Medicines—Tobacco, Cedar, Sage, and Sweetgrass (Benton-Banai, 1988; Buswa & Shawana, 1993). These are by no means the only plants that are used for medicinal purposes by First Nations people, but they are the four that are common to many of our ceremonies and everyday life, particularly among the Anishnabe.

There are many other teachings that come from the Medicine Wheel. I have only outlined certain concepts that are crucial to help to create a good way of being together.

❖ A BROKEN CIRCLE

At the present time, First Nations peoples in Canada are initiating an incredible cultural, social, and political resurgence. This resurgence is incredible for a number of reasons. Most notably, First Nations peoples have been subjected to systematic, purposeful policies and practices carried out by all levels of the Canadian government. These policies and practices have been wholly founded and perpetuated on the misbegotten assumption that the colonizers—initially and most influentially from European nations—were superior to First Nations people. That misbegotten belief, in concert with a world view that saw the world as a supply of resources waiting exploitation for profit, allowed for the construction of the First Nations of Turtle Island as a racial group. According to this spurious, cruel world view, the interests of First Nations peoples were thus minimized, ignored, or disparaged allowing for the socio-economic marginalization and dislocation from their lands and schemes of life. This current resurgence is also incredible because, through colonization, First Nations peoples have retained a sense of identity, some connection to ancestral lands and varying degrees of affinity with the tenets of traditional cultures.

The cultural resurgence of which I am speaking is being played out in differing conceptions and arrangements for self-government within the Canadian polity. Those arrangements for self-government include responsibility for design, implementation, monitoring, and, increasingly, financing of social programs and services to deal with the poignant ramifications of colonization. The effects of the contradictory and long-standing policies of assimilation and social isolation, from my perspective, constitute ritual abuse of a people, genocidal actions, and I am tempted to recount them here. However, there are many other sources that do so, the most comprehensive of which is *The Final Report of the Royal Commission on Aboriginal Peoples* (1996).

Besides detailing the deplorable social conditions that many First Nations peoples face, the Royal Commission on Aboriginal Peoples has also documented the ways in which First Nations peoples are addressing those social conditions, one of which is the Circle.

❖ MENDING THE CIRCLE

The Circle is a not only a symbol but also a ceremony that may be held for various purposes. First Nations organizations and the people working within them are renewing very old traditions like the Circle. Child welfare agencies may call them "family conferences," the Canadian justice system may call them "sentencing circles," and addiction treatment centres may simply call them "healing circles." These approaches are being instituted by indigenous nations that have extensive traditional foundations within their cultures for such uses, and other nations are adapting and adopting circles based upon similar cultural precepts unique to those cultures. These approaches are being instituted with varying degrees of accord with the different levels of Canadian governments.

The use of Circles is not only being reaffirmed in First Nations organizations and institutions. There are those of us who are trying to bring our scheme of life that works to places that have not frequently seen those ways in action. The application that I wish to discuss is a Teaching and Learning Circle. I use this approach in virtually all teaching situations that I facilitate where I am engaged in exploring the impact of colonization and issues of racism in Canadian society, particularly as it relates to First Nations peoples.

The primary basis for regulating our collective behaviour is the Medicine Wheel teachings as I have outlined them above. As I noted earlier, there are many layers to these teachings, but I apply them selectively for our purposes. I also share other cultural teachings that help to guide our learning.

People are seated in a circle, facing each other, and I prefer that barriers such as tables or textbooks are removed from in front of people. Within a circle, you cannot tell who is first or last, and there is no physical separation between student and teacher. There are different ways of facilitating the opportunity for each participant to have his or her say. Often a sacred object will be passed—a feather, "talking stick," or stone—that signifies that whoever holds the sacred object has the sole right to speak without interruption at that time, sharing as much or as little as the person wishes.

When I am inviting students to learn in Circle, I advise them that learning is not just a mental exercise, but is also a physical, emotional, and spiritual undertaking. I suggest that if they are too uncomfortable with this notion, then perhaps they are not ready to learn in this way. Many students in my classes have no problem relating to the first two aspects, but are more hesitant to acknowledge the emotional and spiritual aspects of self. Many others are enthusiastic to engage themselves in other than a purely intellectual or mental sense.

Once students make the choice to participate in the class, then the Four Sacred Medicines are introduced such that they may be used in a purification ceremony. Again, I offer this ceremony to students as part of my personal identity that should be inseparable from the work I hope to do, which, in this case, is to facilitate some learning. Most students have entered my classes with an explicit purpose to learn how to better work with Aboriginal peoples or to develop some understanding of an Aboriginal world view and so are open to beginning each session with this ceremony and are willing to be respectful of its sacredness. I share what I know about the ceremony, the four medicines, and the sacred objects that are present to help people to be respectful.

In laying the foundation for working in circle, I ask students to consider that "the head has no answers and the heart has no questions" and invite them to learn by speaking from the heart rather than simply from the mind. Students are also asked to consider that, when speaking, "there are hard words and soft words" and that there are ways to share a wide variety of opinions and experiences (about delicate issues such as racism, sexism, homophobia, colonization) and still nurture a safe learning environment. We are also challenged to conceive of ourselves as part of Creation and that human beings are custodians of Creation. Our responsibility to Creation means that we are responsible to each other and to the kind of learning environment we create, that our circle is a microcosm of the kind of world we want to see for our children. People come to their own understanding about what is meant by these things and make their choice to participate or not.

Throughout my own social work education I found that the terms "listening" and "respect" were discussed in practice-related courses. We all have a conception of what these terms mean. Yet in no academic course of which I am aware have "listening" and "respect" been considered as integral to learning as they are within Anishnabe culture and within working in Circle. People are reminded that to feel safe to speak from their hearts we need to feel we are listened to and respected. I ask people to listen to others and respect others as they themselves desire. Agreement to allow only one speaker at a time, he or she who is holding the stone or feather, means that people spend much more time listening than they do talking. This gives people the opportunity to simultaneously attend to their own internal processes and people can listen knowing they will have an opportunity to speak if they wish. They are learning about themselves, how they learn, as much as they are learning from other students. They also are learning to find their own voices and to trust in what they know, that what they say will be heard and valued.

One other means to create respect is the idea that we are all teachers and learners. I acknowledge that I have power over students in my responsibility for evaluation and this is specifically a factor when students submit work for evaluation. The trick is to minimize that "power-over" during our discussions in Circle. In my opinion, that requires the facilitator to take some risk to share personal feelings and experiences and not simply be a talking head. I also acknowledge that I am no expert on anything and that we all have thoughts and feelings that we can share. Even though readings may have been assigned and I may take an active role in imparting information, it is impossible to predict where discussion will go when so many people speak about what concerns them at the present time. What is said may not appear to relate in a direct, linear fashion, but what every person says contributes to collective knowledge and wisdom and each one may take something different (or what they are ready to take) as knowledge. If we all tried to mimic one another and reach the same conclusions, that would be boring. Circle is an excellent place to acknowledge that we are all capable of manifestations of genius (Pelletier, 1972) and to open ourselves to learning from one another in an equitable manner.

Learning in this manner proceeds according to the willingness of participants to engage themselves since "learning is considered a personal journey towards wholeness, determined by the individual's own pace of development" (Hart, 1996). Working in Circle, in my experience, may initially be intimidating because people do not have faith in the process and the classroom dynamics reinforced throughout a lifetime of institutionalized education are not deconstructed instantaneously. I remember incidents where I had explained the process and outlined my own personal belief in its benefits, when students asked, "Yeah, but how do we confront someone we disagree with?" I did not provide any kind of answer in those situations as that seemed to be part of learning from a perspective that does not place central value upon confrontation or competition.

Many students have spoken about how the learning is not simply related to content but to process as well. Circle takes on a life of its own. It becomes an organic expression of the lived history of all participants, energized by their volitional belonging in the present, fulfilled in the living out of their individual futures. I often wonder what kind of sharing and learning people could do if their lives were not bound by the institutional structures of where I practice.

❖ RACISM AS A SPIRITUAL FORCE

I choose to work in Circle because I want to affirm my identity as an Anishnabe person and I want to teach others that our scheme of life is relevant and equal to the schemes of life of other peoples. Working in this way allows me to bring in the spiritual aspect of my self, my family, and my nation to how I conduct myself on a daily basis.

What is the approach to this next leg of our history? A noted Aboriginal author and activist, Lee Maracle, recently sat among a small group of Aboriginal social work students at the University of Victoria and asked this question. I found her question and our collective answers to be a suitable guide to my approach here in that I was encouraged to consider racism as a spiritual force.

The world view of Anishnabe people leads us to accept that all of Creation is imbued with spirit, that the world is alive and is one of our relatives. I have wondered if a conceptual parallel to racism existed in our historical Anishnabe society. I was forced to admit that my own belief that First Nations people are no better or worse than other human beings led me to a logical place of discomfort. I have no doubt that Anishnabe and other First Nations peoples have internalized the colonizers' conception of racism and that it is alive and well. So I looked to our traditions to see if I could find a way to understand and engage this contemporary racist society.

In *The Wretched of the Earth*, Franz Fanon (1963) analyzed the decolonization process and found that what began in violence must end in violence. Elsewhere I have described how First Nations peoples have largely not reacted against the colonization process with outward expressions of violence towards the rest of Canadian society, but that we have turned that violence inward upon ourselves (Bruyere, 1999). The ways in which First Nations peoples, and indeed Canadian people in general, have internalized racism, leads me in my heart and mind to view racism as an act of cannibalism. That was my purpose for sharing my story about the Windigo. As hyperbolic as it may be, I wanted to find something within the brand of consciousness that makes me Anishnabe that will allow me to face racism from a place of power, an individual and collective power that is not destructive or exploitative. It is important in the ongoing renewal of our scheme of life that we not only utilize the tools that help us to identify the problem, but also find the means to create solutions. I personally may not be able to perform the ceremonies that Anishnabe ancestors would to deal with the Windigo spirit that afflicted human beings. Yet I can personally take responsibility for working in Circle and describing a scheme of life that works in order to, in some small way, move human beings beyond racial divides.

To maintain our own balance, eradicating racism must follow natural law. By this I mean a number of things. The Medicine Wheel can be a guide.

The Four Directions and the Four Elements illuminate a sense of connection and interdependence that is an invitation to responsibility that emphasises relationship, equality, mutuality and respect. The Four Seasons, while they are distinct faces of Creation, connote gradual change that can be virtually imperceptible until we step back a bit and see changes

over time. This may help us to persist and yet be flexible. Changes in
the seasons suggest that some things are simply beyond human control,
inscrutable, and yet are also necessary. We may learn how to address racism
as a spiritual force with the understanding that everything happens in its
own time and in its own way. Thus eradicating racism should, at times at
least, involve the exercise of patience and the considered recognition of a
fertile situation when dealing with it within ourselves and with others.

In relation to the Four Aspects of human beings, potential is enacted
volitionally. Thus anti-racist work is an act of creation, an act of will to
seek balance. Since we are always in relation, anti-racism begins with
ourselves and moves outward and back to involve the Four Faces of
Human Identity. The Earth is strong and yet the balance is delicate. So
it is when teaching and learning with other human beings. We must be
strong and gentle with ourselves and with others. Fertile situations to
create change, we must recognize, occur throughout our lifetime and must
involve people throughout the Four Stages of Life to stem the ongoing
spread of that cannibal spirit. Viewing racism as a spiritual force means
we have to confront the ways in which our own spirits are malnourished
by the lifestyles we live that allow us to unconsciously and cavalierly use
more of the Earth's sustaining forces than we need to live.

Working to move beyond racial divides, of course, means creating a
Vision, allowing Time for that Vision to unfold and for knowledge to be
built and shared, and to act accordingly. Taking into account the Medicine
Wheel means working in a life-affirming, creative way. Change in human
beings comes from working with the good, the affirmative, in people.
Enacting affirmative aspects creates affirmative change, creates balance,
allowing us to remain balanced within ourselves as we work.

It can mean creating an understanding of the relationship human
beings have with all of Creation and that we are custodians for Creation in
a way that no other living beings are custodians. When we begin to see the
world through a Medicine Wheel, and when we begin to move within the
circle of Creation, "the spiritual and the commonplace are one" (Fire and
Erdoes, 1972) everything becomes sacred. When that recognition happens,
life itself becomes a ceremonial process that is constantly unfolding, and
we are consciously and inevitably participating in ongoing change.

❖ INTERWEAVING CIRCLES

Is this participation, this renewal, limited to the Anishnabe nation or only
to First Nations peoples in Canada? Is this way of relating to life and to
the world limited to one particular kind of people? My belief is that what

makes these teachings resonate within human beings from diverse ethnic and cultural backgrounds is that all human societies have indigenous roots and the teachings of the Medicine Wheel may parallel the root teachings of many past, present, and future human societies. Diverse human beings relate to these teachings because they are *human* teachings, not merely teachings for a particular ethnic group. It would be a mistake to presume that Medicine Wheel teachings are simply categorical in their conception or in who may use them. Medicine Wheel teachings are meant to be universal in conceptualizing diversity simply by virtue of incorporating non-human life into the circle and by conceiving that *everything* is a living being, including supposedly inanimate things like stones, winds, rivers, or volcanoes (Soydan & Williams, 1998).

As such, the Circle, which flows from these teachings, can peacefully coexist with other circles, with other human ways of envisioning equitable relationships. As with most theoretical frameworks or paradigms, it presumes the good will of those who are determined to make use of it.

❖ CONCLUSION

In some ways I have tried to share a particular way of being in the world, one that is intimately bound with my identity as an Anishnabe, a First Nations person. I have attempted to share the root teachings that have led me to practise helping as a social worker and teacher. These roles have led me to try to reaffirm particular cultural, ethnic precepts that may help me, First Nations peoples, and other human beings to move beyond racial divides as equal, conscious participants.

When I consider racism as a manifestation of Windigo, the cannibal spirit, perhaps it is as Fanon says, that what begins in violence must end in violence. However, I have a difficult time reconciling that possibility with what I feel to be the responsibility for the custodianship for the Earth. We are here to do something good for Creation and thus meeting destruction with destruction, exploitation with exploitation, seems futile, damaging and enervating. Yet meeting force with force, spiritual force with spiritual force, conceiving of it in that way, makes more sense to my way of being in the world. Given the history of the relationship between the Indigenous nations of Turtle Island and the colonizing peoples, it may be too easy to forget that Anishnabe people and others are still here, and that despite the racist policies and practices designed to eradicate us as an ethnic and racial group, we continue to assert the right to retain, reaffirm, and renew our schemes of life to again make them work for us. Considered assistance in the decay that leads to renewal—in individuals, communities, societies, the Earth herself—will bear fruit in a garden our children can faithfully inherit. Our roles as custodians of Creation, including human beings, will have been fulfilled in our unique, yet mutual and interdependent ways. We will all have a place.

REFERENCES

Allen, P.G. (1986). *The sacred hoop: Recovering the feminine in American Indian traditions.* Boston: Beacon Press.

Benton-Banai, E. (1988). *The Mishomis book.* Minneapolis: The Red School House.

Black Elk (as told to Neihardt, J.G.). (1932). *Black Elk speaks: Being the life story of a holy man of the Oglala Sioux.* New York: W. Morrow.

Bopp, J., Bopp, M., Brown L., & Lane, P., Jr. (1984). *The sacred tree.* Lethbridge, AB: Four Worlds Development Press.

Bruyere, G. (1999). The decolonization wheel: An Aboriginal perspective on social work practice with Aboriginal peoples. In R. Delaney, K. Brownlee, & M. Sellick (Eds.), *Social Work with Rural and Northern Communities* (pp. 170-181). Thunder Bay, ON: Centre for Northern Studies.

Buswa, E., & Shawana, J. (1993). *Nishnabe bimaadziwin kinoomaadwin: Teachings of the Medicine Wheel.* Manitoulin Island, ON: Ojibwe Cultural Foundation and Nda-Gkenjge Gaming.

Deloria, E. (1944). *Speaking of Indians.* Lincoln, NE: University of Nebraska Press.

Fanon, F. (1963). *The wretched of the earth.* New York: Grove Press.

Fire, J., & Erdoes, R. (1972). *Lame Deer, seeker of visions.* New York: Simon and Schuster.

Hart, M.A. (1996). Sharing circles: Utilizing traditional practice methods for teaching, helping, and supporting. In D. West & S. O'Meara (Eds.), *From our eyes: Learning from Indigenous peoples* (pp. 60-76). Toronto: Garamond Press.

Longclaws, L. (1994). Social work and the medicine wheel framework. In B.R. Compton & B. Galway (Eds.), *Social work processes* (5th ed.), (pp. 24-33). Toronto: McGraw-Hill.

Native Child and Family Services of Toronto. (1990). *Native family well-being in urban settings: A culture-based child and family services model.* Toronto: Native Child and Family Services of Toronto.

Pelletier, W. (1972). Dumb Indian. In R. Osborne (Ed.), *Who is the Chairman of this meeting?* (pp. 1–10). Toronto: Neewin Publishing Company.

Royal Commission on Aboriginal Peoples. (1996). *The final report of the Royal Commission on Aboriginal Peoples.* Ottawa: Canada Communications Group.

Soydan, H., & Williams, C. (1998). Exploring concepts. In C. Williams, H. Soydan, & M. Johnson (Eds.), *Social Work and Minorities: European Perspectives* (pp. 3-35). London: Routledge.

CHAPTER 17

COMMUNITIES IN COOPERATION:

HUMAN SERVICES WORK

WITH OLD ORDER MENNONITES

LINDA SNYDER AND SARAH BOWMAN

This chapter describes some special considerations in human services work with Old Order Mennonites. Because of Old Order Mennonites' beliefs about the importance of living apart from mainstream society and the ethic of taking care of each other within the community, interactions with professional services have considerable potential for misunderstanding. An exploratory research project, using interviews with members of the Old Order Mennonite community and with human services providers, offers insight into the context of practice, the array of services used, and the manner in which services can be provided in order to be helpful to members of the community.

❖ INTRODUCTION

Human services professionals have become increasingly aware of the importance of attention to diversity in providing culturally sensitive and relevant services (Green, 1999; Lie & Este, 1999). In the Waterloo area of southern Ontario, a substantial community of Old Order Mennonites lives and practises a lifestyle that is distinctly different from mainstream society and is tied directly to its religious beliefs. While much has been written about cultural competence with various ethnic and religious groups, and a few articles are available about human service work with some specific branches of the Anabaptist faith (Emery, 1996; Wittmer, 1995), no professional literature addressing either social work or general human services work with the Old Order Mennonite community located near Waterloo, Ontario, was found. Despite the lack of literature on this topic, members of the Old Order Mennonite community require human services from time to time that are only available from the larger society: health services, specialized programs for the developmentally challenged or physically disabled, counselling, etc. Because of the beliefs of Old Order Mennonites about the importance of living apart from mainstream society and the ethic of taking care of each other within the community, these contacts for human services may represent an interaction between groups who do not understand each other very well.

Background

History of the Waterloo Area Old Order Mennonites

The Mennonite religion has its origins in the Protestant Reformation. Its Swiss founders believed that Luther and Zwingli had not gone far enough in their reforms, particularly regarding the practice of infant baptism. The ideas of the Anabaptist movement spread north to Holland where Menno Simons became a well-known leader and, thereafter, the term Mennonite was commonly applied to the movement and its members (Fretz, 1989). Both the Swiss and the Dutch groups met with persecution from the state (principalities) and the established churches, which considered their radical reforms to be heresy (Redekop, 1989). Relocations to various parts of Europe resulted, with the paths of the original Swiss and Dutch groups remaining distinct. In the first half of the 1700s, about 4000 of the Swiss Mennonite group came to North America to settle in Pennsylvania, USA, where pacifist beliefs were respected (Epp, 1974; Fretz, 1989). Around 1800, families began to arrive in Upper Canada (Ontario) to establish farms and agriculturally related enterprises (Fretz, 1989).

The formation of the distinctive Old Order Mennonite group was a response to renewal movements calling for innovations like English preaching and Sunday schools. Although the original church passed resolutions such as those specifying uniformly simple dress and banning musical instruments and photography, in 1872 in the United States and in 1889 in Canada, separate Old Order churches were formed (Epp, 1974).

Needless to say, the Old Order Mennonites are not the only group in the Waterloo area with roots in the Anabaptist Movement. The Amish who had separated from the Swiss Mennonite group in 1693 arrived in 1824 (Fretz, 1989). A group known as David Martin Mennonites separated from the Old Order group in 1917, yet maintain the conservative lifestyle, and the Waterloo-Markham group separated in 1939 to adopt some elements of modern life (Fretz, 1989). A group known as Mexican Mennonites, originally from the Dutch Mennonite stream, began to arrive in the Waterloo area during the 1960s (Fretz, 1989). As well, there are the members of the main Mennonite Church of Eastern Canada who cannot be visually distinguished from non-Mennonite residents of the Waterloo area. The Old Order Mennonite group currently has a baptized adult membership of approximately 2600 (Peters, 2002).

Principles and Practices

In addition to the foundational beliefs regarding infant baptism, non-resistance, and non-swearing of oaths, a number of other beliefs based on biblical scripture undergird the Old Order Mennonite way of life. Winfield Fretz (1989) identified many of these same practices in his criteria for distinguishing the degree of conservatism of various Mennonite church groups.

Separation from the World. The belief in the importance of separation from the world (2 Corinthians 6:17; John 15:19) leads to principles related to living "apart" from mainstream society in an "unworldly" way. Practices such as generating income through farming and related rural enterprises allow for relative economic self-sufficiency. Similarly, retaining traditional methods such as using horse and buggy transportation rather than cars, farming with simple tractors rather than large modern equipment, and producing much of the family food reinforces "unworldliness." Maintaining the use of the German dialect in the home and amongst community members also serves to maintain a life apart from the predominately English-speaking mainstream society. Rejecting radio and television are other illustrations of maintaining separation.

Disobedience May Lead to Damnation. Strong beliefs in obedience to God's will and avoiding the sins of the flesh (Galatians 5:19-21) are the basis of the strong principle of modesty. Clothing covers the full body and is made from increasingly sombre colours as one matures. Men and boys always wear long pants and women and girls always wear dresses. Girls and women keep their hair long, with girls' hair braided and women's hair pulled up and worn under a prayer covering.

Caution Regarding False Doctrine. The admonition to avoid false doctrine (Hebrews 13:9) underlies an emphasis placed on learning the teachings of the Bible and the church. Because of the potential for worldly influences and ideas that conflict with the Mennonite interpretation of the Bible, formal education beyond the elementary level is disallowed for members of the community and outside teachings are viewed with scepticism.

Caring for Each Other. The belief in caring for each other within the community (Galatians 6:2) gave rise to the principle of non-participation in external social or insurance programs. In practice this means that Old Order Mennonites will not accept any universal demogrant (Old Age Security), social insurance (Canada Pension), or social assistance (welfare allowance). Their participation in social programs such as organized residential and home care only takes place when family and community members cannot manage. Similarly other professional human services would only be sought when needs cannot be met within the community.

Social Structure
The Old Order Mennonite social structure is tightly bound by the above beliefs, principles, and practices. The church and the community are one and the same. Winfield Fretz (1989), provides a vivid description of the sociological category of *Gemeinschaft* community, which typifies Old Order Mennonite social structure:

> *Gemeinschaft* (community) ... describes a cohesive society organized on the basis of shared values and norms that command strong allegiance from its members. Members have a kindred feeling for each other and do not easily renounce their membership because it involves deep emotional ties. People tend to be born into this community or grow into it rather than joining voluntarily. Relations tend to be face-to-face. Members tend to have common ancestors. They know who they are and whence they came. (p. 36)

The social structure is hierarchical, following the teaching of St. Paul that "the husband is the head of the wife, even as Christ is the head of the church" (Ephesians 5:23) in a very literal manner. Christ's teachings instruct the church, the church makes resolutions by which the community is to abide, husbands have authority over wives, and parents over children.

❖ RESEARCH METHODOLOGY

The purpose of the current study is to provide some beginning insights into how human services workers can provide culturally sensitive services to a religious community like the Old Order Mennonites in the Waterloo area of southern Ontario. It is an exploratory and descriptive study conducted within the interpretive paradigm. As such, its findings are constructed from the meanings of the participants and it makes no pretence that its conclusions can be generalized beyond its own particular time and place.

Qualitative data were gathered though nine interviews and one focus group with people from the Old Order Mennonite community and from the human services provider community. Data were also gleaned from the researchers' own experiences as a former service provider and a former member in the Old Order Mennonite community. Thus the emic categories and perspectives, identified as essential to full understanding in ethnography by Spradley (1979) and Geertz (1983), were recognizable to the researchers as near-insiders in their respective areas. Each shared relevant emic data with the other who, in turn, was able to apply the "cool assessment" from an etic (outside) researcher perspective (Geertz, 1988).

Prior to seeking participants from the Old Order Mennonite community, the principal researcher spoke with community leaders including a deacon and preacher about the purpose of the study and asked for their assistance in locating Old Order Mennonite participants. Although seven names were provided, only four parties were interested in participating in the study. This probably reflects the reticence to confide in "outsiders," especially regarding mental health service needs that were at issue for all three of the parties who declined to participate. To allay any concerns about confidentiality, the principal researcher interviewed these participants and their identity was not disclosed to the research assistant who maintains close ties with the community.

Participants from the service provider community were sought among an array of agencies operating within the small towns in the rural area in which the Old Order Mennonites live. One of the agencies suggested attendance at a staff meeting rather than an individual interview and, thus, a focus group with six counsellors was possible. The resultant service provider participants (five interviews and one focus group) included health services, general community services, specialized services for the developmentally challenged, and counselling services.

The interviews and focus group were conducted using a flexible interview guide with enough structure (McCracken, 1988) to ensure that pertinent topics were covered as well as Spradley's (1979) suggestions for ethnographic interviewing to allow unanticipated concepts to emerge. The interviews were not taped (out of respect for Old Order Mennonite shunning of electronic technology); notes were taken in all of the interviews and transcribed by the researchers. Data analysis utilized the constant comparative method developed by Glaser and Strauss (1967). The transcribed interviews were searched and coded by themes pertinent to the research purpose. The themes from all of the interviews were then organized into categories for presentation in a draft of preliminary findings.

A follow-up meeting was held with each of the participants (individuals, couples, and the focus group) to ask if they felt the researchers had understood them correctly and if they were comfortable with the presentation of the data. It became apparent that several service providers wanted to be sure that the Old Order Mennonite community would not feel their trust had been betrayed and that the presentation of the findings would not create a reluctance to use professional services. For this reason a second stage of member-checking (Lincoln & Guba, 1985) was developed with a church leader reviewing the full report before it was released publicly.

❖ FINDINGS

The data gathered from the interviews and focus group provided useful information regarding the context of human services practice with Old Order Mennonites, the continuum of services used, and how services were provided.

The Context from the Participants' Perspective

The uncompromising faith that brought the Old Order Mennonite community through religious persecution in Europe and the hardship of pioneering in North America sustains them in their commitment to live a primarily agricultural lifestyle and to remain visibly and culturally separate from the rest of society. Because the Old Order Mennonite community shuns education beyond grade eight, none of their members gain the knowledge and skills necessary for provision of health care, developmental services, or counselling. Consequently, they must depend on the professional human service community for such assistance.

Beyond Theology: The Centrality of Religious Belief

The primacy of religious beliefs to the lives of Old Order Mennonite community members was mentioned by the Old Order Mennonite participants as well as by service providers. An Old Order Mennonite church leader explained:

> We are to be "in the world, but not of the world." It is not our purpose to live in isolation, but to be separate.

A mental health worker noted:

> Many immigrants to Canada are trying to integrate into general society, but Old Order Mennonites do not want to integrate. Thus a very important question for Old Order Mennonites is "Do we want to look to the world for emotional help—for counselling?"

Dilemmas regarding how to live out this separateness are clarified twice yearly at special meetings of the church membership followed by an assembly of the ordained clergy. Church discipline helps define acceptable and unacceptable practices and to maintain the culture. In the words of a mental health professional,

> It's theology, but it's more than that, it's a world view; the [distinct conceptualization of] "us and them" or "church and world" is very strong.

The Community Cares for Its Own

In Canada, as in most Western, industrialized nations, there was a strong movement during the twentieth century toward the establishment of a national welfare state. This policy direction violates the Old Order Mennonite tenet of caring for its own community members. As an Old Order Mennonite church leader described,

> One of our key principles is that the community takes care of its own — this is an integral part of the church's responsibility.

Similarly, a service provider noted,

> Old Order Mennonites have a very high value on mutual aid — of being one's brother's keeper … this is a big contrast with the extreme individualism of general society.

A church leader made it clear, however, that the Old Order Mennonites do not attempt to live completely without professional human services:

> We look inside the community for help — up to a point. We recognize the need for professional help. For example, we would not accept hospital insurance, but hospital care — yes.

Study participants shared some remarkable stories of community care. For example, an Old Order Mennonite family provides a home for children whose own parents are not always able to care for them. As a service provider said:

> It is much better for the children to be cared for in a home within their own culture than for Children's Aid to take them away. The resources of the community that are adaptable and appropriate should be used to solve problems, rather than bringing in external solutions or institutions.

One of the Old Order Mennonite participants described the serious mental health problems that his wife has faced most of her adult life. In mainstream society, she might have needed to be institutionalized. However, because of the Old Order Mennonite traditions (including grandparents living in the attached house, having hired girls from the community, and neighbours rallying in times of crisis), the children were always well cared for and the household tasks were completed.

The research assistant has an example from her own experience, as a person who was born and raised in the Old Order Mennonite community:

> There were very creative community efforts to provide care for my grandmother when she was in the advanced stages of Alzheimer's disease. A special room to accommodate her specific needs was prepared in my parents' home. Her children and neighbours took turns caring for her day and night. Such care for the elderly is a common practice in the community. Emotional support provided by the wider Old Order Mennonite community was exemplified in the relationship that developed between my mother, who was my grandmother's primary caregiver, and a family in Pennsylvania who cared for a parent with a similar condition. Through the exchange of letters and a visit to my parents' home, a special bond developed between my parents and this family.

The example of Old Order Mennonite non-participation in insurance or income security programs illustrates the principles of the community caring for its own and the separation of the church and the state. A church leader described his interchange with a member of the Canadian government during formal discussions regarding the Canada Pension Plan. The government member explained that the government was simply trying to put this same idea of community responsibility for others in place at a national level. The church leader reported telling the government official,

> You can't legislate charity; it has to come from within a community that is tied together with strong bonds of trust—that is bound, out of love, to share.

A further rationale for non-participation in public income security programs was offered by another Old Order Mennonite participant:

> We think it's important to be independent or free from the government. This is related to not wanting the government to expect military service

from us. Our young men did alternative service during the Second World War—some of them stayed at a camp near Sault Ste. Marie where they helped to build the trans-Canada highway (coming home only once a year). We would not want to be expected to serve in the military.

For these reasons, the Old Order Mennonite community has developed a system of financial aid for those who need it. According to an Old Order Mennonite participant: "This [communal aid system] takes care of medical costs or losses in a fire."

Reference was made to situations in which a member of the Old Order Mennonite community is injured in a traffic accident due to the fault of a motor vehicle driver. A church leader explained,

> We do not accept insurance for ongoing needs beyond the costs related to the actual accident. For the immediate costs related to the accident, the treatment for example, we would accept the insurance money of the person who caused the accident—it is important for them to feel that they are attempting to make things right. But not for ongoing needs that constitute a dependency—that help is the responsibility of the church community.

Continuum of Services Used

Although the full spectrum of professional human services is available to Old Order Mennonites, the data revealed a continuum of services that they find more to less comfortable to use. Services related to physical well-being were most easily used while services related to emotional and behavioural issues were more difficult to decide to use, as well as to discuss.

Services with a Physical Focus

Professional human services with a purely physical focus were most readily used by Old Order Mennonites. For example, the parents of a physically and developmentally delayed child were pleased to find professional resources such as physiotherapy to monitor their child's progress and teach them what to do to strengthen the child's limbs. Even people whose spouses had mental health problems often understood the disorder to stem from physical or chemical bases and remembered the treatment to have been oriented toward "getting the medication right." Regarding the interactions with mental health professionals, one man said: "There wasn't much discussion about how we live."

Service providers' comments corroborated this greater ease with physically-based concerns. A nurse in the community provides a broad scope of primary health care to Old Order Mennonite people—care for episodic illnesses like sore throats or for injuries, immunizations, and well-baby check-ups, and home visits to the elderly; but she noted less openness to discussing issues related to stress or relationships. A mental health professional described how it seemed to be harder for Old Order Mennonites to decide to go outside of the community for counselling regarding emotional problems than to seek to outside professional help for a physical problem:

> I don't think they would have any problem going to an outsider for something like getting an appendix out because none of their people have the training.

Schooling for Old Order Mennonite children with special needs is a particular challenge. The Old Order Mennonites operate small parochial schools for their children. Although the parochial schools do make provision for about half of the children with special needs, they do not have the resources to teach children with more severe disabilities. As a result, children with more demanding special needs are often educated within the public school system. Old Order Mennonite participants cited numerous examples of practices within the wider educational system that were not acceptable to them. As the mother of a preschooler involved in a developmental services program mused,

> I think it will come up more if she goes to school there. In the school program, the children go swimming. And we aren't accustomed to having the boys and the girls in the water at the same time. Or the school might have a Hallowe'en party.

Another parent described their family's experience with their son's school Christmas celebration:

> The school tried very hard to include us and the principal came to pick us up for the Christmas concert. But we were very displeased with the emphasis on Santa Claus. For us, we want the children to celebrate the arrival of the Baby Jesus. It was nice that they brought us to be part of their celebration, but we explained afterward that we wouldn't come in the future years.

Adult training programs, as well as schools, may use modern technology like radios and computers. Perhaps most importantly, the wider educational system strives to teach skills for independent living, an objective that is contrary to the interdependent communitarian living practised by Old Order Mennonites. The father of a developmentally challenged young man described these conflicting values:

> Their objective was to try to help [our son] learn so that one day he would be able to live independently. They wanted him to learn about shopping and apartment living. It was as though they wanted to try to get everything into him so he wouldn't ever be dependent on the government. We had to explain that in our community that type of learning is not needed. [Our son] will always be with us—we will provide for him. And after we're gone, his brothers and sisters will take care of him.

More will be said later about the cooperative problem-solving that ensued in these situations.

This reticence to use services with a focus beyond the purely physical to a broader involvement in matters of living was exemplified in the experience of the local association providing services for the developmentally challenged. Old Order Mennonites provide a tremendous amount of assistance with fundraising for the organization, far beyond their level of service utilization. There is some use of the occupational training and the skills development program; however, use of the residential program is rare. Only when the traditional family and community care practices have proven unsuccessful in meeting the needs of a developmentally challenged Old Order Mennonite person has the residential program been used.

Mental Health Services
It has already been noted that it is more difficult for Old Order Mennonites to seek mental health services in comparison with physically or developmentally oriented services. However, the same kinds of emotional problems experienced in the general population are found amongst Old Order Mennonites—relationship and workload stresses, end of life existential issues, situational depression including postpartum depression (referred to as "the baby blues"), and schizophrenia. It was suggested that relationship issues might be difficult for Old Order Mennonites to bring to counselling because of the emphasis on principles of honouring and obeying parents and husbands. As one service provider noted: "It feels like a betrayal of the relationship if they talk about the stresses."

Mental health problems seemed to be more common in women, although there was some suggestion that there may be a greater stigma for a man to be immobilized by depression, as one health professional noted: "Because the value of work is so high [and] if you can't work you're seen as lazy."

When professional services had become necessary for severe mental health problems, the counselling component was not always evident or was not always seen as valuable:

> Well, sometimes the doctors would talk to her alone. And they did suggest counselling at a place in Kitchener—I can't remember the name of the place. They saw her for about a half-hour each time. But it didn't seem to help.

In some instances, Old Order Mennonite preachers have sought consultation for themselves from professional counsellors in order to strengthen their pastoral care abilities.

It is not surprising, given the centrality of Old Order Mennonite belief systems to their manner of living, that these beliefs would be very important in the counselling process. The issue of change was especially noted by service providers, as one remarked:

> For Old Order Mennonites, the dilemma of change versus conserving tradition is highlighted and dramatically enacted every day.

Thus, attempting to bring about positive changes in intrapersonal or interpersonal functioning takes place in the context of strict community parameters regarding acceptable change.

Services Related to Behavioural Matters

Perhaps the most difficult professional services for anyone to admit to needing are services related to behavioural problems such as spousal abuse or sexual assault. As in all communities, the Old Order Mennonite community also experiences these problems and has engaged the help of professionals to deal with them. As a church leader acknowledged,

> We have to admit that this does happen in our community; the knowledge that it is happening is too often suppressed.

Both consultative and direct services are used to ensure that the abuse stops and that the victim is receiving treatment. A consulting professional helped in the development of a support and accountability system for an abuser:

> ... providing information about helpful and non-helpful things the church group could do and avoid doing.

Another professional provided educational workshops for church leaders as well as direct individual, family, and group counselling services for victims of abuse.

Figure 17.1 provides an illustration of the continuum of comfort-discomfort in seeking professional services from people outside of the community.

Figure 17.1 Comfort in seeking outside services

Greatest comfort	Some discomfort	Greatest discomfort
Service with a physical focus	Mental health services	Services related to sensitive behavioural matters

Provision of Services

The way that services are provided is key to how helpful they will be for Old Order Mennonites. A few examples of unhelpful incidents or approaches are described as well as numerous examples of very useful approaches and adaptations.

Unhelpful Approaches

Old Order Mennonite participants in the study described very few incidents where they felt that their ways were not understood. One of the participants who had been a boy during WWII remembered the anti-German and anti-pacifist sentiment of that time, but said that the last years have been really good. He also remembered that perhaps 30 years ago some hospital staff could not comprehend why Old Order Mennonites did not have government health insurance, but that now they understand. Other participants described service providers as very helpful. One couple described their child's years in an outside educational system as "happy times" for him, and the inevitable issues as opportunities for creative problem-solving.

Both church leaders and service providers expressed concerns about inappropriate use of alternative medicines. Old Order Mennonite churches leaders were concerned when the alternative medicines incorporated some incompatible belief systems as in the citing of mantras or incantations. A health service provider worried about the substitution of alternative medicines for seriously needed conventional medications such as insulin for diabetes. This provider was also troubled by reluctance on the part of some Old Order Mennonites to utilize health services in a timely manner.

It was service providers who were forthcoming in the sharing of the non-helpful incidents that had transpired in their practice and that had served as learning experiences for them. In a social skills program for children from a similar conservative Mennonite community, the group leaders described a problem with the examples they used:

> I remember, when we were teaching the children about compromise, we used an example in which one friend wanted to see the movie *Snow Dogs* and the other wanted to see *Harry Potter*. Of course, the children didn't know what we were talking about—so we changed our example activity to board games.

One of the leaders also described an incident where she unthinkingly used the expression "holy cow," causing the children to gasp in surprise. Thereafter, they described being careful in their choice of words and examples.

One of the principal researcher's mistakes as a former residential program director with an association for developmentally challenged people may be instructive here:

> A local service club provided a generous donation of sports equipment to the residential program. To publicly thank them, I organized a baseball game where residents and staff played against the service club members and I invited the local newspaper to come and do a story. To my great surprise, the newspaper published the story with a large photo of the only Old Order Mennonite resident at bat.

Although this and similar errors were committed innocently, she feels that less of them would have improved her effectiveness in working with the association.

Helpful Approaches
Numerous ideas about helpful approaches to service provision were offered by Old Order Mennonite participants and by service providers. They range from very straightforward concepts to more complex arrangements that have developed out of cooperative arrangements.

Accessibility of services. Service accessibility is important because horse and buggy transportation is relatively slow. The service providers included in this study are located in agencies within the small rural towns near the farms where the Old Order Mennonites live and attributed the utilization of their services by Old Order Mennonites to this fact. Participants noted the barrier to service posed by distance. When specialized services were only available in the larger, more distant cities, they appreciated the provision of bus transportation or organized cooperative arrangements amongst themselves.

Attention to Old Order Mennonite lifestyle. Attending to the Old Order Mennonite way of life was apparent in a number of provider practices. Using relevant examples, such as games rather than movies, and recognizing that "Mom cooks dinner for me" may be a more common expression of affection than "Mom hugs me" or "Mom saying 'I love you'" were useful adaptations in the social skills program for children. Two women in counselling roles described being careful about their personal appearance—not wearing pants, bright colours, or make-up. Using language that will be understood was mentioned by counsellors. As one stated,

> I find using agricultural metaphors is great. For example, when I'm talking about boundary issues, I use "line fence" language.

Another counsellor described how in addition to using language that will be understood,

> I ask about activities that would be normal in their lives, to show interest and that I'm aware or understand something of their lifestyle.

Having service providers with a similar background (Mennonite or Amish, although not Old Order) was cited as helpful in a number of situations. A residential program for developmentally challenged people assigned a staff member who was originally from the conservative Mennonite community to provide support services for the group home where an Old Order Mennonite woman lives; this way adherence to Old Order Mennonite dress and grooming could be managed more readily. A counsellor felt that his Mennonite faith helped Old Order Mennonite clients trust that he would understand their ways. However, the similar background is not a guarantee of helpfulness, as one study participant pointed out:

> I took a young woman and her family to the hospital because the young woman appeared to be having a psychotic episode. The psychiatrist had

left the Mennonite church and his prescription was that the young woman
do the same!

In situations where providing services in the home was possible, this
seemed to be a particularly effective way to pay attention to the Old Order
Mennonite manner of living. Home visits from Infant Development staff
provided the added benefit of the worker being able to see what household
items could be used by the family in promoting the child's development.
Visiting nurses were able to see that a mother with mental health problems,
along with her children and household, were well cared for by family and
community members. As a church leader noted,

> Programs that provide home visits are less of a problem because there's
> less exposure to the ways of others.

Another reality of life in the closely-knit Old Order Mennonite
community is that the members know each other and know a lot about
each other. This becomes problematic when individuals want to seek
out professional help for very personal matters. Counsellors provided
a heightened level of confidentiality, such as trying to ensure that
appointments for Old Order Mennonites were not booked sequentially.
Similarly, a group worker described her cautious approach:

> When an individual client is ready to benefit from group involvement, I
> need to ask her if she would like me to share her name with the current
> group members and ask their comfort with her joining. Then I ask them if
> they are comfortable sharing their names with her. I try to be very careful
> about this.

The worker kept the groups very educationally or skills focused, because
the sharing of stories could not been done without others recognizing the
identity of the parties involved.

Approaches relevant to Old Order Mennonite beliefs. Some of the Old
Order Mennonite beliefs that affected human services practice were
general rather than religious beliefs. The belief, for example, that the
counsellor is the expert—someone who "knows"—made it particularly
challenging to assist clients to find their own "expertise" about their own
situation and their own "voice." Counsellors also encountered clients who
were oversensitive to high expectations from the Old Order Mennonite
community that they should have progressed promptly and easily in
their emotional healing processes; this required caution on the part of the
counsellor about suggesting where the client "ought to be" in his/her stage
of healing.

Other beliefs related more to religious teachings. Strong feelings like anger were not readily admitted; expectations that "victims" should forgive their "abuser" and return to normal relations were high; and patterns of being overly self-critical were cited. One counsellor described caution in doing "cognitive" work which would examine belief systems. Another counsellor encourages discussion of scripture verses that Old Order Mennonites clients bring forward in individual and group counselling. Similarly, in educational workshops for church leaders she used material such as that produced by the Mennonite church offices in Winnipeg and Indiana:

> With that material, we could work from a scriptural base in a way that they are comfortable.

Importance of respect. One of the Old Order Mennonites participants indicated that he felt respect was one of the most important things for students in professional human services to learn about working with his community. Similarly, one of the counsellors recalled that one of her clients had said,

> I want to be treated like a normal human being—but, I also want you to respect our differences.

An administrator with the association for people with development challenges emphasized the importance of finding ways of respecting the beliefs of the Old Order Mennonite clients without infringing on the rights of other residents:

> For example, whether or not there is alcohol in a group home is a decision made by the people living in that home. However, we would ensure that an Old Order Mennonite person is living with a group of people who similarly do not want alcohol in the home.

Another counsellor described respecting Old Order Mennonite beliefs as essential because of the potentially severe consequences for Old Order Mennonites who reject them:

> I'm very clear that it is not my intent to get them to leave the church … I'm very aware that if they went against the religious teachings, they might be rejected by their whole community; they could be ex-communicated and possibly "shunned." The consequences are severe. Often what they need

is a "hand" to be able to stay in their own community. Self-determination is very important here.

Respect was also spoken of in terms of the Old Order Mennonites' appreciation for what the agencies were doing. Parents of a developmentally challenged young man described their respect for the well-organized staff in the occupational training program, acknowledging that they had learned that their son needs supervision to keep him busy. Service providers described feeling that their work was respected by a good portion, but not all, of the Old Order Mennonite community:

> I believe it does take a long time to build the relationship with the Mennonite community. I've needed to earn their respect. They need to see that it's working, that it's making a difference.

Importance of trying to understand. The process of "trying to understand" is very closely tied to the matter of respect in participants' comments. For example, a parent of a disabled child said,

> I think it helps that they were respectful, they would try to understand our ways; they accepted that we're only human people too.

The "trying to understand" also was perceived as highly important, as indicated by one of the church leaders:

> I think the most important thing for outside professionals is this: that they be open to considering the teachings of the community and not give the message that "you've been taught wrong."

This same church leader spoke of being able to work well with hospital social workers and a counselling centre director who understood Old Order Mennonite principles, enabling them often to sort through problematic situations together. For example, when individuals who were struggling with the teachings of the church gave permission for their minister to join them in a counselling session, misinterpretations based on very dogmatic perspectives often could be reframed.

One of the counsellors described how she put the principle of "trying to understand" into practice:

> I try to have the Old Order Mennonite people describe their realities. I ask them: "What is possible in your situation?" and "What options are available to you?"

One of the Old Order Mennonite participants described a situation where he felt outside professionals had made an important effort to try to understand his culture. There had been a series of barn fires set by a local youth (not Old Order Mennonite). Each of the farmers was asked to write a letter describing how the fire had affected them and no Old Order Mennonite farmer had to attend court. In his words, "It was handled very well."

There is a reciprocal or two-way dimension to the "trying to understand" in the comments of many of the study participants. Parents of a disabled child, for example, appreciated how the professionals would try to understand Old Order Mennonite culture, as the mother acknowledged: "Most people, not having grown up in it, wouldn't have any way of knowing those things." Parents of a developmentally challenged young man described this mutual "trying to understand" as the most important practice for outside professionals working with Old Order Mennonites:

> I would say it's the "trying to understand"—to try to look at it, as if standing in the other person's shoes. It really goes well when both parties try to understand and value the other's perspective. We really appreciated those who took the time and effort to listen and try to understand—who valued our religious beliefs and opinions.

The reciprocal respect and understanding are critical foundations for the effective problem-solving practices described below.

Problem-solving. Creative problem-solving occurred in many of the examples put forward as issues of differences. As a parent of a developmentally challenged boy described:

> The school wanted the children to wear shorts and T-shirts for gym classes and we are very firm on the importance of modest clothing—being covered. We talked about it for quite a while and we sorted it out that [our son] could bring along a change of clothes (but his own clothes) for gym and change back into his other clothes that weren't sweated after gym.

With this clear understanding of and respect for each other's concerns, options for meeting the needs of both parties emerged.

Another example of creative problem solving involves the uncommon situation where an Old Order Mennonite is utilizing the residential services of an association for persons with developmental challenges. After this woman's parents died, the traditional practice of brothers and sisters caring for her was put into place. However, for this particular person the moving from family to family began to take its toll and the family approached the association to discuss how she could be supported in the residential program. As a result of the discussions, the Old Order Mennonite woman is able to live in a group home with only women and has staff support to help her maintain her traditional practices regarding dress and hair as well as church attendance. Arrangements are made so that she doesn't participate in parties where there is dancing or where there are secular celebrations such as Hallowe'en or Valentine's Day. However, she does participate in picnics and is not sheltered from radio or television in the group home. The association director describes the agency's problem-solving process:

> The decision-making about practices happens at the individual client and family level—not at the organizational policy level. We describe the realities of the program environment and ask how they want it managed. It's a very creative process with a lot of give and take on the part of both parties. It's an equal partnership.

Many service providers emphasized the importance of the principle of client self-determination (within the usual limitation of the law and the obligation to attempt to prevent harm to self or others) because of their own position outside of the Old Order Mennonite culture and belief system. A nurse in the community described her role as a provider of information and the Old Order Mennonite patient's role as the one who decides what to do with that information. As she said: "Everyone has the right to their own beliefs and choices."

Counsellors spoke of the collaborative nature of the process. One counsellor described it as follows:

> I ensure that Old Order Mennonite people control the treatment process. I ask them what they need, how I can work with them and their family, for example.

Other counsellors spoke of how they emphasized their expertise in leading a problem-solving process, not in "knowing" the solutions for individual clients. One described a particular method that she found useful in helping Old Order Mennonite clients, in which the client reflects on their own belief about the problem; this reinforces the client's own capacity to deal with the belief him/herself and, in her words, "They reach their own understanding."

Community responsibility and the professional role. The introduction to this section provided some comments to contextualize the provision of human services to a community with a strong ethic of caring for its own members. Here more detail is provided regarding the working out of the balance between Old Order Mennonite community responsibility and the role of the professional in dealing with the sensitive matter of abuse. Cooperative relationships are evident in more general areas as well.

According to study participants, the leadership in the Old Order Mennonite community realized that they needed professional assistance in dealing with abuse, and service providers realized that they had some useful assistance to offer. The data provide examples of the church leadership seeking consultation and of service providers initiating contact. An early example of service provider outreach was the approach by a community agency to the church leadership to offer general talks about family violence to their members. More recently, workshops on dealing with sexual abuse were offered to those in pastoral care roles. In both instances, the service providers recognized the authority of the church leaders and reviewed the content material for their discussions or workshops with the leaders prior to delivering them, as one described:

> When I'm doing a workshop for Old Order Mennonites, the ministers like to meet in advance and see what handouts I'm planning to use. They rejected some that spoke clearly of feminism.

The church leaders also indicated their recognition of the need for counselling for victims of abuse:

> We are hesitant to take these issues to a court of law. We believe, again, in the important role of the church. A while ago, when we were dealing with such a situation, we took on the responsibility of ensuring that the abuser would not have any contact with the victim and was getting treatment.

They sought out professional consultation, and a clear understanding between the parties ensured that Old Order Mennonite values would be respected by the counsellor and that the law would be respected by the Old Order Mennonites. The church leaders also mandate that some perpetrators participate in a professional treatment program for sexual offenders that was developed by a well-respected Mennonite (not Old Order) practitioner and is offered in a nearby city.

Cooperative relationships between the Old Order Mennonite and human services communities underlie all of the helpful services identified. Parents with a child needing developmental services were not worried about having to work out the differences between Old Order Mennonite and conventional ways as their child continues in the program:

There are other parents from our group and they tell us that these things work out ... we're not worried about it—they find a way.

One of the Old Order Mennonite study participants spoke of the openness of a community health organization to input from the Old Order Mennonite community:

They held exercise and physical fitness classes and wondered why no Old Order Mennonites came. Well—the classes were held when we are still doing chores; it takes a lot longer to get there by horse and buggy; we're getting physical exercise in our work all day long; and we're modest about doing that kind of thing in public. It was good that they asked us and we could help them understand.

Service providers spoke of learning a lot from their experiences in working with Old Order Mennonites. One of the agency administrators described the current process of developing a program idea to explore with the Old Order Mennonite community. As he said,

I believe it is important to offer options and listen to the input from the Old Order Mennonite community.

In summary, the findings highlight unique elements of the context of practice with Old Order Mennonites, the array of services used, and the provision of those services. Contextual factors such as the centrality of religious beliefs and the ethic of the community caring for its own members form the parameters within which human service possibilities are negotiated. An array of services came to light, ranging from those with a purely physical or developmental focus (that were easier to use) to those addressing mental health problems and those which deal with behavioural matters (which were more difficult to use). The findings also emphasize that the way in which services are provided is critical to their effectiveness. Services were most helpful when relationships of mutual respect were developed in which both parties try to understand the other's perspective and collaborative problem-solving could occur.

❖ DISCUSSION AND IMPLICATIONS

The study found much that was congruent with the earlier literature, such as that of Wittmer (1995) and Emery (1996) in their writings about the Old

Order Amish in the United States. Both Wittmer and Emery advocated the importance of respect on the part of human services workers for the beliefs and practices of the community. However, in contrast with Emery's portrayal of the Amish, the Old Order Mennonites in the Waterloo area are somewhat open to the use of some modern amenities such as running water, electricity, and the telephone, as well as selective use of professional counselling services.

Many examples of culturally sensitive practices were found and described in this study. Given the current lack of specific literature regarding human services with Old Order Mennonites, perhaps it is the commitment to professional values that has guided practice in the many situations described (Canadian Association of Social Workers, 1994). This study attests to the importance of these professional values in this particular practice context, and it provides some specific examples of how professional values such as respect and self-determination can be acted upon in human services work with Old Order Mennonites. The study showed that impressive problem-solving in human services practice became possible when work was founded on respect and an understanding of the other's perspective. This fostered a creativity that led to the development of effective solutions to meet the needs of both parties and to balance the rights of all concerned.

The research also provided illustrations of cooperative and collaborative relationships in human services practice with individuals, families, groups, and communities. Some reluctance to use services continues, particularly as the focus of service moves from the purely physical to matters of living. Particularly in the area of counselling, finding the balance between the ethic of "caring for one's own" and recognizing the need for professional help is difficult. Among the preachers there is a variation of opinion with some supporting the use of professional counselling and others rejecting it as a part of shunning worldly influences. The comments from the study also suggest that members of the Old Order Mennonite community need opportunities to consider the results of the work of "outside" professionals and time to build relationships of trust.

The areas of greatest challenge appear to be those in which there are conflicts with Old Order Mennonite values. For example, the deliberations of an individual member about leaving the Old Order Mennonite community bring them into direct confrontation with beliefs about damnation as a potential consequence of disobedience. Thus, a counsellor sought out to help an individual deal with this stressful dilemma is faced with the challenge of respecting the Old Order Mennonite culture and the client's right to self-determination. Similarly, the involvement of legal authorities conflicts with the Old Order Mennonite principles of separation from the world and community care. Thus, human services professionals learning of child abuse or sexual assault face the challenge of respecting Old Order Mennonite values and the professional obligation to report. Yet, in the face of these demanding situations, the study found examples of human services workers respecting both their professional ethics and the Old Order Mennonite culture and beliefs. Through collaborative problem-solving, solutions were developed that provided community support systems to ensure protection for vulnerable persons and the commencement of a healing process.

It is important to acknowledge that this study has made only a modest beginning in exploring these topics. With only nine interviews and one focus group, it was not possible to probe deeply into the areas of deepest challenge; most situations were seen from only one perspective – that of the service user or the service provider. Nor is it possible to generalize from such a small, non-representative sample; however, readers may judge from the degree of similarity with the Old Order Mennonite community described, whether some of the findings of this study may be transferable to human services work with other "plain people"—people led by their religious beliefs to live simply and separately.

Given these disclaimers, a tentative model of principles for practice with conservative religious communities is offered. The various principles for providing helpful services to a conservative religious community seem to begin with some very basic and foundational precepts that must be present in all services and build to ascending levels of service ideals that become necessary in dealing with the most sensitive issues. For example, all services must be accessible or people will not be able to get to them. However, if people are going to continue involvement with a service, the service must attend to community's unique lifestyle and religious beliefs. Respect for the community will be essential to any authentic attempt to understand their situation and to be able to engage in creative, cooperative problem-solving. In the most challenging dilemmas, human services professionals will need to work with the religious community in order to balance and honour both the community's responsibility to its members and the professional's ethical obligations and role. Figure 17.2 provides a graphic representation of this conceptual model.

Perhaps future research can add to this beginning. In-depth case studies of some of the most challenging examples could provide a deeper understanding of the difficulties and useful practices. A clearer picture could be gained by interviewing all of the important actors in a particular

Figure 17.2 Ascending levels of service principles

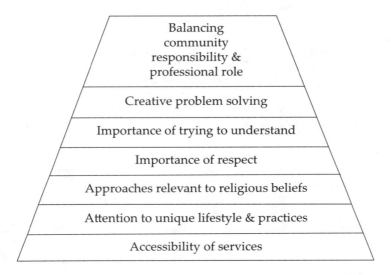

Balancing community responsibility & professional role

Creative problem solving

Importance of trying to understand

Importance of respect

Approaches relevant to religious beliefs

Attention to unique lifestyle & practices

Accessibility of services

case; for example: the service provider, "client," significant others (family members, victim, perpetrator), and religious community leaders. Privacy issues would be a concern in this type of study; however, if the specific case has become a public issue, an accurate representation of all perspectives could be beneficial to those involved as well. Subsequent research regarding human services in the Old Order Mennonite community might also explore possibilities for obtaining more participants from the particular community. Other studies might include additional conservative Anabaptist groups or extend the geographic scope beyond the Waterloo area. Lastly, future research could review some of the literature related to human services and social issues that is prepared for or by members of the Anabaptist faith in order to gain insight into the perspectives most familiar to the Old Order Mennonite community.

Research on human services with Old Order Mennonites and other conservative religious communities that itself adheres to the important human services practice principles revealed in this study (respect, trying to understand, collaborative problem-solving, etc.) can develop a useful body of knowledge regarding the provision of culturally sensitive services for this group.

REFERENCES

Augsburger, D. (1974). *The control and management of hostility in a nonviolent-nonresistant community.* Unpublished doctoral dissertation, School of Theology at Claremont, California.

Canadian Association of Social Workers. (1994). *Social work code of ethics.* Ottawa: CASW.

Emery, E. (1996). Amish families. In M. McGoldrick, J. Giordano, & J. Pearce (Eds.), *Ethnicity and family therapy* (2nd ed., pp. 442–450). New York: The Guilford Press.

Epp, F. (1974). *Mennonites in Canada, 1786–1920.* Toronto: Macmillan.

Fretz, J.W. (1989). *The Waterloo Mennonites: A community in paradox.* Waterloo, ON: Wilfrid Laurier University Press.

Geertz, C. (1983). *Local knowledge.* New York: Basic Books.

Geertz, C. (1988). *Works and lives: The anthropologist as author.* Stanford, CA: Stanford University Press.

Glaser, B., & Strauss, A. (1967). *The discovery of grounded theory: Strategies for qualitative research.* Hawthorne, NY: Aldine de Gruyter.

Green, J. (1999). *Cultural awareness in the human services: A multi-ethnic approach* (3rd ed.). Boston: Allyn & Bacon.

Klaassen, W. (1981). *Anabaptism: Neither Catholic nor Protestant.* Waterloo, ON: Conrad Grebel Press.

Lie, G., & Este, D. (1999). *Professional social services delivery in a multicultural world.* Toronto: Canadian Scholars' Press.

Lincoln, Y.S., & Guba, E.G. (1985). *Naturalistic inquiry.* Beverly Hills, CA: Sage Publications.

McCracken, G. (1988). *The long interview.* Newbury Park, CA: Sage Publications.

Peters, J. (2002). The Ontario Old Order Mennonites as Canadian citizens. *Ontario Mennonite History, 20*(1), 2–8.

Redekop, C. (1989). *Mennonite society.* Baltimore: Johns Hopkins.

Spradley, J. (1979). *The ethnographic interview.* Fort Worth, TX: Harcourt Brace.

Wittmer, J. (1995). Old Order Amish: Culturally different by religion. In N. Vace, S. DeVaney, & J. Wittmer, (Eds.), *Experiencing and counselling multicultural and diverse populations* (pp. 29–61). Bristol, PA: Taylor & Francis.

CHAPTER 18

BLACK CHURCHES IN CANADA: VEHICLES FOR FOSTERING COMMUNITY DEVELOPMENT IN AFRICAN-CANADIAN COMMUNITIES—A HISTORICAL ANALYSIS

DAVID ESTE

Although people of African descent have resided in Canada for over 400 years, the majority of Canadians are not aware of this historical reality. There is a belief that the presence of the black population is a relatively recent phenomenon, especially with the increasing number of newcomers arriving from the Caribbean beginning in the 1970s and, more recently, from Africa.

Until recently, the Canadian social work literature ignored the concerns and issues confronting African Canadians. Even with the contributions of writers such as Christensen (1998, 2005), Bernard (1996), Bernard and Bernard (1999), Este and Bernard (2003), and Danzer (1997), the Eurocentric world view and interventions based on this perspective continue to dominate the material used in Canadian social work education. Comparatively speaking, despite their visibility, African Canadians remain quite "invisible" in the social work curriculum. It is not surprising that the majority of social workers in Canada possess limited or no knowledge of the African-Canadian community and the myriad of challenges, social and economic, that confront this group of Canadians. As a consequence, practitioners are not equipped with the skill set that is required to work effectively with African Canadians as individuals, in families, and at the community level.

In examining the existing body of Canadian social welfare history, it would appear that African Canadians have not contributed to this history. Other racialized minorities are also absent from this history. In fact, one could strongly maintain that Canadian social welfare history is synonymous with the dominant group in Canada.

Throughout their history, many African Canadians have attempted to integrate into Canadian society. For the majority of African Americans, who constituted the largest group of blacks who settled in the country, Canada was perceived, according to Foster (1996), as a "place of heaven." However, these individuals experienced both subtle and explicit forms of racism and discrimination. For example, in the early part of the 20th century, the migration of African Americans to Canada was strongly discouraged by the federal government.

The various ways that African Canadians were excluded by whites served as a catalyst for blacks to develop their own institutions that provided members of the community with feelings of acceptance and belonging, as well as opportunities to develop their leadership and other skills. As Walker (1995) noted,

> The barriers erected by racism encouraged black people to look to their own communities and institutions, permitting the growth and protection of cultural distinctions and generating a conscious black identity. (p. 170)

These institutions proved to be valuable contributors to the ongoing development of African-Canadian communities in all parts of Canada where blacks settled. This chapter is focused on what some scholars (Walker, 1997; Pachai, 1997; Hill, 1981; Gillard, 1997) have called the most important institution—the black church. Using the creation and existence of black churches in Nova Scotia, Ontario, and Montreal as case studies, the central thesis presented in this chapter stresses that the presence of these churches served as a primary vehicle for fostering community development in the early African-Canadian communities.

❖ THE BLACK CHURCH IN CANADA: COMPETING INTERPRETATIONS

Two distinct interpretations have emerged in black Canadian history regarding the influence of the church. Winks (1997), in his book *The Blacks in Canada: A History*, maintained that the church possessed a negative and harmful influence on black Canadians. He asserted that separate black churches acted as barriers to the ultimate goal that black Canadians should have been striving for—integration. Winks (1997) remarked that "the churches too often stressed that final accommodation was to come in the hereafter diverting eyes from the immediate problems of the day" (p. 340).

Winks believed that black churches increased the sense of distance between blacks and whites.

Instead of trying to promote total integration, Winks (1997) concluded the black ministers were basically accommodationist and satisfied to be classified as second-class citizens. Winks also maintained that black preachers held blacks behind by preaching doctrines of patience, subservience, and resignation. He maintained that the preachers should have adopted a militant stand against racism and demanding equal rights and opportunities (p. 480).

Although Winks acknowledged the presence of racism in Canada, he downplayed the impact of this phenomenon on the creation of black churches. Virtually all groups of blacks who migrated to Canada attended white churches. However, the majority of black Canadians were effectively excluded from becoming members of these churches.

Winks's negative interpretation was reinforced by anthropologist Frances Henry in her work *Forgotten Canadians: The Blacks of Nova Scotia* (1973) and by sociologists Donald H. Clairmont and Dennis Magill in their work *Nova Scotia Blacks: An Historical and Structural Overview* (1970). Henry maintains that the creation of black churches furthered the segregation of blacks from the white society. Although Henry acknowledged that the black church was an important institution in the African Nova Scotia Community, she concluded that,

Unlike the United States or the Caribbean, where Blacks have evolved a fairly specific cultural system, Black Nova Scotians, perhaps because of their isolation from these mainstreams of Black culture, could only absorb the values with which they were in contact. The combination of the relative lack of a Black culture and the overriding influence of the values of the dominant society has resulted in a Black population which is characterized also by the values which emphasize conservatism and the status quo. (p. 2)

Clairmont and Magill (1970) in their analysis maintain that the establishment of churches in the black communities laid the basis for the possible growth of a genuine black Nova Scotian subculture. However, they assert that there was little consciousness or evidence of the existence of a distinct black subculture until the late 1960s. They argue that church leaders were in a position to conserve and enrich any distinctive black subculture, but structural limitations imposed by the size of the black population, the scattered distribution of African Nova Scotians, and the isolation of the region contributed to the difficulties the ministers encountered in unifying and giving direction to the black communities. Furthermore, Clairmont and Magill criticized the interlocking directorate of the church leadership in the province by describing the pastors as a small clique who possessed limited general influence. Clairmont and Magill also maintained that the salience of the church in the black community's leadership was over-emphasized (p. 118).

James Walker in various publications dealing with blacks in Canada (1976, 1979, 1980, 1985, 1995) provides a positive interpretation of the role the black church played in African-Canadian communities. Walker maintains that the establishment of separate black churches was a reaction to the racism and discrimination blacks encountered in their efforts to integrate into Canadian society. He interprets the creation of the black churches as a positive and courageous accomplishment. According to Walker (1995) the churches offered blacks a positive identity, a sense of self-worth, and ultimately a base of operations from which to launch attacks against the discriminatory nature of Canadian society (p. 170).

Walker further argues that the black churches offered members of the community opportunities to develop or expose leadership abilities, which were not provided in the dominant society. He stresses that black preachers provided leadership in keeping the communities together, despite the challenges that blacks encountered:

> The Black pastors inevitably became the natural leaders of their local communities for they represented the first all-black institution in lots of their congregations' lives. (Walker, 1979, p. 86)

Walker maintains that the church also provided blacks with a social centre where they could hold an array of activities, especially providing opportunities for youth to develop their skills. He argues that

> for the black pioneers and for generations of their descendents, the core of the community was the church. Church membership defined community, provided opportunities to participate in community affairs, and created networks for cooperative endeavour. (1995, p. 153)

Daniel Hill, in *The Freedom Seekers: Blacks in Early Canada* (1981), reiterates Walker's stance on the importance of black churches in the development of black communities in Canada. He remarks,

Early in the 19th century when some religious groups—particularly the Quakers—undertook to combat slavery by the Underground Railroad movement, Blacks began to come to Canada first in small numbers, later in thousands. Their churches, which had been an important part of their life before they fled from the USA, were quickly transplanted to Canadian soil and carried on their ministry there. The earliest and most important institutions in all Black Upper Canadian communities were the churches. (p. 130)

Hill provides an in-depth account of the formation and contributions of black churches in a number of black communities in southern Ontario. In particular he traces the development of Baptist and Methodist churches.

Dorothy Shreve, in the *AfriCanadian Church: A Stabilizer* (1983), also maintains that the black church played an important role in fostering a sense of community. She comments that

the church was a place where they [blacks] could participate with dignity, pride, and freedom.... On Sunday in the church they became deacons, deaconesses, the lead tenor or soprano in the choir, or superintendent of Sunday school. (p. 13)

Finally, words by Gillard (1997) capture the essence of the value of the black churches:

The Black church has found it necessary to separate from the mainstream in order to afford its members the full participation, lay empowerment, leadership, development, and spiritual dignity. (p. 1)

The experiences of the black churches in Nova Scotia, Ontario, and Montreal provide excellent examples of the positive attributes of these churches, confirming the arguments of those writers who have advanced a positive interpretation of the contributions by these community institutions.

❖ NOVA SCOTIA

The first significant influx of African Americans to what is now Canada occurred after the American Revolution. During the war, the British offered freedom to any slave who would desert their masters and assist the British war effort. At the end of the war the British were forced into keeping their promise, and as a result approximately 3,500 African Americans were sent to different parts of New Brunswick and Nova Scotia, with the majority settling in the latter (Walker, 1976, 1992; Schama, 2005).

However, upon their arrival in Canada, the Black Loyalists were relegated to second-class status while the White Loyalists received preferential treatment. Discrimination prevailed against the free blacks in relation to the distribution of land. Less than a third of the black families who moved to Nova Scotia received land and they received the worst farmland in the province. As well, the land grants they received averaged one-quarter of the size of the farms granted to the whites (Walker, 1976, 1979).

As farming was virtually impossible, most of the blacks were forced to find some other means of employment. Some became tenant farmers renting land from white farmers under sharecropping agreements, while others became indentured servants. The majority of blacks became casual day workers in the major towns. The economic discrimination the Black Loyalists experienced set the stage for over two centuries of ongoing racism and exclusion encountered by African Nova Scotians (Walker, 1976, 1979).

The social environment in Nova Scotia, and in North America in general, during the 1780s was dominated by a fundamentalist religious revival, during which the membership in the Baptist and Methodist churches increased. The Black Loyalists arrived in Nova Scotia with an evident readiness to receive the benefits of religion (Walker, 1976, 1992). Initially the Church of England displayed an early interest in the religious affairs of the Black Loyalists. Blacks attended the white churches, but they were not permitted to mingle with whites in the congregation. In order to maintain this separation, a special gallery was put in place in St. Paul's Church in Halifax in 1784, to which blacks were confined for worship. The Black Loyalists were eventually forced to hold services in private homes, as the large number of white Anglicans made it impossible for all members to attend the church and blacks became the logical choice for exclusion (Walker, 1976; Winks, 1997).

Rejected by the white community in all sectors of society, the African Americans in Nova Scotia turned inwards and created their own churches that rapidly became the focal points in the black communities. Most of the early religious work among the Black Loyalists was carried out by David George, who had escaped from slavery in Virginia. He arrived in Halifax in 1783 and began the mass conversion of African Nova Scotians to the Baptist denomination. George also worked in the communities of

Shelbourne and Birchtown, His presence was not well received by certain whites in those communities, and in 1784 blacks were attacked by former white soldiers. The various meeting houses of the black Baptists were destroyed and George was forced to flee Shelbourne (Walker, 1976; Winks, 1997; Schama 2005). George continued his religious work throughout the province as his reputation as a preacher became known throughout the various black settlements.

Despite the emergence of distinct black communities, the Black Loyalists were economically dependent on the white community. Job opportunities were mostly limited to menial tasks, and for those fortunate enough to possess permanent jobs, the wages they received for the long hours of work were very poor. Overall, blacks encountered ongoing forms of discrimination.

Frustrated by their situation, African Nova Scotians began to organize and protest their status in society. Led by Thomas Peters, who had fought for the British in the American Revolution, members of the community demanded that the British government fulfill the promises made to them. Peters left for England with a petition signed by several black families in both Nova Scotia and New Brunswick who had not received the land they were promised or had lost their land to white settlers. At this time an offer was made by the Sierra Leone Company to the Black Loyalists to relocate to Sierra Leone and establish a homeland. The offer proved to be very attractive to most blacks, as it gave them the chance for complete control over their own affairs (Walker, 1976; Oliver, 1953). On January 15, 1792, 1,200 Black Loyalists sailed from Halifax bound for Sierra Leone (Walker, 1976, 1995; Pachai & Bishop, 2006).

The foundation of the Black Loyalists' society was religion. As Walker (1976) commented,

> Religion gave them much of their vocabulary and determined many of their daily activities, but it also conditioned their attitude towards themselves and towards other people. Religion made them aware of race to a greater extent even than their luckless experience with land had done, for it bound them together as a select all-black group against the encroachments of outsiders considered sinful or at least less pure. (p. 86)

The black community in Nova Scotia—negatively impacted by the departure of the Black Loyalists—was revived during the War of 1812 with the influx of the Black Refugees. The British, adopting the same strategy used during the American Revolution, called upon the slaves of the

Untied States to join them in their struggle against the Americans. Those individuals who heeded the call were to be rewarded by the British.

However, once these Black Refugees arrived in Nova Scotia they were basically left on their own, landless in the majority of cases and ill prepared for the harsh Canadian winters. The majority became dependent on handouts from local government officials. Like the Black Loyalists, the Black Refugees were discriminated against, and the presence of institutional racism resulted in the establishment of separate schools and churches.

The majority of Black Refugees were Baptists, as the result of the Baptist church's successful conversion drive during the religious revival of the last two decades of the 18th century. Initially, most of these new residents of Halifax attended a church organized by a white minister, Reverend John Burton. Eventually most of the congregation consisted of blacks, which was frowned upon by the white community (Oliver, 1953; Pachai & Bishop, 2006).

One of the most active participants at Burton's Church was Richard Preston, an African American who arrived in Preston, Nova Scotia, in search of his mother who had ventured to the province a few years earlier. Preston's mother was living in the black settlement at Preston (Pachai, 1997).

Preston, a devout Baptist, immediately joined Burton's church and during the 1820s he became an important aide to Burton, taking on the responsibility of handling the religious work in the various black communities. In a short period of time Preston's stature in these communities increased as his abilities as a leader and organizer became quite apparent. Supported by members of the congregation, Preston went to England in 1831, where he trained to become a minister. The following year, he was ordained as a Baptist minister (Oliver, 1953; Pachai, 1997; Pachai & Bishop, 2006).

In order to provide Preston with a base from which he could continue his religious and secular duties in the community, the black Baptists in Halifax believed that a fully organized black church needed to be established. The Covenant of the African Churches revealed that African Nova Scotians also desired to be together in their worship:

> Having been as we trust, brought by divine grace to embrace the Lord Jesus Christ, and to give up wholly on him, we do now solemnly and joyfully covenant with each other, To Walk Together In Him with Brotherly Love, to his glory as our common Lord. (quoted in Boyd, 1976, p. xv)

Upon his return to Halifax, Preston became minister of the First African Baptist Church on Cornwallis Street and began his campaign for more conversions to the Baptist faith. During his career, Preston organized 13 churches and he preached in several additional communities throughout the province (Pachai, 1997).

Preston recognized that blacks in Nova Scotia were regarded as second-class citizens and he used every means at his command for the moral and religious advancement of this community. With his crusading spirit and devotion to members of the community, the Baptist faith solidified its position as the most popular denomination among African Nova Scotians.

With the growth and expansion of black Baptist churches throughout the province, Preston, along with Septimus Clarke, a farmer from the town of Preston, recognized the need for a cohesive central organization that would look after the needs of the churches and facilitate communication between them. The dream of the two men materialized in 1854 when they organized the churches into the African United Baptist Association of Nova Scotia (AUBA) (Oliver, 1953; Winks, 1997; Pachai, 1990). At the time of Preston's death in 1861, almost every black settlement had a chapel and preacher.

During the first 25 years of its existence, the AUBA experienced a number of financial challenges. Although community members were very poor, they contributed whatever they could to support their churches. However, the money the churches received was not sufficient, and the leaders of the association received assistance from whites in order to sustain the organization (Oliver, 1953; Winks, 1997).

The AUBA was active in the salient social issues that negatively impacted the black communities in Nova Scotia. The issue of temperance was a main priority, and the ministers constantly stressed the importance of community members maintaining high moral standards. In their view, this would hopefully garner respect from the broader society.

Another major concern centred on the quality of education that black youth received. Educational opportunities were extremely limited. African Nova Scotian youths attended separate schools in the black communities. These schools lacked the facilities common in white educational institutions. In response to this situation, the AUBA demanded better conditions. However, the practice of "Jim Crow" schools in Nova Scotia prevailed well into the 20th century. Despite this situation, the various preachers continued to stress the importance of gaining an education, either formal or informal (Oliver, 1953; Winks, 1969).

From the initial arrival of the Black Loyalists and their exclusion from
virtually all aspects of the dominant society, the black churches emerged
as a critical institution in African Nova Scotian communities. Not only did
these institutions provide African Nova Scotians with a venue in which to
express their spirituality; they also provided opportunities to engage in
social activities and to take on leadership responsibilities.

❖ ONTARIO

The establishment of black churches was similar in Ontario, although the
first significant migration of blacks to the province did not occur until the
War of 1812. An estimated 10,000 African Americans moved to what was
then Upper Canada between 1812 and 1850. They settled along the frontier
facing Detroit and along the Niagara Peninsula. Eventually, significant
numbers of blacks settled in the larger centres of Toronto, London,
Hamilton, and St. Catharines.

Generally, the social conditions for blacks were better in Upper Canada
than they were in Nova Scotia. Commenting on the condition of blacks in
the province one refugee remarked,

> I came into Canada in 1845. Stopped at Toronto where I found the
> coloured people prompt, doing well, ready to help. I went to Oro, where I
> found some 50 person settled, many comfortable and doing well. (quoted
> in Drew, 1972, p. 120)

Another refugee exclaimed,

> I have been through both Upper and Lower Canada and I have found
> the coloured keeping stores, farming, and doing well. I have made more
> money since I came here than I make in the United States. I know several
> coloured people who have become wealthy by industry—owning horses
> and carriages. (quoted in Drew, 1972, p. 96)

Religion was a very important dimension of the social life for the
majority of blacks who settled in Upper Canada. Coming from a society
where slavery and racism prevailed for some, the actual exodus itself was
a religious and liberating experience. As remarked by an African American
who left the United States for Canada,

> On the morning of the third day after their arrival at Detroit, Jarm led
> his old mare into Canada. When he put his foot on the soil the angel of

freedom touched his heart and it leapt for joy.... He felt the divine hand within him and he extinctively exclaimed O'Lord Go, I thank thee/- I am free. (quoted in Lewis, 1965, p. 119)

The majority of refugees in Ontario, like their counterparts in Nova Scotia, were Baptist; therefore it is not surprising that the Baptist Church emerged as the most popular church in Ontario's black communities. Initially, blacks were welcomed in the white churches, but as the number of African Americans settling in the province and attending the churches increased, members of the dominant group felt threatened. Blacks began to feel unwanted by the white congregation members. Moreover, the blacks were also dissatisfied with the quality of education offered by the white Baptist churches. As states by an African American who settled in Canada,

but we must admonish our Baptist and Methodist friends, that they are sadly in fault since they neglected their duty and done nothing for us when they have been earnestly entreated to do something, nor are our "Free Mission Baptist" friends even to be excused in this case. (quoted in Simpson, 1971, p. 43)

The experiences of discrimination, along with the desire to control their own religious affairs as they had in the United States, propelled these African Americans to establish their own churches. Once again, these churches helped to develop a tradition of communal response and mutual response.

The first black Baptist church in Ontario was formed by Elder William Wilks, who entered Canada from the United States in 1818, at Amherstburg, where he remained for one year. He then moved to Colchester, where he purchased 40 acres of land on which was built the First African Baptist Church of Ontario (Hill, 1981). However, Elder Christian was responsible for the rapid expansion of the church in the province as he established more churches than any other black Baptist minister. As Hill stated,

He laboured as a missionary for a time in Boston, Connecticut, and New York. Then he felt the call to go among the refugee slaves in Canada. He entered Canada and organized a coloured Baptist Church at Toronto. Its membership grew to such a size during his pastorate that they had to build a larger church.... He also founded Baptist churches at St. Catharines and Hamilton. (quoted in Hill, 1963, p. 5)

The pastors of these churches became the leaders of their local communities, for often they were the most educated and represented the most important institution in the lives of the refugees. The churches represented a place where members of the community gathered, not only to have their spiritual needs met, but as well to hold a variety of social activities. The churches also served as social welfare institutions providing food, clothing, and housing for newly arrived refugees. In some cases the ministers and congregations helped these new citizens to find jobs. In essence, the church itself became the community for blacks (Simpson, 1971).

The African Americans who settled in Ontario, who strongly believed that academic education was the key to the future, also stressed the importance of spiritual education. Besides the weekly sermons and the work of the home missions, the churches established sabbath schools where Bible reading and the memorization of scriptures were deemed important. Throughout the 19th century, these schools played a vital role in the education of blacks.

By 1841, black Baptist churches were established in virtually every community where blacks had settled. Most of the Black Refugees entered Canada through the Amherstburg area, and members of the Amherstburg Baptist Church recognized their responsibility in helping these African Americans settle in Canada. As the number of refugees increased, the congregation recognized the need to create an organization that would be capable of addressing the needs of the new settlers (Lewis, 1961).

Once established, the Amherstburg Association became active in the major social concerns that blacks encountered in Upper Canada. Each year the association passed resolutions condemning slavery and provided support to abolitionists who were actively involved in the struggle to eradicate the "peculiar institution." A resolution passed by members of the Association in 1842 expressed their position in relation to slavery:

> We see the deformed evil of slavery creeping with its satanic influence with spiritual wickedness in high places, therefore, we recommend our Brethen to stand up against it as strong opposers, wherever they merit it, whether in Church or State: and ever hold forth anti-slavery truth to the world and not to tolerate any person or persons who will hold fellowship with slave holders of their apologists. (quoted in Johanson, 1962, p. 7)

The association consistently stressed the importance of educational advancement of community members and supported the establishment of

Sabbath schools and bible classes. A resolution passed in 1842 revealed the importance the association placed on education:

> Resolved that it is the duty of all ministering Elders and Deacons and church members to search the scriptures for themselves so that they may know the truth concerning the Salvation of their souls for we believe the time has come for us to get out of the Dark in to the light. (quoted in Johanson, 1962, p. 8)

Missionary work was another activity promoted by the association. Members were interested in helping all blacks regardless of their religious denomination and recommended that church members pay one penny a week. Certain communities in the province did not have a trained minister and in order to alleviate this situation, the association appointed a missionary each year. During their year of work, the missionaries travelled extensively, preaching, visiting families, attending church meetings, and baptizing new adherents to the church.

The passing of the *Fugitive Slave Act* in 1850 by the American government initiated a mass exodus of blacks to Canada—an estimated 40,000—with the majority settling in Upper Canada. The *Act* made it possible for individuals suspected of being a runaway slave to be arrested without a warrant and turned over to a claimant on nothing more than the claimant's sworn testimony of ownership. A suspected slave could not ask for a jury trial nor testify on his or her own behalf (Franklin & Schweninger, 1999).

The increased size of Upper Canada's black communities strengthened the Amherstburg Association, and by 1856 the organization reached its peak with several churches becoming new members. The association and the Canadian Anti-Slavery Baptist Association, which was formed in 1850, merged into one entity known as the Amherstburg Regular Baptist Association in 1857.

The Methodist Church also proved to be popular among the early black pioneers in Upper Canada. During the 1830s, African Methodism spread very rapidly in Canada. In recalling the development of the British Methodist Episcopal Church in Ontario, Bishop Markham, former minister of the church in Toronto, remarked,

> We were originally a conference of the African Methodist Episcopal Church headquarters in the United States, but during the 1850s, due in great part the passing of the [Fugitive] Slave Act, and the fear of persecution on the

part of Black Canadians, who had to attend the conferences in the United States, the members of the Canadian conference sought and gained the approval of the mother church to become a distinct and separate organization. It was at that time that the name was changed, and in 1856 we were incorporated as the British Methodist Episcopal Church. (quoted in Walker, 1979, p. 88)

The Methodist churches provided the same services to community members as the black Baptist churches. Because they were not welcomed by the white Methodist churches, blacks found a sense of security and a more cordial atmosphere in their own churches.

The development of black churches continued until the end of the American Civil War. During the war, some community members migrated to the United States to enlist in the Union Army. By 1865, the number of blacks returning to the United States rapidly increased. The desire to rejoin families; the perceived improvement in opportunities, especially during the Reconstruction period; and experiences of discrimination in Canada motivated the majority of these blacks to leave. The migration to the United States directly impacted the development of the black churches in Ontario. With a depleted population, the churches suffered from a decline of income that forced them to curtail some of their programs.

Without question, black churches played an important and vital role in helping blacks adjust to their new homes in Ontario. In looking for support, the black settlers relied on religion and their churches. Samuel Gridley Howe, in a report to the Freedman's Inquiry Commission (1864), captured the importance of religion for community members when he stated, "Whenever a few refugees congregate together the first thing they do in common is to provide for public worship. They have a passion for public worship" (quoted in Simpson, 1971, p. 3).

❖ MONTREAL

The origin of the modern black community in Montreal dates back to the 1880s with the completion of the Grand Trunk and Canadian Pacific Railway lines into the city. Montreal became the centre of railway transportation in Canada when the Canadian Pacific Railway Company made the city its general employment headquarters. Influenced by the American-based Pullman Railway Company to hire blacks as porters and dining car attendants, and by a desire to keep labour costs at a minimum, the Canadian railway companies implemented the same practice.

Initially, African Americans were temporary residents, as most were college students who worked to pay the cost of their education. While working in Montreal, most stayed in lodgings owned by the railway companies, while a small number rented rooms in family residences. With such a transient population, services that emerged in this temporary black community included social clubs, a hotel, barbershops, and restaurants (Potter, 1948, p. 11). The transitory population eventually led to the establishment of a permanent black community during the late 1890s, as many decided to remain in Montreal (Walker, 1997). Two factors were instrumental in this decision. First, African Americans perceived the racial atmosphere to be less hostile than in the United States, especially in the South; and second, the availability of a job on the railway provided a sense of security, even for porters who were fairly well educated. By 1897, an estimated 300 black people lived in Montreal. However, within a relatively short period of time, the influx of new members brought the black population to approximately 500 (Williams, 1997, p. 199).

The social environment in Montreal was not as congenial as many blacks thought it would be (Walker, 1997). Although legal segregation was nonexistent, blacks encountered a more subtle type of racism that was manifested in various segments of society. The theatres and clubs in Montreal also discriminated against blacks. One of the most famous incidents took place in March 1899, when a black man bought tickets for two orchestra chairs in the Academy of Music. Upon arrival with his female companion, the gentleman was denied his seats by the ushers and offered seats in another part of the theatre. He refused the seats and brought legal action against the theatre. He won the case in the Lower Court; the theatre carried the case to the Court of Appeal, which rejected the appeal. However, the decision did not stop the discriminatory practices of the white social establishments (Greaves, 1930).

Religion was vital for the majority of African Americans who settled in Montreal. Although they initially sought religious salvation by attending the local white churches, they were not cordially received, as the whites would neither associate, nor mingle, with them. Blacks were often placed in the choir lofts or in the back pews where they could not be seen. In some instances, the pastors told the blacks that they were not welcome and admittance was refused (Bertley, 1983; Israel, 1928). This alienation was amplified when the blacks, who were accustomed to organizing and controlling the affairs of their own churches in the United States, were allowed no input into the operation of the white churches. Because of the discriminatory seating practices, the blacks also did not feel like part of the congregation, even in those churches where services were active (Bertley, 1976; "Negro Church," 1972).

As a result, members of the black community attempted to organize church services that suited the community's own needs. Their efforts were realized in 1897 when the British Methodist Episcopalian Mission allowed blacks to use its facilities. Services were usually held on Sunday night, officiated by a local resident who served as pastor (Israel, 1928, pp. 113–114). By 1906, a group of blacks, totally frustrated by the failure to organize one central church, organized and established the Union Congregational Church.

Besides providing a place to worship, these organizers recognized the need for the church to be an important institution within the community. To ensure efficient operations of the facility, the constitution provided guidelines for the establishment of an administrative system: "The officers shall be a Pastor, not more than five deacons, seven deaconesses, a clerk, a treasurer, a superintendent of the Sunday School, and an auditor" (Union Congregational Church, 1907). The number of positions clearly indicated that members of the community would be allowed to develop or reveal their leadership abilities. The opportunities for black women reflected their importance in the affairs of the church and the community. Because the majority of men were employed by the railway and spent considerable time away from the community, the female deaconesses provided services to ensure the operation of the church. Even when male deacons were present, the women filled active and important roles (Este, 2004). Women also formed social organizations, such as the Coloured Women's Club of Montreal (CWCM), organized in 1901, which played a vital role in the community (Bertley, 1977). These organizations "aimed to bring blacks together and encouraged and supported family life" (Williams, 1997, p. 2).

The Union Congregational Church was officially opened in the Welsh Dance Hall on September 1, 1907, with Reverend Samuel Brown of Boston and the church's first minister, Reverend Samuel Bowser, presiding over the official activities. Twenty-six people made up the first membership roll (Este, 2004). During Reverend Bowser's term of ministry, from 1907 to 1909, the church concentrated on increasing its membership and serving as a social centre for the community. In its capacity as a welcoming house for new residents in the community, the church received assistance from the CWCM.

Church officials encouraged the active participation of its members to establish a close rapport with the community. Members of the congregation responded by making announcements in the services concerning the illnesses of fellow members and stating times for various meetings and social activities (Israel, 1928). They were involved in community work, visiting members of the congregation who were ill, or helping in the organization of social events (Bertley, 1976).

Younger members of the community were also actively involved in the church's affairs. The church provided opportunities to develop their leadership abilities, as well as a place to display their talents in music, public speaking, dancing, and teaching. The Sunday school emerged as the most attractive institution for young blacks.

After the war in 1918, the influx of West Indians to Montreal resulted in an increased membership for Union Church. The social environment for these new immigrants mirrored that of the early African Americans. Although many were skilled workers—carpenters, shipbuilders, jewellers, and other tradesmen—the majority were forced to seek jobs on the railroads. This was a degrading experience for the trained black workers who expected Canada to be a land of opportunity. As with their American counterparts, religion was an important aspect of their social life. Upon arrival in Montreal, a few of them attended white churches, but the discrimination propelled the majority of them to Union Church (Este, 2004).

The prosperity of the church rapidly declined as Montreal experienced an economic depression. By the middle of 1920, attendance decreased as some members of the community migrated to the United States in search of employment. This resulted in a decrease in church revenue, thus making it difficult to maintain a comfortable place of worship (Este, 2004). By 1923, the church was in danger of closing. However, even during this period of financial difficulty, the church continued in its role as a social welfare institution. The Sunday school continued to be the main attraction for the youth. A Young Peoples' Club was organized and members became involved in community work. The weekly meetings of the United Negro Improvement Association (UNIA) provided opportunities for community members to socialize.

In March 1923, a movement across Canada made up of the Presbyterian, Methodist, and Congregational churches was being organized to discuss the possibility of merging into one church body known as the United Church of Canada. The majority of trustees believed that Union Congregational Church would benefit from the merger, as the church could not continue to operate, and the financial status of the church would be improved if it participated in the union. The major concern was to reverse the decline that the church was experiencing, and the merger proposal appeared to be a very attractive method to help restore the church to prominence in the community (Union Church Trustee Meetings, Montreal, Quebec, 27 March, 1 April, and 2 June 1923).

During his tenure as student pastor (1923–1925), Charles Este took steps to ensue the future of the church and repeatedly stressed the need for cooperation between all organizations and the church committees. His main priority was to pay the operating expenses of the church and seek ways to raise funds. Organizations affiliated with the church contributed as much as they could, and the revenue began to escalate. Este was ordained in Union Church. He assumed his duties as full-time minister and the resurgence of the church continued (Bertley, 1983; Williams, 1997; Este, 2004).

On June 11, 1925, the church union was finalized and Union Congregational Church became known as Union United Church. It was the only black church in Canada that participated in the merger, which proved to be a blessing for the church, as the United Church of Canada reduced the rent of the church property from $25 per month to $1 per year (Union Church Trustee Meeting, Montreal, Quebec, 18 June 1923).

With the leadership of Reverend Este, his contacts with the greater Montreal community, and the efforts of the church-affiliated organizations, the church raised the funds required to keep the church alive. The response of the community to the fundraising campaign reflected the value of the church to the community. As Potter (1948) maintains, members of the community were proud of their "coloured" church, as it was affectionately known.

Besides his spiritual responsibilities, Reverend Este became the secular leader of the black community. Despite improved economic conditions in Montreal, blacks were still plagued with employment difficulties, poor housing, and other social problems. Without a social agency to look after the needs of blacks, members of the community naturally turned to the pastor, as he was regarded as their leader (Este, 2004).

During fall 1927, Este suggested to the congregation that a black community centre be formed. He believed that such a centre would become the focal point of all social activities (Bertley, 1983; Homewood, 1959; Walker, 1997). Este and Golden Darby, an American-born black with considerable experience in community organizations, were the driving forces behind the centre's formation. Because the community lacked the funds to completely finance the project, Darby and Este approached

Montreal businessmen for financial assistance. By February 1928 the Negro Community Centre (NCC) was opened in the basement of Union Church (Bertley, 1983; Williams, 1997).

Of particular concern to the founders of the centre were the barriers to employment encountered by blacks. They were denied employment in the city's department stores and hospitals. In commenting on the centre's role in this domain, Bertley (1983) maintains that

> the Centre was ... naturally directed towards establishing and organizing services and programs for youth and adults, and representing the Negro in the Montreal Community in many ways, breaking down barriers to hiring and employment and seeking better housing accommodation and working with other agencies and government groups and officials in order to correct injustices whenever they appeared. (p. 126)

In a short period of time, the NCC proved to be very beneficial to the black community by increasing community consciousness and socialization. It is not surprising that gym and music classes and a variety of other programs geared toward the youth were the major activities of the centre.

❖ DISCUSSION

Rejected by the dominant community in their efforts to integrate into Canadian society, black Canadians turned inward and formed their own institutions, which provided them with a certain degree of protection from a racist and oppressive society. Upon arrival in Canada, blacks initially sought religious salvation in established white churches. However, being subjected to discriminatory practices in these churches propelled black settlers, primarily African Americans, to establish their own churches. The existence of the churches allowed blacks to control their own religious affairs.

In a short period of time, the black church became the most important institution in African-Canadian communities and was instrumental in providing a sense of stability for community members. The strong ministerial and secular leadership provided blacks with a sense of pride and worth and a community consciousness.

In collaboration with the church, the various church and auxiliary organizations contributed to the development of the community. The organizations, through an array of social and spiritual activities, served as mechanisms whereby community members socialized with each other. The youth in the communities received a considerable amount of attention from elders in the community who regarded the youth as the future leaders. The church also provided opportunities for community members to develop or display their leadership abilities.

The black churches also emerged as advocates on behalf of their communities. Through various means, racism and discrimination were denounced and demands for equity and social justice, especially in the educational and employment domains, were put forth by the ministers and other community members.

The contributions of the black churches to African-Canadian communities represent clear manifestations of community development. An overall purpose of community development is to improve the economic, social, cultural, or environmental well-being of individuals who comprise the community. Biddle and Biddle, two scholars who wrote extensively on community development, noted

> Community development is a social process by which human beings can become more competent to live with and gain some control over local aspects of a frustrating and changing world. (quoted in Mattessich & Monsey, 1997, p. 58)

Voth, another academic who also published literature on community development, remarked:

> Community development is a situation in which some groups, usually locality-based such as a neighbourhood and local community... attempt to improve [their] social and economic situation through their own effort. (Voth, quoted in Mattessich & Monsey, 1997, p. 59)

The various activities organized by the black churches were designed to improve the quality of life experienced by black Canadians. The churches also engaged in different types of advocacy directed at ensuring that members of African-Canadian communities were treated in an equitable and just manner, especially regarding educational and employment opportunities.

Instead of being complacent with their situation, African Canadians created a strong sense of community wherever they settled in Canada. Walker (1995), in describing this phenomenon, remarked,

The early pioneers learned that as individuals they were vulnerable, in the face of mainstream hostility, and they developed a tradition of communal response and mutual support. Community has therefore become a fundamental theme of black history in Canada. (p. 152)

Phillip Daniels, a filmmaker, who produced a documentary about the role of churches in African-Canadian communities, *Seeking Salvation*, argues the following:

I believe that the impact of the institution of the church within black communities across our country [Canada] is probably deeper and its impact is probably a lot wider. Not only in a spiritual sense or in a religious sense.... It has traditionally been involved in education and literary efforts and it has been an organizing point for women in the community. (p. 1)

The creation, maintenance, and survival of the black churches, in a society where blacks were treated as second-class citizens, clearly reveals the importance of the church in the daily lives of African Canadians. Community members strongly believed that the church was the "pillar" of strength in the community, an institution that helped preserve a distinct black Canadian culture.

❖ CONCLUSION

Given the reality that blacks in Canada continue to experience racism and discrimination that results in their exclusion in mainstream society, the black churches continue to be an important institution for African Canadians. In essence, it is still a place that provides a sense of belonging, a gathering point that brings together members of the community, not only as a venue for worship and expressing their spirituality, but also a place where social events are ogranized by church-related groups.

The ministers of these churches continue the proud but necessary tradition of advocating and fighting for equal treatment for African Canadians. These messages are clearly imparted in the documentary *Seeking Salvation: A History of the Black Church in Canada*, which was released in 2005. This film clearly acknowledges and celebrates the array of contributions of black churches in Canada and, more specifically, the role they palyed in the lives of African Canadians.

In his book *The Blacks in Canada: A History*, Winks questioned if these churches were indeed a pillar of strength within the black communities.

Based on the contributions that the black churches played in the individual lives of black Canadians in fighting social and economic inequalities resulting from the presence of "everyday" racism, Winks's question is no longer debatable.

REFERENCES

Bernard, W.T. (1996). *Survival and success: As defined by black men in Sheffield, England and Halifax, Canada*. Unpublished doctoral dissertation, University of Sheffield.

Bernard, W.T., & Bernard, C. (1999). Creative innovation: African centered community support for children and families. *National Child and Youth Care Journal, 15*(1), 73–85.

Bertley, L. (1976). *Montreal's oldest black congregation: Union Church*. Pierrefonds, QC: Bilongo.

Bertley, L. (1977). *Canada and its people of African descent*. Pierrefonds, QC: Bilongo.

Bertley, L. (1983). *The Universal Negro Improvement Association of Montreal 1917–1979* Unpublished doctoral dissertation, Concordia University, Montreal.

Biddle, W., & Biddle, L. (1965). *The community development process: The rediscovery of local initiative*. New York: Holt, Rinchart and Winston.

Boyd, F. (1976) (Ed.). *A brief history of the coloured Baptists of Nova Scotia, 1783–1895*. Halifax, NS: Afro Nova Scotian Enterprises. (Reprint of 1895 ed.)

Christensen, C. (1995). Immigrant minorities in Canada. In J. Turner & F. Turner (Eds.), *Canadian social welfare* (3rd ed. pp. 179–212). Scarborough, ON: Allyn and Bacon.

Christensen, C.P. (1998). Social welfare and social work in Canada: Aspects of the Black experience. In V.P. Oyle & C. James (Eds.), *Re/visioning Canadian perspectives on the education of Africans in the later 20th century* (pp. 36–55). York, ON: Captus Press.

Christensen, C. (2005). Immigrant minorities. In J. Turner & F. Turner (Eds.), *Canadian social welfare* (5th ed. pp. 167–195). Scarborough, ON: Allyn and Bacon.

Clairmont, D., & Magill, D. (1970). *Nova Scotia blacks: An historical and structural overview*. Halifax, NS: Institute of Public Affairs, Dalhousie University.

Clairmont, D. & Magill, D. (1999). *Africville: The Life and death of a Canadian black community*. Toronto, ON: Canadian Scholars' Press.

Danzer, P. (1997). Challenging diversity: Black women and social welfare. In P. Evans & G. Wekerle (Eds.), *Women and the Canadian welfare state: Challenges and changes* (pp. 269–290). Toronto, ON: University of Toronto Press.

Drew, B. (1972). *The narratives of fugitive slaves in Canada*. Toronto: Coles Publishing Company. (First published in 1856.)

Este, D. (2004). The black church as a social welfare institution: Union United Church and the development of Montreal's black community, 1907–1940. *Journal of Black Studies, 35*(1), 3–22.

Este, D., & Bernard, W.T. (2003). Social work practice with African Canadians: An examination of the African Nova Scotian community. In A. Al-Krenawi and J. Graham (Eds.), *Multicultural social work in Canada: Working with diverse ethno-racial communities* (pp. 306–337). Don Mills, ON: Oxford University Press.

Foster, C. (1996). *A place called heaven: The meaning of being black in Canada.* Don Mills, ON: HarperCollins.

Franklin, J.H., & Schweninger, L. (1999). *Runaway slaves: Rebels on the plantation.* New York: Oxford University Press.

Gillard, D. (1997). *The black church in Canada.* Retrieved 8 August 2004 from www.mcmaster.ca/mjtm/1-5.htm.

Greaves, I. (1930). *The Negro in Canada.* Orillia, ON: Pocket Times Press.

Henry, F. (1973). *Forgotten Canadians: The blacks of Nova Scotia.* Toronto: Longham Press.

Hill, D. (1963). *Negroes in Toronto, 1793–1865. Ontario History Society,* 55(2), 73–91.

Hill, D. (1981). *The freedom-seekers: Blacks in early Canada.* Agincourt, ON: Book Society of Canada.

Homewood, E.L. (1959). The preacher was a bookblack. *United Church Observer,* (June), pp. 8-9.

Israel, W. (1928). *The Montreal Negro community.* Unpulished master's thesis, McGill University, Montreal.

Johanson, J. (1962). *The Amherstburg Baptist Association, 1841–1861.* Unpublished bachelor's thesis, McMaster University, Hamilton, ON.

Jones, B. (1982). Nova Scotia Blacks: A quest for a place in the Canadian Mosaic. In V.D. Oyley (Ed.), *Black presence in multi-ethnic Canada* (pp. 54–70). Vancouver: Centre for the Study of Curriculum and Instruction, Faculty of Education, University of British Columbia.

Lewis, J. (1961). Religious nature of the early Negro migration to Canada and the Amherstburg Baptist Association. *Ontario History,* 58, 117–132

Lewis, J. (1965). *Religious life of fugitive slaves and rise of colored Baptist churches, 1820–1865, in what is now known as Ontario.* Unpublished master's thesis, McMaster University, Hamilton, ON.

Mattessich, P., & Monsey, B. (1997). *Community building: What makes it work: A review of factors influencing successful community building.* Saint Paul, MN: Amherst H. Wilder Foundation.

Negro Church. (1972) Marking the 65th anniversary of community leadership. *The Gazette* (May 28), p. 14.

Oliver, P. (1953). *A brief history of the colored Baptists of Nova Scotia, 1782–1953.* Halifax, NS: African United Baptist Association of Nova Scotia.

Pachai, B. (1990). *Beneath the clouds of the promised land: The survival of Nova Scotia's blacks. Volume 2, 1800–1989.* Halifax, NS: Black Educators Association.

Pachai, B. (1997). *Peoples of the Maritimes.* Halifax, NS: Nimbus Publishing.

Pachai, B., & Bishop, H. (2006). *Historic Black Nova Scotia.* Halifax, NS: Nimbus Publishing.

Potter, H. (1948). *The occupational adjustment of Montreal Negroes, 1941–48*. Unpublished Master's Thesis, McGill University, Montreal, PQ.

Schama, S. (2005). *Rough crossings: Britain, the slaves, and the American revolution*. Toronto: Penguin.

Shreve, D. (1983). *The AfriCanadian church: A stabilizer*. Jordon Station, ON: Paideia Press.

Simpson, D. (1971). *Negroes in Ontario from early times to 1870*. Unpublished doctoral dissertation, University of Western Ontario, London, ON.

Union Congregational Church (1907). *Constitution & By-Laws*. Montreal, PQ: Author.

Union Congregational Church (1923). *Union Church Trustee Meeting*. Montreal, PQ: Author.

Walker, J. St. G. (1976). *The Black Loyalists: The search for a promised land in Nova Scotia and Sierra Leone*. Halifax, NS: Dalhousie University Press.

Walker, J. St. G. (1979). *Identity: The black experience in Canada*. Toronto: Ontario Educational Communications Authority.

Walker, J. St. G. (1980). *A history of blacks in Canada: A study guide for teachers and students*. Hull, QC: Minister of State for Multiculturalism.

Walker, J. St. G. (1985). *Racial discrimination in Canada: The black experience*. Ottawa: Canadian Historical Association.

Walker, J. St. G. (1992). *The Black Loyalists: The Search for the Promised Land in Nova Scotia and Sierra Leone, 1783-1870*. 2nd ed. Toronto: University of Toronto Press.

Walker. J. St. G. (1995). African Canadians. In P. Magocsi (Ed.), *Encyclopedia of Canada's Peoples* (pp. 139–176). Toronto: University of Toronto Press.

Walker, J. (1997). *Race, rights and the law in the Supreme Court of Canada: Historical case studies*. Waterloo, ON: Osgoode Society for Canadian Legal History, Wilfred Laurier University Press.

Williams, D. (1997). *The road to now: A history of blacks in Montreal*. Montreal: Vehicule Press.

Winks, R. (1969). Negro school segregation in Ontario and Nova Scotia. *Canadian Historical Review, 50*(2), 164–191.

Winks, R. (1971). *The blacks in Canada: A history*. Montreal & Kingston, ON: McGill-Queen's University Press.

Winks, R. (1997). *The blacks in Canada: A history* (2nd ed.). Montreal & Kingston, ON: McGill-Queen's University Press.

CHAPTER 19

ISLAMIC THEOLOGY AND PRAYER:
RELEVANCE FOR SOCIAL WORK PRACTICE

ALEAN AL-KRENAWI AND JOHN R. GRAHAM

A varied literature outlines the religious basis of the social work profession in the West (Alexander, 1983; Fauri, 1988; Freedberg, 1986; Graham, 1992; Horsburgh, 1988; Leiby, 1985). Social work practice issues in religion and clinical work (Berthold, 1989; Cornett, 1992; Cox, 1985; Goldberg, 1996; Sermabeikian, 1994) and in such fields of practice as health care (Rockowitz, et al., 1981) are also well documented. Practising social workers, however, appear to have little training in religious issues (Sheridan, et al., 1992), and a number of scholars advocate a greater presence of religion in the social work curriculum (Canda, 1988; Netting, et al., 1990; Sheridan, et al., 1994).

To this end, the present chapter analyzes two aspects of knowledge that are particularly valuable for social workers practising among Muslim clients: theology and prayer. It thereby joins a small body of recent research that has started to examine disparate facets of Islam in a social work practice context (Al-Krenawi, 1996; Al-Krenawi & Graham, 1996; Graham & Al-Krenawi, 1996; Haynes, et al., 1997). The first part introduces Islamic theology, followed by the pillars of Islam; a third section examines the individual and group helping significance of prayer. A concluding section briefly discusses implications for social work research and practice.

❖ ISLAM

Islam is the world's fastest growing and second largest religion. In 2007 Muslims represented 19.4 percent of the world's population, numbered 1.1 to 1.2 billion people and were found in 184 of the world's 262 countries (*Encyclopaedia Britannica*, 1997). Muslims constitute a majority in more than 48 countries and are significant minorities in many others. Islam, as will be discussed, is theologically diverse; approximately 83 percent of all Muslims are Sunnis, 16 percent are Shiites, and 1 percent belongs to other traditions in Islam. Although the Arab world is often seen as the heartland of Islam, most Muslims, in fact, are found in Asia and Africa (Esposito, 1995, p. 243). There are 368 million Muslims in Africa and 900 million in Asia (*Encyclopaedia Britannica*, 2007). Moreover, in Western countries, as in non-Western countries, Islam is an increasing presence. By 1990, as an example, the Muslim community in the United States outnumbered its Jewish counterpart (*Britannica 1996 Book of the Year*, 1996, p. 298); likewise in Canada, there were more Muslims than Presbyterians (Bibby, 1987). In 2006 there were 5.54 million Muslims in North America, 33 million in Europe, and 1.75 million in Latin America (*Encyclopaedia Britannica*, 1997). Muslim social institutions in the West have increased in a like proportion. For example, by 1992 the number of North American mosques, Islamic schools, community centres, publishing houses, and media programming units totalled over 2,300 (Haddad & Smith, 1994, p. xx).

The term "Islam," pronounced "al-Islam" in Arabic, refers to the religion based on the doctrine that Muslims believe was revealed in the year AD 610 to the Prophet Muhammad in the city of Mecca. People who adhere to the religion of Islam are called Muslims. Both terms derive from the Arabic root "*salam*," meaning "peace" or "submission." The basis of Islam is the Koran, a Holy Book consisting of 114 chapters: "It is the eternal, uncreated, literal word of God, sent down from heaven, revealed ... to the prophet Muhammad as a guidance for humankind" (*Oxford Encyclopedia of the Modern Islamic World*, 1995, p. 244). A second valid religious authority is the *Hadith*, the tradition of the Prophet Muhammad's words and deeds as well as those of many of the early Muslims; while transmitted originally orally, these have been written in direct, conversational prose.

Religious Thought

Islam is diverse, and has two key religious aspects that bear particular attention. The first is a distinction between Sunni and Shiite adherents. Unfortunately, a rift exists between the two Islamic sects. The term "Shiite" or "Shia" refers to "party" or "sect," and the party of Muslims who are followers of Ali, a descendant of Muhammad, the prophet (Winters, 1995). Ali is seen as the ultimate religious master (Esposito, 1995). Extreme political transformation has been a cornerstone of Shiism throughout history (Esposito, 1995). Ayatollah Khomeini was one of the most politically successful revolutionary Shiites, and he was able to bring about the destruction of the Persian monarchy (Esposito, 1995). Shiite Muslims tend to be less economically advantaged and some Western commentators characterize them as proponents of the Islamic movement. Shiite Muslims view history wherein the beliefs of Ali can be spread all over the world, for God's rule to be re-established on earth (Esposito, 1995). Shiite Islam is the state religion of Iran (Parrinder, 1971) and, in fact, Iran is considered the head of Shiite Islam (Vohra, 1995). It has a strong influence in Iraq, Pakistan, India, and Yemen. The Shiites comprise approximately 15 percent of the world Muslim population (Swatos, 1998).

The term "Sunna" or "Sunni" is translated as "path," referring to the majority denomination of Muslim people (Winters, 1995). Sunni Muslims follow the traditional practices of Muhammad closely. They believe in, and adhere to, one of four orthodox schools of law. Sunni Muslims comprise approximately 85 percent of the world Muslim population (Swatos, 1998). Sunni Muslims are usually characterized as moderate and more economically advantaged than their Shiite rivals and less inclined toward the Islamic movement. They conceive of community achievement, such as early Islamic growth, and individual achievement, such as prosperity, as a reward from God for being faithful. They see themselves as traditionalists who "distinguish themselves from other Islamic sects whose views, they maintain, constitute … departures from what the community at large holds." Saudi Arabia is considered the head of Sunni Islam (Vohra, 1995).

Challenges shared by Shiite and Sunni Muslims continue to include emphasizing the validity and relevance of their beliefs, in the context of a changing modern world, without losing track of what each group believes to be authentic Islamic practice and beliefs. The origins of the Shiite/ Sunni conflict are based in the differences of religious beliefs. Revivalist movements of the 19th century, although quite diverse in their specifics, collectively felt that Muslim society required purification, and that there should be a more chaste return to the practice of Islam, the wisdom of the Koran, and the example of the Prophet (Esposito, 1995).

The Islamic movement has also presented challenges for the Muslim community, as it has afforded Islam and its followers somewhat negative attention. The Islamic movement has, in the past, been referred to as Islamic fundamentalism. Fundamentalism is defined as faith that is absolute and literal in manner. It involves a "self-conscious effort to avoid compromise, adaptation, or critical reinterpretation of the basic texts and sources of belief." Applying the term "fundamentalism" to Muslims is subject to controversy, since it may be considered derogatory and may imply notions of fanaticism and radical behaviour. Preferred terms for Muslim activist movements include "Islamism, integrism, neonormative Islam, neo-traditional Islam, Islamic revivalism, and Islamic nativism" (Voll, 1995, p. 33), and the Islamic movement. Scholars such as Rahman, Hrair Dekmejian and Voll (cited by Esposito, 1995) believe that the Islamic movement has existed throughout history and has continued to promote a return to the pure essentials of the religion. An example of this type of movement is provided by the jihad actions of Sufis in Southeast Asia. Other scholars such Marty, Lawrence, and Appleby (cited by Esposito, 1995) believe that the Islamic movement has pre-modern origins but is for the most part a product of the modern era. An example of the latter would be the Muslim Brotherhood, which has evolved in Egypt in this century. Major issues for Muslims continue to be their communication with the West, and actions towards reviving and strengthening Islam (Esposito, 1995). Islamic activist movements vary widely in their methods of bringing about change. Organizations run the gamut from those who operate publicly within the law (the Muslim Brotherhoods and the Jama'at'i) to those who use violence and terrorism to see their aims brought to fruition (Islamic Jihad and the Society of Muslims) (Esposito, 1995). Although fundamentalists are not totally anti-modern, modernization does cause concern in that it inherently implies a departure from old, traditional, and trusted ways. To this end, fundamentalists attempt to maintain the religious practices of the past.

Social Consequences

In anthropological terms, Muslim society tends to be high-context: it emphasizes the collective over the individual; it has a slower pace of societal change and a higher sense of social stability. Its opposite is a low-context society, frequently found in the West: one which reveres the individual over the collective, and is a fast-paced society in transition (Hall, 1976). Not surprisingly, the Muslim religion reflects and reinforces the high-context disposition of its societies.

Social stability, for example, is understood by Muslims as the achievement of social peace. This imperative is reinforced by an emphasis upon the collective over the individual; a mutually responsive brother-and sisterhood extending an ummatic bond to a global level. "Help each other in the acts of goodness and piety and do not extend help to each other in sinful acts or transgression behaviours" (Koran, 5, v. 2). The Prophet Muhammad advised Muslims, "Help your brother [the Muslim] whether he is the oppressor or the oppressed." When the Prophet was asked how to help him if he is the oppressor, he replied: "Hold his hand from oppression" (Al-Juzuyyah, 1993). The *Hadith* points out: "Every one of you is a shepherd and each one of you is responsible for his flock" (Nagati, 1993).

This sense of collective responsibility is further reinforced by how the Muslim views his or her place within society. Islam, it should be emphasized, is not concerned with the welfare of the individual alone; it seeks to achieve a wider societal well-being. While ensuring the individual's freedom, it places equal stress on mutual responsibility. This principle, in turn, is two-dimensional. The individual achieves balance between thought and action (internal), while caring for the collective welfare of society (external) (Azmi, 1991; El-Azayem & Zari, 1994). But this internal individual-societal consonance is best realized by a third party: through total submission to the will and pleasure of God. As stated in the Koran: "My worship and my sacrifice and my living and my dying are all for Allah, Lord of worlds" (Koran, 6, v. 163).

The Islamic perspective of the person emphasizes selflessness, healthy altruism, perfection of self, and giving happiness to others (Al-Bostani, 1988; Al-Issawi, 1988). It has a high ideal of the ultimate good, but also a means of being within reach of all adherents, for Islam promises forgiveness to anyone who is committed to fulfilling its conditions: "He is the one that accepts repentance from His servants and forgives sin and he knows all that ye do" (Koran, 42, v. 25). Although the sin may not be condoned, the sinner is nonetheless provided an opportunity to turn from sin and to obtain spiritual purification (Mohamed, 1995; Rizvi, 1989). The following section will provide insight into some of these Islamic mechanisms.

THE PILLARS OF ISLAM

Islam is considered a way of life. Its tenets are to be integrated holistically into a follower's life, and also within society as a whole (Qutib, 1967). Muslims believe in the existence of angels, the devil, a day of judgement, destiny, heaven, and hell (Mohamed, 1995; Rizvi, 1989). Of particular theological significance, however, are the five pillars of faith. These bear upon the reciprocal relationships between an individual's physical, spiritual, psychological, and emotional well-being (Azmi, 1991; El-Azayem & Zari, 1994). From a strictly individual perspective, there is not only an eschatological imperative for following Islam. Muslims also hold that to deviate from the faith is tantamount to being less than a fully authentic human being. As stated in the Koran, oblivion occurs when humanity loses touch with this fundamental truth: "And be not like those who forgot God and He caused them to be oblivious of their own selves or souls" (Koran, 49, v. 19). And so a Muslim is required to adhere to the following pillars.

1. The *shahada*, or profession of faith, is the belief that there is no other god but Allah and that Muhammad is His last prophet. Thus, Islam insists on the submission of the faithful to the oneness of God. "Say: He is God, the one and only" (Koran, 112, v. 1–4) is one of many Koranic verses emphasizing the monotheistic character of Islam.
2. The *salat* is the imperative to pray five times daily: at dawn, noon, mid-afternoon, sunset, and evening. The prayers can be performed anywhere, and although individual prayer is allowed, group prayer is preferred.
3. The *zakat* is the requirement to pay alms to the needy on behalf of one's family and business. "It was customarily calculated as an annual payment of two-and-one-half percent of all capital assets, savings, and current income above a specified threshold" (Azmi, 1991). The exact rate, however, could be flexible, in part according to the need established by the *imam*, or local Muslim cleric.
4. The *siam* is the imperative to fast from food, drink, and sex during daylight hours during the month of Ramadan, which immediately precedes the celebration of the date upon which Allah revealed the Koran to the Prophet Muhammad. Ramadan thus ends with a three-day celebration, Id Al-Fitr, the breaking of the fast. Self-discipline and reflection, rather than abstinence and self-mortification, are emphasized.
5. The *hajj* is a pilgrimage to Mecca, a holy city of Islam located where Allah revealed the Koran to the Prophet Muhammad. The pilgrimage should be undertaken at least once in a Muslim's lifetime, if financially, mentally, and physically capable. The beginning of the pilgrimage season is the end of Ramadan; the end of the season is the celebration of the Great Feast Id Al-Adha (see below).

Praying

Prayer five times daily, a main principle within the five pillars of Islam, assists the devotee to submit to Allah's will. Although the individual can undertake daily prayer alone, it is preferable, if possible, to pray with others; an obvious place for this to occur is within the mosque, led either by the *imam* or any Muslim. In bringing an individual closer to God, the *Hadith* indicates that group prayer is 27 times more effective than praying alone (Al-Radi & Al-Mahdy, 1989). Group prayer likewise reinforces a sense of belonging to a single, worldwide community of believers. Larger assemblies of prayer, in mosques, are especially prevalent at noon on Fridays, the Muslim Holy Day; this is preceded by a *khutba*, sermon, delivered by the *imam*.

Muslims also celebrate major and minor religious feasts in a group setting; these begin with group prayer in a mosque, and end in the sharing of a meal amongst family members. One of two major feasts, the Id Al-Fitr is the feast at the end of Ramadan. In the mosque, it includes the corporate recitation of prayers, and ends in people exchanging greetings; even enemies are encouraged to settle their differences and to exchange the peace.

The second major feast, the Al-Adha, commemorates the Koranic story in which Abraham was told by Allah to slaughter his son Ishmael; as his knife was drawn towards the son's neck, the angel Gabriel intervened by the will of Allah, putting a sheep in place of the son and thereby allowing the sheep to be sacrificed in Ishmael's stead. Each year, after mosque prayer, Muslims slaughter an animal and then consume it in a family meal, in honour of this event; if it is available, the animal is a sheep.

❖ SIGNIFICANCE TO SOCIAL WORK OF PRAYER AND THE FIVE PILLARS

A social worker should comprehend the helping benefits, at several levels, of the above forms of prayers and the five pillars of Islam. All have a strong group element, reflecting and reinforcing Muslim society's high-context nature; as a popular Muslim saying has it, "God's hand [is] with the group." At the group level, emotional support and exchange of ideas or difficulties take place, most often in the mosque, with other worshippers or with the imam. As emphasized by the *Hadith*, "The Prophet Muhammad remarked: Those who interact with people and express their hardships are better than those who do not interact with people and do not express their pains" (Ibn-Majah, 1975).

Group prayers help to create a sense of familiarity, friendliness, selflessness, and equality among the faithful. This is entirely consistent with the *Hadith* edict of the equality of believers regardless of colour, social strata, or wealth; the Prophet Muhammad said: "All the people are equal as the comb's teeth" (Nagati, 1993). Group prayers also reinforce a potential for natural support networks, and provide a rationale for breaking down barriers that would normally interfere with the mutual exchange of social support. The group nature of prayer can thus influence the thought and behaviour of their members, in the context of group intervention (Yalom, 1975).

Group prayers mirror a wide range of instrumental and social support outside the mosque, such as family or marital advice, assistance with building a home or extension to a home, or assistance during times of sickness and other traumatic events. An excellent example is the in-mosque greetings of peace during major feast celebrations. Even enemies are compelled to be cordial. The feast seasons themselves often provide the context for settling instances of marital or family discord, very often with the assistance of concerned family members, neighbours or friends. Major feasts also include the imperative to visit relatives and close friends; visits are extended over a four-day period for the sacrifice holiday, and three days for the Id Al-Fitr. The feast periods preceding fasting periods are also associated with various good works, such as visiting sick friends or relatives, which themselves also provide the basis for natural social support.

On the level of the person-to-group, the practice catapults the praying individual into a worldwide body of believers, both dead and alive, thus reinforcing a sense of the integrity and strength of the religion. Group cohesion is reinforced by Muslim scholars, the religious rituals and Islamic theology: "Hold fast together by the rope of Allah and not by being divisive among yourselves.... Believers are like a building, strengthening and supporting each other.... God helps him who helps his brother" (Koran, cited in Al- Radi & Al-Mahdy, 1989, p. 274). The individual in Islam is also considered an independent member of the group, who makes decisions to satisfy his or her needs and interests without hurting the group (Al-Radi & Al-Mahdy, 1989). So the interests of the individual and the group do not necessarily contradict one another; rather, they are supposed to be mutually reinforcing. The individual's voice is not silenced, and group members are always expected to express personal views (Al-Krenawi, 1995).

The recitation of the Koran during prayer, either silently or aloud, represents a continuous chain of teaching, listening, and memorizing Koranic sayings. On the individual level, the prayer is a reminder that a Muslim's daily life and faith are continuously intertwined. Praying can be viewed as both a preventative and an inexpensive psychological guard against anxiety and depression (Al-Krenawi, 1995; Azhar, et al., 1994). The practice of prayer, meditation, and other forms of religious devotion can lead to balance in the Muslim personality (Nagati, 1982), increasing the person's sense of well-being, relief, and anxiety-reduction (Azhar, et al., 1994). To put it in religious terms, the institutions of prayer and the Muslim five pillars "enable the believer to turn away from evil and to enhance his/her consciousness of God—an essential process in the actualization of human nature (*fitrah*)" (Mohamed, 1995, p. 14).

Likewise, but on a different level, the individual encounters religion diachronically, in the sense of the immediate temporal and spatial context of treatment, but also synchronically, that is, in the transcendence of time and space and in the encounter with an omnipotent and omnipresent Deity. This assumption of religiosity, then, provides an opportunity for transcending one's historical circumstances, by making allowance for that ultimate hope that is the core of Islamic salvation (Al-Krenawi & Graham, 1997). On a final level, then, prayer itself, for the believer, allows the individual to encounter the omniscient wisdom and omnipotent healing powers of Allah (Abramowitz, 1993; Ranganathan, 1994; Saucer, 1991).

Sacred places are also important to Muslim spirituality. For instance, Muslims typically visit dead saints' tombs, which are holy places associated with stories of relieving personal anxiety, healing physical and mental ailments, and mediating requests to God (Al-Krenawi and Graham, 1996). There are particularly sacred *maqam*, or holy places—for example, the burial places of such prophets as Moses—where Muslims undergo addictions recovery, among other forms of help for personal problems (Al-Krenawi & Graham, 1997). A highly important sacred place for Muslims is Mecca, the destination of the *hajj* pilgrimage.

The *hajj* to Mecca is not just a trip, but a journey to a particularly sacred and auspicious spot to obtain the spiritual gains of purification and redemption (Eliade, 1964; Turner, 1979). Before undertaking the *hajj*, individuals have to reconcile with anyone with whom they have had a dispute; this in itself is yet another natural locus of conflict resolution. The pilgrimage often takes place in a group, and once at Mecca, the supplicants ask God to forgive their sins and grant them His blessings. During the performance of the *hajj*, Muslims help each other, gathering together for prayers.

Close to Mecca is Medina, the burial place of Muhammad, and at the tomb, supplicants commonly cry, pray, and experience much psychological release and catharsis (Al-Krenawi, personal communication, 1998). During the *hajj* performance, in order to expel evil forces each pilgrim throws seven *jamrats* (stones) at a site in Mecca called Iblis, named after the fallen angel who had been expelled from the Garden of Eden and who was the original source of all evil spirits (Koran, Surah Al-Hijr, v. 28–40). This process symbolizes a freeing of the self from guilt feelings and sins. Moreover, the process of tangible actions — of doing something — symbolizes and reinforces the overall sense of sin propitiation. From the Islamic perspective, after participating in the *hajj*, a person is considered "born again," which means that all his/her sins are erased by God's will. This leads to satisfaction, relaxation, and release (Al-Issawi, 1988; Nagati, 1982); for many Muslims it can be the symbolic beginning of major life changes. For the rest of their lives, the pilgrim assumes the title *hajj*, one who has undertaken the *hajj* pilgrimage. Their social status consequently increases, and their personal conduct is expected to reflect kindness, devotion, and other virtuous attributes.

Beyond these considerations, research in social work and allied disciplines reveals several direct practice considerations for working with Muslim individuals and families. Practitioners, the literature points out, should

1. have an understanding of Muslim family arrangements as more hierarchical and less flexible, with a communication style that tends to be implicit and indirect, rather than explicit and direct (Daneshpour, 1998).
2. have an understanding of the implications of gender construction within Muslim society, which limits women's movements outside the home and their women's vocational choices, encourages women's domesticity, and creates an ethos of the breadwinner male (Mass & Al-Krenawi, 1994; Al-Krenawi, 1996). In contrast to men, women's sometimes limited geographic mobility precludes seeking help outside their home communities.
3. appreciate that the client may be reluctant to work with a practitioner of the opposite sex. Where opposite-sex clients occur, reduced eye contact, greater physical distance, and culturally appropriate and consciously non-sexual terms such as "my brother" or "my sister" may be used (Al-Krenawi, 1996).
4. have a basic understanding of Islam, including Shiite, Sunni, and Islamic movement traditions, as well as their common practices and implications.
5. have a clear understanding of the Muslim world view on sociocultural and psychosocial phenomena, which may be encountered during social work practice. Examples include, but

are not limited to, social prohibitions against suicide and social constructions of sexuality that affirm heterosexual lifestyles (Haynes, et al., 1997).

6. comprehend the cultural and personal significance of polygamy to family members, appreciate the significance of polygamy to children's and mothers' functioning. In order to motivate the father to accept help, children may be selected as a target system for intervention (Al-Krenawi, et al., 1997). Muslim family structures may be polygamous, which may create economic loss to women and children, lower academic achievement among children, poor relations with wives and husband, and competition and jealousy between co-wives and among the co-wives' children (Al-Krenawi, et al., 1997).

7. appreciate the explicit link between a Muslim's religious identity and his or her individual identity.

8. appreciate the potential use of such natural support networks as traditional healers (Al-Krenawi & Graham, 1996) and high-status members of society. Traditional healers in Muslim society, such as the dervish, often operate with strong reference to the Koran, and intercede in a wide variety of psychosocial and somatic complaints (Al-Krenawi, et al., 1996).

❖ CONCLUSION

Islam is a total, all-embracing way of life for Muslims. It includes both specific religious rituals and prayers and a large body of works setting out the words and commands of the Prophet and subsequent religious leaders. As several researchers have argued, social workers (Al-Dabbagh, 1993; Abdul-Hadi, 1989; Lum, 1992; Canda, 1988) and mental health practitioners working among religious clients (Bilu & Witzum, 1993, 1995; Galanter, et al., 1991; Johnson & Ridley, 1992; Lipsker & Ordt, 1990) must comprehend their clients' spiritual dimensions and incorporate these into treatment. This is a particular imperative in work with Muslim peoples. Even if they do have access to helping professionals, Muslims inside or outside the West may under-utilize or prematurely terminate services (Al-Krenawi & Graham, 1996; Savaya, 1995, 1998). As well, despite the historic role of social welfare institutions, social work has a limited presence in the Islamic world (Al-Dabbagh, 1993; Ragab, 1995). Social work should not be yet another instrument of Western colonialism. As Lila Ahmad, among other scholars, has argued, the forces of globalization have created a "fear," present throughout the Arab-Islamic world, "of losing an indigenous 'authentic' Islamic-Arab culture" (1992, cited in Shalhoub-Kevorkian, 1997, p. 61). For these reasons, social work with Muslim peoples therefore needs to be adapted according to Muslim values, rather than added as a graft upon prevailing social work knowledge (Devore & Schlesinger, 1994).

As a starting point, this can occur in three ways. Firstly, social workers should be familiar with the basic beliefs, values, and rituals of Islam as it is practised in the client's milieu. This chapter sheds light on some important aspects in this regard. Future research might develop a second, related area of inquiry: the myriad processes in which social workers could learn from the client the relative significance of religion, and the manner in which it could be integrated into a helping relationship. In both cases, social work practice enters into a still richer sense of the depth and breadth of the Muslim human condition. Finally, research could begin to think about generic cross-cultural principles of working with religious clients, and the lessons that can be mutually applied transculturally, transnationally, and across religious traditions.

REFERENCES

Abdul-Hadi, M.A. (1989). Islamic social work. In S. Abdul-Menaim (Ed.), *Social Work* (pp. 319–352). Cairo: Al-Nahdah Al-Messriah (in Arabic).

Abramowitz, L. (1993). Prayer as therapy among the frail Jewish elderly. *Journal of Gerontological Social Work, 19*(3/4), 69–75.

Al-Bostani, M. (1988). *Studies in Islamic psychology*. Beirut: Dar Al-Blaah Press (in Arabic).

Al-Dabbagh, A. (1993). Islamic perspectives on social work practice. *American Journal of Islamic Social Sciences, 10*(4), 536–537.

Alexander, L.B. (1983). The graduate school for Jewish social work, 1924–1940: Training for social work in an ethnic community. *Journal of Education for Social Work, 19*(2), 5–15.

Al-Issawi, A.R. (1988). *Islam and psychotherapy*. Beirut: Daar Al-Blaah Press (in Arabic).

Al-Juzuyyah, I.Q. (1993). *Natural healing with the medicine of the Prophet* (Muhammad Al-Akili, Trans.). Philadelphia: Pearl.

Al-Krenawi, A. (1995). *A study of dual use of modern and traditional mental health systems by the Bedouin of the Negev*. Unpublished PhD dissertation, University of Toronto.

Al-Krenawi, A. (1996). Group work with Bedouin widows in a medical clinic. *Affilia: Journal of Women and Social Work, 11*(3), 303–318.

Al-Krenawi, A. (1998). Personal communication with a Mecca pilgrim, F. Al-Krenawi.

Al-Krenawi, A., & Graham, J.R. (1996). Social work practice and traditional healing rituals among the Bedouin of the Negev, Israel. *International Social Work, 39*(2), 177–188.

Al-Krenawi, A., & Graham, J.R. (1997). Nebi-Musa: A therapeutic community for drug addicts in a Muslim context, *Transcultural Psychiatry, 34*(3), 377–391.

Al-Krenawi, A., Graham, J.R.. & Al-Krenawi, S. (1997). Social work practice with polygamous families. *Child and Adolescent Social Work Journal, 14*(6), 444–458.

Al-Krenawi, A., Graham, J.R., & Maoz, B. (1996). The healing significance of the Negevs Bedouin Dervish. *Social Science and Medicine, 43*(1), 13–21.

Al-Radi, O.M., & Al-Mahdy, M.A. (1989). Group therapy: An Islamic approach. *Transcultural Psychiatric Research Review, 26*(4), 273–276.

Azhar, M.Z., Varma, S.L., & Dharap, A.S. (1994). Religious psychotherapy in anxiety disorder patients. *Acta Psychiatrica Scandinavica, 90*(1), 1–3.

Azmi, S.H. (1991). Traditional Islamic social welfare: Its meaning, history, and contemporary relevance. *Islamic Quarterly, 35*(3), 165–180.

Berthold, S.M. (1989). Spiritism as a form of psychotherapy: Implications for social work practice. *Social Casework, 70*(8), 502–509.

Bibby, R.W. (1987). *Fragmented gods: The poverty and potential of religion in Canada.* Toronto: Irwin.

Bilu, Y., & Witzum, E. (1993). Working with ultra-orthodox patients: Guidelines for culturally sensitive therapy. *Culture, Medicine, and Psychiatry, 17*(2), 197–233.

Bilu, Y., & Witzum, E. (1995). Between sacred and medical realities: Culturally-sensitive therapy with Jewish ultra-orthodox patients. *Science in Context, 8*(1), 159–173.

Britannica 1996 Book of the Year. (1996). London: Oxford University Press.

Canda, E.R. (1988). Spirituality, religious diversity, and social work practice. *Social Casework, 69*(4), 238–247.

Cornett, C. (1992). Toward a more comprehensive personology: Integrating a spiritual perspective into social work practice. *Social Work, 37*(2), 101–102.

Cox, D. (1985). The missing dimension in social work practice. *Australian Social Work, 38*(4), 5–11.

Daneshpour, M. (1998). Muslim families and family therapy. *Journal of Marriage and Family Counseling, 24*(3), 355–368.

Devore, W., & Schlesinger, E. (1994). *Ethnic-sensitive social work practice* (3rd ed.). New York: Macmillan.

El-Azayem, G.A., & Zari, H.D. (1994). The psychological aspects of Islam: Basic principles of Islam and their psychological corollary. *International Journal for the Psychology of Religion, 4*(1), 41–50.

Eliade, M. (1964). *Shamanism.* Princeton, NJ: Princeton University Press.

Encyclopedia Britannica. (2007). 2007 Britannica Online. Chicago: Encyclopedia Britannica Inc.

Esposito, J.L. (Ed.). (1995). *Oxford Encyclopedia of the Modern Islamic World* (4 Vols.). New York and Oxford: Oxford University Press.

Fauri, D.P. (1988). Applying historical themes of the profession in the foundation curriculum. *Journal of Teaching in Social Work, 2*(1), 17–31.

Freedberg, S. (1986). Religion, profession, and politics: Bertha Capen Reynolds challenge to social work. *Smith College Studies in Social Work, 56*(2), 95–110.

Galanter, M., Larson, D., & Rubenstone, E. (1991). Christian psychiatry: The impact of evangelical belief on clinical practice. *American Journal of Psychiatry, 148*(1), 90–95.

Goldberg, C. (1996). The privileged position of religion in the clinical dialogue. *Clinical Social Work Journal, 24*(2), 125–136.

Graham, J.R. (1992). The Haven, 1878–1930: A Toronto charity's transition from a religious to a professional ethos. *Histoire Sociale/Social History, 25*(50), 283–306.

Graham, J.R., & Al-Krenawi, A. (1996). A comparison study of traditional helpers in a late nineteenth-century English Canadian (Christian) society in Toronto, Canada, and in a late twentieth-century bedouin (Muslim) society in the Negev, Israel. *Journal of Multicultural Social Work, 4*(2), 31–45.

Haddad, Y.Y., & Smith, J.I. (1994). *Muslim communities in North America*. Albany, NY: State University of New York Press.

Hall, E.T. (1976). *Beyond culture*. New York: Doubleday.

Haynes, A., Eweiis, M.M.I., Mageed, L.M.A., & Chung, D.K. (1997). Islamic social transformation: Considerations for the social worker. *International Social Work, 40*(3), 265–275.

Horsburgh, M. (1988). Words and deeds: Christianity and social welfare. *Australian Social Work, 41*(2), 17–23.

Ibn-Majah, A. (1975). *Sunan Ibn-Majah*, Vol. 2, p. 1338, #4032. Cairo: Dar Ihya Atturath Al-Arabi (in Arabic).

Johnson, W.B., & Ridley, C.R. (1992). Brief Christian and Non-Christian rational-emotive therapy with depressed Christian clients: An exploratory study. *Counseling and Values, 36*(3), 220–229.

Leiby, J. (1985). Moral foundations of social welfare and social work: A historical view. *Social Work, 30*(4), 323–330.

Lipsker, L.E., & Ordt, R.M. (1990). Treatment of depression in adolescents: A Christian cognitive-behavior therapy approach. *Journal of Psychology and Christianity, 9*(4), 25–33.

Lum, D. (1992). *Social work practice and people of color*. Monterey, CA: Brooks/Cole Publishing.

Mass, M., & Al-Krenawi, A. (1994). When a man encounters a woman Satan is also present: Clinical relationships in Bedouin Society. *American Journal of Orthopsychiatry, 64*, 357–367.

Mohamed, Y. (1995). Fitrah and its bearing on the principles of psychology. *American Journal of Islamic Social Sciences, 12*(1), 1–18.

Nagati, M.A. (1982). *The Koran and Psychology*. Beirut: Dar Al-Shorok Press (in Arabic).

Nagati, M.A. (1993). *The Tradition of the Prophet and psychology*. Cairo: Dar Al-Shorok Press (in Arabic).

Netting, F.E., Thibault, J.M., & Ellor, J.W. (1990). Integrating content on organized religion into macropractice courses. *Journal of Social Work Education, 26*(1), 15–24.

Parrinder, G. (1971). *A Dictionary of Non-Christian Religions*. Philadelphia: Westminster Press.

Qutib, S. (1967). *In the shadow of the Koran.* Beirut, Lebanon: Dar Ihya Atturath Al-Arabi (in Arabic).

Ragab, I.A. (1995). Middle East and Egypt. In T.D. Watts, D. Elliott, & N.S. Mayadas (Eds.), *International Handbook on Social Work Education* (pp. 281–304). Westview, CT: Greenwood Press.

Ranganathan, S. (1994). The Manjakkudi experience: A camp approach towards treating alcoholics. *Addiction, 89*(9), 1071–1075.

Rizvi, A.A. (1989). *Muslim traditions in psychotherapy.* Lahore: Institute of Islamic Culture.

Rockowitz, R.J., Korpela, J.W., & Hunter, K.C. (1981). Social work dilemma: When religion and medicine clash. *Health and Social Work, 6*(4), 5–11.

Saucer, P.R. (1991). Evangelical renewal therapy: A proposal for integration of religious values into psychotherapy. *Psychological Reports, 69*(3, Pt. 2), 1099–1106.

Savaya, R. (1995). Attitudes towards family and marital counseling among Israeli Arab women. *Journal of Social Service Research, 21*(1), 35–51.

Savaya, R. (1998). The under-use of psychological services by Israeli Arabs: An examination of negative attitudes and the use of alternative sources of help. *International Social Work, 41*(2), 195–209.

Sermabeikian, P. (1994). Our clients, ourselves: The spiritual perspective and social work practice. *Social Work, 39*(2), 178–183.

Shalhoub-Kevorkian, N. (1997). Wife-Abuse: A method of social control. *Israeli Social Science Research, 12*(1), 59–72.

Sheridan, M.J., Bullis, R.K., Adcock, C.R., Berlin, S.D., & Miller, P.C. (1992). Practitioners personal and professional attitudes and behaviors toward religion and spirituality: Issues for education and practice. *Journal of Social Work Education, 28*(2), 190–203.

Sheridan, M.J., Wilmer, C.M., & Atcheson, L. (1994). Inclusion of content on religion and spirituality in the social work curriculum: A study of faculty views. *Journal of Social Work Education, 30*(3), 363–376.

Swatos, W.H. (Ed.). (1998). *Encyclopedia of religion and society.* Walnut Creek, CA: AltaMira Press.

Turner, V. (1979). *Process, performance and pilgrimage.* New Delhi: Concept Publishing.

Vohra, S. (1995). Iran and the world, *Strategic Analysis, 18*(5), 729–736.

Winters, P. (Ed.). (1995). *Islam: Opposing viewpoints.* San Diego, CA: Greenhaven Press.

Yalom, I.D. (1975). *The theory and practice of group psychotherapy.* New York: Basic Books.

CONCLUSION

BARBARA SWARTZENTRUBER

This book provides a provisional overview of the current state of Canadian scholarship in the area of social work and spirituality. As we continue to trace the religious and spiritual threads that have wound their way through the evolution of social work theory and practice, we gain new perspectives on our collective professional response to the modern and postmodern eras. In doing so, we are forced to look, along with our colleagues in other disciplines, at areas of value dissonance, the limitations of our present discourse, and the potential way forward. Within this context, spirituality—as a guiding construct, praxis orientation, and connecting principle—holds both promise and challenge for exploring this path. It clearly enables, however, a growing capacity for an inclusive and at times difficult dialogue; one that does not sidestep previously dismissed questions of religious and spiritual importance to individuals and communities.

Our reflections and research have taught us that our understandings of religion and spirituality are historically situated and socially constructed, and as such are best understood from the vantage point of the broader socio-cultural context. Whether one views the emergence of spirituality in academic and popular discourse as part of a progressive, spiritual, and cultural evolution or as a reaction to the arid rationality of modernity and Western culture, or both, it is difficult not to make the connections to a broader societal transformation. Globalization, secularization, and fundamentalism are powerful and emergent actors in this postmodern transformation. Together with spirituality, they are engaged in a critical dialogue, one in which, as this collection would suggest, social work must now participate actively.

What then might the unique contributions of social work be to this dialogue? The chapters in this volume suggest that our historical roots, knowledge, and praxis commitments have a great deal to offer in shaping and grounding this larger conversation. Understanding these emergent actors in relation to individual and social change will require a number of things. Among them are direct engagement with the tacit knowledge and "lived experience" of individuals, in the context of global political and economic forces; an understanding of the need for, and complexities of, a shared ethical and moral framework; and a level of comfort with praxis perspectives that seek to maintain a creative tension between the scientific-rational and sacred-existential positions.[1] As such, social work is well positioned to provide leadership to the ongoing exploration of these issues through practice and research at the local and global levels.

Much of this dialogue will require that social work build alliances across disciplinary boundaries, as well as between the academy and various fields of practice, in order to further a knowledge base about spirituality that is essentially transdisciplinary in nature. This book is intended to serve as a foundation for expanding this conversation within the social work community and beyond; for solidifying spirituality as an emerging field of study within Canada; and for enabling future research, which will no doubt be increasingly international in nature.

❖ CHALLENGING SECULARIZATION: SPIRITUALITY AS AN EMANCIPATORY PROJECT

One of the most significant presuppositions of modernity has been that the process of secularization that began with the Enlightenment has resulted in an increasingly private and individualized relationship with religion, and a consequent decline of religion as an authoritative presence in public space. Current events and research emerging from several disciplines imply that religion and spirituality are of fundamental relevance to contemporary life and to theories of social change and development (see the introduction to this volume). From a postmodern view, the secularization hypothesis might in fact be a construction of Western scientific-rational discourse, one that is not necessarily upheld by either quantitative evidence or localized experience in Canada or throughout the world.[2] Secularization may be better understood as more myth than reality, a myth that supports an "emotionally coherent picture of a modern world in which religion and spirituality are not 'real forces'" (Thomas, 2005, p. 53). As one scholar argues, we accept the many implications of secularization theory (rise of reason, potential of progress, decline of faith, etc.) because it holds "powerful images and assumptions of what many people in the West want to believe modernity is" (Thomas, p. 53).

Many of the writings in this volume serve to emancipate social work from this prevailing discourse and to destabilize this commonly held theory and related assumptions, and in so doing offer new images and resources for the future. By bringing together both fresh historical perspectives and contemporary research on spirituality and religion, the myths and constraints of current societal (and social work) discourse are made more clearly visible. This reconstructed view acknowledges that while individual and collective relationships to religion and religious institutions are changing, they are doing so in ways that are richly varied by culture and location.[3] New forms of religion and evolving expressions of spirituality remain powerful and significant forces in the world and can no longer be ignored. Further research will be required to fully explicate these new forms and to understand their many implications for individual and social change. For example, what role do religion and spirituality play in contemporary social movements and global civil society? What resources do they bring and what is their impact? How can an interfaith dialogue improve human rights and social justice? Does an "engaged spirituality" lead to increased health and well-being?

How the secular and religious/spiritual might be properly reconciled with the realities of a global, postmodern world clearly remains a dilemma. Falk (2002), for example, criticizes the anti-religious trend of modernity as a kind of "secular fundamentalism" (p. 55) and calls for a "reconstructed secularism" that includes a "recovery of the sacred" (pp. 61–62). This reconciliation of the secular and spiritual is better able to respond to the denationalizing and dehumanizing aspects of global capitalism and the challenges of globalization. Falk goes so far as to propose that the reversal of the separation of church and state may be required, particularly in the West. Recent controversies about allowing faith-based arbitration in Canada imply that this is a highly complicated, multi-layered issue that will not be easily addressed.[4]

Globalization has meant that cultures, religious groups, and various spiritual traditions now exist in increasing "proximity" — producing the greater "moral" challenge of how to "live with others amid powerful forces shaping one's own society and identity" (Schweiker, 2004, p. 6). What is at issue is "how we 'picture' or imagine the moral space of life" (p. 15). In a postmodern world, moral space is highly contested and increasingly monopolized by powerful geopolitical and corporate interests. With a renewed interest in the relevance of spirituality, there are now possibilities for introducing moral values and ethical principles to issues of social and economic policy, politics, and development.[5] For social work, such a "politically engaged" spirituality (Falk, 2003) offers the opportunity to form coalitions based on mutual goals such as poverty reduction, climate change, Indigenous rights, and land use. As an illustration of this line of thinking, emerging social work practice perspectives, as noted in this collection, apply spiritual and ethical principles to a critical analysis of sustainability and the generation of policy alternatives.

There are some who see potential in a critical project of social transformation to both envision and realize a "just society" (Leonard, 1997; Midgley, 2001; Naidoo, 2004).[6] This includes proposals for national and global social welfare and social development agendas built on moral and spiritual values that counter the perceived hegemony of the neo-liberal economic paradigm (Falk, 1995, 2003; Holland, 1988; Brecher, Costello, & Smith, 2000; Desai, 2002). This "new social movement" draws on postmodern notions of spirituality to uncover visions of hope and possibility that can be realized through an active global civil society and grassroots democratic engagement.[7] Participating as well in this project are religious groups and faith-based organizations that combine, to various degrees, religious commitments with political activism (see, for example, Cerny, 2004). As an evolving "group-in-fusion" (Thompson, 2002) the nature and implications of this secular and religio-spiritual movement for social welfare, social services, and global social policy is still unfolding.

In response to the current context, then, spirituality may function as a *mediating discourse* providing a counter-hegemonic response to the prevailing ideals of modernization and secularization; as a *mobilizing factor* in the development of new social movements focused on global social justice issues; as a *connecting factor* coalescing a diverse mix secular and (inter-) religious actors and discourses at the local and global levels; and as a *transformative factor* in bringing about a new relation between self and society. Questions remain as to how the spiritual perspective, in each of these iterations, can address the diverse and the particular to avoid replicating a universalizing grand vision and a dogmatic moral agenda—whether it be secular or sacred (Tenbruck, 1990; Casanova, 1999; Mo Sung, 2004). Explorations of spirituality's relation to sustainable development, internationalization, and indigenization of social work theory and practice are perhaps at the forefront of wrestling with these issues (see, for example, Coates, Gray, & Hetherington, 2006; Yip, 2005; Daniels, 2001; Gardner, 2006).

❖ FUNDAMENTALISM, SOCIAL WORK, AND SOCIAL WELFARE

Strangely, those who see in spirituality the potential for recovering the sacred might find themselves "strange bedfellows" with fundamentalist religious groups that are equally disenchanted with the modern secular world view. Both fundamentalism and the emergent spirituality movement share some common ground in their critique of extreme secularization that relegates religio-spiritual world views to the margins. Certainly, there are significant points of departure between the proponents of fundamentalism and spirituality. Each of course, is not a homogeneous category. It makes a tremendous difference whether we are referring to Protestant fundamentalism, evangelicalism, or political Islam; and there are just as many differences between Christian mysticism, eco-spirituality, or indigenous spirituality. While all of these tendencies may share certain characteristics that cross faith and national boundaries, their manifestations vary through historical development within a particular cultural context and their relative capacity for critical reflexivity.

These points are raised to suggest that the struggle to understand spirituality and fundamentalism in our current context might *begin* with a historical understanding of the commonalities shared by fundamentalisms and spiritualities as the "disappointed prodigy" of a modern world,[8] but it must *proceed* with a greater level of specificity and analytic clarity.[9]

Dinerman (2003), in an editorial on the subject of social work and fundamentalism, reflects the state of collective worry within the profession about the ability of "fundamentalist" social workers or those with strongly held religious stances to uphold professional ethics and values in practice. This heated debate[10] is an important reminder that important areas of difference and potential bias continue to exist within our current understandings of social work in relation to spirituality and religion; while the spiritual perspective prompts a revisiting of our ethical principles, it does not necessarily provide a unifying framework.

Running just under the surface here is perhaps a greater fear that the re-emergence of spirituality has opened a Pandora's box of issues that will no longer be easily reconciled by our present notions of professional practice. Inevitably, social work, along with other professions, will be forced to struggle with limitations and consequences of having been conceived in a modern paradigm that is inadequate to address emergent issues (Coates, 2003; Ferguson & Lavalette, 2006; Thompson, 2002). This includes a growing awareness that "as participants in a larger system of governmentality and social control, social workers, like their clients are also victims—victims of burnout, deception, denial, the repression of contradictions " (Denzin, 2002, p. 35). The way forward here will require further dialogue on the broader limitations inherent in our current conceptualizations of professional practice and the potential contribution of spiritual perspectives to an "enriched ethical foundation" (Walz & Ritchie, 2000, p. 213).

Bonnycastle (2004) provides a cogent analysis of the important differences between "religious collective engagement in a politics of hope, focused on justice and democratic alignment" and those that lead to a "culture of charity" (p. 69). Of particular concern here is the trend in the United States "to fuse religion and family institutions to free market capitalism" (p. 71) through policies such as the Charitable Choice law.[11] In Canada there is a similar shift towards allowing the market to fund social services and public institutions,[12] and a growth in prevalence of faith-based organizations (FBOs) involved the delivery of social services. In Canada, FBOs tend to function much as secular social agencies at the present time, but rely on a mix of financial support from religious affiliates and government sources.

Of particular interest is the more noticeable presence of "theological conservatives" in the Canadian political arena and their affiliation with the "religious right" in the United States. McDonald (2006) provides an overview of their strategic, organized, and concerted efforts to influence public policy in Canada under the mentorship of US counterparts, and their alignment with the ideology of the dominant tendency within the Conservative Party of Canada. The influence of this growing political-religious alliance (encompassing like-minded Christians and Jews) stretches to world politics through a common belief in "end of time" prophecy— the "rapture," "tribulation," and second coming of Christ—a belief in "premillennial dispensationalism" popularized into contemporary fiction in the *Left Behind* series of novels (Gribben, 2004, p. 80; McDonald, 2006).

❖ NEW CONSTRUCTIONS OF RELIGION AND SPIRITUALITY

While there are many ways to distinguish religion and spirituality, they remain best thought of as interrelated and non-exclusive concepts dependant upon each other in a variety of ways. The appeal and consequence of this approach is that it allows for spirituality that emanates from a religious tradition (whether monotheistic, theistic, pantheistic, or non-theistic), as well as for spiritual expression/practice within a secular or atheistic belief system.[13] In this way, spirituality becomes a common, universal experience of non-believers and believers alike, one that appears to rise "beyond culture" as an "essential dimension of human life" (Ortiz, Villereal, & Engel, 2000, p. 22). It is the draw of these claims and the manner in which the relationship of religion and spirituality has been socially constructed and historically situated that requires further discussion.

Flood (1999) suggests that "'religion' is an emic, Western category that originated in late antiquity and developed within Christianity" (p. 44). He notes that the abstraction "religion"—along with the abstractions culture, mysticism, and spirituality—developed in the context of the Enlightenment's critique of Christianity and the rise of the modern individual (p. 45). While we have freely applied the term "religion" to traditions outside Christianity, the validity of utilizing a primarily Western construct in considering cross-cultural phenomena is questionable. One of the clear consequences of this particular view of religion, dealt with by several authors in this volume, has been the displacement and oppression of traditional indigenous spiritualities.

Examinations of religion tend to focus on the substance of "what religion is" or on the function of "what religion does"—that is, the purpose religiousness serves in individual and communal life (Zinnabauer & Pargament, 2005, pp. 22–23; Beyer, 2001, p. 422). Spirituality has increasingly become associated with the more functional elements of this role, those that are concerned with efforts of individuals to find meaning, truth, and interconnection, while the more substantive aspects of religion have been relegated to formal, institutionalized beliefs and practices (Zinnabauer & Pargament, 2005). In this conceptualization, religion becomes easily viewed as static, conservative, traditional, and a potential source of interfaith tension. Spirituality becomes connected with the dynamic, personal, creative aspect of human nature, and, to the extent that we can legitimately consider it to be universal, is given the ability to float above and across cultural categories enabling a non-conflictual source of collectivity. This approach to differentiating spirituality from religion parallels a clear cultural preference for the "subjective view" and a pushing aside of religion as an anachronism of a bygone era.

King (1996) suggests that the "popularity of the word spirituality is in part a symptom of the movement towards a global society and global consciousness" and the preoccupation to create a more tolerant pluralist society (p. 346). As noted earlier, globalization and internationalization have meant that religious, cultural, and spiritual traditions are brought into greater proximity. In response to this diversity it is tempting to look to spirituality for a connecting thread or unifying principle that ignores difference. Noting the varied and complex nature of spiritualities, and the ambiguity of the concept itself, King warns against the "essentialist trap" in a view of spirituality that is "broken free" of the cultural boundedness of religion and religious traditions (p. 350). This is an important reminder that the study of spirituality should also be rooted in time and place, and in relation to the broader religious and cultural context.

❖ NOTIONS OF TRANSCENDENCE AND SOCIAL TRANSFORMATION

When spirituality becomes solely focused on the interior, or confined to an individual's personal relationship to a "higher power" (however defined), it forgoes opportunities to function as a source for social change and social transformation. To move towards a more politically and socially engaged spirituality will require "overcoming egoism" (Giri, 2004) and the illusion of self-mastery:

> The forces of secularization have dismissed all but intra-mundane forms of self-transcendence. As a consequence, spirituality has shrunk and become increasingly shallow, indeed, self-serving. This dwarfed spirituality is further aggravated by a propensity to Promethean arrogance in which people are urged to delusional grandeur regarding self-mastery. (Boyd, 1994, pp. 97–98)

As many point out in this collection, transcending the self is not an end in itself, but a path to a spirituality of engagement through a realization of connectedness with others and the natural world. Here, transcendence, functioning as "radical alterity" (Schrag, 1997), provides resources for both removing the boundaries of self/society/natural world and unifying the divisiveness created by modernity.

While conceptually transcendence has broader meaning in religious and spiritual traditions, it has been brought down to earth by a secular social science that does not "acknowledge transcendence" as a distinct sphere of values, science, art, or morality (Quarles van Ufford & Kumar Giri, 2003, p. 267). As such, the commonly held social-scientific approach to the study of religion and spirituality generally contains "materialist assumptions about the nature of the world and about the mythic (i.e., false) nature of religious claims to transcendence" (Flood, 1999, p. 69). This secularized view of spirituality leaves out many of the complexities inherent in the notion of transcendence, and precludes its potential as a transformative factor in relation to self and society.

❖ REVISIONING THEORY, PRACTICE, AND RESEARCH

Many of the chapters in this volume include important reflections upon the dynamic relationship between the moral and ethical frames of reference of the profession, individual practitioners, and those with whom they work. They explore how the helping relationship and intervention practices change when spirituality is included and recognized as a dynamic force. What seems to be emerging is a fundamental reconceptualization of this relationship, a transcending of the Western dichotomies of giver/receiver and self/other, and an opening to alternative knowledge and practices.

There is a growing understanding that the realization of progressive social change will require the healing of much of the dualistic thinking embedded in modernity—private/public, local/global, social/economic development, sacred/secular, spiritual/material, immanent/transcendent (Baudot, 2002). Echoed in the discussions throughout this book, the incorporation of a spiritual perspective has significant implications for social work theory and practice—it "requires a radical revision of very fundamental knowledges and values, even a revision of consciousness" (Chile & Simpson, 2004, p. 8). This will entail opening the door to multiple paths of knowledge creation and "post-secular" approaches to intervention that are best suited to addressing issues of ultimate meaning and concern.

Our present moment, the seventh and future moment that shapes the field of qualitative research (Denzin & Lincoln, 2000) can be characterized by the discernable paradigm shift that is occurring within the social sciences and humanities. The roots of this change can be found in the traditions of the previous six moments—in the rational, universalizing truth claims of the modernist era and the decentring response of the postmodern refusal to reify any particular knowledge claims. While not yet fully articulated, the seventh moment revisits pre-Enlightenment ideas through a concern with moral and ethical discourse, considerations of "sacred epistemologies," a turn to reflexivity and praxis, and an acknowledgement of the ethical and social responsibilities of inquiry in relation to community transformation (Denzin & Lincoln, 2000, p. 3). Complementing the important contributions of quantitative research (see, for example, Bibby, 2002), this emerging context of inquiry enables a broad agenda of further research in spirituality and social work.

The spirituality research agenda will require methodological approaches that allow for areas of inquiry that push beyond the traditional limits of the current social-scientific perspective. As Denzin (2002) notes "there is a pressing need to ask questions and to seek ways of knowing that cannot, or will not, be asked" (p. 35). Research approaches will need to explore alternative, grassroots, and at times contradictory knowledge perspectives (p. 33). In this regard both feminist and critical theorists have pointed to paths for deconstructing prevailing methodological ideologies while working to recover marginalized perspectives and delineating research models that build alternative ethical and moral visions for academic inquiry.

Christians (2000), for example, suggests the need for a "feminist communitarian" model for interpretive inquiry that involves the inclusion of "multivocal and cross-cultural representation," the enhancement of the "moral discernment" of the individual and the community, and the promotion of social transformation through resistance and empowerment (pp. 144–149). This revisioning of interpretive inquiry is attuned to the needs of a spirituality research agenda that seeks to recognize the significant contributions of positivistic/rational inquiry but also the limitations of its application to questions of ultimate meaning and conceptualizations of the sacred.

In conclusion, this book is situated at the vanguard of a new conversation between social work and spirituality, a conversation set just at the edge of a new era of tentative rapprochement in the great historical debates between science and religion.[14] With a strong historical grounding in the nuances of this debate, social work has much to contribute. In providing an orientation to the current Canadian literature on spirituality from a social work perspective, this text positions the profession to engage with colleagues in other disciplines, and with society itself, in this broader global conversation. The agenda for further research offers opportunities for a multitude of perspectives in addressing issues that transgress time-honoured boundaries of all kinds and defy well-worn paths to resolution. In that and other respects "the spiritual project remains an ongoing one, always somehow incomplete" (King, 1998, p. 10).

NOTES

1.   Denzin (2002) suggests that social work is well positioned to translate the broader discourse into an effective approach to inquiry and social change based

on a "sacred, existential epistemology that locates persons in a noncompetitive, nonhierarchical relationship" to the earth, nature, and the "larger moral universe" (p. 31).

2.   See Bramadat & Seljak (2005), for instance, for a comprehensive look at the vitality of religious groups in Canada today.

3.   Turner (2006) suggests that "secularization may simply be the transformation (metamorphosis) of religion as it adjusts to new conditions" (p. 440).

4.   The Ontario Association of Social Workers strongly objected to the use of Sharia law in family law disputes, noting that "there is a very real possibility of eroding women's equality rights and giving primacy to group rights over individual rights and thereby creating a power imbalance contrary to the intent of the Canadian Charter of Rights and Freedoms" (OASW, n.d.).

5.   For example, this idea has been forwarded by the UN with regard to social development: see UN Secretariat (1995).

6.   Closely related to this work, and an underlying aspect of many of the proposals in this volume, is the development of a new normative architecture built on an ethics of social justice and equity (Mittleman, 2004, p. 228). Schweiker (2004) outlines two emergent approaches to thinking about global ethics: the "Declaration Toward a Global Ethic" developed by Hans Kung and the Parliament of the World's Religions, which attempts to isolate common values, standards, and attitudes found among the worlds religions, and "the turn to human rights" and cosmopolitan citizenship.

7.   See Baudot (2002) for a range of essays on this topic and Griffin (1988) for a discussion of postmodern spirituality.

8.   I take this idea from Schwartzentruber (2006), who refers to spirituality and fundamentalism as postmodern "orphans" of religious traditions.

9.   The Fundamentalist Project was a international comparative project of the American Academy of Arts and Sciences involving an interdisciplinary, geographically dispersed group of more than 100 scholars who developed an identifiable "cluster of characteristics" or "family resemblances," one or more of which might be shared by contemporary fundamentalist religious groups. Among other things, they tackle some common misperceptions, such as the idea that fundamentalism leads to violence, is limited to monotheism, or is necessarily conservative in nature (Herbert, 2003, p. 48–49; Appleby & Marty, 2002).

10. See Hodge (2002) and Jimenez (2006) for a further elaboration of this issue.

11. Enacted in 1996, the Charitable Choice law allows for direct government funding for religious groups to deliver social services. See Cnaan & Boddie (2002) for an overview.

12. For example, the current Conservative federal government amended the taxation rules in 2006 to remove the capital gains tax on transfers of stock to charitable organizations.

13. For further discussion of this conceptual approach, see, for example, Canda & Furman (1999).

14. There are now many examples of academic endeavours to explore what E.O. Wilson (2003) calls the "consilience" of knowledge. See, for example, Watts &

Dutton (2006). For an example of how this conversation is evolving in the popular media see the articles on "God vs. Science" in the October/November 2006 issue of *SEED* magazine.

REFERENCES

Appleby, S., & Marty, M. (2002). Fundamentalism. *Foreign Policy*, (Jan./Feb. 2002) 16–22.

Astell, A.W. (Ed.). (1994). *Divine representations: Postmodernism and spirituality*. New York: Paulist Press.

Baudot, B.S. (Ed.). (2002). *Candles in the dark: A new spirit for a plural world*. Seattle, Washington: University of Washington Press.

Beyer, P. (1994). *Religion and globalization*. London: SAGE Publications.

Beyer, P. (2001). Contemporary social theory as it applies to the understanding of religion in cross-cultural perspective. In R. Fenn (Ed.), *The Blackwell companion to the sociology of religion* (pp. 418–432). Oxford: Blackwell Publishers.

Bibby, R. (2002). *Restless Gods: The renaissance of religion in Canada*. Toronto: Stoddart Publishing Company.

Bonnycastle, C. (2004). The role of religion in contemporary social service: Reemerging democratic alignment or false hope. *Canadian Review of Social Policy*, 53, 68–88.

Boyd, T. (1994). Is spirituality possible without religion? A query for the postmodern era. In A.W. Astell (Ed.), *Divine representations: Postmodernism and spirituality* (pp. 83–101). New York: Paulist Press.

Bramadat, P., & Seljak, D. (Eds.). (2005). *Religion and ethnicity in Canada*. Toronto: Pearson.

Brecher, J., Costello, T., & Smith, B. (Eds.). (2000). *Globalization from below: The power of solidarity*. Cambridge, MA: South End Press.

Candland, C. (2000). Faith as social capital: Religion and community development in Southern Asia. *Policy Sciences*, 33, 355–374.

Canda, E.R., & Furman, L.D. (1999). *Spiritual diversity in social work practice: The heart of helping*. New York: The Free Press.

Casanova, J. (1999). The sacralization of the *humanum*: A theology for a global age. *International Journal of Politics, Culture and Society*, 13(1), 21–40.

Cerny, J. (2004). Social change and spirituality: Planting seeds of hope and promise from spiritual roots. *Canadian Review of Social Policy*, 54, 135–142.

Chile, L., & Simpson, G. (2004). Spirituality and community development: Exploring the link between the individual and the collective. *Community Development Journal*, 39(4), 318–331.

Christians, C.G. (2000). Ethics and politics in qualitative research. In Denzin, N.K. and Lincoln, Y.S. (Eds.), *Handbook of Qualitative Research*, 2nd ed. (pp. 133-155). Thousand Oaks, CA: Sage Publications.

Cnaan, R. & Boddie, S. (2002). Charitable choice and faith-based welfare: A call for social work. *Social Work*, 47(3), 224–236.

Coates, J. (2003). *Ecology and social work: Toward a new paradigm*. Halifax, NS: Fernwood Publishing.

Coates, J., Gray, M., & Hetherington, T. (2006). Ecology and spirituality: Finally, a place for Indigenous social work. *British Journal of Social Work, 36*, 381–399.

Daniels, J.E. (2001). Africentric social work practice: The new approach for social work practice intervention in the 21st century. *International Social Work, 44*(3), 301–309.

Denzin, N.K. (2002). Social work in the seventh moment. *Qualitative Social Work, 1*(1), 25–38.

Denzin, N.K., & Lincoln, Y.S. (Eds.). (2000). *Handbook of qualitative research* (2nd ed.). Thousand Oaks, CA: Sage Publications.

Desai, N. (2002). Global ethics in a plural world. In B.S. Baudot (Ed.), *Candles in the dark* (pp. 83–95). Seattle: University of Washington Press.

Dinerman, M. (2003). Fundamentalism and social work. *AFFILIA, 18*(3), 249–253.

Falk, R. (1995). *On humane governance: Toward a new global politics*. University Park, PA: Pennsylvania State University Press.

Falk, R. (2002). Secularism, globalization, and the role of the state: A plea for renewal. In B.S Baudot (Ed.), *Candles in the dark* (pp. 47–61). Seattle: University of Washington Press.

Falk, R. (2003). Politically engaged spirituality in an emerging global civil society *ReVision, 25*(4), 1–10.

Ferguson, I., & Lavalette, M. (2006). Globalization and global justice: Towards a social work of resistance. *International Social Work, 49*(3), 309–318.

Flood, G. (1999). *Beyond phenomenology: Rethinking the study of religion*. London: Cassell.

Gardner, G. (2006). *Inspiring progress: Religions' contributions to sustainable development*. New York: W.W. Norton.

Giri, A.K. (2004). Knowledge and human liberation. *European Journal of Social Theory, 7*(1), 85–103.

Gribben, C. (2004). Rapture fictions and the changing evangelical condition. *Literature & Theology, 18*(1), 77–94.

Griffin, D. (Ed.). (1988). *Spirituality and society: Postmodern visions*. Albany, NY: State University of New York Press.

Herbert, D. (2003). *Religion and civil society*. Hampshire, England: Ashgate Publishing.

Hodge, D.R. (2002). Does social work oppress Evangelical Christians? A "new class" analysis of society and social work. *Social Work, 47*(4), 401–414.

Holland, J. (1988). A postmodern vision of spirituality and society. In D. Griffin (Ed.), *Spirituality and society: Postmodern visions* (pp. 99–107). Albany, NY: State University of New York Press.

Jimenez, J. (2006). Epistemological frameworks, homosexuality, and religion: A response to Hodge. *Social Work, 51*(2), 185–188.

King, A. (1996). Spirituality: Transformation and metamorphosis. *Religion, 26*, 343–351.

King, U. (Ed.). (1998). *Faith and praxis in a postmodern age*. London: Cassell.

King, U. (Ed.). (2001). *Spirituality and society in the new millennium*. Brighton, England: Sussex Academic Press.

Leonard, P. (1997). *Postmodern welfare: Reconstructing an emancipatory project*. London: SAGE Publications.

McDonald, M. (2006, October). Jesus in the House: Is the religious right taking over Stephen Harper's government? *The Walrus*, 45–61.

Midgley, J. (2001). The critical perspective in social development. *Social Development Issues, 23*(1), 42–50.

Mittleman, J. (2004). What is critical globalization studies? *International Studies Perspectives, 5*, 219–230.

Mo Sung, J. (2004). Economics and spirituality. In L. Susin, J. Sobrino, & F. Wilfred (Eds.), *Concilium 2004/5: A different world is possible* (pp. 96–105). London: SCM Press.

Naidoo, K. (2004). It's time to act. *Canadian Review of Social Policy, 53*, 11–18.

Ontario Association of Social Workers. (n.d.). *Consultation on Sharia law in Ontario*. Retrieved 29 October 29 2006 from http://www.oasw.org/en/communitysite/oaswinaction/advocacy.asp.

Ortiz, L., Villereal, S., & Engel, M. (2000). Culture and spirituality: A review of the literature. *Social Thought, 19*(4) 21-36.

Schrag, C. (1997). *The self after postmodernity*. New Haven, CT: Yale University Press.

Schwartzentruber, P. (2006, September). *Spirituality as the root of tolerance: Religion practiced at the Retreat Centre*. Paper presented at the World Religions Conference, Montreal.

Schweiker, W. (2004). *Theological ethics and global dynamics: In the time of many worlds*. Oxford: Blackwell Publishing.

Selinger, Leah. (2004). The forgotten factor: The uneasy relationship between religion and development. *Social Compass, 51*(4), 523–543.

Smith, C. (1996). *Disruptive religion: The force of faith in social movement activism*. New York: Routledge.

Tenbruck, R. (1990). The dream of a secular ecumene: The meaning and limits of policies of development. *Theory, Culture & Society, 7*, 193–206.

Thomas, S. (2005). *The global resurgence of religion and the transformation of international relations*. New York: Palgrave Macmillan.

Thompson, N. (2002). Social movements, social justice and social work. *British Journal of Social Work, 32*, 711–722.

Turner, B. (2001). Cosmopolitan virtue: On religion in a global age. *European Journal of Social Theory, 4*(2), 131–152.

Turner, B. (2006). Religion. *Theory, Culture & Society, 23*(2/3), 437–455.

UN Secretariat. (1995). *Ethical and Spiritual Dimensions of Social Development* (Report prepared for the World Summit for Social Development, 6–12 March 1995, Copenhagen). New York: United Nations Publication.

Quarles van Ufford, P., & Kumar Giri, A. (Eds.). (2003). *A moral critique of development: In search of global responsibilities*. New York: Routledge.

Walz, T., & Ritchie, H. (2000). Gandhian principles in social work practice: Ethics revisited. *Social Work, 45*(3), 213–223.

Watts, F., & Dutton, K. (Eds.). (2006). *Dialogue matters: Voices from the international society for science and religion.* West Conshohocken, PA: Templeton Foundation Press.

Wilson, E.O. (2003). *Consilience: The unity of knowledge.* New York: Knopf.

Yip, Kam-shing. (2005). A dynamic Asian response to globalization in cross-cultural social work. *International Social Work, 48*(5), 593–607.

Zinnbauer, B.J., & Pargament, K.I. (2005). Religiousness and spirituality. In R.F. Paloutzian & C.L. Park (Eds.), *Handbook of the psychology of religion and spirituality* (pp. 21–39). New York: The Guilford Press

COPYRIGHT ACKNOWLEDGEMENTS

Chapter 10 by Sarah Todd, "Feminist Community Organizing: The Spectre of the Sacred and the Secular," from *Currents: New Scholarship in the Human Services* 3:1 (2004). Reprinted by permission of Currents: New Scholarship in the Human Services.

Chapter 11 by Susan J. Cadell, Linda Janzen, and Dennis J. Haubrich, "Engaging with Spirituality: A Qualitative Study of Grief and HIV/AIDS," from *Critical Social Work* 7:1 (2006). Reprinted by permission of Critical Social Work. http://cronus.uwindsor.ca/units/socialwork/critical.nsf/main/AA48 AC493B651963852571790071B3EF?OpenDocument

Chapter 12 by Cindy Baskin, "Circles of Resistance: Spirituality in Social Work Practice, Education and Transformative Change," from *Currents: New Scholarship in the Human Services* 1:1 (2002). Reprinted by permission of Currents: New Scholarship in the Human Services. http://fsw.ucalgary.ca/ currents/articles/baskin_v1_n1.htm

Chapter 13 by John Coates, "From Ecology to Spirituality and Social Justice," from *Currents: New Scholarship in the Human Services* 3:1 (2004). Reprinted by permission of Currents: New Scholarship in the Human Services. http://fsw.ucalgary.ca/currents/articles/coates_v3_n1.htm

Chapter 14 by Michael Kim Zapf, "Profound Connections Between Person and Place," from *Critical Social Work* 6:2 (2005). Reprinted by permission of Critical Social Work. http://cronus.uwindsor.ca/units/socialwork/critical. nsf/EditDoNotShowInTOC/62C3C075C4133F288525701900280CFB

Chapter 15 by Rick Csiernik and David Adams, "Spirituality, Stress and Work," from *Employee Assistance Quarterly* 18:2 (2002): 29–37. Reprinted by permission of Haworth Press Inc.

Chapter 16 by Gord Bruyere, "Making Circles: Renewing First Nations Ways of Helping," from *Beyond Racial Divides: Ethnicities in Social Work Practice*, Lena Dominelli, Walter Lorenz and Haluk Soydan, eds. (London: Ashgate Publishing, 2000): 213–227. Reprinted by permission of Ashgate Publishing.

Chapter 17 by Linda Snyder and Sarah Bowman, "Communities in Cooperation: Human Services Work with Old Order Mennonites," from *Journal of Ethnic & Cultural Diversity in Social Work* 13:2 (2004): 91–118. Reprinted by permission of Haworth Press Inc.

Chapter 18 by David Este, adaptation of "The Black Church as a Social Welfare Institution: Union United Church and the Development of Montreal's Black Community, 1907-1940," from *Journal of Black Studies* 35:1 (2004): 3–22. Reprinted by permission of Sage Publications.

Chapter 19 by Alean Al-Krenawi and John R. Graham, "Islamic Theology and Prayer: Relevance for Social Practice," from *International Social Work* 43:3 (2000): 289–304. Reprinted by permission of Sage Publications.